Dia Center for the Arts
Discussions in Contemporary Culture
Number 8

D0089631

Black Popular Culture

Moira Roth

A Project by Michele Wallace

Edited by Gina Dent

Bay Press · Seattle · 1992

Printed in the United States of America
First printing 1992

Library of Congress Number 89-650815
ISSN 1047-6806
ISBN 0-941920-24-0

Designed by Bethany Johns with Georgie Stout
Typesetting by Strong Silent Type
Printing by Malloy Lithographing

"Nihilism in Black America" by Cornel West was originally published in *Dissent* (Spring 1991). Reprinted by permission of the author and the Foundation for the Study of Independent Social Ideas, Inc.

"The Body in Question" by Lisa Kennedy was originally published in *The Village Voice* (October 16, 1990). Reprinted by permission of the author.

Contents

VII   **A Note on the Series**

IX   **Editor's Note**

1   **Black Pleasure, Black Joy: An Introduction**   *Gina Dent*

21   **What is this "Black" in Black Popular Culture?**   *Stuart Hall*

I. Popular Culture: Theory and Criticism

37   **Nihilism in Black America**   *Cornel West*

48   **Dialectically Down with the Critical Program**   *bell hooks*

56   **The Documentary Impulse in Contemporary U.S. African-American Film**   *Valerie Smith*

65   **The Politics of Interpretation: Black Critics, Filmmakers, Audiences**   *Jacqueline Bobo*

75   **The Black Man's Burden**   *Henry Louis Gates, Jr.*

85   **Discussion**

II. Gender, Sexuality, and Black Images in Popular Culture

95   **The Accusatory Space**   *Jacquie Jones*

99   **Unleash the Queen**   *Marlon T. Riggs*

106   **The Body in Question**   *Lisa Kennedy*

112   **Getting Down to Get Over: Romare Bearden's**   *Judith Wilson*
      Use of Pornography and the Problem of the
      Black Female Body in Afro-U.S. Art

123   ***Boyz N the Hood* and *Jungle Fever***   *Michele Wallace*

132   **"You Cain't Trus' It":**   *Houston A. Baker, Jr.*
      Experts Witnessing in the Case of Rap

139   **Discussion**

III. The Urban Context

153   **Toward a Redefinition of the Urban:**   *John Jeffries*
      The Collision of Culture

164   **Two Words on Music: Black Community**   *Sherley Anne Williams*

173   **Nostalgia for the Present:**   *Kofi Natambu*
      Cultural Resistance in Detroit 1977–1987

187   **The Multicultural Wars**   *Hazel V. Carby*

200   **Popular Culture and the Economics**   *Julianne Malveaux*
      of Alienation

209   **Discussion**

IV. The Production of Black Popular Culture

223   **Black Texts/Black Contexts**   *Tricia Rose*

228   **Seizing the Moving Image:**   *Ada Gay Griffin*
      Reflections of a Black Independent Producer

234   **About Face:**   *Thomas Allen Harris*
      The Evolution of a Black Producer

243 **Preface to a One-Hundred-and-Eighty Volume**   *Greg Tate*
Patricide Note: Yet Another Few Thousand
Words on the Death of Miles Davis and the
Problem of the Black Male Genius

249 **69**   *Arthur Jafa*

255 **"Black Is, Black Ain't":**   *Isaac Julien*
Notes on De-Essentializing Black Identities

264 **Discussion**

V. Do the Right Thing:
Postnationalism and Essentialism

279 **Pan-American Postnationalism:**   *Coco Fusco*
Another World Order

285 **Afro-Kitsch**   *Manthia Diawara*

292 **Race, Identity, and Political Culture**   *Manning Marable*

303 **It's a Family Affair**   *Paul Gilroy*

317 **Black Nationalism:**   *Angela Y. Davis*
The Sixties and the Nineties

325 **Discussion**

333 **Afterword: "Why Are There No Great**   *Michele Wallace*
Black Artists?" The Problem of Visuality
in African-American Culture

347 *Bibliography of Related Sources*

367 *Notes on Contributors*

373 *Photo Credits*

A Note on the Series

Our aim for the "Discussions in Contemporary Culture" series is to reflect on aspects of our culture which are emerging or in flux. Often we are in uncharted territory. The symposia are opportunities for many voices to take part in new conversations and are organized to encourage informal presentations and audience participation. The books that grow out of these symposia are similarly meant as explorations, open and informal.

This book, the eighth in the "Discussions in Contemporary Culture" series, includes texts prepared by the participants in a three-day conference held at The Studio Museum in Harlem and at Dia's space in SoHo on December 8–10, 1991. Michele Wallace first conceived of a conference event to acknowledge the growing presence of a politicized popular culture and to explore debates on participation by black communities in the creation and critique of popular culture. Her thoughts on the structure of the conference took shape with the assistance primarily of Phil Mariani. Michele has participated before in events in this series and Phil has had a long-standing role in conceiving and organizing symposia with Dia; it was a great pleasure to work with both of them again. Of course, we owe a great debt of thanks to the participants in the conference for their presentations and for the prepared texts.

The event as it was structured would not have been possible without the collaborative participation of The Studio Museum in Harlem, and I would especially like to thank Kinshasha Conwill, Director; Pat Cruz, Deputy Director of Programming; and George Calderaro, Public Relations Manager for their support and active participation in the organization of the conference. Sara Schnittjer at Dia was also instrumental in the coordination of the conference.

This publication is the result of considerable further effort to transcribe and edit presentations from the conference, and to craft the whole into one coherent volume. Gina Dent, as editor of this publication, energetically and ably took on these responsibilities. She was assisted principally by Karen Kelly of Dia's staff, who has overseen the project from start to finish. I would like to thank Thatcher Bailey at Bay Press for his enthusiasm in publishing this book.

We are particularly grateful to The Nathan Cummings Foundation for generous funding for this project.

Charles B. Wright

Executive Director, Dia Center for the Arts

Editor's Note

In recognition of the contest within African diasporic intellectual production over the meaning of the term "blackness," we have allowed a small subset of that debate to live on in the use of both Black with a capital "B" and black with a lowercase "b" in the essays that follow. Bay Press's standard style, which calls for the latter practice, has been observed, however, in all the discussions and in every case where an author has not otherwise stated a preference. For those unfamiliar with the dynamics of such a debate, let it suffice to say that this apparently minor distinction can indicate subtle differences in the way scholars and artists think about the issues of black nationalism, essentialism, and Pan-Africanism, just to name a few, as is revealed in the various essays and exchanges presented here. There is no definitive way this choice should be evaluated. It speaks to our personal histories and the diversity of thought and practice influencing our work.

In addition to the contributors, I would like to thank the following individuals for their contributions to this volume: Michele Wallace, for having the audacity to propose such a project and for the lengthy discussions we had at various stages in this process; and Karen Kelly, at Dia Center for the Arts, for her assistance in everything, but especially in the pursuit of elusive footnotes and the selection of images.

Gina Dent

Gina Dent

Black Pleasure, Black Joy: An Introduction

Every gathering has its points of profound collective understanding, never to be fully grasped except in the elusive phrases with which we attempt to reconstruct them. These phrases serve to remind us of our collective goals for the future, and yet point continually to our distance from them—for they can never be matched in the habits of our daily lives, our constant negotiations through the contradictory spaces of identity and history, our imperfect access to the "real." One of the challenges for cultural criticism today is to learn to grasp the full range of questions and problems proposed in media where the modes of expression are not easily captured within language. It is, then, not surprising that at a conference on black popular culture, one figure came to stand in for this complexity, returning again and again in variants on a single refrain, a single elusive phrase: black pleasure, black joy.

No one could have expected that in responding to a question about pleasure in our own work, Cornel West could, in elucidating the differences between our conceptions of pleasure and joy, so compellingly provide a context for reading this volume. As he described them then,

> ...pleasure, under commodified conditions, tends to be inward. You take it with you, and it's a highly individuated unit...But joy tries to cut across that. Joy tries to get at those non-market values—love, care, kindness, service, solidarity, the struggle for justice—values that provide the possibility of bringing people together.

This formulation became, in fact, the theme of the conference. Or, more precisely, it became the text of call and response that was consistently rewritten over the next two days. That a conference on black popular culture comprised of the work of some thirty black artists, critics, and scholars, could hold to an agenda so explicitly concerned with the issues of collective struggle, and the politics of gender and sexuality that factor into any discussion of the economies of pleasure, is a powerful comment on the possibilities for new bases of collective engagement in this historical moment.

Joy, as West says, is a collective experience, or at least provides the possibility of one. For me, this definition revises the discussion of woman's pleasure inherited from feminism and psychoanalysis and places it within a black progressive context. Like pleasure, joy still speaks, though not exclusively, to that locus of sensation and activity around which so much contemporary black anxiety is produced—the erotic. But I refer to the erotic here not in its most general, colloquial sense, but in the way that Audre Lorde has defined it: as our deepest knowledge, a power that, unlike other spheres of power, we all have access to, and that can lessen the threat of our individual difference.[1]

I.

Joy is about the potential for our coexistence within another sphere of knowledge. Alluding to this potential forces us to question what the practices might be within that alternative space and to examine what current conflicts prevent us from entering its realm. At this moment, joy is another mythic construction, one that has recently been engagingly deployed in Alice Walker's *Possessing the Secret of Joy,* a novel that at once appropriates and recontextualizes the restrictive neocolonial adage that gives Walker her title—"Black people are natural, they possess the secret of joy."[2] And in transposing this essentialist version of blackness, Walker plunges us into what may be considered the most uncompromising nexus of confusion in the black diasporic intellectual tradition: those issues gathered around gender, sexuality, and cultural or national difference.

In Walker's novel, these issues coalesce around the very particular concern of female circumcision, a subject that she rightly identifies as at the center of a structure of myth. The question becomes, of course, whose myth are we reading? Is this an essential African cultural symbolic exposed for the gaze of African descendants in the West or, rather, a mythic construction shedding light on the syncretic nature of our own ambivalent situation in the black diaspora? We must take it as the latter. As Stuart Hall writes,

...popular culture, commodified and stereotyped as it often is, is not at all, as we sometimes think of it, the arena where we find who we really are, the truth of our experience. It is an arena that is *profoundly* mythic...It is where we discover and play with the identifications of ourselves, where we are imagined, where we are represented, not only to the audiences out there who do not get the message, but to ourselves for the first time.

Walker's novel forces us to confront not the history of female circumcision, but the mythical use of that particularity as a point of entry into the analysis of our ever elusive connections to Africa. And like other contemporary efforts, such as Afrocentrism, this novel struggles to rebuild the story of Africa only to satisfy the intense desires for an oppositional politics unleashed within the United States.

We could read the gesture of an African-American woman writing from the United States about an issue that primarily affects black women living in Africa as an extension of the imperial eye, as the thoroughly acritical absorption of a classic western feminist paradigm, or as a liberatory move to shed light not only on the painful practice of circumcision, but on the strange marriage of "traditional" African and colonial culture that is the post-colonial condition. But the choice among these three limited readings is already, perhaps, a false one. However we see it, Walker locks the proverbial feminist personal-is-political into battle with that notorious black manifesto—we will not have our business put in the streets—and cuts close to the communal nerve. The scene of this battle is that legacy of western hegemony in the world, the courtroom; its protagonist is a black woman, a woman both African and American in the truest sense, on trial for murder. But this is where the story begins to trouble our most intransigent notions of collective responsibility and personal agency exercised in the interest of justice: she has not murdered a European or a village elder, but an older African woman; she is never absolved of and never denies her responsibility in this; and in the end she herself is put to death. In fact, she tells us her story from "the other side," through Walker as author and medium.

Tashi, Walker's protagonist, has returned from Europe and the United States to Africa to murder the woman who performed her circumcision (an operation that was performed late in Tashi's life due to the earlier intervention of the African-American missionaries who challenged the common practices of her native heritage). It was Tashi herself who insisted, once the missionaries were gone, on having this ritual performed. But its legacies were years of physical and emotional pain, altered and reduced possibilities for her sexual pleasure, and brain damage for the only child to whom she was able to give birth. Within the structure of the novel, Tashi's assertion of individual agency, her choice to be circumcised, is supported by the nationalist call to traditional culture, within which the sexual economy places restrictions on pleasure that disproportionately impact on the lives of women. Her later rebellion against this decision is a specific feminist act against those discriminatory structures of gender subordination.

But this "choice"—between modern, feminist, U.S.–based black culture and traditional African culture—is the paradigm we must learn to unread. The now more familiar error of western feminism, of extending the category of woman across time and space with little regard for cultural or historical specificity, is no longer at issue; it is the ground for defining that specificity that must be questioned. On the basis of the premise that the personal is political, the category of experience allows Walker to extend a narrative of personal pain into a larger story of gender oppression, colonial expansion, and post-colonial cultural conflict. To deconstruct the paradox of Tashi's choice between Africa and America, between culture and gender, between woman's acceptability and woman's pleasure is not merely to state that within the context of western rationalism she can exert no agency. It is to go even further than complicating the means by which we determine an action, and more significantly here, a cultural text, to be progressive or conservative, positive or negative. It is to begin dismantling our understanding of the very means by which we are said to come to know, to decide, and to act.

Tashi is unable to answer questions in the courtroom according to a direct, rational line of thought. Instead, her response to interrogation is to begin to tell a story. We come to understand that her habit of telling stories in these crucial moments is not simply a reflection of her essential African nature or Walker's acritical reproduction of one; it is the result of a very specific psychic trauma that prevents her, until she is "returned to actionality" (as Frantz Fanon might have said), from finding peace. *Possessing the Secret of Joy* is the story of the recovery of that trauma through a series of therapies: psychoanalysis, dreamwork, and Tashi's own creative reconstruction of her unconscious life in endless outpourings, including a mural that eventually takes over her living space. Out of her dreampainting is produced a narrative of gender subordination in its mythic form, interpreted as the cultural symbolic of her native Africa. This extension of the personal symbolic directly into the cultural symbolic (the Jungian approach) relies on belief in a system of therapy that derives meanings from dreams and interprets them as reflections not only of our inescapably singular *experience* of culture but applies them unself-consciously to the collective imagining, and therefore to the collective reality as well.

II.

Taken to the extreme, the elision from the personal into the cultural symbolic is consistent with the tendency toward one of two opposing vectors of logic in contemporary cultural criticism. In this direction, interpersonal relationships are translated directly into structural oppressions, and the remedies for any antagonisms can be found within the private spheres of personal examination and family confrontation. In the other direction, structural oppressions *determine* interpersonal dynamics, such that all interactions that attempt to transcend these barriers become suspect unless they are subsumed under the larger project of structural reform. These habits parallel the modes of the two critical camps Cornel West describes here in setting out his thesis on nihilism in black America—the conservative behaviorists and the liberal structuralists, respectively.

West's attention to these political critiques points out that in both tendencies an analysis of our cultural products is largely absent. We will have to be reminded again and again that any successful cultural critique must take account not only of the movements in both these directions, but of the myriad cross-connections and dislocations that occur and prevent us from making any such overdetermined causal links. In attending to the domain of culture and in articulating a variety of points of ambivalence, this volume points past the conclusions drawn in the game of positive and negative image-making and toward the context in which this game is played out. But it also refuses to strand us in that ambivalent zone; recognizing our mandate to "do the right thing," these essays return us to the ground of intervention equipped with that "other knowledge."

In the year of the televised trial of four Los Angeles police officers for the beating of Rodney King, and in the wake of such cataclysmic public events as the Anita Hill–Clarence Thomas confrontation, it has become increasingly clear that black criticism will have to begin to make use of the more sophisticated cultural analyses that depend on understanding the complexities of video imaging, the dynamics of representation, and reception theories. These analyses take for their example the full range of colors available on the screen and deploy the now habitual but nonetheless crucial triad, gender-race-class, to describe the politics for the constituencies of color encoded there. This volume reaches beyond the model of black criticism that posits blackness as the antidote to whiteness within the limited but predominant sphere of American popular culture. It speaks to the ways black cultures have begun to revise the dynamics inherited from other periods of intense cultural production and reassembled vision in terms that extend beyond the illusory poles of black and white. And it references the various movements, political and cultural, struggling to build "the new cultural politics of difference," as Cornel West has recently named them.[3]

These new cultural politics depend on our reconfiguring the field of representation, on creating another context for cultural and political activity as we reconstitute the ground of difference. That is to say, some differences we habitually construct, as Stuart Hall says here, might not make any difference at all. The newness in any cultural politics of difference also depends on our being able to distinguish between these *habits* of difference, read through the mythic realm of culture, and the emerging differences we must *learn* to read. Despite the anxieties that Walker's novel produces for those of us interested in the areas of black culture, feminism, and post-colonial international conflict and negotiation it is incumbent upon us to produce the context that will, I believe, not only allow a discussion of her novel, but provide a basis for making our way through the nexus of complexes, both psychological and social, that she describes. I repeat: she rightly identifies the center of a structure of myth—our myth. But how do we read that myth? And what do we *do* once we can read it?

Walker's novel encourages a political reading that, when attributed to one specific version of the joined discourses of feminism and psychoanalysis, allows us to see Tashi's dreampainting but not its frame, the projection without its context, the myth but not our coimplication in it. We do not, for example, necessarily recognize, until Walker makes it clear in her closing address to the reader, that Tashi is one of many invented "African" names, that the Olinkans are not an existing African tribe, that the village and the nation in which this story takes place are the products of Walker's imagination. We do not recognize this either, because our knowledge of Africa is so severely limited or, because conceiving of this as the stuff of fiction so entirely transgresses our notion of just representation.

Do we, peoples of the African diaspora, any longer have the right to invent an Africa? Certainly, argue some of the cultural workers in this volume, we have the right to attend creatively to any of the domains we find within our view. And this may follow even if what we see exists only inside of our own heads. But how, in black popular culture and criticism, are we, as Coco Fusco writes, to "avoid retracing 'intercultural' patterns established by modernism, surrealism, and ethnography"? The answer lies perhaps not in policing the areas over which our gaze may trespass, but, rather, in making it clear that what we reveal there are the effects of that gaze. This is the significant political move this volume makes: rather than policing the borders of black culture, these critics attend to the high and the low, the progressive and conservative, the general and the particular. In doing so, airing our dirty laundry so to speak, they challenge the resurrection of communal privacy that relies on extending the paradigm of the bourgeois family to that of the "race." And they go against the version of Afrocentrism that, in inscribing privacy at the level of the community, attempts to hide the gender relations that benefit "our men," calling it the protection of "our women." Or, worse yet, that treat our cultural circumstances as so distinct and isolated from the larger community's that the gender economy no longer applies.

Afrocentrists and feminists, then, are struggling with each other over whether or not we can extend the paradigm of the family to the black nation. This group of cultural critics overwhelmingly sides with the feminist critique. It is interesting, however, considering the current tendency to set the methods and practices of Afrocentricity and feminism against each other, to discover that they can sometimes operate in the same mode. That is, the personal-is-political should involve breaking down the rigid distinctions between public and private space so that all dominations are submitted to critique, and therefore are available to structural, political, *and* personal redress. Instead, in practice, the personal-is-political often results in overexamination of that single set of experiential narratives within a diverse but simultaneously oppressed community that are privileged along another axis (*white* female, black *male,* gay *white,* even black gay *male*). That is, behind the express attention to the conditions of the entire community, one set of narratives gets sanctioned over another because it can exert authority elsewhere. Thus, the category of experience is not always opened to all comers, and the analysis of that experience too often follows a particularly narrow formula.

Paul Gilroy's discussion of the trope of the family in contemporary black music struggles with recent nationalist articulations, describing them as a set of therapies and not a coherent ideology:

> Afrocentricity names itself "systematic nationalism"...but it is stubbornly focused around the reconstitution of individual consciousness rather than around the reconstruction of the black nation in exile or elsewhere...the flow is always inward, never outward; the truth of racialized being is sought, not in the world, but in the psyche.

What this tells us is perhaps something we already know: whatever its register, colloquial or academic, the discourse of psychoanalysis permeates our lives. It also tells us that we must work to overcome that inward movement both Gilroy and West comment upon.

For black studies, this may mean that we need to grapple with the legacy of Frantz Fanon's fusion of anti-colonial activism and psychiatric practice. For Fanon, though there were always individuals in need of treatment, the entire social body shared in the psychological—now sociological—complex. All were imbricated in its structure. All drew similar meanings from diverse appearances coded consistently. And yet the question was *how* individuals came to share in the common understanding, or, how they came to participate in the collective unconscious through "the unreflected imposition of a culture."[4] Returning individuals to actionality, to the realm of affect *and* effect, was about determining the ground of collective action, about the restoration of a whole number of individual dream-events taking place at the same time, in the same place, toward the same end—what we now call a movement.

For black peoples, overcoming this inward tendency—our attempt to construct a politics on the basis of our individual wants and not our collective needs—necessitates evaluating our relationship to the economies of pleasure. And in so doing, we must confront what Michele Wallace calls our "gap around the psychoanalytic," our collective resistance not to being psychoanalyzed, or to the academic discourses of psychoanalysis, but to recognizing the significance of our centrality especially in the American psyche. This is to approach the issue of our relative power as central figures in the national imagination, which is to point neither to our continued victimization nor to our successes in spite of it (the two continuous grand counternarratives Stuart Hall notes have consumed us). Most importantly, redirecting that inward movement is to confront our submergence in the discursive system of psychoanalysis, the evidence of which comes forward in our everyday meaning-making and in our cultural products. As Lisa Kennedy writes, commenting on 1991 as "the year of black film," the T-shirt would read: "It's an Oedipal Thing. You Wouldn't Understand."

III.

To begin to understand how this inward/outward tension forms a context for this volume, we must examine the archaeology of our current use of the terms pleasure and joy, since these serve as reminders here of a hidden discourse. In speaking of pleasure, contemporary feminist theory, especially feminist film theory (and film is the favorite topic, it seems, for these cultural critics), derives much of its language from readings of Jacques Lacan on feminine sexuality, in which the phallic order assigns woman to a position of fantasy. According to Lacan, the sexual relation, that is, our narration of the act of sex, hangs on a fantasy of oneness—phallocentrism, but also our longing to be "as one with another"—that the idea of woman comes to support.

Lacan posits a feminine pleasure, *jouissance* (literally, "coming," from the verb "to enjoy"), outside of this phallocentric circuit and against this fantasy, or rather, as its excess. Connecting this directly to the problem of "man" as a speaking being, Lacan describes *jouissance* as a language of the body; it is pure *signifiance*. (The translation of the latter term to "signifying" is a happy coincidence we should not ignore here.[5]) But he also connects this feminine pleasure to the realm of God. For who experiences this pleasure? Not women, as defined by rigid gender economies, but all those who say no to the phallic—and invite the possibility of love, not the *act* of love, but love itself:

You only have to go and look at Bernini's statue in Rome to understand immediately that she's coming, there is no doubt about it. And what is her *jouissance,* her *coming* from? It is clear that the essential testimony of the mystics is that they are experiencing it but know nothing about it.[6]

Finally, this is the reason the photo of jazz singer Maxine Sullivan, a still from Greta Schiller's film biography *Love To Be in Love,* begins a volume on black popular culture. To me, it expresses something of what Greg Tate has called our "romance with being black." Set against Bernini's *The Ecstasy of Saint Theresa,* it speaks to the agenda for control of our own images, to the history of the exclusion of black pleasure in dominant narratives, to the collective basis of our conception of joy, and to the difficulty of describing what we feel when we experience it.

What is the experience Sullivan expresses in what Gilroy calls here the "ethics of antiphony—a kind of ideal moment in the relationship between the performer and the crowd that surpasses anything the structures of the family can provide"? What is she signifying that we cannot *know,* in the sense that it will always exceed the words we have to describe it? It is something always outside, but that we move closer and closer to incorporating. Or, rather, it is inside, an interior knowledge that we must struggle to bring into use. We have always recognized it in our experience of black music. We are only just beginning to feel its effects, and the resistance to them, in literature and film and the other arts.

How do we recognize "it" when we find it? How do we translate the experience we have that we cannot know? Even to discuss it, to call it up in a single phrase—black pleasure, black joy—is to risk the essentialist gesture, just as to think of feminine *jouissance* as women's pleasure is to miss the significance of that intervention in women's politics. It is a question of love, of ethics, and not of sexual difference, not even of the regimes—culture and politics—that accrue value to either side of that difference unequally. *Jouissance* is not the complement to sexual pleasure; it is its supplement. It is not only oppositional but alternative.

Similarly, in West's formulation, we must ask whether joy is on the other side of pleasure, its complement, or, like *jouissance,* its supplement. If joy is the domain of non-market values—love, care, kindness, service, solidarity, the struggle for justice—what must we do with our knowledge of how eminently marketable these values can be? We will have to distinguish between those moments when cultural products take the place of oppositional practices, the oppositional practices themselves, and that other, alternative space where we glimpse our infinite possibilities. Hazel Carby's comments on feminist uses of black women's texts in the new curricula might serve as a lesson for ourselves as well:

> Black cultural texts have become fictional substitutes for the lack of any sustained social or political relationships with black people in a society that has retained many of its historical practices of apartheid...

To extend the discussion of pleasure and joy into a black context is to shift back and forth continually between the political and ethical registers. It is to shift between the material domain in which our identities are constructed for us and where we play them out, and that "other side" where we play with the many possibilities of identification, where we possess the secret of joy. The ethical register is never entirely present to us; we can experience it, but we cannot know it. But the potential for ethical love takes us outside of the circuit of oppositional practices and gives us a hint of that other knowledge, the erotic, propelling us back into action. Remembering that the move from pleasure to joy takes us from a notion of political agency to an examination of how we come to know, to decide, and to act, we reinvestigate the grounds of consciousness and address not only the subject matter of black life, but also its modes, aesthetic and cultural.

In other words, how do these oppositional practices work? As Arthur Jafa asks,

> Black pleasure (not joy)—what are its parameters, what are its primal sites...How do those strategies in Black music play out the rupture and repair of African-American life on the structural level?...How can we interrogate the medium [film] to find a way Black movement in itself could carry, for example, the weight of sheer tonality in Black song? And I'm not talking about the lyrics that Aretha Franklin sang. I'm talking about *how she sang them.*

Jafa distinguishes here between these questions, which are about the different bases of our pleasure, and those about joy, which would shift us into the alternative ethical domain. But drawing on this other, alternative knowledge also helps us to understand the structure of the oppositions we make.

Certain critiques of popular culture depend on our willingness to privilege language in our criticism when we privilege other aesthetic domains in our experience of popular culture. Can we, for example, analyze rap production, see it as positive or negative, and discuss the ways it affects our communities by attending to its lyrics and by pointing to their reflection of negative sociological indicators? And if so, what then should we do about rap—censor it, study it, struggle to change it? Sherley Anne Williams, Houston A. Baker, and Tricia Rose debate these questions here. Williams's criticism of the content of rap lyrics calls for us to take responsibility for black cultural production, to address the nihilism expressed in this cultural form. Baker, unwilling to relinquish rap music to the interpretations based on an inadequate knowledge of the form and to the transgressions of certain of its practitioners, points to our failure as cultural critics to account for the *range* of rap products. Rose, finally, reads both of these as responses to rap music based on an imbalance in our attention to both the sociohistorical and the *aesthetic* contexts of black practices.

Arthur Jafa's questions lead us into thinking about the modes of black popular culture, about the ways a more sophisticated understanding of the black aesthetic can alter our approach to its forms and enhance our ability to make use of all of the sources of our hybrid tradition, not just those that privilege its western heritage. In an analysis of what she calls the "documentary mode" in contemporary black fiction film, Valerie Smith displays some of the political consequences of adhering to the political requirements of one western form: "Directors, studios, and their marketing experts collude in shrinking the distance between referent and representation…thereby delimiting what counts, or sells, as black film." But she also shows us examples of contemporary black documentarians who "trouble the boundary between fact and fiction" through techniques that expose or break down the distinctions between private and public, filmmaker and audience, history and myth.

Of course, whether cultural critics assign black cultural products the labels of progressive or conservative, black audiences can never be said to absorb them in this rigid way, as Jacqueline Bobo demonstrates in her discussion of the "unruly" responses of black women to popular films. There, we find that even the most well-intentioned political critiques too often assume a paradigm of audience reception that never holds true in every individual case. What we "know" cannot exclusively determine our experience of culture.

Still, we continue to circumscribe the limits of our cultural production, distinguishing what is authentically ours from what is not. As Ada Gay Griffin states, "Black films, Black videos, and Black media are those productions directed by Black artists on subjects and forms that reference the Black experience and imagination...Why is it important to make that distinction?...Ultimately, it is about power over the image." Griffin's definition, which relies on an identification both of the author *and* of the subject matter, assumes, in fact, a *position* on black culture. And it is a position that we sometimes enforce, or that we perceive to be in force, to our detriment, which is to say: sometimes we only pretend to know what black culture is.

Again, how do we recognize "it" when we find it? There is, as Stuart Hall notes, a test of black popular culture, to which we submit all of its products. It is sometimes a test as to where it fits on the increasingly conservative ideological spectrum of blackness. But it is also another kind of test—against what Jafa refers to as the deepest level at which we carry culture, our "core stability," our sense that what we are experiencing is, as Hall says, right on. Isaac Julien, however, asks us to go further in de-essentializing blackness, and the cultural critics in this volume overwhelmingly adhere to that philosophy. Still, as Greg Tate comments, "I don't think anyone, even someone who is self-defined as an antiessentialist, wants to give up a certain kind of romance we have with being black."

We love to be in love.

IV.

There are conflicts, however, that disturb our love and prevent us from entering that alternative collective space. The event that those who contributed to this volume probably remember most vividly speaks to the other side of this potential for a more expansive criticism and a more diversified experience. There was, at this conference, an overt agreement on a feminist and anti-homophobic agenda. But that stated agreement does nothing to untangle the vicious web of resistant personal habits and complicit practices with which we are all so familiar—habits that lie, as they did for Fanon, under both our black skins and our white masks. Quite ironically, the sometimes antagonistic discussion of sexuality in black communities grew out of a question inspired by Henry Louis Gates's elegy on Isaac Julien's film *Looking for Langston,* an essay that, in its meanderings through the thickets of black historical responses to black gay interventions, attacked our disciplinary (in both senses) practices of black representation.

The conflict that ensued, in the panel on gender, sexuality, and black images in popular culture, is evidence of our incomplete understanding of the phrase "black pleasure, black joy." It is a reflection of the way that our critical, cultural, and personal habits can sometimes obscure our common goals and impede our progress toward a more inclusive definition of blackness. In the end, it became largely a debate between those men seen to have secured prominent positions in the academy (and elsewhere) and those who remain outside; that is, as much as it was a debate about the quality of attention to our diverse sexualities, it was also an intergenerational dialogue. As Lisa Kennedy remarked, another Oedipal reenactment. But, as such, it also begins the necessary process of resolving that conflict. Paradoxically, for example, both Houston Baker and Thomas Harris, who were taken to have set out divergent agendas on sexuality, bravely brought up the difficult subject of black father-son relations and the cycle of violence that gets passed on there as the grammar of love. Perhaps we should heed Paul Gilroy's cautionary tale about the seemingly ideologically opposed John Singleton's *Boyz N the Hood* and Marlon Riggs's *Tongues Untied*: "Aren't there also similarities and convergences in the way that love between men is the common focus of both of these 'texts'?"

We are forced to wonder, then: Where are black women positioned in this dialogue between men? Perhaps in what Jacquie Jones calls here "the space of accusation." My invocation of Walker's novel was precisely to combat that positioning. On the other side of her story of female circumcision lies the quiet projection of a fantasy of an alternative sexual universe, challenging the rituals of sexual behavior that restrict us to some very specific notions of pleasure. Uncovering the taboo area of sexual practices outside the sphere of the so-called norm, *Possessing the Secret of Joy* explicitly addresses that circumscribed area Michele Wallace deconstructs for us here in her discussion of Spike Lee's *Jungle Fever*—namely, oral sex—as a code for black women's pleasure, gay sexuality, and other illicit practices, including drug use in black communities.

But attending to the questions of gender and sexuality, even of the popular, often produces conservative black reactions to culture. The erotic, like all transgressive attempts to move into the alternative domain, also moves us toward the possibility of its spectacularization, as in, for example, pornography. Judith Wilson's essay on the work of Romare Bearden and the subject of the black female nude in black art history is courageous in its effort to situate black high art production within the context of our popular aesthetic and moral battles. But I only became aware of how courageous she had been when we were denied permission from the Bearden estate, the Bearden family, and the Bearden foundation to reprint the artworks for this volume. In their estimation, Wilson's argument is "offensive, inaccurate and...damaging to the reputation of the late Mr. Bearden."[7]

The response of the Bearden estate, their desire both to protect Bearden's reputation from the association with pornography and to restrict the use of those images to high art formats, speaks to the specific cultural and political circumstances of this particular historical moment. As Greg Tate argues in his exaltation of the legacy of Miles Davis (despite Davis's sexual politics):

> Miles was a holdover from a time when Black intellectual and artistic achievement was a major currency through which racial progress could be bought and symbolically sold—on a rarified, individual basis—a time distinct from the postnationalist present where Black representation is a market force capable of raking in corporate profits without being allied to our agendas of social advancement and reform.

Tate, of course, is speaking largely of U.S. African-American culture, which at one time, as Manthia Diawara testifies here, formed a powerful enough oppositional critique that it served as an alternative cultural capital for African youth. But as Coco Fusco remarks, "For black peoples, at this historical moment, the postmodern fetishizing of the exchange of cultural property seems less like emancipation and more like intensified alienation."

Black Americans in the United States now have unprecedented access to cultural and economic capital "by fair means or foul," as bell hooks points out. We must, therefore, begin to analyze the relative power derived from our position as citizens, however unsatisfied, of these United States. And this means thinking through the hall of mirrors in which our cultural power gets projected as political power, but also the ways our cultural power allows the projection of one national black culture around the world as what Coco Fusco calls the "prototype of blackness." We must mark the dangers not only of an Afrocentrism that reinvents Africa to satisfy our need to fight our own internal national cultural battles, but of what Paul Gilroy renames it as—Americocentrism. How often, for example, do we think of what it means to have those other privileges, like the ability, barring the economic contingencies that overwhelmingly plague us yet, to travel where we want? Unlike the Haitians and the Sudanese and other African and diasporic peoples who cannot enter the United States and certainly are not invited to stay, we can visit the Africa we want to reinvent.

In the end, this volume points to our need to begin to build politics, cultural and otherwise, that remain cognizant of the variety of axes along which we may be oppressed and empowered differentially. Manning Marable and Angela Davis call for these new politics here. We can consider it a gift that Davis writes back, not only to the sixties' nationalists with whom she struggled to define a movement that was internationalist, feminist, and attentive to class, but to the current crop of culture producers, hip-hop consumers, and budding activists who are forced to draw on an unfortunately narrow range of representations of that era. Along with Marable, who makes concrete suggestions toward a program for new political engagement, Davis establishes the basis for another intergenerational dialogue, one in which many of the participants have never had the opportunity to live in a time when black capacity was so vehemently asserted in the face of the forces that continue to deny it.

To build new bases for political engagement, for oppositional critique, we must take into account the variety of intersecting oppressions that structure our collective life. Remembering all of our differences and remaining attentive to their cross-connections and dislocations depends on our willingness to negotiate the difficulties brought to our attention by that other knowledge. It necessitates our imagining not just what we want but what the others we represent may need. And in the same way that addressing blackness transnationally provides a context for better understanding our own internal hierarchies, the knowledge of the distance between pleasure and joy, though provisional, reminds us that our choices are always overdetermined. In our eagerness to do the right thing, we must ask again and again: How do we come to know, to decide, and to act? How do we learn to do what is right? And how do we remember that justice is an experience of the moment, that its definition will continue to shift depending on the time and the location we are in?

V.

If we possessed the secret of joy, we could always access the domain of love and thereby always be assured of doing the right, the ethical, thing. Instead, what we have is a provisional understanding of the possibilities for a more democratic existence and a recognition of the necessity to intervene in the political sphere in a firmly oppositional stance. Taking care as to how we form these oppositions, an analysis of culture allows us to attend to representation in both its senses—as aesthetic presentation and political delegation.[8] We must remain mindful that the basis of the popular is its association with the people. And we must never forget that the mirage of representativeness is merely a symptom of our experience of that powerful and profoundly mythic realm—our culture.

It may seem curious to some that a volume on black popular culture invokes the work of those who are not usually considered "popular" artists, whose work either partakes of high art's formulas or has audiences narrow enough to preclude the routine application of that label. Inasmuch as the definition of the popular employed here assumes that all our cultural products provide arenas for populist intellectual critique, this volume responds to the persistent perception that all black cultural products are marginal to the mainstream, that they are, therefore, of the masses—at the low end of the high/low pole. And it writes back against the flip side of that perception, namely, that those of us who are in a position to publicly critique our cultural production are by definition in the service of the masses, and when they are perceived to have failed, have betrayed them.

The role of the cultural worker may be, as bell hooks argues, to point to what we see that others do not and call it out. But just as we can no longer assume that blackness is a positive modulating force in our lives, remaining with us no matter where we go and what we do (as the song says, "Black Meaning Good"), we can no longer rely on a model of false consciousness to describe the situation of the oppressed. We cannot privilege one way of knowing over another.

The experience of joy, of the erotic, is another kind of knowledge, and we must learn to account for its insights because, in theory, it is a domain to which we all have access. To trace our movement in and out of it, from pleasure to joy and back again, is to go beyond the framework even of what we have called for almost a century our double consciousness—the capacity to speak and think dialogically and in more than one register at the same time. The reference to joy exceeds this capacity precisely because double consciousness has always implied the articulation of two *identifiable* and *opposing* modes of consciousness—blackness and whiteness. In other words, it has remained inside the sphere of its invention: the twentieth-century American color line. And because of this, it has always hidden the ambiguous yet privileged national class position of the truly double-conscious. This is, after all, how W.E.B. Du Bois first defined it. The experience of joy, on the other hand, provides another context for these oppositions; remaining alternative and outside, it signals our more democratic hopes and dreams for the future.

Joy is a knowledge that by definition critiques some of the oppositions we persist in making, and even goes against the very habits we sometimes confuse as the basis of our collective experience. Blackness, as we deploy it, is not coincident with that other knowledge. It is still a mythic construction; and our love of it must be recognized as the fantasy that it is—which is not to say that we must now fall out of love. Nor is it to encourage us to end our romance with being black. It is to remind us that there is, as Houston Baker says here, no innocence "as in puppy love or as in non-overdetermined by market conditions." When Stuart Hall speaks of the black subject having emerged from the age of innocence, he refers to the necessity for rethinking these politics of representation, and within them, the still more fraught arenas of gender and sexuality.

This emergent critical consciousness will do precisely what hooks says it will—change the nature of our pleasure. But it is possible that this change in the habits of our satisfaction will bring us closer to the collective domain of joy, where more of us will find what we need and where some of us will find less of what we are accustomed to. What we might find is that we can exchange our current habit of catharsis in vision—vision replacing action—for what Michele Wallace calls a revolution in vision. But for that we must continually remind ourselves of the possibilities for collective responsibility and personal agency exercised in the interest of justice, the potential hidden in that elusive phrase: black pleasure, black joy.

1. Audre Lorde, "Uses of the Erotic: The Erotic as Power" in *Sister Outsider* (Trumansburg, N.Y.: The Crossing Press, 1984).

2. Alice Walker, *Possessing the Secret of Joy* (New York: Harcourt, Brace, Jovanovich, 1992). The epigraph is from Mirella Ricciardi, *African Saga* (London: Collins, 1981).

3. Cornel West, "The New Cultural Politics of Difference," in *Out There: Marginalization and Contemporary Cultures,* ed. Russell Ferguson, et al. (Cambridge: MIT Press in association with The New Museum of Contemporary Art, 1990), 19–36.

4. Frantz Fanon, *Black Skin, White Masks,* trans. Charles Lam Markmann (New York: Grove Press, 1967), 188.

5. Henry Louis Gates, Jr. has posited the signifying tradition as the contribution of black peoples to the American literary tradition. See Gates, *The Signifying Monkey: A Theory of African-American Literary Criticism* (New York: Oxford University Press, 1988).

6. Juliet Mitchell and Jacqueline Rose, eds., *Feminine Sexuality: Jacques Lacan and the école freudienne* (New York: W. W. Norton & Co., 1982), 147.

7. From a letter signed by the attorney to the Bearden estate and dated October 14, 1992.

8. The articulation of the two senses of representation, and their implications, is derived from Gayatri Spivak, "Can the Subaltern Speak?" in *Marxism and the Interpretation of Culture,* ed. Lawrence Grossberg and Cary Nelson (Urbana: University of Illinois Press, 1988), 271–308.

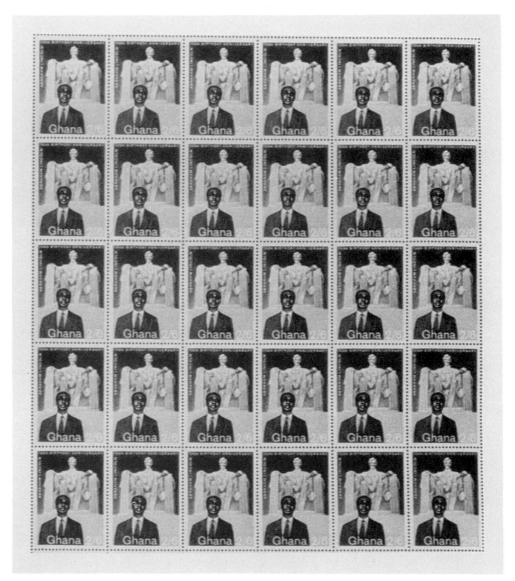

20   Postage stamps of Kwame Nkrumah commemorating Lincoln's Birthday, 1959.

Stuart Hall

What Is This "Black" in Black Popular Culture?

I begin with a question: what sort of moment is this in which to pose the question of black popular culture? These moments are always conjunctural. They have their historical specificity; and although they always exhibit similarities and continuities with the other moments in which we pose a question like this, they are never the same moment. And the combination of what is similar and what is different defines not only the specificity of the moment, but the specificity of the question, and therefore the strategies of cultural politics with which we attempt to intervene in popular culture, and the form and style of cultural theory and criticizing that has to go along with such an intermatch. In his important essay, "The New Cultural Politics of Difference,"[1] Cornel West offers a genealogy of what this moment is, a genealogy of the present that I find brilliantly concise and insightful. His genealogy follows, to some extent, positions I tried to outline in an article that has become somewhat notorious,[2] but it also usefully maps the moment into an American context and in relation to the cognitive and intellectual philosophical traditions with which it engages.

According to Cornel, the moment, this moment, has three general coordinates. The first is the displacement of European models of high culture, of Europe as the universal subject of culture, and of culture itself in its old Arnoldian reading as the last refuge...I nearly said of scoundrels, but I won't say who it is of. At least we know who it was against—culture against the barbarians, against the people rattling the gates as the deathless prose of anarchy flowed away from Arnold's pen. The second coordinate is the emergence of the United States as a world power and, consequently, as the center of global cultural production and circulation. This emergence is both a displacement and a hegemonic shift in the *definition* of culture—a movement from high culture to American mainstream popular culture and its mass-cultural, image-mediated, technological forms. The third coordinate is the decolonization of the third world, culturally marked by the emergence of the decolonized sensibilities. And I read the decolonization of the third world in Frantz Fanon's sense: I include in it the impact of civil rights and black struggles on the decolo-nization of the minds of the peoples of the black diaspora.

Let me add some qualifications to that general picture, qualifications that, in my view, make this present moment a very distinctive one in which to ask the question about black popular culture. First, I remind you of the ambiguities of that shift from Europe to America, since it includes America's ambivalent relationship to European high culture and the ambiguity of America's relationship to its own internal ethnic hierarchies. Western Europe did not have, until recently, any ethnicity at all. Or didn't recognize it had any. America has always had a series of ethnicities, and consequently, the construction of ethnic hierarchies has always defined its cultural politics. And, of course, silenced and unacknowledged, the fact of American popular culture itself, which has always contained within it, whether silenced or not, black American popular vernacular traditions. It may be hard to remember that, when viewed from outside of the United States, American mainstream popular culture has always involved certain traditions that could only be attributed to black cultural vernacular traditions.

The second qualification concerns the nature of the period of cultural globalization in progress now. I hate the term "the global postmodern," so empty and sliding a signifier that it can be taken to mean virtually anything you like. And, certainly, blacks are as ambiguously placed in relation to postmodernism as they were in relation to high modernism: even when denuded of its wide-European, disenchanted Marxist, French intellectual provenance and scaled down to a more modest descriptive status, postmodernism remains extremely unevenly developed as a phenomenon in which the old center/peripheries of high modernity consistently reappear. The only places where one can genuinely experience the postmodern ethnic cuisine are Manhattan and London, not Calcutta. And yet it is impossible to refuse "the global postmodern" entirely, insofar as it registers certain stylistic shifts in what I want to call the cultural dominant. Even if postmodernism is not a new cultural epoch, but only modernism in the streets, that, in itself, represents an important shifting of the terrain of culture toward the popular—toward popular practices, toward everyday practices, toward local narratives, toward the decentering of old hierarchies and the grand narratives. This decentering or displacement opens up new spaces of contestation and affects a momentous shift in the high culture of popular culture relations, thus presenting us with a strategic and important opportunity for intervention in the popular cultural field.

Third, we must bear in mind postmodernism's deep and ambivalent fascination with difference—sexual difference, cultural difference, racial difference, and above all, ethnic difference. Quite in opposition to the blindness and hostility that European high culture evidenced on the whole toward ethnic difference—its inability even to speak ethnicity when it was so manifestly registering its effects—there's nothing that global postmodernism loves better than a certain kind of difference: a touch of ethnicity, a taste of the exotic, as we say in England, "a bit of the other" (which in the United Kingdom has a sexual as well as an ethnic connotation). Michele Wallace was quite right, in her seminal essay "Modernism, Postmodernism and the Problem of the Visual in Afro-American Culture,"[3] to ask whether this reappearance of a proliferation of difference, of a certain kind of ascent of the global postmodern, isn't a repeat of that "now you see it, now you don't" game that modernism once played with primitivism, to ask whether it is not once again achieved at the expense of the vast silencing about the West's fascination with the bodies of black men and women of other ethnicities. And we must ask about that continuing silence within postmodernism's shifting terrain, about whether the forms of licensing of the gaze that this proliferation of difference invites and allows, at the same time as it disavows, is not really, along with Benetton and the mixed male models of the face, a kind of difference that doesn't make a difference of any kind.

Hal Foster writes—Wallace quotes him in her essay—"the primitive is a modern problem, a crisis in cultural identity"[4]—hence, the modernist construction of primitivism, the fetishistic recognition and disavowal of the primitive difference. But this resolution is only a repression; delayed into our political unconscious, the primitive returns uncannily at the moment of its apparent political eclipse. This rupture of primitivism, managed by modernism, becomes another postmodern event. That managing is certainly evident in the difference that may not make a difference, which marks the ambiguous appearance of ethnicity at the heart of global postmodernism. But it cannot be only that. For we cannot forget how cultural life, above all in the West, but elsewhere as well, has been transformed in our lifetimes by the voicing of the margins.

Within culture, marginality, though it remains peripheral to the broader mainstream, has never been such a productive space as it is now. And that is not simply the opening within the dominant of spaces that those outside it can occupy. It is also the result of the cultural politics of difference, of the struggles around difference, of the production of new identities, of the appearance of new subjects on the political and cultural stage. This is true not only in regard to race, but also for other marginalized ethnicities, as well as around feminism and around sexual politics in the gay and lesbian movement, as a result of a new kind of cultural politics. Of course, I don't want to suggest that we can counter-pose some easy sense of victories won to the eternal story of our own marginalization—I'm tired of those two continuous grand counternarratives. To remain within them is to become trapped in that endless either/or, either total victory or total incorporation, which almost never happens in cultural politics, but with which cultural critics always put themselves to bed.

What we are talking about is the struggle over cultural hegemony, which is these days waged as much in popular culture as anywhere else. That high/popular distinction is precisely what the global postmodern is displacing. Cultural hegemony is never about pure victory or pure domination (that's not what the term means); it is never a zero-sum cultural game; it is always about shifting the balance of power in the relations of culture; it is always about changing the dispositions and the configurations of cultural power, not getting out of it. There is a kind of "nothing ever changes, the system always wins" attitude, which I read as the cynical protective shell that, I'm sorry to say, American cultural critics frequently wear, a shell that sometimes prevents them from developing cultural strategies that can make a difference. It is as if, in order to protect themselves against the occasional defeat, they have to pretend they can see right through everything—and it's just the same as it always was.

Now, cultural strategies that can make a difference, that's what I'm interested in—those that can make a difference and can shift the dispositions of power. I acknowledge that the spaces "won" for difference are few and far between, that they are very carefully policed and regulated. I believe they are limited. I know, to my cost, that they are grossly underfunded, that there is always a price of incorporation to be paid when the cutting edge of difference and transgression is blunted into spectacularization. I know that what replaces invisibility is a kind of carefully regulated, segregated visibility. But it does not help simply to name-call it "the same." That name-calling merely reflects the particular model of cultural politics to which we remain attached, precisely, the zero-sum game—our model replacing their model, our identities in place of their identities—what Antonio Gramsci called culture as a once and for all "war of maneuver," when, in fact, the only game in town worth playing is the game of cultural "wars of position."

Lest you think, to paraphrase Gramsci, my optimism of the will has now completely outstripped my pessimism of the intellect, let me add a fourth element that comments on the moment. For, if the global postmodern represents an ambiguous opening to difference and to the margins and makes a certain kind of decentering of the Western narrative a likely possibility, it is matched, from the very heartland of cultural politics, by the backlash: the aggressive resistance to difference; the attempt to restore the canon of Western civilization; the assault, direct and indirect, on multiculturalism; the return to grand narratives of history, language, and literature (the three great supporting pillars of national identity and national culture); the defense of ethnic absolutism, of a cultural racism that has marked the Thatcher and the Reagan eras; and the new xenophobias that are about to overwhelm fortress Europe. The last thing to do is read me as saying the cultural dialectic is finished. Part of the problem is that we have forgotten what sort of space the space of popular culture is. And black popular culture is not exempt from that dialectic, which is historical, not a matter of bad faith. It is therefore necessary to deconstruct the popular once and for all. There is no going back to an innocent view of what it consists of.

Popular culture carries that affirmative ring because of the prominence of the word "popular." And, in one sense, popular culture always has its base in the experiences, the pleasures, the memories, the traditions of the people. It has connections with local hopes and local aspirations, local tragedies and local scenarios that are the everyday practices and the everyday experiences of ordinary folks. Hence, it links with what Mikhail Bakhtin calls "the vulgar"—the popular, the informal, the underside, the grotesque. That is why it has always been counterposed to elite or high culture, and is thus a site of alternative traditions. And that is why the dominant tradition has always been deeply suspicious of it, quite rightly. They suspect that they are about to be overtaken by what Bakhtin calls "the carnivalesque." This fundamental mapping of culture between the high and the low has been charted into four symbolic domains by Peter

Stallybrass and Allon White in their important book *The Politics and Poetics of Transgression.* They talk about the mapping of high and low in psychic forms, in the human body, in space, and in the social order.[5] And they discuss the high/low distinction as a fundamental basis to the mechanisms of ordering and of sense-making in European and other cultures despite the fact that the contents of what is high and what is low change from one historical moment to another.

The important point is the ordering of different aesthetic morals, social aesthetics, the orderings of culture that open up culture to the play of power, not an inventory of what is high versus what is low at any particular moment. That is why Gramsci, who has a side of common sense on which, above all, cultural hegemony is made, lost, and struggled over, gave the question of what he called "the national popular" such strategic importance. The role of the "popular" in popular culture is to fix the authenticity of popular forms, rooting them in the experiences of popular communities from which they draw their strength, allowing us to see them as expressive of a particular subordinate social life that resists its being constantly made over as low and outside.

However, as popular culture has historically become the dominant form of global culture, so it is at the same time the scene, par excellence, of commodification, of the industries where culture enters directly into the circuits of a dominant technology—the circuits of power and capital. It is the space of homogenization where stereotyping and the formulaic mercilessly process the material and experiences it draws into its web, where control over narratives and representations passes into the hands of the established cultural bureaucracies, sometimes without a murmur. It is rooted in popular experience and available for expropriation at one and the same time. I want to argue that this is necessarily and inevitably so. And this goes for black popular culture as well. Black popular culture, like all popular cultures in the modern world, is bound to be contradictory, and this is not because we haven't fought the cultural battle well enough.

By definition, black popular culture is a contradictory space. It is a sight of strategic contestation. But it can never be simplified or explained in terms of the simple binary oppositions that are still habitually used to map it out: high and low; resistance versus incorporation; authentic versus inauthentic; experiential versus formal; opposition versus homogenization. There are always positions to be won in popular culture, but no struggle can capture popular culture itself for our side or theirs. Why is that so? What consequences does this have for strategies of intervention in cultural politics? How does it shift the basis for black cultural criticism?

However deformed, incorporated, and inauthentic are the forms in which black people and black communities and traditions appear and are represented in popular culture, we continue to see, in the figures and the repertoires on which popular culture draws, the experiences that stand behind them. In its expressivity, its musicality, its orality, in its rich, deep, and varied attention to speech, in its inflections toward the vernacular and the local, in its rich production of counternarratives, and above all, in its metaphorical use of the musical vocabulary, black popular culture has enabled the surfacing, inside the mixed and contradictory modes even of some mainstream popular culture, of elements of a discourse that is different—other forms of life, other traditions of representation.

I do not propose to repeat the work of those who have devoted their scholarly, critical, and creative lives to identifying the distinctiveness of these diasporic traditions, to exploring their modes and the historical experiences and memories they encode. I say only three inadequate things about these traditions, since they are germane to the point I want to develop. First, I ask you to note how, within the black repertoire, *style*—which mainstream cultural critics often believe to be the mere husk, the wrapping, the sugar coating on the pill—has become *itself* the subject of what is going on. Second, mark how, displaced from a logocentric world—where the direct mastery of cultural modes meant the mastery of writing, and hence, both of the criticism of writing (logocentric criticism) and the deconstruction of writing—the people of the black diaspora have, in opposition to all of that, found the deep form, the deep structure of their cultural life in music. Third, think of how these cultures have used the body—as if it was, and it often was, the only cultural capital we had. We have worked on ourselves as the canvases of representation.

There are deep questions here of cultural transmission and inheritance, and of the complex relations between African origins and the irreversible scatterings of the diaspora, questions I cannot go into. But I do believe that these repertoires of black popular culture, which, since we were excluded from the cultural mainstream, were often the only performative spaces we had left, were overdetermined from at least two directions: they were partly determined from their inheritances; but they were also critically determined by the diasporic conditions in which the connections were forged. Selective appropriation, incorporation, and rearticulation of European ideologies, cultures, and institutions, alongside an African heritage—this is Cornel West again—led to linguistic innovations in rhetorical stylization of the body, forms of occupying an alien social space, heightened expressions, hairstyles, ways of walking, standing, and talking, and a means of constituting and sustaining camaraderie and community.

The point of underlying overdetermination—black cultural repertoires constituted from two directions at once—is perhaps more subversive than you think. It is to insist that in black popular culture, strictly speaking, ethnographically speaking, there are no pure forms at all. Always these forms are the product of partial synchronization, of engagement across cultural boundaries, of the confluence of more than one cultural tradition, of the negotiations of dominant and subordinate positions, of the subterranean strategies of recoding and transcoding, of critical signification, of signifying. Always these forms are impure, to some degree hybridized from a vernacular base. Thus, they must always be heard, not simply as the recovery of a lost dialogue bearing clues for the production of new musics (because there is never any going back to the old in a simple way), but as what they are—adaptations, molded to the mixed, contradictory, hybrid spaces of popular culture. They are not the recovery of something pure that we can, at last, live by. In what Kobena Mercer calls the necessity for a diaspora aesthetic, we are obliged to acknowledge they are what the modern is.

It is this mark of difference *inside* forms of popular culture—which are by definition contradictory and which therefore appear as impure, threatened by incorporation or exclusion—that is carried by the signifier "black" in the term "black popular culture." It has come to signify the black community, where these traditions were kept, and whose struggles survive in the persistence of the black experience (the historical experience of black people in the diaspora), of the black aesthetic (the distinctive cultural repertoires out of which popular representations were made), and of the black counternarratives we have struggled to voice. Here, black popular culture returns to the ground I defined earlier. "Good" black popular culture can pass the test of authenticity—the reference to black experience and to black expressivity. These serve as the guarantees in the determination of which black popular culture is right on, which is ours and which is not.

I have the feeling that, historically, nothing could have been done to intervene in the dominated field of mainstream popular culture, to try to win some space there, without the strategies through which those dimensions were condensed onto the signifier "black." Where would we be, as bell hooks once remarked, without a touch of essentialism? Or, what Gayatri Spivak calls strategic essentialism, a necessary moment? The question is whether we are any longer in that moment, whether that is still a sufficient basis for the strategies of new interventions. Let me try to set forth what seem to me to be the weaknesses of this essentializing moment and the strategies, creative and critical, that flow from it.

This moment essentializes differences in several senses. It sees difference as "their traditions versus ours," not in a positional way, but in a mutually exclusive, autonomous, and self-sufficient one. And it is therefore unable to grasp the dialogic strategies and hybrid forms essential to the diaspora aesthetic. A movement beyond this essentialism is not an aesthetic or critical strategy without a cultural politics, without a marking of difference. It is not simply rearticulation and reappropriation for the sake of it. What it evades is the essentializing of difference into two mutually opposed either/or's. What it does is to reorganize us into a new kind of cultural positionality, a different logic of difference. To encapsulate what Paul Gilroy has so vividly put on the political and cultural agenda of black politics in the United Kingdom: blacks in the British diaspora must, at this historical moment, refuse the binary black *or* British. They must refuse it because the "or" remains the sight of *constant contestation* when the aim of the struggle must be, instead, to replace the "or" with the potentiality or the possibility of an "and." That is the logic of coupling rather than the logic of a binary opposition. You can be black *and* British, not only because that is a necessary position to take in 1992, but because even those two terms, joined now by the coupler "and" instead of opposed to one another, do not exhaust all of our identities. Only some of our identities are sometimes caught in that particular struggle.

The essentializing moment is weak because it naturalizes and dehistoricizes difference, mistaking what is historical and cultural for what is natural, biological, and genetic. The moment the signifier "black" is torn from its historical, cultural, and political embedding and lodged in a biologically constituted racial category, we valorize, by inversion, the very ground of the racism we are trying to deconstruct. In addition, as always happens when we naturalize historical categories (think about gender and sexuality), we fix that signifier outside of history, outside of change, outside of political intervention. And once it is fixed, we are tempted to use "black" as sufficient in itself to guarantee the progressive character of the politics we fight under the banner—as if we don't have any other politics to argue about except whether something's black or not. We are tempted to display that signifier as a device which can purify the impure, bring the straying brothers and sisters who don't know what they ought to be doing into line, and police the boundaries—which are of course political, symbolic, and positional boundaries—as if they were genetic. For which, I'm sorry to say, read "jungle fever"—as if we can translate from nature to politics using a racial category to warrant the politics of a cultural text and as a line against which to measure deviation.

Moreover, we tend to privilege experience itself, as if black life is lived experience outside of representation. We have only, as it were, to express what we already know we are. Instead, it is only through the way in which we represent and imagine ourselves that we come to know how we are constituted and who we are. There is no escape from the politics of representation, and we cannot wield "how life really is out there" as a kind of test against which the political rightness or wrongness of a particular cultural strategy or text can be measured. It will not be a mystery to you that I think that "black" is none of these things in reality. It is not a category of essence and, hence, this way of understanding the floating signifier in black popular culture now will not do.

There is, of course, a very profound set of distinctive, historically defined black experiences that contribute to those alternative repertoires I spoke about earlier. But it is to the diversity, not the homogeneity, of black experience that we must now give our undivided creative attention. This is not simply to appreciate the historical and experiential differences within and between communities, regions, country and city, across national cultures, between diasporas, but also to recognize the other kinds of difference that place, position, and locate black people. The point is not simply that, since our racial differences do not constitute all of us, we are always different, negotiating different kinds of differences—of gender, of sexuality, of class. It is also that these antagonisms

Pat Ward Williams, *Accused/Blowtorch/Padlock*, 1987.

refuse to be neatly aligned; they are simply not reducible to one another; they refuse to coalesce around a single axis of differentiation. We are always in negotiation, not with a single set of oppositions that place us always in the same relation to others, but with a series of different positionalities. Each has for us its point of profound subjective identification. And that is the most difficult thing about this proliferation of the field of identities and antagonisms: they are often dislocating in relation to one another.

Thus, to put it crudely, certain ways in which black men continue to live out their counter-identities as black masculinities and replay those fantasies of black masculinities in the theaters of popular culture are, when viewed from along other axes of difference, the very masculine identities that are oppressive to women, that claim visibility for their hardness only at the expense of the vulnerability of black women and the feminization of gay black men. The way in which a transgressive politics in one domain is constantly sutured and stabilized by reactionary or unexamined politics in another is only to be explained by this continuous cross-dislocation of one identity by another, one structure by another. Dominant ethnicities are always underpinned by a particular sexual economy, a particular figured masculinity, a particular class identity. There is no guarantee, in reaching for an essentialized racial identity of which we think we can be certain, that it will always turn out to be mutually liberating and progressive on all the other dimensions. It *can* be won. There *is* a politics there to be struggled for. But the invocation of a guaranteed black experience behind it will not produce that politics. Indeed, the plurality of antagonisms and differences that now seek to destroy the unity of black politics, given the complexities of the structures of subordination that have been formed by the way in which we were inserted into the black diaspora, is not at all surprising.

These are the thoughts that drove me to speak, in an unguarded moment, of the end of the innocence of the black subject or the end of the innocent notion of an essential black subject. And I want to end simply by reminding you that this end is also a beginning. As Isaac Julien said in an interview with bell hooks in which they discussed his new film *Young Soul Rebels,* his attempt in his own work to portray a number of different racial bodies, to constitute a range of different black subjectivities, and to engage with the positionalities of a number of different kinds of black masculinities:

> ...blackness as a sign is never enough. What does that black subject do, how does it act, how does it think politically...being black isn't really good enough for me: I want to know what your cultural politics are.[6]

I want to end with two thoughts that take that point back to the subject of popular culture. The first is to remind you that popular culture, commodified and stereotyped as it often is, is not at all, as we sometimes think of it, the arena where we find who we really are, the truth of our experience. It is an arena that is *profoundly* mythic. It is a theater of popular desires, a theater of popular fantasies. It is where we discover and play with the identifications of ourselves, where we are imagined, where we are represented, not only to the audiences out there who do not get the message, but to ourselves for the first time. As Freud said, sex (and representation) mainly takes place in the head. Second, though the terrain of the popular looks as if it is constructed with single binaries, it is not. I reminded you about the importance of the structuring of cultural space in terms of high and low, and the threat of the Bakhtinian carnivalesque. I think Bakhtin has been profoundly misread. The carnivalesque is not simply an upturning of two things which remain locked within their oppositional frameworks; it is also crosscut by what Bakhtin calls the dialogic.

I simply want to end with an account of what is involved in understanding popular culture, in a dialogic rather than in a strictly oppositional way, from *The Politics and Poetics of Transgression* by Stallybrass and White:

> A recurrent pattern emerges: the "top" attempts to reject and eliminate the "bottom" for reasons of prestige and status, only to discover, not only that it is in some way frequently dependent upon the low-Other...but also that the top *includes* that low symbolically, as a primary eroticized constituent of its own fantasy life. The result is a mobile, conflictual fusion of power, fear, and desire in the construction of subjectivity: a psychological dependence upon precisely those others which are being rigorously opposed and excluded at the social level. It is for this reason that what is socially peripheral is so frequently *symbolically* central...[7]

1. Cornel West, "The New Cultural Politics of Difference," in *Out There: Marginalization and Contemporary Cultures,* ed. Russell Ferguson, et al. (Cambridge: MIT Press in association with the New Museum of Contemporary Art, 1990), 19–36.
2. Stuart Hall, "New Ethnicities," *Black Film/British Cinema, ICA Document 7,* ed. Kobena Mercer (London: Institute of Contemporary Arts, 1988), 27–31.
3. Michele Wallace, "Modernism, Postmodernism and the Problem of the Visual in Afro-American Culture," in *Out There: Marginalization and Contemporary Cultures,* 39–50.
4. Hal Foster, *Recodings: Art, Spectacle, and Cultural Politics* (Port Townsend, Wash.: Bay Press, 1985), 204.
5. Peter Stallybrass and Allon White, *The Politics and Poetics of Transgression* (Ithaca: Cornell University Press, 1986), 3.
6. bell hooks. "States of Desire" (interview with Isaac Julien), *Transition* 1, no. 3, 175.
7. Stallybrass and White, *The Politics and Poetics of Transgression,* 5.

Daniel Tisdale, *Paul Robeson*, from the "Post Plantation Pop" series, 1988.

Popular Culture: Theory and Criticism

36   Robert Sengstacke, *Savior's Day Gathering, Chicago Colosseum*, 1966.

Cornel West

Nihilism in Black America

Recent discussions about the plight of African Americans—especially those at the bottom of the social ladder—tend to divide into two camps. On the one hand, there are those who highlight the *structural* constraints on the life chances of black people. This point of view involves a subtle historical and sociological analysis of slavery, Jim Crowism, job and residential discrimination, skewed unemployment rates, inadequate health care, and poor education. On the other hand, there are those who stress the *behavioral* impediments to black upward mobility. They focus on the waning of the Protestant ethic—hard work, deferred gratification, frugality, and responsibility—in much of black America.

Those in the first camp—the liberal structuralists—call for full employment, health, education and child-care programs, and broad affirmative action practices. In short, a new, more sober version of the best of the New Deal and the Great Society: more government money, better bureaucrats, and an active citizenry. Those in the second camp—the conservative behaviorists—promote self-help programs, black business expansion, and non-preferential job practices. They support vigorous "free market" strategies that depend on fundamental changes in how black people act and live. To put it bluntly, their projects rest largely upon a cultural revival of the Protestant ethic in black America.

Unfortunately, these two camps have nearly suffocated the crucial debate that should be taking place about the prospects for black America. This debate must go far beyond the liberal and conservative positions in three fundamental ways. First, we must acknowledge that structures and behavior are inseparable, that institutions and values go hand in hand. How people act and live is shaped—though in no way dictated or determined—by the larger circumstances in which they find themselves. These circumstances can be changed, their limits attenuated, by positive actions to elevate living conditions.

Second, we should reject the idea that structures are primarily economic and political creatures—an idea that sees culture as an ephemeral set of behavioral attitudes and values. Culture is quite as structural as the economy or politics; it is rooted in institutions like families, schools, churches, synagogues, mosques, and communication industries (television, radio, video, music). Similarly, the economy and politics are not only influenced by values, they also promote particular cultural ideals of the good life and good society.

Third, and most important, we must delve into the depths where neither liberals nor conservatives dare to tread, namely, into the murky waters of despair and dread that now flood the streets of black America. To talk about the depressing statistics of unemployment, infant mortality, incarceration, teenage pregnancy, and violent crime is one thing. But to face up to the monumental eclipse of hope, the unprecedented collapse of meaning, the incredible disregard for human (especially black) life and property in much of black America is something else.

The liberal-conservative discussion conceals the most basic issue now facing black America: *the nihilistic threat to its very existence.* This threat is not simply a matter of relative economic deprivation and political powerlessness—though economic well-being and political clout are requisites for meaningful black progress. It is primarily a question of speaking to the profound sense of psychological depression, personal worthlessness, and social despair so widespread in black America.

The liberal structuralists fail to grapple with this threat for two reasons. First, their focus on structural constraints relates almost exclusively to the economy and politics. They show no understanding of the structural character of culture. Why? Because they tend to view people in egoistic and rationalist terms, according to which they are motivated primarily by self-interest and self-preservation. Needless to say, this is partly true about most of us. Yet, people, especially degraded and oppressed people, are also hungry for identity, meaning, and self-worth.

The second reason liberal structuralists overlook the nihilistic threat is a sheer failure of nerve. They hesitate to talk honestly about culture, the realm of meanings and values, because to do so may seem to lend itself too readily to conservative conclusions in the narrow way Americans discuss race. If there is a hidden taboo among liberals, it is to resist talking about values *too much* because it takes the focus away from structures, especially the positive role of government. But this failure leaves the existential and psychological realities of black people in the lurch. In this way, liberal structuralists neglect the battered identities rampant in black America.

As for the conservative behaviorists, they not only misconstrue the nihilistic threat, but inadvertently contribute to it. This is a serious charge, and it rests upon three claims. First, conservative behaviorists talk about values and attitudes as if political and economic structures hardly exist. They rarely, if ever, examine the innumerable cases in which black people do act on the Protestant ethic and still remain at the bottom of the social ladder. Instead, they highlight the few instances in which blacks ascend to the top, as if such success is available to all blacks, regardless of circumstances. Such a vulgar rendition of Horatio Alger in blackface may serve as a source of inspiration to some—a kind of model for those already on the right track. But it cannot serve as a substitute for serious historical and social analysis of the predicaments of and prospects for all black people, especially the grossly disadvantaged ones.

Second, conservative behaviorists discuss black culture as if acknowledging one's obvious victimization by white supremacist practices (compounded by sexism and class condition) is taboo. They tell black people to see themselves as agents, not victims. And on the surface, this is comforting advice, a nice cliché for downtrodden people. But inspirational slogans cannot substitute for substantive historical and social analysis. Although black people have never been simply victims, wallowing in self-pity and begging for white giveaways, they have been—and are—*victimized.* Therefore, to call on black people to be agents makes sense only if we also examine the dynamics of this victimization against which their agency will, in part, be exercised. What is particularly naive and peculiarly vicious about the conservative behavioral outlook is that it tends to deny the lingering effect of black history—a history inseparable from though not reducible to victimization. In this way, crucial and indispensable themes of self-help and personal responsibility are wrenched out of historical context and contemporary circumstances—as if it is all a matter of personal will.

This ahistorical perspective contributes to the nihilistic threat within black America in that it can be used to justify right-wing cutbacks for poor people struggling for decent housing, child care, health care, and education. And, as I pointed out earlier, although liberals are deficient in important ways, they are right on target in their critique of conservative government cutbacks for services to the poor. These ghastly cutbacks are one cause of the nihilistic threat to black America.

The proper starting point for the crucial debate about the prospects for black America is the nihilism that increasingly pervades black communities. *Nihilism is to be understood here not as a philosophic doctrine that there are no rational grounds for legitimate standards or authority; it is, far more, the lived experience of coping with a life of horrifying meaninglessness, hopelessness, and (most important) lovelessness.* This usually results in a numbing detachment from others and a self-destructive disposition toward the world. Life without meaning, hope, and love breeds a coldhearted, mean-spirited outlook that destroys both the individual and others.

Nihilism is not new in black America. The first African encounter with the New World was an encounter with a distinctive form of the Absurd. The initial black struggle against degradation and devaluation in the enslaved circumstances of the New World was, in part, a struggle against nihilism. In fact, the major enemy of black survival in America has been, and is, neither oppression nor exploitation but rather the nihilistic threat—that is, loss of hope and absence of meaning. For as long as hope remains and meaning is preserved, the possibility of overcoming oppression stays alive. The self-fulfilling prophecy of the nihilistic threat is that without hope there can be no struggle.

The genius of our black foremothers and forefathers was to create powerful buffers to ward off the nihilistic threat, to equip black folk with cultural armor to beat back the demons of hopelessness, meaninglessness, and lovelessness. These buffers consisted of cultural structures of meaning and feeling that created and sustained communities; this armor constituted ways of life and struggle that embodied values of service and sacrifice, love and care, discipline and excellence. In other words, traditions for black surviving and thriving under usually adverse New World conditions were major barriers against the nihilistic threat. These traditions consist primarily of black religious and civic institutions that sustained familial and communal networks of support. If cultures are, in part, what human beings create (out of antecedent fragments of other cultures) in order to convince themselves not to commit suicide, then black foremothers and forefathers are to be applauded. In fact, until the early seventies black Americans had the lowest suicide rate in the United States. But, now young black people lead the nation in suicides.

What has changed? What went wrong? The bitter irony of integration? The cumulative effects of a genocidal conspiracy? The virtual collapse of rising expectations after the optimistic sixties? None of us fully understands why the nihilistic threat is more powerful now than ever before. I believe that the commodification of black life and the crisis of black leadership are two basic reasons. The recent shattering of black civil society—black families, neighborhoods, schools, churches, mosques—leaves more and more black people vulnerable to the nihilistic threat. This shattering spawns a deracinated and denuded people with little sense of self and few existential moorings.

Black people have always been in America's wilderness in search of a promised land. Yet many black folk now reside in a jungle with a cutthroat morality devoid of any faith in deliverance or hope for freedom. Contrary to the superficial claims of conservative behaviorists, these jungles are not primarily the result of pathological behavior. Rather, this behavior is the tragic response of a people bereft of resources to confront the workings of U.S. capitalist society. This does not mean that individual black people are not responsible for their actions—black murderers and rapists should go to jail. But it does mean that the nihilistic threat contributes to criminal behavior—a threat that feeds on poverty *and* shattered cultural institutions. The nihilistic threat is now more powerful than ever before because the armor to ward against it is weaker.

But why this shattering of black civil society, this weakening of black cultural institutions in asphalt jungles? *Corporate market institutions* have contributed greatly to this situation. By corporate market institutions I mean that complex set of interlocking enterprises that have a disproportionate amount of capital, power, and influence on how our society is shaped. Needless to say, the primary motivation of these institutions is to make profits, and their basic strategy is to convince the public to consume. These institutions have helped create a seductive way of life, a culture of consumption that capitalizes on every opportunity to make money. Market calculations and cost-benefit analyses hold sway in almost every sphere of U.S. society.

The common denominator in these calculations and analyses is usually the provision, expansion, and intensification of *pleasure*. Pleasure is a multivalent term; it means different things to many people. In our way of life it involves comfort, convenience, and sexual stimulation. This mentality pays little heed to the past, and views the future as no more than a repetition of a hedonistically driven present. This market morality stigmatizes others as objects for personal pleasure or bodily stimulation. In this view, traditional morality is not undermined by radical feminists, cultural radicals in the sixties, or libertarians, as alleged by conservative behaviorists. Rather, corporate market institutions have greatly contributed to undermining traditional morality in order to stay in business and make a profit. This is especially evident in the culture industries—television, radio, video, music—in which gestures of foreplay and orgiastic pleasure flood the marketplace.

Like all Americans, African Americans are influenced greatly by the images of comfort, convenience, machismo, femininity, violence, and sexual stimulation that bombard consumers. These seductive images contribute to the predominance of the market-inspired way of life over all others—and thereby edge out nonmarket values—love, care, service to others—handed down by preceding generations. The predominance of this way of life among those living in poverty-ridden conditions, with a limited capacity to ward off self-contempt and self-hatred, results in the possible triumph of the nihilistic threat in black America.

A major contemporary strategy for holding the nihilistic threat at bay is to attack directly the sense of worthlessness and self-loathing in black America. The angst resembles a kind of collective clinical depression in significant pockets of black America. The eclipse of hope and collapse of meaning in much of black America is linked to the structural dynamics of corporate market institutions that affect all Americans. Under these circumstances, black existential angst derives from the lived experience of ontological wounds and emotional scars inflicted by white supremacist beliefs and images permeating U.S. society and culture. These wounds and scars attack black intelligence, black ability, black beauty, and black character daily in subtle and not-so-subtle ways.

The accumulated effect of these wounds and scars produces a deep-seated anger, a boiling sense of rage, and a passionate pessimism regarding America's will to justice. Under conditions of slavery and Jim Crow segregation, this anger, rage, and pessimism remained relatively muted because of a well-justified fear of brutal white retaliation. The major breakthroughs of the sixties—more psychically than politically—swept this fear away. Sadly, the combination of the market way of life, poverty-ridden conditions, black existential angst, and the lessening of fear toward white authorities has directed most of the anger, rage, and despair toward fellow black citizens, especially black women. Only recently has this nihilistic threat—and its ugly inhuman outlook and actions—surfaced in the larger American society. And it surely reveals one of the many instances of cultural decay in a declining empire.

What is to be done about this nihilistic threat? Is there really any hope, given our shattered civil society, market-driven corporate enterprises, and white supremacism? If one begins with the threat of concrete nihilism, then one must talk about some kind of *politics of conversion*. New models of collective black leadership must promote a version of this politics. Like alcoholism and drug addiction, nihilism is a disease of the soul. It can never be completely cured, and there is always the possibility of relapse. But there is always a chance for conversion—a chance for people to believe that there is hope for the future and a meaning to struggle. This chance rests neither on an agreement about what justice consists of nor on an analysis of how racism, sexism, or class subordination operate. Such arguments and analyses are indispensable, but a politics of conversion requires more. Nihilism is not overcome by arguments or analyses; it is tamed by love and care. Any disease of the soul must be conquered by a turning of one's soul. This turning is done by one's own affirmation of one's worth—an affirmation fueled by the concern of others. This is why a love ethic must be at the center of a politics of conversion.

This love ethic has nothing to do with sentimental feelings or tribal connections. Rather it is a last attempt at generating a sense of agency among a downtrodden people. The best exemplar of this love ethic is depicted on a number of levels in Toni Morrison's novel *Beloved*. Self-love and love of others are both modes toward increasing self-valuation and encouraging political resistance in one's community. These modes of valuation and resistance are rooted in a subversive memory—the best of one's past without romantic nostalgia—and guided by a universal love ethic. For my purposes here, *Beloved* can be construed as bringing together the loving yet critical affirmation of black humanity found in the best of black nationalist movements, the perennial hope against hope for transracial coalition in progressive movements, and the painful struggle for self-affirming sanity in a history in which the nihilistic threat *seems* insurmountable.

The politics of conversion proceed principally on the local level—in those institutions in civil society still vital enough to promote self-worth and self-affirmation. It surfaces on the state and national levels only when grass-roots democratic organizations put forward a collective leadership that has earned the love and respect of and, most important, that has proved itself *accountable* to these organizations. This collective leadership must exemplify moral integrity, character, and democratic statesmanship within itself and within its organizations.

Like liberal structuralists, the advocates of a politics of conversion never lose sight of the structural conditions that shape the sufferings and lives of people. Yet, unlike liberal structuralism, the politics of conversion meet the nihilistic threat head-on. Like conservative behaviorism, the politics of conversion openly confronts the self-destructive and inhumane actions of black people. Unlike conservative behaviorists, the politics of conversion situates (not exonerates) these actions within inhumane circumstances. The politics of conversion shuns the limelight—a limelight that solicits status seekers and ingratiates egomaniacs. Instead, it stays on the ground among the toiling everyday people, ushering forth humble freedom fighters—both followers and leaders—who have the audacity to take the nihilistic threat by the neck and turn back its deadly assaults.

The nihilistic threat to black America is inseparable from a crisis in black leadership. This crisis is threefold. First, at the national level, the courageous yet problematic example of Jesse Jackson looms large. On the one hand, his presidential campaigns based on a progressive multiracial coalition were *the* major left-liberal response to Reagan's conservative policies. For the first time since the last days of Martin Luther King, Jr.—with the grand exception of Harold Washington—the nearly de facto segregation in U.S. progressive politics was confronted and surmounted. On the other hand, Jackson's televisual style resists grass-roots organizing and, most important, democratic accountability. His brilliance, energy, and charisma sustain his public visibility—but at the expense of programmatic follow-through. We are approaching the moment in which this style exhausts its progressive potential.

Other national nonelectoral black leaders—like Benjamin Hooks of the NAACP and John Jacobs of the National Urban League—rightly highlight the traditional problems of racial discrimination, racial violence, and slow racial

progress. Yet their preoccupation with race—the mandate from their organizations—downplays the crucial class, environmental, and patriarchal deter-
minants of black life chances. Black politicians—especially new victors like
Mayor David Dinkins of New York City and Governor Douglas Wilder of
Virginia—are part of a larger, lethargic electoral system riddled with decreasing revenues, loss of public confidence, self-perpetuating mediocrity, and
pervasive corruption. Like most American elected officials, few black politicians can sidestep these seductive traps. So black leadership at the national level
tends to lack a moral vision that can organize (not just periodically energize)
subtle analyses that enlighten (not simply intermittently awaken), and exemplary practices that uplift (not merely convey status that awes), black people.

Second, this relative failure in leadership creates vacuums to be filled by bold
and defiant black nationalist figures with even narrower visions, one-note racial
analyses, and sensationalist practices. Louis Farrakhan, Al Sharpton, and others
vigorously attempt to be protest leaders in this myopic mode—a mode often,
though not always, reeking of immoral xenophobia. This kind of black leadership not only is symptomatic of black alienation and desperation in a country
more and more indifferent or hostile to the quality of life among black working
and poor people, it also reinforces the fragmentation of U.S. progressive efforts
that could reverse this deplorable plight. In this way, black nationalist leaders
often inadvertently contribute to the very impasse they are trying to overcome:
inadequate social attention and action to change the plight of America's "invisible people," especially disadvantaged black people.

Third, this crisis of black leadership contributes to political cynicism among
black people; it encourages the idea that we cannot really make a difference in
changing our society. This cynicism   already promoted by the larger political
culture—dampens the fire of engaged *local* activists who have made a difference, yet who also have little interest in being in the national limelight. Rather
they engage in protracted grass-roots organizing in principled coalitions that
bring power and pressure to bear on specific issues.

Without such activists there can be no progressive politics. Yet state, re-
gional, and national networks are also required for an effective progressive
politics. That is why local-based collective (and especially multigendered)
models of black leadership are needed. These models must shun the idea of
one black national leader; they also should put a premium on critical dialogue

Jesse Jackson and Congresswoman Maxine Waters in Los Angeles after the verdict in the trial of
the four police officers charged in the beating of Rodney King, April 30, 1992.

and democratic accountability in black organizations.

Work must get done. Decisions must be made. But charismatic presence is no legitimate substitute for collective responsibility. Only a charisma of humility and accountability is worthy of a leadership grounded in a genuine democratic struggle for greater freedom and equality. This indeed may be the best—and last—hope to hold back the nihilistic threat to black America.

bell hooks

Dialectically Down with the Critical Program

When contemporary black intellectuals speak about the plight of African Americans, the mounting despair and nihilism, they usually invoke images of a dehumanized underclass ravaged by external and internal genocidal forces. Rarely do any of us, frankly and without shame, dare to name our own struggles to ward off depression, despair, suicidal impulses, and addictions, exposing the reality of our own lives. Despite certain levels of material privilege and status and relative tolerance of our presence in predominately white spheres of power, the feelings of hopelessness and helplessness, of powerlessness in the face of structures of domination, often pervade our lives. We insurgent black critical thinkers able to break through denial and testify to the crisis of meaning in our own lives need not see ourselves as estranged and alienated from suffering underclass black folks who are in crisis. We know: we too are in crisis.

Recognizing that our fate is inextricably linked to that of all African Americans, we must remain committed to the progressive struggle for black liberation. That struggle has been hindered by our collective willingness to accept the dominant culture's insistence that there be no vital, reciprocal, transformative connection between the work of intellectuals and the work of masses of people in everyday life. At the same time, black folks of all classes, including academics, have nurtured the profound anti-intellectualism that we are all socialized to perpetuate in a white supremacist, capitalist patriarchy.

Coupling this anti-intellectualism with the naive assumption that liberation is determined solely by the extent to which individuals have access to material goods, masses of black people assume that anything we can do for money is somehow an act of resistance, a challenge to racist domination. Black intellectuals, scholars, cultural workers, and artists are as involved in the lust for money and power as any other group of black folks. Although we may not be shooting folks in the streets for a pair of tennis shoes, many of us willingly participate in the commodification of blackness in ways that ultimately perpetuate the existing social order. In methods akin to strip-mining, we have appropriated and exploited those essential and unique aspects of black culture that have been life-affirming, leaving masses of black people without the resources and skills that would enable them to effectively resist domination. Even those among us who may feel the emptiness of material success—which is never in any way aligned with our capacity to live meaningful lives—help perpetuate the false assumption that material acquisition is the quintessential expression of "making it," of liberation.

Tragically, even though black folks have historically unprecedented access to the realm of material acquisition (by fair means or foul), we have been systematically losing ground when it comes to making political interventions that would fundamentally transform the lives of African Americans and the society as a whole. Indeed, the traditional political focus on institutionalized reform in the realm of civil rights has become increasingly detached from a progressive vision of social change that would oppose the status quo. As long as black people embrace the status quo, believing that our collective liberation lies in aping bourgeois and ruling-class white culture, we help to perpetuate white supremacist, capitalist patriarchy and condone the dehumanization and marginalization endemic to it. And this collaboration is the breeding ground for the profound disillusionment, hopelessness, despair, and life-threatening nihilism.

In his recent essay, "Nihilism in Black America" [reprinted in this volume], Cornel West comments on this situation, suggesting that,

> If one begins with the threat of concrete nihilism, then one must talk about some kind of politics of *conversion* ... Nihilism is not overcome by arguments or analyses; it is tamed by love and care. Any disease of the soul must be conquered by a turning of one's soul. This turning is done by one's own affirmation of one's worth—an affirmation fueled by the concern of others. This is why a love ethic must be at the center of a politics of conversion.

Only by systematic resistance to the existing social order, which denies our worth, can we, as African Americans, fully affirm ourselves as a people or as

Joint Chiefs of Staff Chairman General Colin Powell and First Lady Barbara Bush enjoy a dance at a reception for Black appointees to the Bush Administration. Photograph by Jason Miccolo Johnson.

individuals. We must posit an oppositional worldview that offers practical strategies for political and social transformation, concrete ways of thinking and living differently. In white supremacist, capitalist patriarchy, black folk can most effectively resist and transform by breaking with internalized racism, by decolonizing our minds and actions. A politics of conversion that has liberatory possibility for black people must begin with a renewed focus on revolutionary black politics, an emphasis on decolonization as a necessary stage in the process of transformation. As we undergo this process, we acquire an oppositional perspective, a standpoint that can guide and direct our radical and revolutionary agendas.

The process of decolonization requires participation in the kind of critical and analytical thinking that is at the root of all intellectual activity. Understanding this, it should be evident that insurgent black intellectuals, critical thinkers, cultural workers, and others can best serve diverse black communities by developing and practicing pedagogies of resistance that aim to share knowledge. That means talking with folks about what decolonization is and why it is important. It means teaching folks how to think critically and analytically. Given the widespread conservative thrust of contemporary black social and political thought and practice, we are in dire need of a pedagogy of liberation, a politics of conversion that would re-radicalize our collective critical consciousness.

Because critical pedagogy can and must take place in every sphere of black life, street corners, beauty parlors, movie theaters, and any other places we hang out are sites as important for dialogue, for teaching, and for learning as classroom settings. Black intellectuals, artists, and critical thinkers must be willing to spread the word beyond institutionalized settings. Increasingly, the conservative nature of most institutions makes subversion a more difficult task; yet we cannot give up on academic settings, even as we cannot behave as though these are the only relevant locations for discussion and dialogue. The effort to radicalize is equally important within and outside the academy.

At the same time, we must resist widespread anti-intellectualism by showing, in practical ways, how we improve the quality of our lives through analysis and critique, through oppositional work. This is no easy task; hostility and resentment toward black intellectuals abounds. Since so many black academics, intellectuals, and critical thinkers offer their insights in ways that often reflect little or no concern for the black masses, it is not surprising that our presence and our words are received with suspicion and distrust. It is our task to demonstrate that we are committed to those forms of intellectual practice that aim to enhance the quality of black life across class lines, and that fully reflect our concern for renewed black liberation struggle.

Since black popular culture continues to be a vital location for the dissemination of black thought—shaping and informing our ethics, values, and politics—useful critical dialogues can and should emerge as black intellectuals engage this work. Such engagement forges a bond between the work of black critical thinkers and artists and the audiences who receive and affirm that work. Yet, any attempt to bring intellectual critique to bear on such work is often resisted and resented. As a cultural critic who writes and talks about black popular culture, film in particular, I often confront audiences that are enraged

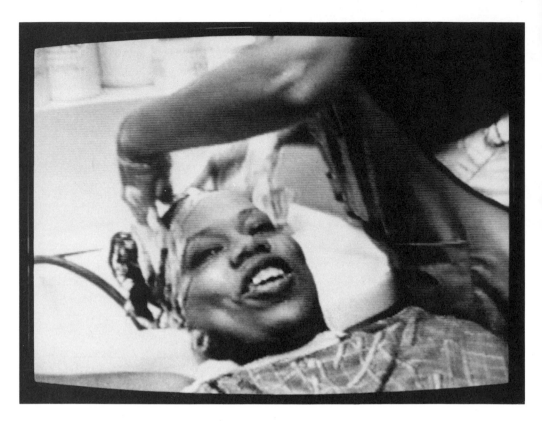

Still from *DiAna's Hair Ego*, directed by Ellen Spiro, 1990. Videotape documenting the formation and growth of the South Carolina AIDS Education Network, which operates out of DiAna's
Hair Ego beauty salon.

by rigorous critique that does not simply celebrate any work done by a black
artist or cultural worker. This hostility surfaces for several reasons. It is rooted
both in the general fear and suspicion of intellectuals and in the traditional
black modes of practicing the art of critique, that which make it appear solely a
negative act.

Critical practices in everyday black life are most often deconstructive; they
aim to unpack, take apart, dismember. In personal conversation, they are usually used to unmask and expose, often with the intent to belittle, berate,
ridicule, or rebuke. Whether one is talking about signifying, "reading," or just
plain "dissin" and "dogging out," these deconstructive practices are often seen as

threatening, as in "I been played," or "she put me on the front street."

In the old days, the black vernacular for "reading" was to get somebody told. I was reminded of this when I was home recently and my mama was talking about my brother overstepping boundaries. She had that particular inflection in her voice she used to use to let us know that she was not *even* playing when she said, "I had to get him told." And I can hear myself using that same inflection when I say, "Girl, I had to read his ass." Despite the element of humor and jest usually involved in a good "read," there is no disputing that "reads" often lead to the belittling and humiliation of the listening subject. And although the essence of a good read is that it is insightful, brilliant, and, most of the time, right on target, it does not, as a form of critique, always emerge from benevolent intent. Even in those cases where folks feel a "read" is deserved, it is still sometimes seen as harsh criticism.

As long as many black folks see critique solely in negative terms, the work of black critics will be misunderstood and devalued. Last week, I was watching television with my sisters and being the cultural critic. One of my sisters began ragging on me about being the Crit. In a later conversation, I asked why there was that contemptuous edge in her voice when she teased me. Her comment was, "We are not as critical. We don't see the same things. We do feel threatened. And it's like, I think, I'm really missing out 'cause I didn't see that." I responded by telling her that she had named the function of the critic, to see things that other folks don't and to call them out. This critical calling-out will be resented if we do not have, in diverse black communities, a critical pedagogy that can foster an appreciation for the sharing of critical insight. Without such a framework, the ideas of critics, particularly when they go against the grain, will be resented and oftentimes dismissed.

My sister G. asserts, "People resent the critic cause you are making them work mentally. They don't wanna work." Thinking critically about a cultural product is often seen as a threat to the pleasure we may feel in consuming a work. In the introduction to *Yearning,* I described the struggle of teaching students, in courses on black women writers, to see rigorous critical thought and analysis as practices that make us more aware and that can potentially enhance our pleasure in a text, rather than take it away. Their fear of criticism, particularly of critical ideas about black popular culture, is that it will destroy their ability to enjoy work. Experiencing black cultural production from the stand-point of progressive critique does, in fact, change the nature of our pleasure. It compels the black consumer to make a break with modes of passive consumption. It intervenes in the kind of essentialist thinking that would have us assume anything done in the name of blackness is righteous and should be celebrated. As well, it breaks with that other critical tradition that merely raises the simple questions of negative and positive representation. Ironically, it is this power to intervene and disrupt that renders criticism so essential to cultural production and yet leads it to be regarded with fear and suspicion.

When black cultural critics write about black popular culture in ways that expose the inadequacies of a particular work, we are often seen as betraying the cause and failing to provide an affirmative context that would foster production. Recently, I have been particularly critical of John Singleton's film *Boyz N the Hood*. Speaking on the subject of race, gender, and representation, I have talked about how the film constructs black gender relations in such a way that it pits black women and men against one another. I have talked about the way the film attacks black single mothers, the way it suggests that black professional women are white-identified (more so than black professional men). I have called attention to the way its cinematic treatment of black women crack addicts, who are also mothers, reinscribes the white right's conservative position. All the while, I have acknowledged it as a powerful and compelling movie. Yet, many black folks have responded angrily to my critique. They call attention to the filmmaker's age, to the fact that it is his first feature-length work, to the need for more black films—all to aggressively assert that this film should not be subjected to rigorous critique.

These experiences made me think about why critique appears to be so threatening to many black folks, why there is the desire to silence and censor radical dissenting voices, and why we are not creating a cultural space that would promote rigorous analysis. Most audiences seem not to recognize that critical feedback can and must encourage black producers of popular culture to strive for excellence. There really needs to be a space where black artists and cultural workers can talk about how critique informs and influences their work.

As an artist and critic, I know that we are not just inspired by affirming, celebratory feedback. We are also inspired by that vital engagement with our work that is critical, that dares to lovingly unmask, expose, challenge. Such engagement is a gesture of respect; it indicates that the work has been taken seriously. Useful critical commentary offers insights that both reveal aspects of a work—how it is what it is, what it does or does not do—as well as suggest new directions, new possibilities. We need to distinguish between criticism that merely acts to trash a work, and that thoughtful reflection rooted in the love ethic Cornel West offers as the foundation of a renewed politics of black liberation. Insightful criticism may make use of deconstructive critical strategies, but if it is truly visionary, it will go beyond mere taking apart. It will make critique a space where work is illuminated and where our understanding of its value is enhanced, not diminished.

Valerie Smith

The Documentary Impulse in Contemporary
African-American Film

In her essay, "History, Fiction, and the Ground Between: The Uses of the Documentary Mode in Black Literature," Barbara Foley argues that an emphasis on the factual has been a persistent presence throughout the history of African-American narrative writing. Foley notes, as have numerous other critics, that during the period of U.S. slavery, African-American writers of slave narratives incorporated various kinds of authenticating documents into their tales to verify their own authority before a skeptical, largely white reading public. Foley suggests that this preoccupation with facticity, or with the "documentary mode," is part of the legacy that slave narrators bequeathed to subsequent generations of African-American writers.[1]

The use of the factual has taken a variety of forms throughout the history of black narrative writing. For instance, Richard Wright introduced several of his works with prefatory statements to authenticate the fictional narratives that followed. Arna Bontemps, David Bradley, and Toni Morrison imaginatively recreated real-life episodes found in the public record of slavery in *Black Thunder, The Chaneysville Incident,* and *Beloved,* respectively, and Margaret Walker constructed an elaborate written context for the oral accounts of slavery that her own great grandmother passed along in *Jubilee.* In *Dessa Rose,* Sherley Anne Williams created an opportunity for two real-life antebellum women to join forces. Each of these authors gestures toward a knowable set of facts to anchor his or her accounts between history and fiction.

In contrast to this tradition, Foley argues, there exists a countertradition of literary works that masquerade as true in order to prompt interrogations of prevailing notions of historical fact. This technique is employed, for example, by Sutton Griggs in *Imperium in Imperio,* Ishmael Reed in *Mumbo Jumbo* and *Flight to Canada,* and John A. Williams in *Captain Blackman,* and is at least partly the impulse behind pseudo-factual autobiographies such as James Weldon Johnson's *The Autobiography of an Ex-Coloured Man* and Ernest J. Gaines's *The Autobiography of Miss Jane Pittman.*

Recent films by African-American directors are likewise positioned at the generic crossroads between fact and fiction. I want to consider briefly the implications of gestures toward the "real" in contemporary African-American cinema. I am concerned here with examining not only the ways in which certain narrative films construct themselves as part of a widely shared and widely recognizable reality, but also the ways that critics and reviewers participate in such constructions. I argue also that, conversely, recent black-directed documentaries gesture toward the fictional or the artificial in an attempt to enter suppressed narratives into public discourse.

It should not surprise us that a strong documentary impulse is evident in much contemporary black filmmaking, given the more recent antecedents of this movement. Key figures in the development of black film such as William Greaves and St. Clair Bourne produced their early work in the television documentary format. Clyde Taylor has identified what he calls a "realness dimension"—the use of techniques associated with nonfiction cinema—in the black-directed independent films of the 1970s.[2] And indeed, documentaries by Ayoka Chenzira, Warrington Hudlin, Michelle Parkerson, Debra Robinson, and many others from the mid-seventies through the early eighties display the possibilities for the comparatively inexpensive and convenient techniques of cinema verité to preserve otherwise suppressed narratives for posterity.

As virtually every major newspaper in the country has reminded us, in 1991 more black-directed films were commercially released than in any previous year. Indeed, since the mid-eighties—with the surprise success of *She's Gotta Have It* in 1986, studio acknowledgment of the size of the black moviegoing public, and the demonstrated crossover appeal and commercial viability of at least certain black-directed films—increasing numbers of black male directors have achieved access to studio support and distribution and mass audiences. Given the plethora of films since the mid-eighties, now is an opportune time to examine how these films construct themselves as a genre and are, in turn, being constructed by critics, reviewers, and viewers.

Several of the most commercially successful films of this recent crop—Spike Lee's *Do the Right Thing,* Mario Van Peebles's *New Jack City,* John Singleton's *Boyz N the Hood,* and Matty Rich's *Straight Outta Brooklyn*—contain markers or referents that gesture toward an externally verifiable "real life."[3] In her persuasive article on *Do the Right Thing,* Wahneema Lubiano problematizes Lee's use of such markers—references to black vernacular culture—to encode his films as authentic black documents.[4] Her observations about Lee's films might usefully be applied to Van Peebles's, Singleton's, and Rich's films as well. Lubiano shows that the reviews of Lee's *School Daze* and *Do the Right Thing* return repeatedly to the issue of the films' faithfulness to a monolithic black experience.

Lubiano questions the way in which Lee and his work have been called upon to stand and speak for "the black community." This kind of fetishization, she argues, eclipses other kinds of oppositional cinematic work. Moreover, she writes that such fetishization insulates vernacularity from critique. As she puts it, "vernacular language and cultural productions allow the possibility of discursive power disruptions, of cultural resistance—they do not guarantee it."[5]

Directors, studios, and their marketing experts collude in shrinking the distance between referent and representation in films such as those I mentioned earlier, thereby delimiting what counts, or sells, as black film. The marketing of these films provides one way in which they are constructed as "real life." For instance, press kits for films such as *Boyz, Brooklyn,* Joseph Vasquez's *Hangin' with the Homeboys,* and Wendell Harris, Jr.'s *Chameleon Street* recall the authenticating documents that accompany slave narratives. Repeatedly, we read that John Singleton grew up in South Central Los Angeles under circumstances similar to those experienced by Tre Styles, his protagonist; that Matty Rich grew up in the Red Hook housing projects in which his film is set and that he shot much of *Brooklyn* in his grandmother's apartment; that Vasquez grew up in the Bronx neighborhood in which *Homeboys* is set; and that the critically acclaimed but poorly distributed *Chameleon Street* is based on the true story of William Douglas Street. In short, most reviews of or feature articles on these films assure us that the directors are in positions of authority relative to their material.

In contrast to the sanitized visions of contemporary urban life commonly circulated by mainstream Hollywood movies, these films contain markers of contemporary urban problems. To cite but one example, the opening credits of *Boyz N the Hood* unfold against the insistent, sinister whirring of police helicopters; the soundtrack is flooded with the sound of gunfire, the visuals punctuated with flashing searchlights. Actual gangs are named, and characters wear clothing and colors appropriate to those organizations.

These films contain not only signifiers of gang and drug culture often excised from images of the city in Hollywood films, but also markers that historicize and position them as interventions in the construction of a multifaceted contemporary urban African-American culture of resistance. The markers locate the films in relation to black achievements in sports and music, and to ongoing cultural debates around constructions of race.

References to Mookie Wilson, Jackie Robinson, and Magic Johnson in *Do the Right Thing* recall popular black sports figures. These references simultaneously invoke the presence of teams with a history of comparatively progressive racial politics—the Mets, Dodgers, and Lakers—and indict by their absence their more intransigent counterparts: the Yankees and the Celtics.

The directors position themselves in a common enterprise with black musicians in the frequent use of rap and hip hop in soundtracks, and with the visible presence of rappers on screen as actors. In the case of *Do the Right Thing,* Lee also uses what W. J. T. Mitchell calls a "musical Wall of Fame," a litany of the names of R&B and jazz musicians.[6] By means of such markers, the directors locate their films in the context of a cross-generic history of cultural resistance.

Furthermore, the visuals, dedications, and narratives place these films in relation to present-day debates around race, gender, sexuality, and economics. In *Do the Right Thing,* Tawana Brawley's name is among the graffiti on the wall of Sal's pizzeria, and the pizza parlor, baseball bat, and police chokehold are referents resonant with the stories of Howard Beach and Michael Stewart. It thus comes as no surprise that the film is dedicated to the families of victims of police brutality.

The problematic of interracial romance, as well as the geography of *Jungle Fever,* invoke a recent episode of racial violence; this film was dedicated to the memory of Yusef Hawkins. And *Boyz N the Hood* might be seen as intervening directly in the discourse around black males as an "endangered species." Jacquie Jones argues that black mothers in that film are shown to be at best neglectful; at worst, they bear primary responsibility for their sons' problems and suffering.[7] Our protagonist rises above the conditions of his peers because he alone has a strong, present, and neonationalist black father. The techniques and narratives of these films thus conceal their status as mediations and suggest that they occupy an intimate, if not contiguous, relation to an externally verifiable reality.[8]

Reviewers and certain viewers grant these films a proximity to and power over real life that is rarely seen in discussions of other types of films.[9] Perhaps the most salient example of this sort of conflation is evident in the panic that surrounded the release of *Do the Right Thing.* Likewise, law enforcement officers, theater owners, and local merchants all voiced concern that the release of *New Jack City* and *Boyz N the Hood* would precipitate gang wars. Thus the marketing of these films went beyond standard strategies of identifying target audiences and attempted to monitor the word and action on the street. In Los Angeles, for example, Columbia Pictures showed *Boyz N the Hood* before audiences of youth gang services counselors, social workers, politicians, psychiatrists, and police officers to ensure that young black viewers would understand that the film was not encouraging them to perpetrate destructive behavior.

Both bell hooks and Henry Louis Gates, Jr. addressed the absurdity of much of the concern around the impact of *Boyz N the Hood.* hooks writes:

It is highly unlikely that black people in this society who have been subjected to colonizing brainwashing designed to keep us in one place and to teach us how to submit to all manner of racist assault and injustice would see a film that merely hints at the intensity and pain of this experience and feel compelled to respond with rage.[10]

And in a published conversation on the reception of the film, Gates says, "There's no simple relationship between the representation of images of ethnic groups and social relationships."[11]

Both statements suggest that the focus on "real world" consequences presupposes some kind of direct, unmediated relationship between black viewers and black films. As Lubiano argues, this focus ignores both the complex processes of signification constructed within the films as well as the possibility of black critical engagement.[12] And as Jacquie Jones also notes, the fetishization of these films eclipses other kinds of black-directed work currently being produced.[13]

I am especially interested here in the fact that among the crop of films that have been overshadowed by films such as those by Lee, Singleton, and Rich, are black-directed documentaries. On the one hand, one should not be surprised that black-directed documentaries enjoy only limited circulation, since non-fiction films in general are considered less commercially viable than fiction films. Given the interest of the general public in consuming "black life" through the medium of black film, however, one might expect that black documen-taries, films that "show us situations and events that are recognizably part of a realm of shared experience,"[14] would enjoy particular visibility.

Ironically, even as Lee et al. construct their films as "true," documentarians such as Camille Billops and James V. Hatch, Marlon T. Riggs, and Marco Williams trouble the boundary between fact and fiction within the context of their nonfiction films. These directors experiment with the artificiality of their medium to defamiliarize assumptions about family, sexuality, gender, race, and identity. Various aspects of the fiction films may point to the "real world," but at least certain black documentary filmmakers self-reflexively point to the "made-upness" of what passes as truth both in cinematic practice and in con-temporary culture.

Billops and Hatch's *Suzanne Suzanne* and *Finding Christa* dismantle the author-ity of documentary filmmaking as they explode ideologies of family. In *Suzanne Suzanne,* Billops and Hatch juxtapose home movies and family photographs with interviews with family members to expose the coercive and ubiquitous nature of myths of family respectability. Billops's sister's family, the subject of the film, struggles to maintain the veneer of respectability, but the orderly surface is shown to conceal a history of family violence and substance abuse. The familiar domestic locations resonate with the secrets, silences, and deceptions of the past. The wrenching, pivotal confrontation between mother and daughter in the film is thus facilitated by the move to the self-consciously artificial setting of a darkened soundstage.[15]

In *Finding Christa,* Billops and Hatch explore Billops's decision to give her daughter up for adoption in the mid-fifties when the child was four years old. Here, the filmmakers interweave dramatic re-enactments, pantomime, and fantasy sequences with archival footage and interviews to question ideologies of motherhood and the adequacy of realist techniques of representation. The directors' use of strategies associated with fiction films questions the very meaning of documentary filmmaking. They frustrate the viewers' desire to observe Billops's private emotions and challenge the voyeuristic relationship

Still from *Tongues Untied*, directed by Marlon Riggs, 1989.

between viewer and documentary subject.

In *Tongues Untied,* Marlon T. Riggs interweaves personal narrative with songs, interviews, dance, and performance pieces in an exploration of gay black male subjectivity in contemporary U.S. culture. The film shows how homophobia among black and non-black heterosexuals, racism among white gays, and the AIDS epidemic have combined to silence the voices of black gay men. The multiplicity of voices in the film both illustrates the diversity of gay black male perspectives and dramatizes the insistence of the forces that seek to obliterate them. Visuals and soundtrack alike in this film deconstruct viewers' expectations of linear narrative and the authoritative voice-over, thereby challenging monolithic notions of black gay identity.

Riggs's *Color Adjustment,* a video on the history of blacks in television, seems at first to have little in common thematically with *Tongues Untied.* However, just as *Tongues Untied* detaches compulsory heterosexism from the category of blackness, *Color Adjustment* critiques the insidious mythologizing of family circulated by network television along with repressive ideologies of race. In *Color Adjustment,* Riggs employs excerpts from television series, footage from the Civil Rights Movement, interviews, and photographs to explode popular notions of historical change and racial progress. His use of moving television images within still photographs of families watching television, and the superimposition of slow-motion images with still photographs and racist caricatures, blurs the distinctions between "real history" and media constructions.

Marco Williams's *In Search of Our Fathers* tells the story of the director's nine-year search to find his father. The film is composed of family photographs and footage of interviews with family members accumulated during the nine-year search. The process of composition gives each scene a quality of authenticity. However, Williams includes slates (places that mark the synchronicity of soundtrack and visuals) and moments where the film and the tape run out in order to undermine the illusion of cinematic transparency. The technical difficulties suggest the inability of media to capture the complexity of real life, just as mainstream media fails to represent adequately the lives of black single-parent households like the one of which Williams himself is a part.

Because they work in a genre that lacks the marketability of fiction films, documentarians are unlikely to achieve the popularity of directors of fiction films. Nevertheless, I would advocate increased critical attention to black documentary filmmaking in order to expand the discourse around the topic of black film and to bridge the space between more mainstream and more marginalized genres. Although I may be optimistic, I would like to think that, to the extent that we participate in the expansion of a critical discourse around black film, we contribute to the growth of an audience for black film. I would like, as well, to believe that as audiences expand, so too will opportunities for a more diverse group of black filmmakers and cinematic products.

1. Barbara Foley, "History, Fiction, and the Ground Between: The Uses of the Documentary Mode in Black Literature," *PMLA* 95 (May 1980), 389–403.

2. Clyde Taylor, "Decolonizing the Image: New U.S. Black Cinema," in *Jump Cut,* ed. Peter Steven (New York: Praeger, 1985), 166–178.

3. bell hooks, Jacquie Jones, Julianne Malveaux, and Michele Wallace have all noted that these films share as well a profoundly misogynist view of African-American culture. See hooks, *Yearning: Race, Gender, and Cultural Politics* (Boston: South End Press, 1990); Jones, "The New Ghetto Aesthetic," *Wide Angle* 13, nos. 3 and 4 (July–October

1991), 32–43; Malveaux, "Spike's Spite—Women at the Periphery," *Ms.* (September, October 1991), 78–80; and Wallace, *Invisibility Blues: From Pop to Theory* (New York: Verso, 1990), 100–106.

4. Wahneema Lubiano, "But Compared to What?: Reading Realism, Representation, and Essentialism in *School Daze, Do the Right Thing,* and the Spike Lee Discourse," *Black American Literature Forum* 25 (Summer 1991), 253–282.

5. Ibid., 264.

6. W. J. T. Mitchell, "The Violence of Public Art: *Do the Right Thing,*" *Critical Inquiry* 16 (Summer 1990), 894.

7. Jones, "The New Ghetto Aesthetic," 41.

8. *Boyz N the Hood, Hangin' With the Homeboys, Straight Outta Brooklyn,* and *Chameleon Street* employ cinema verité techniques that contribute to the sense that they are constructed to be read, at least in part, as "true to life." The cinematography, art direction, and strategies of characterization that Lee employs in *Do the Right Thing* introduce a hyper-real, almost self-parodic quality to the film that threatens to undermine its historical specificity. The self-consciously artificial dimension of the film thus complicates its relation to the category of "the real."

9. Obvious exceptions to this formulation would be films such as *The Last Temptation of Christ; Angel Heart; The Cook, The Thief, His Wife and Her Lover,* which religious fundamentalists and/or conservatives find degraded or sacrilegious and which, to their minds, threaten the very stability of the social order.

10. hooks, *Yearning: Race, Gender, and Cultural Politics,* 175.

11. "'*Do the Right Thing*': Issues and Images" (a conversation among Mary Schmidt Campbell, Henry Louis Gates, Jr., Nathan Glazer, Alvin Poussaint, Burton Roberts, Paul Schrader, Betty Shabazz, and editors of the Arts and Leisure section of the *New York Times*), *New York Times,* July 9, 1989, H1.

12. Lubiano, "But Compared to What?: Reading Realism, Representation, and Essentialism in *School Daze, Do the Right Thing,* and the Spike Lee Discourse," 264.

13. Jones, "The New Ghetto Aesthetic," 33. Jones cites *Chameleon Street, A Rage in Harlem,* and *Livin' Large* as examples of films that have been marginalized because they fail to conform to the conventions of representing black urban life.

14. Bill Nichols, *Representing Reality: Issues and Concepts in Documentary* (Bloomington: Indiana University Press, 1991), ix–x.

15. Valerie Smith, "Telling Family Secrets: Narrative and Ideology in *Suzanne Suzanne* by Camille Billops and James V. Hatch," in *Multiple Voices in Feminist Film Criticism,* ed. Diane Carson, Linda Dittmar, and Janice Welsch (Minneapolis: University of Minnesota Press, 1993), forthcoming; "*Finding Christa,*" *Black Film Review* 7, no. 2 (May 1992), 12–15.

Jacqueline Bobo

The Politics of Interpretation:
Black Critics, Filmmakers, Audiences

In the film *Cotton Comes to Harlem* (1970), Calvin Lockhart plays a conniving black minister who holds sway over his large congregation through continual recourse to the liturgical refrain "Is that Black enough for you?" The affirmative response from his following, and from the film audience, was a demonstration of a particular understanding of the implications of Lockhart's question and of the specific historical moment in which it was asked. Black people had emerged from a time of nonviolent resistance in the face of social and economic oppression into an active and vocal stance—Black, proud, and visible. Even the politically charged designation of the racial group had gained widespread acceptance: Black people had advanced from being "colored" to "Negro" to "Black." Other manifestations of this change were the clothes that displayed African origins, the "natural" hairstyles, and the conspicuous use of Black "folk" language. When the film's question—"Is that Black enough for you?"—was asked of a newly politically aware Black audience, implicit in the question was a prior knowledge that the response would be a figurative "five on the Black hand side" and a boisterous "right on."

We are no longer in a heady time of high expectations when the sheer novelty of seeing Black people on film, in a work directed by a Black person, makes it simpler, on a surface level, to ascertain when Black cultural representation is "Black enough." In the present historical moment, neither Black cultural representation nor Black cultural criticism is as wholeheartedly accepted or beyond challenge. The politics of representation present many problems and obstacles, especially those regarding the multidimensions of race, class, gender, and sexual orientation. I will address some of the debates surrounding Black cultural representation as well as those around Black cultural criticism. And finally, I will discuss how Black film audiences fit into the equation.

In his article "New Ethnicities," Stuart Hall, the British cultural studies scholar, writes of the evolution of Black cultural representation.[1] As presented by way of the dominant regimes of representation, Black people had been treated as objects, rarely as subjects. Through contestation and struggle, Black artists and cultural workers gained access to the means of representing Black people. Hall writes of the power of image creation and the potency of representation. Although events, relations, and structures do exist separately from the discursive, Hall submits that it is only within the discursive that they can be "constructed within meaning." These meanings, or "how things are represented and the 'machineries' and regimes of representation," play a formative, not simply an expressive or reflective, place in the "constitution of social and political life."[2]

As Hall is indicating, the way a group of people is represented can play a determining role in how those people are treated socially and politically. This means that the process of representation is a politically charged act. That being the case, the process of criticism has ramifications as well. In Black culture, Hall states, once a person enters the politics of criticism, that person leaves the age of critical innocence. And in perhaps one of his most debated statements of the late 1980s, Hall states that "films are not necessarily good because black people make them. They are not necessarily 'right-on' by virtue of the fact that they deal with the black experience."[3]

I want to start with a reference to the discussions concerning Black independent filmmakers that took place in *Black Film Review* from 1988 through 1990. The first article was by Clyde Taylor, a veteran Black film analyst and the person who coined the term "the L.A. Rebellion" to describe the group of young Black filmmakers making films at University of California, Los Angeles in the early 1970s.[4] Taylor wrote about the paradox of Black film: there are now more university-trained filmmakers than ever, and yet there are fewer Black films. Taylor challenged the filmmakers to go beyond amateurish auteurism—one person as actor, writer, producer, director, cameraperson, and editor. He reminded them of their stated desires to reach the larger Black community, rather than limit themselves exclusively to film festivals, museum showings, and the art cinema circuit.

A later article in *Black Film Review,* written by the founding editor, David Nicholson, went much further than Taylor's observations and severely criticized Black independent filmmakers for the shoddiness of their products.[5] Nicholson felt the films were bland and overpersonalized "tone poems." As the debates in *Black Film Review* were reprinted in *Wide Angle,* Nicholson extended his critique to the current crop of commercial films.[6] He acknowledged that there were more films by Black filmmakers coming out of Hollywood, but he said, "Only a fool would call it progress." Nicholson felt that the films celebrated the "worst aspects of Black culture" and that critics, Black and white, were afraid to discuss the films honestly, "one group because of some mistaken need to maintain solidarity, the other out of a reluctant patronizing that is the worst kind of racism."

Nicholson also noted that Black independent filmmakers have faulted Black people for not being able to understand their films. For Nicholson, this rationale is merely "a resort to some incomprehensible academic mumbo-jumbo." But, whether we agree with Nicholson or not, he does make a telling point about the Black film audience:

> This is, at worst, blaming the audience. At best it is condescension, for it fails to take into account the extent to which the black American audience is visually sophisticated—most of us, in urban centers, at least, grew up watching movies. Most of us, no matter how poor, grew up with television. We are, then, for better or worse, visually sophisticated, though we may not be visually literate. How, then, can we expect to attract an audience with poorly constructed (and poorly made) films, when the audience is used to a product that is, in every way except perhaps content, superior?[7]

In a published rebuttal to Nicholson's argument, Zeinabu Davis, a Black independent filmmaker, writes about the financial and economic constraints within which Black independents work.[8] She discusses the virtual lock-out they experience in attempting to simply get their films and videos to a Black audience. Davis does not use this as an excuse; she presents this as information that should be used in evaluating the work of Black independents. She also raises two critical points about the Black film audience and the Black film producer.

The first is that Black independents are creating a new cinematic language in their films:

> We are asking the audience to see things anew. If one really looks at the recent development in Hollywood films, one can see that there are no new explorations of narrative style or any real innovations in terms of content. Studio films are feeding us a pablum of multimillion dollar visual effects that only momentarily dazzle the eye. When was the last time you felt impassioned and moved to discussion after seeing a Hollywood film?[9]

Davis goes on to say that Black filmmakers are dealing with new themes and subjects, allowing different perspectives on topics that have not been explored in film and that have been silenced, in part, in the community—topics such as sexuality, sexism, slavery, migration, religious fanaticism, the color line, and campus politics.

Davis's second point is the one I want to explore further in the remainder of this essay:

> As a filmmaker, I have found that Black American audiences are … hungry to see their own image or the image of any Black person on the screen, that they can make that jump, that suspension of disbelief, and accept a film that has a style radically different than what they are used to.[10]

It seems to me that both Nicholson and Davis agree that the content of mainstream Hollywood films is woefully deficient. What they do not agree on are the production values of Black independent filmmakers, as well as whether or not a Black film audience will accept an unfamiliar style of presentation that presents an alternative view of critical elements in Black people's lives. I agree with Davis when she suggests, elsewhere in her article, that critics and filmmakers need a stronger collaboration, but what I think also needs to be analyzed further is the Black film audience. The collaboration is, in fact, threefold: the makers, the critics, and the audience.

Although the most important part of gleaning information about how Black people watch films is interacting with the audience, the first work of the critic is just to get the word out. Many films by Black independent filmmakers do not have mainstream distribution. They travel the film festival/select theater/art cinema circuit, or, as in the case of *To Sleep with Anger,* are given limited distribution and minimal marketing. If Black people do not know the films are available, how can they watch them? The second task confronting the critic is preparing the audience to watch. Zeinabu Davis is right on target when she faults the Hollywood industry for feeding the audience the mere dazzle of multimillion dollar special effects. The audience may be hungry for more substance, but there is a formula involved in viewing mainstream films, as much as in their making. A third task, and perhaps the most important work of the critic, is to develop a better understanding of the Black film audience.

In cultural studies, there now seems to be a move away from attempting to understand media audiences and back to an analysis exclusively of the text. Charlotte Brunsdon, writing in *Remote Control,* a collection of essays about television audiences, details the evolution of audience analysis within the disciplines of film and television studies, noting the proliferation of textual analyses in the 1970s.[11] These were primarily political readings of texts—what Brunsdon labels "redemptive readings." The critic was searching out the incoherencies and inconsistencies within the text in order to salvage the work for a particular audience. This form of critical practice soon became a problem. As Brunsdon states, "The redemptive reading frequently meets with a certain skepticism, a doubt that real readers read like that."[12] There was a move toward finding out how nonacademic readers actually made sense of texts.

Media researcher Jane Feuer commented, then, that the media text was being replaced by the "text of audience." Brunsdon sees a problem with this over-reliance on audience responses at the expense of textual analysis because she feels the critic simply suspends judgment of the text. Consequently, there is little need to change textual practices since creative audiences are astute enough to circumvent the harmful meanings of the media product. I agree with her that critics should not abandon an analysis of texts, but we need much more insight into how a film audience creates meaning from these works. I think this is especially important in considering the Black film audience.[13]

Black people watch a lot of television and spend a lot of money going to see commercial films. And these may not be films that they find particularly useful, or that they even enjoy. Consequently, I believe that if more works produced by black film and video makers were available, the Black audience would cultivate the habit of watching, and watching critically. It is, of course, difficult to assess any group's reactions to specific cultural works. Media audiences in general, not just Black audiences, have proven to be unruly and unpredictable. Because they do not always follow a prescribed ideological route, there is a tendency for the researcher to flatten out the contradictions, to smooth over statements where members of the audience appear as "cultural dupes."

In interviews with Black women about their reactions to the film *The Color Purple,* I received, at times, responses that taught me to go beyond a quick and superficial analysis. There was, of course, more to my assessment of their reactions than just the interviews. I did a comprehensive review of the literature in an effort to chart Black women's responses in print, on radio and television talk shows, and in conversation with each other. I then conducted several sets of unstructured interviews with selected Black women in different parts of the country. From my research and interviews, I found that many Black women had an overwhelmingly favorable response to the film.[14]

Whether we, as filmmakers or as critics, agree with the sentiments expressed by members of the audience, it is important to consider their reactions within the totality of their lives. The meanings embedded in mainstream cultural works are deeply ingrained in this culture. They are designed according to formulas that can elicit conditioned responses from viewers. I am reminded of Lorraine Hansberry's comments about a review of her play *A Raisin in the Sun*:

> My colleagues and I were reduced to mirth and tears by that gentleman writing his review of our play in a Connecticut paper who remarked of his pleasure at seeing how "our dusky brethren" could "come up with a song and hum their troubles away." It did not disturb the writer in the least that there is no such implication in the entire three acts. He did not need it in the play; he had it in his head.[15]

Just as mainstream reviewers, such as the one referred to by Hansberry, draw on their own social/cultural backgrounds and media memories in the analysis of cultural works, mainstream producers are also under "ideological pressure" to reproduce the familiar. For Black audiences the struggle to resist the pull of certain works is the same struggle waged against domination and oppression in everyday life. Their work of resistance involves acknowledging that mainstream works will at some point present caricatures of Black people's lives and balancing that knowledge with their more personal responses to the parts of the films that resonate with other elements in their lives.

For example, some of the women I interviewed reacted favorably to the

Margaret Avery as Shug leading a procession from the Juke Joint to the church. From a scene in *The Color Purple*, 1985.

musical interlude in *The Color Purple* where Shug and the juke jointers sing and dance on their way from the jukejoint to the church. In analyzing these women's reactions, it is important to consider how music is and has been an integral part of Black people's lives. Religion, of course, is also contested terrain in Black communities. Although we are well aware, as Stuart Hall reminds us, that religion has been used to maintain ideological control over many societies in numerous epochs,[16] religion is vitally important in Black people's lives. Research data show that there are 65,000 Black churches in this country with membership totaling 24 million people.[17] This explains, in part, many of the women's reactions to the scene with Shug and the juke-jointers.

My interviews allowed me to glimpse some of the more complicated ways in which Black women negotiate these two aspects of their lives—the centrality of Black music and the role of the church. One of the women I interviewed talked about the scene and her experiences:

I didn't ever think I would feel that way when I was in church. I noticed that when I was going through my deepest, hardest time, if I would go to church and get involved in the service, and they start singing like that, I could feel the spirit.

Another woman responded that it was "God's spirit or somebody else's, but it was some spirit." To this statement the first woman responded that she did believe in a Creator:

I have a difficulty believing in the kind of God that I see lots of people worship. But I know there's a Creator. But my view is probably different from what they would say the Creator is supposed to be.

Yet another woman articulated a similar belief:

Nobody can have as many good things happen to them as have happened to me (without a whole lot of effort on my part) without something, some single spirit, some collective spirit, or something, providing some support and guidance. I don't know that I believe in, what is it? The one, the two, and the three? The trinity, and all of that, or in a real literal interpretation of the Bible, but I do believe there is something.

The reconciliation scene between Shug and her preacher father was another moment in the film that elicited a strong response from the women I interviewed. As we know, this segment differed from the novel and was invented for the film. During the interviews with Black women, I shared with them some Black critics' reaction to the contrast in Shug as presented in the novel and as presented in the film. In the novel, Shug's strength was that she did what she wanted and was not affected by others' judgment of her actions. According to the critics, the invention of the preacher father in the film was a way of controlling Shug and rendering a negative evaluation of her independent nature. The women I interviewed were in general agreement with one woman's comment:

It didn't have that effect on me. Shug was still a strong woman. It didn't neutralize her to me. Now if that's what they (the producers) wanted to do, they missed the boat, because it didn't do that for me. You go back and tell the critics they missed their point.

That many Black women stood firm in their stated positive engagement with *The Color Purple* in the face of enormous public criticism of the film demonstrates that audience members are not the unthinking pawns, manipulated at will by the mainstream media, that many critics make them out to be. It is a mistake to value the comments of the critics at the expense of a more wide-ranging examination of the ways in which audiences make sense of cultural products. As an article in the film journal *Close-Up* suggested in 1933, the ideal is a thinking audience. And we must be the ones who bring that thinking audience's views into circulation.

Not until that happens can we expect a consistently high standard of film production. For we know well enough that in the last instance it is the audience, not the artist, that makes the film; the artist can only supply a demand which is already there.[18]

It is the responsibility of those of us in audience studies to give voice to members of the audience who otherwise would not be considered in any analysis of Black cultural works.

1. Stuart Hall, "New Ethnicities," in *Black Film/British Cinema, ICA Document 7,* ed. Kobena Mercer (London: Institute of Contemporary Arts, 1988), 27–31.
2. Ibid., 27.
3. Ibid., 28.
4. Clyde Taylor, "The Paradox of Black Independent Cinema," *Black Film Review* 4, no. 4 (Fall 1988), 2–3, 17–19.
5. David Nicholson, "Which Way the Black Film Movement?" *Black Film Review* 5, no. 2 (Spring 1989), 4–5, 16–17.
6. David Nicholson, "Voices," *Wide Angle* 13, nos. 3 and 4 (July–October 1991), 120–125.
7. Nicholson, "Which Way the Black Film Movement?" 5.
8. Zeinabu Irene Davis, "The Future of Black Film: The Debate Continues," *Black Film Review* 5, no. 3 (1990), 6, 8, 26, 28.
9. Ibid., 8.
10. Ibid., 28.
11. Charlotte Brunsdon, "Text and Audience," in *Remote Control: Television, Audiences, and Cultural Power,* ed. Ellen Seiter, et al. (London: Routledge, 1989), 116–129.
12. Ibid., 122.
13. There is a complex process of negotiation that occurs when viewers watch a film or television program. Viewers will interpret a text based upon elements in their background that prompt them to dismiss what is being presented, to accept it, or to travel the continuum between the two. For a discussion of this process, see David Morley, "Texts, Readers, Subjects," in *Culture, Media, Language,* eds. Stuart Hall, et al. (London: Hutchinson, 1980), 163–173.
14. See Jacqueline Bobo, "*The Color Purple:* Black Women as Cultural Readers," in *Female Spectators Looking at Film and Television,* ed.

E. Deidre Pribram (London: Verso, 1988), 90–109; and "Sifting Through the Controversy: Reading *The Color Purple,*" *Callaloo* 12, no. 2 (Spring 1989), 332–342.

15. Lorraine Hansberry, "An Author's Reflections: Willy Loman, Walter Younger, and He Who Must Live," reprinted in *The Village Voice Reader,* ed. Daniel Wolf and Edwin Fancher (New York: Doubleday, 1962), 194–199.

16. In Lawrence Grossberg, ed., "On Postmodernism and Articulation: An Interview with Stuart Hall," *Journal of Communication Inquiry* 10, no. 2 (1986), 45–60.

17. Cited in "The Black Church in America," *Progressions: A Lilly Endowment Occasional Report* 4, no. 1 (February 1992).

18. E. Coxhead, "Towards a Cooperative Cinema," *Close-Up: A Quarterly Devoted to the Art of Films* (June 1933), 133–137.

Henry Louis Gates, Jr.

The Black Man's Burden

The strictures of "representation" have had wide and varied permutations in the black community. For as we know, the history of African Americans is marked not only by its noble demands for political tolerance from the larger society, but also by its paradoxical tendency to censure its own. W. E. B. Du Bois was rebuked by the NAACP for his nationalism in the 1930s, and then again for his socialism a decade or so later. James Baldwin and Ralph Ellison were victims of the Black Arts Movement in the sixties, the former because of his sexuality, the latter for his insistence upon individualism. Martin Luther King and Eartha Kitt, strange bedfellows at best, were roundly condemned for their early protests against the Vietnam war. Amiri Baraka repudiated a whole slew of writers in the sixties for being too "assimilationist," then invented a whole new canon of black targets when he became a Marxist a few years later. Michele Wallace, Ntozake Shange, and Alice Walker have been called black male bashers and accused of calculated complicity with white racists. Not surprisingly, many black intellectuals are acutely aware of the hazards of falling out of favor with the thought-police, whether in whiteface or black.

In the case of artistic elites, the issues of representation arise with a vengeance. I want to talk about a revisioning of the Harlem Renaissance in which such issues become particularly acute, the film *Looking for Langston*, which was directed by Isaac Julien and produced by the black British film collective Sankofa in 1988.

Distance and displacement have their benefits, as the literature of migrancy reminds us; so it is not altogether surprising that one of the most provocative and insightful reflections on the Harlem Renaissance and the cultural politics of black America should come from across the Atlantic. I want to take a look at New York from the standpoint of black London; I want to examine the rela-

National Guard bayonets block street while protest marchers pass, March 29, 1968.

tionship between a New York–based cultural movement in the 1920s and one in London in the 1980s. Of course, the question of modernism has always also been one of a cultural vanguard or elite. And that means that the old "burden of representation" is always present. "The ordinary Negro never heard of the Harlem Renaissance," Langston Hughes remarked ruefully, "or if he did, it hadn't raised his wages any." Always, there is the question: what have you done for us?

But to see *Looking for Langston* as an act of historical reclamation, we might begin with the retheorizing of identity politics and black British cultural studies among such critics and theorists as Stuart Hall, Paul Gilroy, Hazel Carby, and Kobena Mercer.

Hall insists, rightly, on distinguishing between a conception of identity founded in an archaeology—in the sense of *res gestae*—and one produced by a narrative, even if an archaeological narrative. For him, that "partnership of past and present" (in Edmund Burke's phrase) is always an "imaginary reunification."[1] But he also insists—something forgotten too quickly in the postmodernist urge to exalt indeterminacy—that "cultural identities come from somewhere, have histories." In a rather nice formulation, Hall observes that "identities are the names we give to the different ways we are positioned by, and position ourselves in, the narratives of the past."

There is a certain reciprocity here I want to hold onto. It says our social identities represent the way we participate in an historical narrative. Our histories may be irretrievable, but they invite imaginative reconstruction. In this spirit, diasporic feminist critics like Hazel Carby have made the call for a "usable past." This call for cultural retrieval—tempered by a sense of its lability, its contingency, its constructedness—has sponsored a remarkable time of black creativity. I am talking, of course, about the work of recent black British film collectives, which really can be seen to deepen and expand these arguments. This is not a relation of mirroring, however, but of productive dialogue.

To talk about the way *Looking for Langston* sets in play history, identity, and desire, let's begin with the fact that it is avowedly a meditation on the Harlem Renaissance. And, let me emphasize, historical particularity is an essential part of the film's texture, rather splendidly realized, I think, by Derek Brown, the film's art director. Throughout the film, archival footage, including film extracts from Oscar Micheaux and period footage of Bessie Smith's "St. Louis Blues," is interspersed with Nina Kellgren's cinematography. What I want to argue is that the film's evocation of the historical Harlem Renaissance is, among other things, a self-reflexive gesture; there is a relation, even a typology, established between black British cinema of the 1980s and the cultural movement of the 1920s that we call the Harlem Renaissance. By its choice of subject, the film brings out, in a very self-conscious way, the analogy between this contemporary ambit of black creativity and an historical precursor.

We look for Langston, I submit, but we discover Isaac.

It is an association represented quite literally in one of the opening images of the film, where the film's director makes his sole appearance. He is the corpse in the casket. With six mourners presiding, Hughes's wake is a black tie affair. The film, of course, is also an act of mourning, in memory of three men who died in 1987—Bruce Nugent, James Baldwin, and Joseph Beam. ("This nut might kill us," we hear Essex Hemphill say in one sequence, reflecting on the AIDS epidemic; "This kiss could turn to stone.")

Visually, there's a circulation of images between the filmic present and the archival past. Textually, something of the same interplay is enacted, with poetry and prose from Bruce Nugent ("Smoke, Lilies and Jade," which receives perhaps the most elaborate and effecting *tableau vivant* in the film), Langston Hughes (including selections from "The Negro Artist and the Racial Mountain," *The Big Sea*, *Montage of a Dream Deferred*, and other works), James Baldwin (from *The Price of the Ticket*), an essay by critic and journalist Hilton Als, and six poems by Essex Hemphill. We hear an interchange of voices, inflections, and accents, including Stuart Hall reading, I believe, Hilton Als; Langston Hughes reading his own work; Toni Morrison reading Baldwin; and Erick Ray Evans reading Bruce Nugent. The result is an interlacement, an enmeshment of past and present, the blues, jazz, Motown, and contemporary dance music, London and New York: a transtemporal dialogue on the nature of identity and desire and history.

But the typology to which the film is devoted also enables another critique of the identity politics we have inherited from the black nationalisms of our youth, a critique that focuses on a maligned sexual politics. Like the self-proclaimed "aesthetic movement" of England's yellow 1890s, chronicled by Arthur Symonds, parodied by Robert Hitchens, promulgated by such "born antinomians" as Oscar Wilde, Alfred Douglas, and Lionel Johnson, the Harlem Renaissance was, in fact, just a handful of people. The usual roll call would invoke figures such as Langston Hughes, Claude McKay, Alain Locke, Countee Cullen, Wallace Thurman, and Bruce Nugent—which is to say that it was surely as gay as it was black, not that it was exclusively either of these. This constituency, in view of the Renaissance's emblematic importance to later movements of black creativity in this country, particularly the Black Arts Movement of the 1960s, is what makes the powerful current of homophobia in black letters a matter of particular interest and concern.

If *Looking for Langston* is a meditation on the Harlem Renaissance, it is equally an impassioned rebuttal to the virulent homophobia associated with the Black Power and black aesthetic movements. On this topic, the perfervid tone that Eldridge Cleaver adopts famously toward James Baldwin (to whom *Looking for Langston* is dedicated) indicates only a sense of what was perceived to be at stake in policing black male sexuality. We see the same obsession running through the early works of Sonia Sanchez and, of course, Amiri Baraka. "Most white men are trained to be fags," Baraka writes in the collection of essays *Home*. "For this reason it is no wonder their faces are weak and blank, left without the hurt that reality makes … " Amid the racial battlefield, a line is drawn, but it is drawn on the shifting sands of sexuality. To cross that line, Baraka told us, would be an act of betrayal. And it is worth noting that, at least in a literal sense, the film opens in the year 1967, with the death of Hughes and the playing of a Riverside radio program in memoriam. It is difficult to read his words today: "without the hurt that reality makes."

Baldwin once remarked that being attacked by white people only made him flare hotly into eloquence; being attacked by blacks, he confessed, made him want to break down and cry. Baldwin hardly emerged from the efflorescence of black nationalism in the 1960s unscathed. Baldwin and Beam could have told LeRoi Jones a great deal about "the hurt that reality makes," as could have a lot of black gay men in Harlem today who are tired of being used for batting practice. And in the wake of a rising epidemic of physical violence against gays, violence of the sort that Melvin Dixon has affectingly depicted in his new novel *Vanishing Rooms*, it is difficult to say that we have progressed very far since *Home*.

That is not to say that the idealogues of black nationalism in this country have any unique claim on homophobia. But it is an almost obsessive motif that runs through the major authors of the black aesthetic and the Black Power movements. In short, national identity became sexualized in the sixties in such a way as to engender a curious subterraneous connection between homophobia and nationalism. It is important to confront this head on to make sense of the ways *Looking for Langston* both fosters and transcends a kind of identity politics.

Surely one of the salient features of the work is its attitude toward the body, the way in which the black body is sexualized. bell hooks has noted that Nina Kellgren's camera presents the black male body as vulnerable, soft, even passive, in marked contrast to its usual representations in American film. It is a way of disrupting a visual order, a hardened convention of representation. There is a scene where we see slides of Robert Mapplethorpe's photos projected on a backdrop while a white man walks through them. And I think there is a tacit contrast between those images, with their marmoreal surfaces and primitivist evocations, and Kellgren's own vision of masculinity unmasked. Indeed, this may be the film's most powerful assault on the well-policed arena of black masculinity. "*And soft*," Nugent writes of his character, Beauty, "*soft*."

In short, by insistently foregrounding—and then refiguring—issues of gender and desire, filmmakers like Rhees August, Maureen Blackwood, Isaac Julien, and others are engaged in an act both of cultural retrieval and reconstruction. The historicity of that act—the way it takes form as a search for a usable past—is, as Hazel Carby and Houston Baker show, entirely characteristic of diaspora culture. So the dialogue with the past, even a past figured as non-recuperable, turns out to be a salient feature of what might be called the Black London Renaissance. The "partnership of past and present" is recast across the distances of exile through territories of the imagination and of space.

And a film like *Looking for Langston* is able to respond to the hurtfully exclusionary obsessions of the black nationalist moment, and our own cultural moment as well, by constructing a counter-history in which desire and mourning and identity can interact in their full complexity, but in a way that registers the violence of history. There are two reductive ways of viewing the film, therefore. The first is preoccupied with fixing the historical question about Hughes's sex life. The second says that the film is an imaginative meditation and, therefore, "real" history is completely immaterial to it. On their own, both approaches are misguided. A more instructive approach is emblematized nicely by the Akan figure of "sankofa" itself (the word literally means "go back and retrieve it"), which refers to a bird with its head turned backward: again, the "partnership of past and present." Obviously, the film is not positivist history; and yet history, and the status of history, are its immediate concerns. So we need to take seriously what Kobena Mercer calls "the artistic commitment to archaeological inquiry"[2] that is at work and at play in this film. And, of course, Stuart Hall's insistence that "cultural identities come from somewhere, have histories" is very much to the point here.

Although the film is not a simple exercise in identity politics, it cannot dispense with the moment of narcissism, of self-recognition. Hence, the use of the mirror tableaux, which thematize the film critic's concern with the dialectic of identification and spectatorship. A man in the club sees himself in the mirror and is caught up short. Water—ponds and puddles—is used as reflecting surface. Indeed, toward the film's end, we are presented with a series of men who lie, Narcissus-like, with their faces to a reflective surface. A belated version of the Lacanian mirror stage? Self-recognition? Or something else entirely? In the prose poem, "The Disciple," Oscar Wilde writes:

> When Narcissus died the pool of his pleasure changed from a cup of sweet waters into a cup of salt tears, and the Oreads came weeping through the woodland that they might sing to the pool and give it comfort..."We do not wonder that you should mourn in this manner for Narcissus, so beautiful was he."
>
> "But was Narcissus beautiful?" said the pool [...] "I loved Narcissus because, as he lay on my banks and looked down at me, in the mirror of his eyes I saw my ever own beauty mirrored."

The film, we should remember, is called *Looking for Langston*; it does not promise he will be found. In fact, I think *Looking for Langston* leads us away from the ensolacement of identity politics, the simple exaltation of identity. We are to go behind the mirror, as Wilde urged. The film gives us angels—there are six of them, including the musician Jimmy Sommerville, with wings of netting and wire—but they are fallen angels, as Essex Hemphill tells us. There are moments of carnival—a club with spirited dancing amid the smashing of champagne glasses—but there are no utopias here. An angel holds a photograph of Langston Hughes, of James Baldwin, but history remains, in a phrase that Stuart Hall repeats: "the smiler with the knife." The carnival is disrupted by a group of men who are described by the credits as "thugs and police" and who represent both the authority of the state and the skinhead malevolence that is its funhouse reflection. In films like *Looking for Langston*, cultural studies becomes cultural work.

At the same time, the controversy that surrounds the productions of Sankofa and Black Audio, to mention the two most prominent black British collectives, leads to what has become *the* central problem for cultural criticism in our day. It is a theoretical terrain that can be taken either as a gold mine or a minefield, depending on your point of view. I speak of the "new politics of representation," and the way these politics impinge on the normative self-image of the so-called oppositional intellectual.

To the extent that black British cinema is represented as an act of cultural politics, it then becomes vulnerable to a political reproach as elitist, Europeanized, overly highbrow; as a black cultural product without a significant black audience, its very "blackness" becomes suspect.

This line of reproach ought to ring a bell: as I suggested at the start, it reprises one of the oldest debates in the history of African-American letters, which is usually framed as the Responsibilities of the Negro Artist. But the populist critique always operates in tandem as a statement about artists and critics.

The centrality of the issue is shown in the fact that a synoptic manifesto on the "new politics of representation" has been issued jointly by Isaac Julien and Kobena Mercer. Their argument follows Paul Gilroy, Pierre Bourdieu, and Ernesto Laclau in linking the critique of essentialism to the critique of the paradigm of representation as delegation. That is, Julien and Mercer recast the ancient debate over "black representation" by focusing on the tension between representation as a practice of depicting and representation as a practice of delegation. Representational democracy, like the classic realist text, is premised on an implicitly mimetic theory of representation as correspondence with the "real."[3]

It has been argued that we should supplant the vanguardist paradigm of "representation" with the "articulation of interests." In such a way, we can lighten the "burden of representation," even if we cannot dispense with it. But whose interest is being articulated?

Worrying that independent black British cinema has become too estranged from the black community, Paul Gilroy has recently proposed what he calls "populist modernism"—which some have decried as a highbrow version of the NAACP Image Awards. There are worries that normative proposals such as "populist modernism" can become techniques for policing artistic boundaries, for separating the collaborationist sheep from the oppositional goats, or perhaps the other way around. Gilroy cites Richard Wright's *The Outsider* as a model for black art, but the poetic career of Langston Hughes might be an even more appropriate candidate for the category.

Perhaps more than any other African American of this century, Langston Hughes was elected popularly to serve as our "representative Negro," the poet of his race. As we know, the burden of representation bore heavily upon him, profoundly shaping his career and his preoccupations, propelling and restraining his own involvement with literary modernism. Nor is it surprising that his image should be, even in our own day, subject to censorship and restriction;

Julien's difficulties with appropriating Hughes's text reflect, in an ironic way, the central argument of the film.

How "modernist" is Julien's own technique? Manthia Diawara, a leading intellectual champion of black British cinema and black British cultural studies, has observed that *Looking for Langston* has evident affinities with many avant-garde and experimental films of the 1970s. And yet, he argues, the film "appropriates the forms of avant-garde cinema not for mere inclusion in the genre, but in order to redefine it by changing its content, and reordering its formal disposition."[4] In Isaac Julien's hands, he suggests, the techniques of the avant garde are made to "reveal that which the genre itself represses."[5] Nor is it an uncritical act of reclamation. Diawara notes that "the dependency of artists and writers upon their white patrons, and the links between the movement and Modernist Primitivism are revealed as moments of ambiguity and ambivalence."[6]

Indeed, the importance of open-textured films such as *Looking for Langston* is in presenting an aesthetics that can embrace ambiguity. Perhaps it is not without its reverential moments, but neither is it a work of naive celebration. It presents an identitarian history as a locus of discontinuities and affinities, of shared pleasures and perils. Perhaps the real achievement of this film is not simply that it rewrites the history of African-American modernism, but that it compels its audience to participate in this rewriting.

1. Stuart Hall, "Cultural Identity and Cinematic Representation," *Framework* 36, 70.
2. Kobena Mercer, "Travelling Theory: The Cultural Politics of Race and Representation: An Interview with Kobena Mercer," *Afterimage* 18, no. 2, 9–90.
3. Isaac Julien and Kobena Mercer, "Introduction—De Margin and De Centre," *Screen* 29, no. 4 (Autumn 1988), 4.
4. From an unpublished essay by Manthia Diawara.
5. Ibid.
6. Ibid.

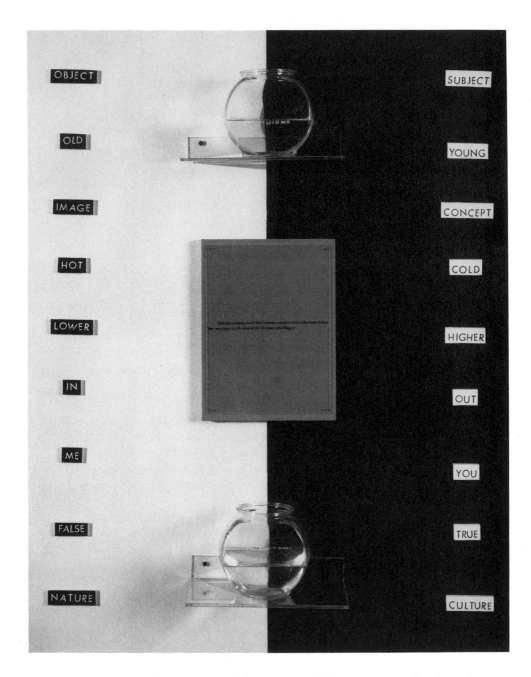

Renée Green, *Which?* (detail), 1990. "Did that woman, could that woman, somehow know that here before her very eyes on the roof of the Drayton sat a Negro?"

Wahneema Lubiano I know that most of you have articulated considerable urgency about the nature of your work and the problems of your work, so I want to ask a frivolous question. There's enough pessimism of intellect being articulated tonight. I want to ask those of you on the panel about pleasure and what part pleasure has played in your work, including your engaged cultural analysis. Since "popular" implies that many people find pleasure there, and since, as cultural critics, you are all also part of an audience (you don't just work on the work, the work works on you), I want to know, is there a way in which you can fit pleasure into your analysis?

bell hooks I did say, Wahneema, that I felt certain kinds of critique change the nature of our pleasure. I also thought about why I didn't go on to talk more about that question of change. I find a lot of people concerned that criticism will destroy pleasure in the text completely. But I am just beginning to formulate what I mean by "changing the nature of pleasure."

Cornel West Professor Lubiano has raised a very difficult question. First, we have to ask what we mean by pleasure: How is it different from joy? And what are the commodified conditions under which people are engaged in pleasure-making and pleasure-giving? For example, when I listen to Anita Baker, is it pleasure or joy?

Joy forces you to look out and make connections so that there's the possibility of collective engagement, whereas pleasure, under commodified conditions, tends to be inward. You take it with you, and it's a highly individuated unit. Now, of course, we don't make choices about this. When I talked about museums and concerts, it wasn't to trash them.* It was to describe the production, distribution, and consumption of pleasure in capitalist society. There's no escape from it. And we do the best we can under these conditions.

*Refers to unpublished remarks that do not appear in the current collection.

But joy tries to cut across that. Joy tries to get at those non-market values—love, care, kindness, service, solidarity, the struggle for justice—values that provide the possibility of bringing people together. So, when Anita Baker sings, "you bring me joy," rather than, "you bring me pleasure," I think that's what she has in mind.

bell hooks And now we know how pleasure is changed into joy, Wahneema.

Thomas Harris My question is for Henry Louis Gates. First of all, I thought the way you read Isaac Julien's film *Looking for Langston* was in the spirit of the hour—in that your construction of the black gay man and the black straight man shows that there's a fluidity in black male sexuality. But this fluidity wasn't really taken into account when you spoke of the black gay man as a "soft" prototype that could teach the black straight man something, and teach him from the outside. Second, I was interested in your involvement in the film (I don't know what your involvement was as far as Langston Hughes's estate), in how you felt personally about the film, and in how you could address issues of black men's sexuality, especially at this time when thirty percent of the population with AIDS is black. I think the issue of sexuality has to be addressed, not so much gay sexuality, but our sexuality in general. As a man, how did you feel about the film? How did you feel about seeing two black men together?

Henry Louis Gates I'll tell you about my personal involvement in the film—which I'm tempted to say was zero, except for the fact that I did know George Bass—the executor of the Hughes estate—fairly well. At the time, we were working on the editing of *Mulebone,* the play by Hughes and Zora Neale Hurston, so I spent a lot of time lobbying George to permit Isaac Julien to use the poetry. As you well know, those efforts weren't very effective.

I find the question about my personal response to the film a very interesting one. I happen to love the film. And part of what I admire in it are the fluid relations between its politics, aesthetics, and erotics. I saw it in public for the first time with Houston Baker and Manthia Diawara at the University of Pennsylvania when I was delivering the Richard Wright lectures. I was thinking about writing about it after having seen it in my living room with a couple of friends, both of whom happen to be gay. After we screened it to the audience, Houston said he was trying to figure out why he found the film to be as erotic as it was. And if he hadn't said it, I would have said the same thing. I found it very erotic, and I enjoyed that experience of joyful—is that right, Cornel?—joyful rather than pleasurable eroticism.

If my work has been consistent in any way, it's been consistent in the sense of puzzling over modes of representation within black discourse of different kinds. And I'm interested that nobody that I know of in black American cinema has taken an historical era and turned it inside out the way that Isaac did. It's wonderful. Ishmael Reed plays with time and history in *Mumbo Jumbo* (and on any other occasion that he can), but in film, if you look at who the dominant filmmakers are in the black American community, and then look at what's happening in independent film in England, it's very, very different. That kind of risk, that kind of excitement, that kind of energy is something I want to see float across the Atlantic Ocean and inform the making of films by black men and black women in the United States. We have too much of a reverence for "history"—not recognizing the nature of "history" in its textuality.

I'm also very interested in our dealing with the homophobia in the black tradition—which is rampant—and in the need to understand our homophobia in relation to our homosexuality. Valerie Smith could very well have expanded her piece in that direction using the same films she analyzed. For example, there was an interesting black gay sequence in the rough cut of *Jungle Fever*. Consequently, the essay I wrote on *Jungle Fever* in *Five for Five* is actually about a film that doesn't exist. I was hoping that, at Cannes, Spike Lee and Isaac Julien would have this great encounter. You know, it would be like DuBois meeting Marcus Garvey, right? But from what I understand, it didn't exactly happen.

I think that coming to an understanding of the homophobia in the black artistic tradition, and enacting its critique, is one of the most important challenges for our generation. I'm trying to understand my own homophobia and my own, as it were, homosexuality simultaneously, if you see what I mean. And I'm working it through. I should point out, though, that when bell hooks commended Isaac for introducing a "soft" image of black masculinity in contrast to the militarized "hardness" she saw in the work of a prominent American black gay filmmaker, she wasn't propounding any simpleminded opposition between the two, and I don't think I was reinstating one, either. More generally, I was trying to point to the porousness of the film, the ambiguities that were made possible there, and the way ambiguity itself becomes its mode of representation.

Eddie Glaude I wanted to ask a question following Professor Hall's lecture. With the fragmentation of the black community at this particular juncture—along the faultlines of class, gender, region, and other specific differences—to what extent have mass movements been displaced by these other constituencies?

Stuart Hall I don't think these other constituencies displace mass movements in the sense of making them impossible. What I think they do is change the terms under which mass political movements come together. We used to assume they came together on the basis of preconstituted social and political identities (as if these were constituted outside of the political processes that brought them together), and then politics was simply mobilizing what already existed. I'm not sure whether mass politics ever were like that, but what I'm bloody sure of is that they're no longer like that, and there's no going back.

What this means is that unity and questions of unity and of mobilization are now always questions of articulations of difference. There are no political programs that can be constructed around issues which try to subsume, within their own terms, all the other identities and antagonisms they're attempting to mobilize around. Therefore, political programs will have to be programs that don't assume that the problems of gender are resolved by the same movement directed toward addressing the questions of racism or of economic inequalities. There have to be specific articulations of different forms of politics that win the identification of either different communities or—what is much more problematic, but I think much more real—the different identities all struggling for articulation within our own heads.

Now, I understand what I think is the problem behind what you're asking: this is a very different sort of politics from the automatic politics we're accustomed to. We know how to engage in a kind of automaticity; the subjects are already duly constituted and attached to particular portions of the political spectrum, and we're either good at getting them out to the ballot box or on the street or we're bad at getting them out. But I don't think we quite know what the new form of politics is that has the necessarily more differentiated shape I am trying to describe. We are still in the process of experimenting with a new form of politics where the constitution of identities, the winning of identification, is itself part of the political struggle, not something preliminary to that struggle. The situation, moreover, is extremely dramatic when the forms of resistance and political mobilization required to address this crisis are difficult to understand. That is the gap I feel—between theoretically understanding the political moment we're in and not yet having a practical grip on the concrete forms in which to conduct the urgent political struggles we have to wage.

Still, I don't think there's any going back to another kind of politics that forgets, or tries to disavow, the necessary entry into the proliferation of difference. That is where modern societies are at now. I don't want to generalize it for the world as a whole, but I think people in the black diaspora are irrevocably committed to struggling in their own way and from their own positions within these forms of modern (postmodern?) politics. So we've got to try to understand the nature of the new cultural politics that are appropriate to that change.

Tiffany Patterson I want to underscore some of the panelists' comments as well as bring out the last question even more. bell's comments, which I agree with, spoke to the native intellectual reaction to criticism within the African-American community. I think we need to grapple with a cultural conservatism that not only is shaping politics in the country as a whole, but is clearly a part of the African-American experience as well. A kind of mythic construction of a progressive African-American community exists that fails to incorporate the ways African Americans can be blind to some of the important observations bell made about *Boyz N the Hood*—about the way women were treated, about the way the welfare mother was treated—because these images fit within their conservative cultural vision. African Americans, as an oppressed or marginalized people who have, in many historical instances, taken a progressive position, can be very conservative at the same time. And this leads me back to Eddie's question.

The question was framed as if fragmentation along class and gender lines in the African-American experience of the United States were a contemporary reality. It is not a contemporary reality; it is an historical one: there has always been fragmentation along class lines, though the specificity of history changes the ways in which that fragmentation is articulated. Class divisions appeared, for example, in slavery. Of course, the dominant within slavery would then shape and suppress that fragmentation. As well, in the period of the Civil Rights Movement, the virulent violence of racism against black people would suppress this fragmentation, even though it continued to smoulder. But we know from the historical studies—works like Robin D. G. Kelley's study of black participation in the Communist party in Alabama, *Hammer and Hoe*—that there was always fragmentation in the African-American experience.

I think it's time for us to stop viewing the African-American community in its monolithic image and view it instead in its very fragmented and diverse image. That doesn't take away from examining the ways in which mass movements get constructed. But I agree with Professor Hall. They are going to be constructed very differently today because of the changes in the economy, the changes in the United States, and in the world. I end by saying that, as an historian, I would push us to be more historical—not in the sense of a grand narrative but in the sense of a more complicated history, of attacking African-American culture in a more complicated way.

Cornel West I think Tiffany's right on the mark. And I think we have to raise the question about why a significant number of black people would associate critique and criticism with put-down and castigation. There is sometimes a healthy impulse behind anti-intellectualism in the black community—even though I reject anti-intellectualism. What's behind it are too many black intellectuals who have been arrogant and haughty and have looked down upon ordinary people—as if we were bringing the goodies, so to speak. Therefore, we have a responsibility to associate critique with enabling and equipping and empowering people in a democratic manner. By democratic, I mean on the ground with them—not being ashamed that we're intellectuals, but recognizing at the same time that the self-critical mode forces us to acknowledge the degree to which they would look on elites as having access to special knowledge, which affords us high status in organizations and movements and so forth. We've got to walk along that narrow ridge. That's a real challenge because there's something democratic about looking at intellectuals critically (and that's what they do in the barbershops and the beauty salons), but, on the other hand, we have to be critical of their self-righteousness and dogmatism.

Gender, Sexuality, and Black Images
in Popular Culture

Still from *Looking for Langston*,
directed by Isaac Julien, 1988.

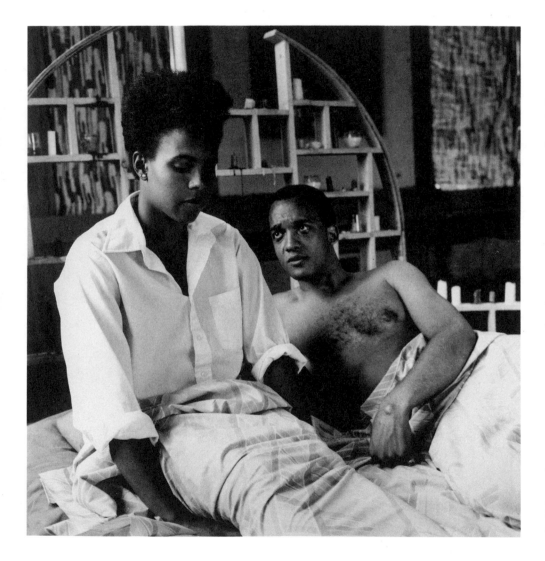

Tracy Camila Johns as Nola Darling and Redmond Hicks as Jamie Overstreet in a still from *She's*
94   *Gotta Have It*, directed by Spike Lee, 1986.

Jacquie Jones

The Accusatory Space

Over the few months following the release of *New Jack City* and *Boyz N the Hood,* I wrote a lot about the relationships of Black women to Black men and to power within the narratives. I found that what was missing for me was a general context out of which I understood the women in these films to be functioning. What I offer here is a kind of personal meditation, an effort to understand that place.

In his *History of Sexuality,* Michel Foucault wrote,

> Sexuality must not be described as a stubborn drive, by nature alien and of necessity disobedient...It appears rather as an especially dense transfer point for relations of power...Sexuality is not the most intractable element in power relations, but rather one of those endowed with the greatest instrumentality: useful for the greatest number of maneuvers and capable of serving as a point of support, as a linchpin, for the most varied strategies.[1]

Nowhere has his point been proven better than in contemporary Black culture of the past year. In fact, what has emerged in the last year's commercial Black film mirrors the prevailing tide in all of our cultural products: a unified credo espousing racial solidarity (nationalism), an appropriated Americanism (vigilantism), and a uniform sexual politic (male-dominated heterosexism).

I wrote recently, in an article for *Wide Angle,*[2] that it is ironic to me that Nola Darling—of Spike Lee's first film *She's Gotta Have It*—is the mother of the Black female character in contemporary mainstream film. And it is eerie to watch Tracy Camila Johns, the actress who animated Lee's fantastic Nola (and I mean that in the fantasy sense of the word), stripping down to red satin lingerie in Mario Van Peeble's *New Jack City.* The commentary that can be made by juxtaposing Johns's two significant roles is profound because, unfortunately, the two express the range of female representation in commercial film. In both instances, Johns's roles best represent the ambiguity between and the narrowness of the two categories that Black women are allowed to occupy in this cinema—that of the bitch and that of the 'ho. I now realize that this positioning is not ironic at all. It's functional. It assigns the accusatory space from which representation in the media, and more generally in society, can continually be reprogrammed along gender lines. And incidentally, the same is true of the way recent Black popular culture has tried to codify words like "punk" and "faggot" in order to segment and control desire, and leave open spaces for blame.

It occurred to me that the stories that predestined 1991's summer ghetto blockbusters, *New Jack City* and *Boyz N the Hood,* as well as upcoming ones like *Juice* and *Make Me Want to Holler,* first came to the American public in the form of television news. From the advent of drive-by shootings in L.A. and leather-jackets-for-lives in Detroit, gangs, drugs, and the accompanying violence became an expected fixture from six to seven, and then again at eleven, in American homes. The news became the factory for Black mass media imagery in cautious, conservative times. The boys, of course, were in the forefront, but always behind them, just inside the frame, was the corps of silent girls, standing on the curb or sitting on a couch. Somehow these girls seemed to me to exist in the space of the accused. After all, according to the news of the early eighties, it was those teenage, female-headed households that produced these boys. So I am used to thinking of current events in terms of cultural commodities, in terms of when the next TV movie will be made.

Plus, I had lived through Rasheeda Moore; and I remembered how, a week after the covert videotape of Moore and former D.C. Mayor Marion Barry was released—and the world watched them drinking a bottle of Courvoisier and smoking crack—vendors in D.C. were peddling T-shirts and cassettes blaring, "goddamn bitch set him up." So, as soon as I heard about Anita Hill, I figured that this, too, would be the stuff of popular culture. Still, I was not prepared for Anita Hill as a media event. I can't forget the staging, the color, the lighting—behind her, a row of Black women whose faces sometimes betrayed her evenness, and in front of her, a row of middle-aged white men: some kind, some vicious, determining the context for our assessment of who Anita Hill was. And all of this for the purpose of situating Clarence Thomas, a Black man, squarely in a white male context. Ultimately, Anita Hill became to me that pitiful, castigated mother in *Boyz N the Hood,* that poor, wronged wife in *Jungle Fever,* and that pathetic, abandoned lover in *Livin' Large*: one of the female accusers cast to the side while her accusations are weighed by the men and, ultimately, reconfigured to blame her.

By insisting, in their cultural products, that Black women, on the basis of an abstracted femaleness, are unfit, Black men have been able to maintain cultural dominance in an albeit limited sphere. In just the past year, we, as Black women, have been accused of being too attainable (whores), as in *Jungle Fever,* being incapable of parenting, as in *Boyz N the Hood,* causing unmendable rifts between Black men, as in *New Jack City,* and, in short, of destroying the Black community. A decade ago, the word "bitch" was generally used, when voiced, to punctuate an extremely heated argument, or as a last pleading effort to muddy an opponent. Today, it is the word used openly to define our image in popular media.

In her essay "The Oppositional Gaze: Black Female Spectators," bell hooks says,

> Conventional representations of Black women have done violence to the image. Responding to this assault, many Black women spectators shut out the image, looked the other way, accorded cinema no importance in their lives.[3]

But, according to the most recent Nielsen ratings, the average Black household watches eleven hours of television every day—about two-thirds of their waking hours. In addition, they spend at nearly five times their proportion of the population at movie theaters. Distinctions no longer exist between movies and news, television and real life. There is nowhere left to avert the gaze.

Still it is impossible for me to lose hope. By looking directly at these images and not only naming the politicized sexuality, but resisting it as well, by claiming nontraditional cinema as a space to articulate and develop transformative ideas which are destined to be incorporated into the language of the cinema, we move ahead. The bombardment of accusatory images in the past year will eventually be met and, at that time, I will be able to write a more satisfying conclusion.

1. Michel Foucault, *History of Sexuality,* Volume I (New York: Vintage, 1980), 103.

2. Jacquie Jones, "The New Ghetto Aesthetic," *Wide Angle* 13, nos. 3 and 4 (July–October 1991), 32–43.

3. bell hooks, "The Oppositional Gaze: Black Female Spectators" in *Black American Cinema: History, Theory and Criticism,* ed. Manthia Diawara (London: Routledge, 1992), forthcoming.

Marlon T. Riggs

Unleash the Queen

Preface: The stage is hers, but she is not yet ready. He knows his audience awaits. What will she say? This queer, this queen, this radical black sissy-fag who won't shut up. Of course, Miss Girl will have to read somebody: that's part of the performance we all expect. But can she transcend the well-rehearsed roles she and her audience (sister and fellow performers yourselves) so naturally slip into? Can I/you transcend our mutual masks—the easy, witty, critical rhetoric with which we so deftly camouflage our deeper mixed emotions, ambivalences, aversions, secrets?

He surveys the faces in front of him, to the left and the right. What do they see, what do they hear inside? Can/will they give voice to these submerged, troubling, interior truths?

Ahh, time for quiet rumination must be temporarily suspended. For this moment, silence is not in order, only words—a waterfall of words. And being the sometimes Loud Snap-Happy Signifying Butch-Girl that he/she is, she beats her face, affixes the appropriate conference queen tiara, assumes the throne, that is, the center stage of your attention, rejoicing in rhetorical gender-fuck—my preferred expression of drag—and commences the show.

ACT I

The Scene: Last July. The night of the national PBS broadcast of *Tongues Untied*. The program has just ended, and I am sitting in a San Francisco studio. My image is beamed by satellite to Minneapolis public TV station KTCA. On the other end, a panel has been assembled, moderated by a local black male journalist, whom I do not know, but whose credentials as a moderator, it quickly becomes apparent, seem to be solely that he is black and has a reputation as a consumer reporter.

100 Assoto Saint in *Non, Je Ne Regrette Rien (No Regrets)*, directed by Marlon Riggs, 1992.

Interesting, I think, let's see how Miss Thing consumes *this*. Interestingly, as well, the panel and moderator can see me. I cannot see them. Talk about the privileged gaze. Within five minutes into this scheduled hour-long broadcast, what I hear, however, tells me enough: Miss Thing is straight, very straight, and intent on letting her audience in on this important fact.

"I just want to clarify one point," Thing announces in an abrupt non sequitur. "You said in your video, 'Everybody on the block did that.' Well I don't know about your block, but my father was a Presbyterian minister, and it didn't happen on my block. Just a clarification."

Well.

Within twenty minutes of the program, Thing's voice betrays acute anxiety. The panel is not falling prey to his most obvious rhetorical traps: Would you let your children see this? Why such language of the street? Is this lifestyle appropriate for the black community? Finally, in exasperation, Thing abandons his strategy of leading questions and simply blurts out that this "documentary, if that's what it was, failed to educate a mainstream audience. A documentary," he goes on to explain, "is supposed to instruct, to take you from A to B and so on. This program clearly didn't do that; hence," he concludes, a rare double-negative driving home his point: "I couldn't get nothing out of it."

For the remainder of the program, Black Macho Recapitulated grew increasingly immoderate. And though his naïve bluntness was atypical for a public forum, his attitude, you and I know, is all too familiar. "Mainstream audience." "The black community." "From A to B." "Lifestyle." All terms denoting an ideological frame of reference that enforces a rigorous exclusion of certain kinds of difference, that erects stifling enclosures around a whole range of necessary debates, or, alternately, confines them within an easily recognizable—and controllable—psychosocial arena.

Can we talk? But of course we can, queer diva darling, if you abide by the rules of the dominant discourse, which means, in short, you must ultimately sing somebody else's tune to be heard. That somebody is, of course, most often in part responsible for the historic gag in your communal mouth.

Performance Break: Theatric aside. Do they now know where girlfriend's going? Do you really think he/she/I would let you off so easily with such an amusing anecdote? Continue performance.

In the last two years I have become a conference queen. Not with much deliberate intent, mind you. But my video, *Tongues Untied,* in a way I frankly never envisioned while making it, has catapulted me into a society of theory divas and culture queens—and yes, my het-brothers, that includes you too, you especially—a society I must admit I barely knew existed three years ago.

Performance Break: Theatric effect: whispered aside. In my former ignorance, I suspect I am not unlike the overwhelming majority of black cultural workers in this country, and the blame for this sorry state of producer-critic relations, I now know, lies not just with a semi-literate producing proletariat. Continue performance.

At these conferences, I am typically called upon to speak on matters of race and sexuality in queer media; race and sexuality in black culture; race and sex-uality in Western cinema. I have become the Race and Sexuality Resident Expert. The assumption, it seems, is that girlfriend can talk about nothing else—that is, with authority. Indeed, based on what I gather from the majority of those who invite me to tea, it's easy to imagine a homo promo video on my behalf with these lines: Wanna find out what it's like to be black and gay, how it looks, how it feels, to live and think that way? Call 976-DIVA.

But increasingly, of late, this Snap Queen harbors the sneaking suspicion that the measure of her acceptance into various critical in-crowds, which solicit her membership with the regularity of Visa and MasterCard companies ("member-ship has its privileges"), has less to do with any vital concern with black gay subjectivity and its intrinsic value in black social/cultural expression than with how well she has mastered, and now mimics, the critical language of her new-found tribe of crit queens.

Le Butch-Girl wonders, for instance, if her/his permission to say gender-fuck is contingent upon knowing and articulating Fanon, Foucault, Gates, Gilroy, hooks, Hall, West, and the rest, as well.

Parenthetical Notation: Forgive the masculinist bent of this pantheon, but this, it seems, is the present predominant nature of the tribe. Continue performance.

Among you, someone no doubt is thinking: Miss Thing can certainly throw down her verbal drag schtick, but does she comprehend discursive intertextual analysis, can she engage in postfeminist, neo-Marxist, postmodern deconstruc-tionist critique? Does she understand the difference between text, subtext, and metatext? Does she know she's part of a subaltern universe? Can she, in a word, *really* read?

Discomforting questions ricochet in the Snap Queen's mind, and she wonders/ponders further whether his/her tongue is at times, in effect, not her tongue, if her tongue (to gain validation, an audience) has really become their tongues, and if, in fact (yes! to trope sweet Zora), it is their tongues that are in his mouth, pressing against, crowding out his own, if he is choking. A different kind of voicelessness.

My mouth moves, but you hear your own words.

What nature of ventriloquism is this?

ACT II

Here we sit assembled, the newest of the New Negroes (the Niggerati of the Nineties?), preening and posturing in our fanciful display of cultural literacy, the command of language, the strategic deployment of so many elegant words. But I wonder: where were the words when Joe Beam really needed them?—when he was alive, when *In the Life* was first published, and black bookstores refused to carry it, and not one—count—not one black, ostensibly straight critic opened his or her mouth to acknowledge Joe's monumental breach of our historic literary silence. Where were the oh-so-pretty words, then?

Performance Break: Race-sexuality-gender. Race-sexuality-gender. Race-sexuality-gender. The mantra now flows so trippingly off formerly silent tongues I am still astonished by the rapid metamorphosis. What interior psycho-ideological adjustment enables such new progressive, inclusive articulation? Or is it really just facility at verbiage? Continue performance.

Miss Girl increasingly doubts those who now effortlessly invoke her name, her community. He doubts because he hears little, beyond lip service, that affirms his status as something other than Other. And what he sees from time to time evidences his intuition that she is perhaps a pawn in somebody else's cultural war game, and is thus expendable. As in: black like who?

Excitedly, she turns the page to the series of *Village Voice* essays, anticipating, in the words of Essex Hemphill, some "evidence of being," only to find a single phrase (and a short one at that) that speaks explicitly to queer black identity. Again, I witness how casually, how unself-consciously, the faggots and dykes have been left in the woodshed—or is it the closet?

The insult is compounded as I turn to the back pages, appropriately enough, of the same issue, where another essay addresses the ghettoization of homo culture. Thus stand our choices: het lip-service, cultural ghetto, or total erasure. Black like who? Implicit answer: not like you!

ACT III

Performance Break: Brief Digression. Miss Thing has some questions she must get out of his system, or I will just scream. She apologizes if it doesn't fit some grand unitary flow of analysis and ideas, but sometimes you can't just fit it all in a neat perfect package, laced just so.

Digression One: Why is it that the majority of us still engage in that most traditional form of cultural review and criticism in which single works and single authors are continuously privileged above anything and everyone else? If not Spike Lee, then John Singleton, if not Singleton, then Julien, and so on. What about more complicated analyses of how multiple black cultural narratives compete, intersect, complement, collide? Wouldn't it stop this oh-so-tiresome process of centering a few of us while marginalizing the rest?

Digression Two: What is, after all, the "black" in black pop culture? Or more specifically, how do Marky Mark and Vanilla Ice and Charlie Pride and Living Colour fit within our frames of reference? That is, the first two kinda sound black but ain't, and the last two are black but don't sound like it, if you know what I mean. So—I mean this seriously—what is the marker of blackness in our pop culture?

Digression Three: What is the "pop" in black pop culture? On a common-sense level, pop culture usually translates as mass culture, which, quite frankly, does not typically include folks like me, Julie Dash, Isaac Julien (pre–*Young Soul Rebels*, that is), Charles Burnett, Camille Billops, Zeinabu Davis, and—you get the picture. So is "pop" a misnomer, or is it that I'm just a dizzy queen, ignorant of recently expanded definitions of the term?

Digression Four: Where is Latifah?!? Where are Ice Cube, Ice-T, Spike Lee, John Singleton, Matty Rich, Salt-n-Pepa, Bytches with Problems, Cosby, namely, the kind of folks one normally associates with the phrase, "pop culture producer"? If criticism, to paraphrase Cornel West, is to enable and transform, then why aren't these divas here in dialogue, too? Are they too busy? Were they invited?

Digression Five: Who ultimately are we writing for, talking to? End digressions. (Sigh). We feel so much better now that that's off our chest, don't we? Continue mainstage performance. Resume Act III.

Gaze upon me. Gaze upon this deviant, defiant, diseased Other. T-cell count less than 150. The collapse of kidney function imminent from interior ravaging by multiplying microbes. Disease consumes me.

Gaze upon your self. Dis-ease grips you as well. We are all mutually bound, sick, trapped. Except you, many of you, persist in the illusion of safe, sage detachment.

Do you honestly think you can so closely, critically examine me without studying or revealing yourself? Or do you really think your progressive, collective "we" is all that's necessary in your performance of reflexivity?

Miss Girl must now abandon your/her stage. Indeed, she suspects she has overstayed, by just a bit, her welcome. But what bona fide queen conforms to expected time limits? Before he/she tosses his/her tiara to the next diva in the wings, I ask you—no, beg—no, demand: a little more realness from each of us. Please.

Lisa Kennedy

The Body in Question

Before I studied the art, a punch to me was just a punch, a kick was just a kick. After I studied the art, a punch was no longer a punch, a kick no longer a kick. Now that I understand the art, a punch is a punch, a kick is just a kick.

—The Tao of Jeet Kune Do, *Bruce Lee, the chapter on "Tools"*

The master's tools cannot dismantle the master's house.

—*Audre Lorde*

The collective body—that phantasm with which I share blood, history, and hips—goes for a stroll. Ambling, lumbering, hobbling in a monstrous mass, more male than female, urban than rural, angry than forgiving, the collective body is reminiscent of some creature from a fifties sci-fi flick, bigger than a house. Familiar and endearing to some, scary to others, the body in question shall remain surnameless, has to, which is no doubt one reason Malcolm took on the X. But let's give it a handle anyway, call it the "black community" this time around, knowing full well, though forgetting all the time, that there is more than one collective body roaming the American landscape at any given moment.

Anyway, it's a humid day in Brooklyn, so the collective body decides to take in a movie. *Terminator 2* has just opened at the Fulton Street Mall. The collective body (working the affirmative-action tip by bringing along Julian and Jeff, who are white) digs deep into its pocket for seven dollars, the price of the ticket for a flick with a decidedly nonblack lead—though his name does seem to say "black," two times.

Without a doubt, the Metropolitan Cinemas is one of the best places to see an action pic. The excellent "Awwh shit…Kill him!" call and response of the audience makes it movie-going like it oughta be. But still, who couldn't be thrown by the sight of an African-American scientist, played by Joe Morton, being chastised ("It's you people who have destroyed the world!") and not scream "Whoa!" ("Who, black men?!?"), and then wonder why the collective body continued to root and respond after that moment. Is there some more compelling (though perhaps unconscious) logic than the simple "that's entertainment"?

Something in controversial black scholar Leonard Jeffries's deployment of history suggests there is. And then somersaults to throw light on Jeffries's own debacle. (And by "debacle" I mean not only his delusions-of-personal-grandeur, pseudoscience, quasireligious filibuster, but also the anxiety-driven, censorious paranoia with which it's been met. Forget the *New York Post* and go directly to the more subtle *Time* magazine piece by Lance Morrow and Thomas McCarroll, who use Jeffries to slip in a cursory critique of the "intellectually troubling" aspects of Afrocentrism, that new religion, which they intimate has no greater goal than to declare ancient Egypt as black and the rightful cradle of civilization.) Where Jeffries and *T2* rebel John Connor meet is in their advocacy of history as something that "can be processed in a way to make it work for you." And that is time travel, pure and simple.

Well, not so simple. *Terminator 2*'s back and forth between the past and the postapocalyptic present is sexy but convoluted. Even so, the conceit of an adult hero reprogramming a cybertool to save his boy-self (making him more his father than his own father could be) is easily the most groovy metaphor for the work of postmodern history available. This is what history is like for the collective body; it is a tool to reengineer the past, get in there, fix it up, guarantee a future. (That some, like Leonard Jeffries, I venture, believe that the iterations have a natural stopping point, a "truth," "our truth," is a problem of a different stripe.)

With history conveniently declared deceased—an untimely death to say the least—even the less conspiracy-minded of us can't help feeling that it's been murdered in order to prevent us, the collective body, from resuscitating it, exhuming it, performing an autopsy, doing whatever it takes to get it to bear witness to the atrocities and triumphs to which it's been privy. This is, of course, one of the aims not only of Afrocentrism, but of multiculturalism and feminism.

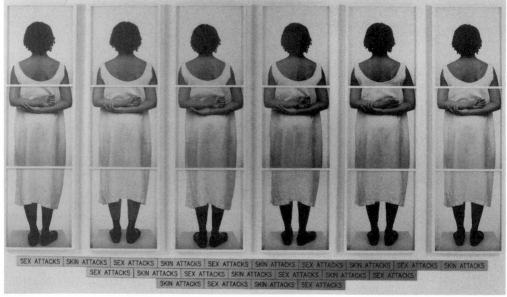

Lorna Simpson, *Guarded Conditions*, 1989.

The collective body wants to know.

But what? Nothing less than its past, present, and future. The time when uttering a historical gem meant announcing a "fact" has slipped by. Not because events themselves are malleable, but because their "meaning" is, from here on out, painfully contestable. This is embedded in Jeffries's rail as well (though his history is more divisive than a device). But there is something truer than all the bogus "frameworks" about sun and ice evoked to show people of color (and whites) that we've had our hand in this world from the get-go, which is that there is certainty no more.

We need look no further than Spike Lee's and Amiri Baraka's brawl over Malcolm's legacy or Jeffries's spiel on the dastardly deeds of a Jewish Hollywood, or even the uproar about Clarence Thomas and African-American Republicans, to see that the collective body, the black community, hasn't a cohesive identity. You don't have to be a psychoanalyst to know how difficult and painful questions of identity can be. If one lone subject spends a lifetime of language trying to represent herself in total, all the while slip-sliding over a world of communication, it's not difficult to imagine the hell (and high points) a nation of millions wades through to express itself in one voice.

Was there ever a time when the collective body moved and spoke as one? Not likely. And is that one-hand, one-heart feeling desirable, or even possible? Racism and inequality make it feel thus—make it seem necessary, but would it be so in a world of undifferentiated difference? A world where race is neither the "master's house" nor a tool to dismantle it. There is a tremendous push (ours) and an opportunity (let's not forget the pangs of a hungry marketplace) for more representation, more film, more images, more, more, more. With this lurch forward comes a flood of anxiety as well. Competition for one: if individual blacks can speak only for the collective body, then exactly how much of it is there to be carved up and sold off? But also a more visceral fear: will we become slaves to the collective body? Forced always to speak for it and to its needs? And scared to death that if we don't, we won't be allowed to say anything; or if we misrepresent it for the sake of ourselves we will be expelled, we will not exist? We will be "Toms," or "house Negroes," or "not black," when clearly we remain in our skins.

It's not a surprise to find film in the midst of this growing discussion of the collective's identity. Film because it feels extraordinarily powerful—all that money and narrative and pleasure—and because historically it is how America looks at itself. Although Leonard Jeffries was not wrong to assail "Sambo images" of black folk in early Hollywood films (though black film historian Donald Bogle has done better work of it in *Toms, Coons, Mulattoes, Mammies, and Bucks,* locating the subversive in the submissive, finding the residue of the black actors' resistance to demeaning roles), he couldn't have chosen an odder time to do it, 1991 being the year of black film and all. If in the recent past, Spike Lee's films have been treated as something of a hand-held mirror by the collective body—many of us drawn to his images less like Narcissus than like people who have seldom seen themselves— the cinema has now become a house of mirrors. *New Jack City, Chameleon Street, Jungle Fever, Boyz N the Hood,* and *True Identity* all speak of, to, and/or for the collective body. With every viewing, the black community gets an inkling of its shape, its texture, even its age and gender (mostly young, mostly male these days).

Indeed many of the African-American films of 1991 did the work of retooling, demonstrating how that activity creates new, compelling difficulties for the collective body. In short: *where are the women?!?* From *House Party* to *To Sleep with Anger* to *Mo' Better Blues* to *Boyz N the Hood,* the sons are working overtime to secure the place of the father, and in doing so, themselves. If ever there was a symbolic effort to counteract a sociological assertion—that of paternal abandonment—it has been these films, which depict a world of fathers and sons. Need I add, this does not take care of all of us who partake and make the collective body's life 24–7.

(Word to the brother: I will not have some twenty-three-year-old manchild in LaLa land telling me I must forgo a career to be a good mother, that it's my responsibility to the embattled black family, just because he made a moving film.)

If one were to seize the entrepreneurial moment, the T-shirt would read: "It's an Oedipal Thing. You Wouldn't Understand." This is less a complaint, more an observation about the failure inherent in casting the collective over the individual or mistaking the individual vision for the collective reality. If we Americans weren't going through such a xenophobic moment in relation to French thought, I would suggest that when discussing black film, we put a slash through the "black" just to make a distinction between a tool with a handle and...us.

That an essay about the identity of the black community can teeter just this side of being a film piece is a testament to our living in a uniquely American moment, when political activism, liberation activity, is more often than not bound up with questions of representation. When the real lives of people are substantiated by their reel lives. The U.S. is at once a semiotic semiotic semiotic semiotic world and a material one; a place where we become the actors, the acted upon, and no one in particular.

No doubt, our bodies are shot through with meaning, riddled with definitions and qualities not of our own choosing. Sometimes the most positive thing to do in that instance is to choose wholeheartedly the meanings, embrace them dramatically, turn the joint upside down. Hip hop does this aggressively. Film bobs and weaves. Identity politics...well, at its best, it's like social work at its best, a strategy employed on the way to a different place.

The collective body is at a weird stage. The question is, will it become the cyborg that we construct, tend, love and hate, breathe life into, and can't bear to part with (though its existence may doom us ultimately)? Or will we let it

Tyra Ferrell as Mrs. Baker in a still from *Boyz N the Hood*, directed by John Singleton, 1991.

pass when the time comes? The fights over who will speak, what will be said and recounted, the "real" blackness suggest that the moment of relinquishing will not be an easy one. But in avoiding it we confound ourselves, throttle our artists, repress our meaning as people who, unlike the collective body, have proper names and rich personal histories. What exactly is the purpose of a politics based on racial identity, any identity? To prove the other guy wrong? Make him yell uncle? Or to deliver the subject from the jaws of a limited/limiting discourse into a meaty narrative, however painful, joyous, and lousy, of her own?

Judith Wilson

Getting Down to Get Over:
Romare Bearden's Use of Pornography and the
Problem of the Black Female Body in Afro-U.S. Art

I want to address the topic of sexuality and black images in popular culture by linking it to what I know best: the record of U.S. black artists' efforts to assert themselves in the language of Western high culture. In seeking to bridge these two quite disparate discourses, that of black high art and that of the black image in popular culture, I have begun to see a central problem in the history of African-American art, the problem of the black nude, in different terms than I had previously.[1] The following remarks are therefore exploratory. They reflect a process of rereading I have just begun.

Now, let me lay out the intended contents of my title.

"Getting down" alludes to cultural hierarchy. It either speaks pejoratively of a descent from some more elevated plane into the "abyss" of popular culture, or it approvingly describes the act of dismounting one's high horse to commune with the masses. In U.S. black vernacular, "getting down" has long been associated with funk, that is to say, with manifestations of an aesthetic that celebrates and requires sweat as evidence of putatively honest feeling. Given this tendency to equate the aromatic pungency of body odors with what is emotionally compelling in cultural products, it is not surprising that "getting down" has also been associated with a particularly pleasurable form of sweat-inducing physical exertion, namely, you guessed it, sexual intercourse.

To "get over" has a different set of meanings, different but related. Transcendence—as described by the black spiritual "How I Got Over," for example —is one of them. On a more mundane level, to "get over" an illness or some other setback denotes recovery. And in yet another black contribution to contemporary English, to "get over" refers to the achievement of success through some form of duplicity. (That the latter use of this term also frequently implies sexual conquest is not irrelevant here.)

In my subtitle, "Romare Bearden's Use of Pornography and the Problem of the Black Female Body in Afro-U.S. Art," I have purposely inserted several troubling terms. By "pornography," I mean the entire spectrum of representations that fetishize the body and objectify desire for public consumption. I have employed the slightly awkward, unfamiliar label "Afro-U.S." to clearly localize my frame of reference.[2]

What I am trying to suggest with this title is that by "getting low," culling images from pornography,[3] the least reputable of pop cultural sources, and dealing with black sexuality in an unusually explicit manner—Romare Bearden managed to transcend the widespread stigmatization of black sexuality.[4] He was able to recuperate the nude black female body, wresting it from the clutches of white purveyors of erotic fantasies about exotic Others,[5] and reposition it in relation to black vernacular culture. By juxtaposing the black female body with such resonant figures as the train[6] (see *Work Train*, 1966) and the patchwork quilt[7] (see *Patchwork Quilt*, 1970), Bearden visualized the historic conjunctions of black female beauty and eroticism with jazz, blues, African-American folklore and religion, as well as African-derived visual practices.[8]

As both image and idea, the black body has long been a contested site. In antiquity, Herodotus retailed rumors that certain parts of the African continent were inhabited by a race of monstrous-looking humans.[9] A millennium or so later, southern Europe was brought face to face with dark-skinned peoples as Spain fell to the Moors.[10] At first, thanks to the combination of Christian symbolism—with its stark equations of good and evil with light and dark—and the tendency of conquered peoples to demonize their foes, medieval European art often represented blacks as grotesque figures whose defining features were impossibly thick lips, bulbous noses, and receding chins, along with prominent cheekbones and curly hair.[11]

By the eighteenth century, according to David Dabydeen, the author of a study of William Hogarth's images of blacks, some European artists and intellectuals had begun to recognize the subjectivity of their own beauty standards *and* to observe that Africans showed a corresponding preference for their own physical traits.[12] For the most part, however, we must speak of the black body as "haunting" the artistic production of both white and black artists in modern times—either in the form of what George Nelson Preston has dubbed "the peripheral Negro" (in reference to the legions of black servants who loom in the shadows of European and Euro-American aristocratic portraiture and to those blacks perpetually cast in supporting roles in allegorical works like William Blake's 1793 print *Europe Supported by Africa and America*) or, as a set of compulsively repeated stereotypes (such as nineteenth-century American painting's genial watermelon eaters and banjo pluckers, or the twentieth-century electronic media's favorite emblems of poverty, physical prowess, and emotional abandon).

The ghosts I have just listed are, of course, white inventions. Nonetheless, they also haunt black visual artists, for whom these apparitions have provoked a different, often antithetical, set of responses. For much of the two-hundred-year history of fine art production by North American blacks, the chief reaction was avoidance of one of high art's favorite categories—the nude.

I must acknowledge my debt to the African-American art historian Sylvia Ardyn Boone. The paucity of black nudes in U.S. black artistic production prior to 1960 has intrigued me ever since Dr. Boone first called my attention to it as an unexamined problem in the history of African-American art. To my knowledge, nineteenth-century black artists produced no counterparts to works like Giacomo Ginotti's monument to black emancipation.[13] I do not mean that nineteenth-century blacks produced no emancipation monuments. They did, but not with quite this tone! Apparently, the black nude only becomes a permissible subject for black artists in the twentieth century.

I say "apparently" because we currently know far too little about nineteenth-century black artistic production to enumerate its repertoires with certainty. Who knew that nineteenth-century New England had possessed a black specialist in fruit and flower still lifes until the Connecticut Gallery mounted a survey of Charles Ethan Porter's career a few years ago?[14] Who knew that a black marine painter had operated in nineteenth-century Chicago until Derrick Beard unearthed James Bolivar Needham a couple of years ago?[15] And surely we can expect the work of a new generation of black scholars, like Juanita Holland, to further expand our conceptions of nineteenth-century black artistic production.[16]

By 1931, with the Harlem Renaissance well under way, we find images like Archibald Motley's *Brown Girl After the Bath,* in which Motley borrows a theme

Left: Hiram Powers, *The Greek Slave*, 1846. In the collection of The Corcoran Gallery of Art, Gift of William Wilson Corcoran.
Right: Giacomo Ginotti, *Abolition de l'esclavage*, 1877. Museo e Gallerie Nazionali di Capodimonte. **115**

from seventeenth-century Dutch art—the harlot performing her toilet.[17] Motley strips the Dutch image of its occupational specificity, but does so without entirely erasing its voyeuristic prurience. By the late 1930s, William H. Johnson and Francisco Lord were painting and sculpting nudes, respectively. At some point, Lord's teacher, Augusta Savage, would also produce her own nudes. Throughout the 1940s, Eldzier Cortor would mine his memories of a stay in the Georgia Sea Islands for statuesque images of dark black women like the ones in his *Southern Gate* and *Room No. 6*. Yet, none of these works openly confront the various legends surrounding the black female body—except for the charge of its aesthetic unworthiness. Merely by making it their subject, all of these artists proclaim the beauty of the black nude. But none of them focus on the volatile conjunction of gender and race or the inflammatory myths of black sexuality that the black nude also inscribes.

Bearden had begun grappling with the nude early in his career and, subsequently, reported his initial frustrations with working from the live model.[18] His 1981 collage *Artist with Painting and Model* seems to reflect this struggle. It shows an early work, *The Annunciation* (1942),[19] mounted on an easel and flanked by the artist and a black model, whose figure is clad only with a bit of drapery. The 1942 painting exemplifies the artist's attempt to "universalize" black subject matter, that is, to shift from the sort of social realist imagery seen in his 1941–42 *Folk Musicians* to a Christian story told in blackface. Both *The Annunciation* and *Folk Musicians* demonstrate Bearden's early assimilation of geometric stylization derived from cubism and traditional African sculpture.[20] The artist's subsequent exploration of cubist fragmentation and a jazz-inspired visual syncopation would, ultimately, lead to his shift to collage in the early 1960s. And his unique contribution to this fundamentally modernist medium, of course, was the conflation of high-art references with pop cultural images, in the form of mass media photography, in order to represent black history and culture.

Obviously, Bearden's use of images derived from pornography, as well as his use of the conventions of the high-art nude, is not unproblematic. There are issues here that I do not have time to unpack. But, in conclusion, I would like to at least enumerate some of them.

First, his reproduction of pornographic strategies, such as the voyeuristic gaze. For example, by representing, in *Dream Images* (1976), both the Peeping

William H. Johnson, *Nude*, ca. 1939. National Museum of American Art, Smithsonian Institution. Gift of the Harmon Foundation.

Tom and the mirrored image of the sexually aroused male, at whom the supine nude directs her gaze but who is positioned outside our view, does the image "expose itself" or merely multiply the viewer/voyeur's trespass, locking us into an obscene triangle of vision?[21]

Second, his representation of prostitution. *Mamie Cole's Living Room* (1978) is one of a number of works based on Bearden's childhood memories, which included contact with a boy who was the son of a prostitute. Does the artist romanticize the condition of sex workers, their commodification, or the various forms of alienation involved in their provision of sexual services?

Third, what I call his domestication of the nude. By placing the female nude in an interior and juxtaposing her form with that of an older, clothed black woman engaged in some routine domestic activity, does Bearden level distinctions between the sexualized female (femme fatale) and the "angel of the hearth," that wife/mother/guardian of the domestic sphere? Do these images offer a simultaneous view of opposite faces of Eve? Or do they simply reinforce a psychosocially restrictive dichotomy?

And finally, his reiteration of the standard gender trope equating Woman with Nature, and the female body with the landscape (see *Memories*, 1970). In what ways does this naturalization of female nudity render "the feminine" a passive site, presumably awaiting creative exploitation by men?

That is just a sample of the kinds of questions I think need to be explored with respect to the gender politics of Bearden's nudes. We have seen that, by undoing the erasure, marginalization, and fetishistic exoticizing of the black female nude, he participated in an important recuperative project of twentieth-century African-American art. We have seen, too, that his specific contribution to this project was the reinscription of black beauty and eroticism *in the context of African-American vernacular culture.* Yet, we have also seen how, insofar as Bearden's nudes replicate some of pornography's standard tropes—its voyeurism, romanticizing of sex work, reliance upon dualistic stereotypes, and naturalization of female nudity, for example—these images suggest the insufficiency of efforts to revise a high-art category by importing into it elements of either popular or vernacular culture, while leaving unexamined the politics of formations at both ends of the spectrum.

It might be argued that the sort of feminist interrogation to which I have subjected these images is inappropriate because their author's views are the products of a pre-feminist generation. But I am as troubled by the fact that *we do not know* his views on this subject as I am by anything else. The general silence about this disturbing aspect of Bearden's oeuvre is symptomatic of the state of criticism on African-American visual artists—the almost exclusively celebratory discourse produced by blacks and the intellectually ghettoizing discourse produced by whites. Here, too, we need to think about "getting down to get over"—"getting down," in this instance, in the sense of shedding inhibitions and risking descent to uncharted depths in order to transcend (or "get over") existing cultural barriers.

1. The resulting adjustments include a heightened awareness of the necessity of specifying gender with respect to "the" black nude. Within both the pop-cultural and fine-art realms, black male nudity and black female nudity have generally functioned incommensurately. Thus, it would be instructive to consider, for example, the implications of Edmonia Lewis's decision to pair a seminude African-American male with a tunic-clad African-American female figure in her 1867 emancipation group *Forever Free,* or to compare Richmond Barthé's treatment of black female nudity in his 1933 *Wetta* with his treatment of black male nudity in his 1935 *Feral Benga.* Such analyses, however, are beyond the scope of the present discussion, which is limited to representations of the black *female* nude.

2. I am preceded in this usage by black cultural critic Albert Murray. See Murray, *Stomping the Blues* (1976; New York: Da Capo, 1989), 65.

3. Tom Wesselman's *Great American Nudes* series, begun in 1961, can be seen as a precedent for Bearden's use of images from porno magazines. But, whereas Wesselman's schematic, painted renditions of the nude employed the grammar of contemporary pornography—its languid poses, bikini marks, and lipsticked open mouths—Bearden used fragments of porno magazine photos, as well as other materials, to construct his female figures' anatomies—as if they were quilts pieced together from scraps of various discarded fabrics. For a discussion of Wesselman's early nudes, see Irving Sandler, *American Art of the 1960s* (New York: Harper Icon, 1988), 180–182. For a description of Bearden's use of photographic material, see Sharon F. Patton, "Memory and Metaphor: The Art of Romare Bearden, 1940–1987," in *Memory and Metaphor: The Art of Romare Bearden, 1940–1987,* ed. Kinshasha Conwill, Mary Schmidt Campbell, and Sharon F. Patton (New York: Oxford University Press in association with Studio Museum in Harlem, 1991), 44–45.

4. See, for example, the discussion of English and American views of black sexuality during the colonial and antebellum eras in Winthrop D. Jordan, *White Over Black: American Attitudes Toward the Negro, 1550–1812* (New York: W. W. Norton, 1977), 32–43, 150–163.

5. For a rare examination of this eroticization of the black body in the visual arts, see the

third chapter, "The Seductions of Slavery," in Hugh Honour, ed., *The Image of the Black in Western Art,* Vol. IV: *From the American Revolution to World War I,* Part 2: *Black Models and White Myths* (Cambridge, Mass.: Harvard University Press, 1989), 145–186.

6. Elton Fax quotes the artist as stating: "I use the train as a symbol of the other civilization—the *white* civilization and its encroachment upon the lives of the blacks. The train was always something that could take you away and could also bring you to where you were. And in the little towns it's the black people who live near the trains." Bearden quoted in Fax, *17 Black Artists* (New York: Dodd, Mead & Co., 1970), 143. For the frequent occurrence of the train motif in African-American folklore, see Albert Murray's brief references to the mythic, functional, and historic dimensions of "railroad imagery in blues titles, not to mention blues lyrics"; Harold Courlander's remarks on the train as a "widespread image" in black sacred music; and Lawrence W. Levine's discussion of the railroad as "a persistent image of change, transcendence, and the possibilities of beginning again." Murray, *Stomping the Blues,* 118, 124. Courlander, *A Treasury of Afro-American Folklore* (New York: Crown, 1976), 305–308. Levine, *Black Culture and Black Consciousness: Afro-American Folk Thought from Slavery to Freedom* (New York: Oxford University Press, 1978), 262–267.

7. For an overview of African-American quilt traditions in the antebellum South, see Gladys-Marie Fry, *Stitched from the Soul: Slave Quilts from the Antebellum South* (New York: Dutton Studio Books, 1990).

8. Bearden's *Storyville* (1974), a collage from his *Of the Blues* series, pays homage to the birthplace of jazz—New Orleans's fabled pre-1917 red-light district—by showing a piano player at work in a brothel, the inhabitants of which include several white and at least one possibly mixed-race nude female. In *Conjur Woman as an Angel* (1964) from his *Prevalence of Ritual* series, Bearden includes a seated nude in an image that makes reference to African-American folk spiritual beliefs. And, of course, the stuttering, staggering rhythms of the bits of striped cloth in *Patchwork Quilt* (1970) are typical of a peculiarly African design preference for "interruption" in pattern sequences, as discussed by Marie-Jeanne Adams in regard to Kuba textiles in Central Africa and by Roy Sieber and Robert Farris Thompson with respect to textiles from various parts of West Africa. *Storyville* appears in Myron Schwartzman, *Romare Bearden: His Life and Art* (New York: Harry N. Abrams, 1990), 229. *Conjur Woman as an Angel* is reproduced in Conwill, Campbell, and Patton, *Memory and Metaphor,* 41. Marie-Jeanne Adams, "Kuba Embroidered Cloth," *African Arts,* 12 no. 1 (November 1978), 24–39, 106–107. Roy Sieber, *African Textiles and Decorative Arts* (New York: Museum of Modern Art, 1972), 190. Robert Farris Thompson, *African Art in Motion* (Berkeley: University of California Press, 1974), 10–13.

9. Herodotus, *The Histories,* trans. Aubrey de Sélincourt (Baltimore, Md.: Penguin Books, 1971), 306.

10. According to Peter Mark, this took place during the eleventh century AD, when the Iberian peninsula was occupied by Almoravid forces that included black Africans. Mark, *Africans in European Eyes: The Portrayal of Black Africans in Fourteenth and Fifteenth Century Europe,* Monograph XVI: *Foreign and Comparative Studies/Eastern Africa* (Syracuse, N.Y.: Maxwell School of Citizenship and Public Affairs, Syracuse University, 1974), 14.

11. For a discussion of the relationship between medieval Christian color symbolism

and European attitudes toward Africans, see
Jean Devisse, *The Image of the Black in Western
Art,* Vol. II: *From the Early Christian Era to the
"Age of Discovery,"* Part 1: *From the Demonic
Threat to the Incarnation of Sainthood* (New
York: William Morrow, 1979), 39–80.

12. David Dabydeen, *Hogarth's Blacks: Images
of Blacks in Eighteenth Century English Art*
(Athens, Ga.: University of Georgia Press,
1987), 41–46.

13. This is *not* to say that African-American
artists failed to produce an emancipation
monument during the nineteenth century.
But the one extant work in this category,
Edmonia Lewis's 1867 marble group *Forever
Free,* pairs a bare-chested male with a fully
robed female figure. To my knowledge the
only nineteenth-century *nudes* by a black
artist are statues of non-black children—
Lewis's 1876 *Poor Cupid,* her 1871 *Asleep,* and
one of the two children in her 1872 *Awake.*

14. Organized by the Connecticut Gallery,
the exhibition took place at the Old State
House in Hartford from October
9–November 8, 1987. The show featured
sixty-eight canvases by Porter, who was born
around 1847, in or near Hartford,
Connecticut, and died there in 1923. The exhibition was accompanied by a 113-page
catalogue with numerous black-and-white
and color reproductions documenting the
artist's career.

15. Beard, a young dealer who currently operates a gallery in San Francisco, was director
of Chicago's Galerie Americana in 1988
when Needham's work first came to his attention. For more information on the
painter, who was born in Canada in 1850 and
died in Chicago in 1931, see Judith Wilson,
"Art," *Black Arts Annual 1988/89,* ed. Donald
Bogle (New York: Garland Publishing,
1990), 20–21.

16. A doctoral candidate in art history at

Columbia University, Ms. Holland is con-
ducting research on the lives of several
African-American artists who were active in
Boston during the nineteenth century in an
attempt to determine what effects their location had upon their careers. She has also
curated a major survey of the work of the
great nineteenth-century Afro–New England
landscape painter, Edward Mitchell
Bannister, which opened in New York in May
1992 at the Kenkeleba Gallery.

17. The similarity of Motley's composition to
a 1663 painting by Jan Steen currently located at Buckingham Palace was pointed out
to me by a student in the undergraduate survey of African-American art that I taught at
Syracuse University in spring 1990. I am in-
debted to Dr. Wayne Franits for supplying
information about the date and location of
Steen's image of a prostitute at her toilet. Dr.
Jontyle Robinson has noted Motley's admira-
tion of various seventeenth-century Dutch
painters. Jontyle Theresa Robinson, "Archibald John Motley, Jr.: A Notable Anniversary
for a Pioneer," in *Three Masters: Eldzier Cortor,
Hughie Lee-Smith, Archibald John Motley, Jr.,*
exhibition catalogue (New York: Kenkeleba
Gallery, May 22–July 17, 1988), 45.

18. Sharon Patton mentions that "four draw-
ings of nudes were shown at his '306'
exhibition in 1940." This show, which took
place at 306 W. 141st St., the Harlem stu-
dio/atelier *cum* salon of painter Charles
Alston, sculptor Henry "Mike" Bannarn, and
dancer Ad Bates, was Bearden's first. The exhibition brochure lists twenty-four examples
of the artist's work—seven oils, six
gouaches, five watercolors, and six draw-
ings—dating from 1937 to 1940. The same
year as the "306" exhibition, Bearden leased
his first studio, a floor above Jacob
Lawrence's at 33 W. 125th St. It was there,
in 1940, that a reproach from a failed prosti-

tute-turned-model spurred the young artist to overcome a creative block. Bearden's account of this crucial experience is reported with slight variations by several authors, including Calvin Tomkins, Avis Berman, and Myron Schwartzman. According to Schwartzman, this encounter initiated the artist's subsequent preoccupation with "the black female form." Conwill, Campbell, and Patton, "Memory and Metaphor," 67. "306" exhibition brochure, Romare Bearden papers, Archives of American Art, New York (Roll N68–87). Calvin Tomkins, "Putting Something Over Something Else," *The New Yorker* (November 28, 1977), 56, 58. Avis Berman, "Romare Bearden: 'I Paint Out of the Tradition of the Blues,'" *Artnews* (December 1980), 64–65. Myron Schwartzman, *Romare Bearden: His Life and Art,* 114–116.

19. *The Annunciation* is the title that accompanies a reproduction of this work in a 1972 monograph on Bearden. Clearly, the composition is *not* an Annunciation scene, but represents the Virgin Mary's visit to her cousin Elizabeth instead. Thus, it has become *The Visitation* in Schwartzman. M. Bunch Washington, *The Art of Romare Bearden: The Prevalence of Ritual* (New York: Harry N.

Abrams, 1972), 34–35. Schwartzman, *Romare Bearden: His Life and Art,* 114–117.

20. See Romare Bearden, "Rectangular Structure in My Montage Paintings," *Leonardo* 2 (1969), 11–15.

21. Other pornographic strategies that appear in his work include a kind of eroticized synoptic vision—the optical equivalent of the "grope." In *Conjur Woman as an Angel* (1964) from his *Prevalence of Ritual* series, for example, Bearden includes a seated nude whose anatomy consists of fragments of various photographs pieced together so that the resulting figure seems simultaneously visible from a variety of perspectives. That is, much like some of Picasso's nudes or one of Hans Bellmer's dolls, the image totalizes viewer access to the depicted female body, which therefore becomes a cipher of sexual availability. In *Work Train* (1966), a length of chain looped around one of the nude female's wrists conveys a hint of sadomasochistic bondage. And in *Susannah at the Bath* (1969), the contrast of silhouetted areas of the central figure's face and body with her photographed breasts and one bare thigh operates like some Fredrick's of Hollywood costume—heightening the thrill of exposed flesh by juxtaposing it with partial concealments.

Michele Wallace

Boyz N the Hood and *Jungle Fever*

The first time I saw John Singleton's *Boyz N the Hood,* I was completely swept away by the drama and the tragedy. It was like watching the last act of *Hamlet* or *Titus Andronicus* for the first time. When I left the theater, I was crying for all the dead black men in my family.

In the neighborhood in Brooklyn where I live, I began to see *Boyz N the Hood* T-shirts instead of the "Stop the Violence" T-shirts of the months before. Unlike *New Jack City,* which celebrated violence with all the abandon of the old cowboy movies, *Boyz N the Hood* really seemed to try to take a critical stance toward violence. It could even be seen as a valid symbolic response to the then-recent beating of Rodney King by the Los Angeles Police Department. Moreover, through the popularity of this film, space for the acknowledgment of the alarming rates of black male homicide and incarceration grew in the dominant discourse.

But then, a black single mother brought the demonization of black single mothers in the film to my attention. In a second viewing of *Boyz N the Hood,* what made me most uneasy about the portrayal of these single black mothers was how little we're told about them, how we, as viewers, are encouraged, on the basis of crucial visual cues, to come to stereotypical conclusions about these women. We never find out what Tre's mother does for a living, whether or not Doughboy's mother works, is on welfare, or has ever been married, or anything whatsoever about the single black mother whose babies run in the street.

I began to think about some other alarming trends in relation to the new black films:

First, black women filmmakers, not to mention black feminist film criticism, were becoming unimaginable.[1]

Second, the focus on violence against black men in particular only serves to further mystify the plight of women and girls in black communities. It's as though their condition were somehow subsidiary and derivative. As usual, it is the people who control the guns (and the phalluses) who hog the limelight.

Before *Boyz N the Hood,* there were two kinds of black female characters in film—whores and good girls. Following "race" film conventions set in the days of *Cabin in the Sky* and *Stormy Weather,* these women were all portrayed as light-weight (and more often than not, light-skinned) cartoon characters. The peak of this trend is Robin Givens's recent performance in *A Rage in Harlem,* where she plays the ebony femme fatale.

In *Boyz N the Hood,* however, a third kind of black female character appears. I call her the Shahrazad Ali nightmare: single black mothers who are white-identified and drink espresso (the Buppie version), or who call their sons "fat fucks" and allow their children to run in the streets while they offer blow jobs in exchange for drugs (the underclass version).

Shahrazad Ali, in case you've forgotten, was the big hit of the summer of 1990 with her book, *The Blackman's Guide to Understanding the Blackwoman.*[2] This book offered its target reader—the black man—insight into the secret workings of the black female mind. Yet, despite Ali's insistence that the book was "the culmination of many years of study, observation and research," it was almost impossible to deduce what her sources were from reading it.

She never refers to a single text, other than the Bible, even in passing, much less by title or author or in a footnote. Although we might well expect such an author to rely heavily upon personal experience, testimony, and observation, she never uses the first person singular. You know as little about Ali when you finish the book as you did when you picked it up.

And she is no journalist either. She never describes the communities she's visited and observed or points out relevant items in the news. From this book, you would never know that Jesse Jackson was narrowly defeated in the race for the Democratic nomination for president, that Spike Lee made movies, or that playwright August Wilson wins Pulitzer Prizes. Nor would you know that the highways and byways of our major cities are flooded with the homeless—man, woman, and child—because of a depraved economic sensibility that values wealth and ostentatious consumption in all races and both genders over decency to the poor.

There isn't a glimmer of contemporary culture or society, just a vague yet insuperable cloud called the "problem with black women." Although she calls the black woman "nearly psychotic" and liberally resorts to all sorts of pseudopsychological terminology to describe the black woman's affliction (which often sounds a lot like chronic depression), she doesn't refer to a single case study or even an interview with a friend. Her style is declamatory. For 180 pages, she insists upon the shortcomings of the black woman by the sheer force of argument. In the process, she becomes an omniscient narrator with a vengeance—as though she was gifted with the power to read all black women's minds.

If mistaken for "real life" instead of symbolic representation, I am afraid that a movie like *Boyz N the Hood* engages in the same brand of opaque cultural analysis. Its formula is simple and straightforward. The boys who don't have fathers fail. The boys who do have fathers succeed. And the success of such a movie at the box office reflects its power to confirm hegemonic family values.

Spike Lee's *Jungle Fever,* although a much more complicated film, made me even more uncomfortable for much the same reason. Especially in the context of symbolic representations, gender and race have no essential, irreducible meanings, only the ones we assign them to get from "here" to "there." But neither John Singleton nor Spike Lee is aware of how gender and race are socially and culturally constructed. And whereas Singleton is highly effective in naturalizing his black postnationalist essentialism in *Boyz N the Hood,* Lee is less successful at the same project when he takes on interracial sex.

Jungle Fever is not as easy to decode as *Boyz N the Hood.* At the narrative level, the film tells three interrelated stories. In the first and most important of these, a black male architect, Flipper Purify (Wesley Snipes) is married to Drew (Lonette McKee), a buyer at Bloomingdale's. Their pre-adolescent daughter attends a public school in Harlem, and the family lives in a brownstone on Strivers Row, one of two middle-class blocks in the middle of the worst section of Harlem.

At the architectural firm where he works, Flipper becomes sexually involved with Angie Tucci (Annabella Sciorra), a white temporary secretary who lives with her father and brothers in Bensonhurst. Working late evenings, in a series of extremely brief scenes—one never gets the impression that they either know or really like each other—Angie and Flipper end up having sex on Flipper's drawing board.

In the outdoor night scene that follows, Flipper tells his best friend, Cyrus (Spike Lee), a high school teacher, that he is "cheating on Drew" with a white woman. "You got the fever—the both of yous!" Cyrus responds, meaning "Jungle fever." Jungle fever turns out to be a condition in which blacks and whites (Asians, Native Americans, and Latinos appear to be both immune to the disease and irrelevant to the narrative) become intimately involved because of their curiosity about racial difference (perish the thought) rather than for love.

From this moment on, the film treats Angie's and Flipper's jungle fever much like a crime. In two dramatic parallel scenes, Drew evicts Flipper from their Harlem apartment, and Angie's father beats her up and throws her out of the house in Bensonhurst. Flipper is even forced out of his white architectural firm. Self-described "outcasts" in their own communities, Angie and Flipper take an apartment together. When it doesn't work out (and there was never any possibility that it would), Flipper goes back to Drew, and Angie goes back to her family.

The film's second story concerns Flipper's crack-addict brother, Gator (Sam Jackson), and his relationship to their mother, a housewife, and father, The Good Doctor Reverend Purify, a fanatical born-again Christian who forbids Gator to enter the house. Yet, Gator is always at the door seeking money for crack from his mother (played by Ruby Dee). The eery *mise en scène* of the parents' home—the mausoleum decor, the constant playing of Mahalia Jackson records, even the frightened sexually repressed demeanor of the reverend's wife—hint strongly that Gator's addiction was caused by the reverend's criminally bad fathering.

The third story revolves around Paulie (John Turturro), Angie's boyfriend, who lives with his father (Anthony Quinn) and runs a candy store in Bensonhurst that also serves as a hangout for a group of Italian-American men. These men are extremely vocal about their racial attitudes.

They hate blacks, we come to understand, partly because of their own fear that as Italians they don't look as white as they should. Their envy of whiteness and blondeness is viewed as an integral part of their loathing of blackness. But their hatred of blackness doesn't preclude their sexual interest in black women. In one of the most striking lines of the film, one of them says, "You know colored women, they love to fuck. You put a saddle on them and ride them into the sunset."

From the beginning, it is clear that Paulie is uncomfortable with the virulent, expressive racism of his clientele and is interested in Orin Goode (Tyra Ferrell), a black woman who comes into the store to ask him to order the *New York Times* and to encourage him to apply to Brooklyn College. Although Paulie receives a cursory beating from his friends while on his way to visit Orin, he gives as good as he gets. And when he arrives at Orin's door, the implication is that he's finally been successful in throwing off the burden of his father's restrictive view of marriage and family.

But what this film is really about is the threat of a female or aberrant sexuality to traditional family values. The film begins with a series of shots that establish The Cosby Show family–type locale of a middle-class urban environment in the early morning. The camera tracks a little boy on a bike delivering newspapers. After a close-up of a rolled copy of the *New York Times* being thrown onto the sidewalk in front of the house, the next shot zooms up and into the house. Reminiscent of the more impressive opening shot of *Psycho*, this shot takes us directly into Drew and Flipper's bedroom where they are having sexual intercourse. Drew's screams get progressively louder as she begins to shout, "Don't wake the baby!" The camera cuts to their daughter Ming's bedroom, where Ming sits up in bed, her eyes wide open, and slowly smiles.

Later, when father, mother, and daughter are having breakfast together, Ming asks, "Why is Daddy always hurting Mommy?" When Drew explains that they were making love, Ming says she was only testing to see whether or not they would tell the truth. Flipper then walks Ming to school. On the street, Ming's and Flipper's expensive, neat attire is juxtaposed with the garbage and graffiti, the drug addicts and abandoned buildings.

This short sequence of shots, which goes from Drew's and Flipper's bedroom to Ming's bedroom to the kitchen and then to the streets of Harlem, can be viewed as a preview of the film's double agenda on race and sexuality. On the one hand, we are supposed to read Drew's cries during sexual intercourse as idiosyncratic, Ming's mock curiosity about it as cute, and Drew's forthrightness in her explanation as progressive. But, on the other hand, there is a problem being subtly (and perhaps unconsciously) delineated: the little black

128   Wesley Snipes as Flipper and Veronica Timbers as Ming in *Jungle Fever*, directed by Spike Lee, 1991.

girl who already knows too much through her premature entry into the mysteries of sexuality.

From the outset, the daughter is triangulated into the sexuality of the parents. The way in which heterosexual phallic (married) sex is problematized in this film is better understood in light of the history of oral sex as a crime, even for heterosexual married couples, in some states. In *Jungle Fever,* oral sex emerges again and again not only as a code for "gay" sexuality (which comes up only once in *Jungle Fever* in the black female war council scene), but also for the rest of the vast range of illicit sexual practices and psychosocial developments beyond the pale of compulsory heterosexuality, in which such perverse passions as interracial sex and drug addiction are included.

In another walk to school later in the film, Flipper and Ming run head-on into Vivian (Halle Berry), Gator's crack addict girlfriend (who looks like a grown-up version of Ming), who tells Flipper, "I'll suck your dick good for $5 ... $3!" A startled Flipper turns to Ming (she's a girl, right?) and shakes her, shouting, "Don't you ever do anything like that!"

The studied phallocentricism of the key scenes in the film (both the opening and closing scenes, which mirror one another, as well as Flipper's first seduction of Angie), which stands against the ongoing threat of oral sex (inexplicably coupled throughout the film with crack addiction), seems too palpable to ignore. Not only is Flipper deeply threatened by the prospect of dominant female sexuality—Angie's, as well as Drew's, Vivian's, and his daughter Ming's—but the yawning threat of female sexuality somehow also becomes, within the film's larger narrative, responsible for the devastation and the insularity of ghettos, both Italian and black America.

Later in the film, when Flipper finds Gator in the dark, teeming Taj Mahal—a mythical crack factory supposedly located in Harlem on 145th Street and Convent Avenue (actually there's a very old and famous Baptist Church on that corner)—Flipper calls Vivian a whore. Vivian responds by yelling, "Eat my pussy!" This confrontation becomes yet another pretext for Flipper to be afraid his daughter will grow up to be like Vivian. After all, Ming already knows too much about sex.

Meanwhile, a crucial visual strategy in the film, undergirding the theme of uncontrolled female sexuality, is Lee's instrumentalization of skin color and lighting effects. In a technique borrowed from the noir tradition, many of the scenes were filmed at night, the strong lighting increasing the play of light and dark. As the film progresses, the shadows around both Flipper and Angie grow more and more dense and obfuscating.

Annabella Sciorra, Lonette McKee, and Wesley Snipes, despite their noteworthy individual talents, were all apparently cast for hair color and complexion: Sciorra because she's a dark-skinned white woman; McKee because she's a light-skinned black woman (visually, the racial difference between Sciorra and McKee is nill); and Snipes because he is dark. The striking visual contrast of dark and light skin is worthy of a Benetton ad.

In the film itself, Snipes is often dressed in strong bright colors—persimmon, red, or purple (an unusual palette for a man represented as so middle-class and dull)—whereas almost everybody else who appears with him, especially the women, wears black, presumably to further heighten the color contrasts. As Flipper's relationship with Angie progresses, its deterioration is signaled not so much through dialogue as by the way his face grows darker and is increasingly cast in menacing shadows. In some of their later scenes together, only his teeth and the whites of his eyes are visible. And sometimes, he is merely a black silhouette.

Revealingly, Lee's meticulous attention to visual effects isn't supported by correspondences in plot, dialogue, or characterization. As the film progresses, Drew, Flipper, and Angie become slick aestheticized surfaces, too slippery to get a handle on. The strongest characters in this film are Vivian, who epitomizes the negative threat of out-of-control sexuality and passion, and Gator, the crack addict who, nevertheless, comes across as straightforward and successful in his manipulation of the entire family system.

When Reverend Purify murders Gator in a veritable Oedipalfest, the patriarchy is the loser. His killing of Gator only serves to confirm the symbolic death of the father in African-American discourse and his descent into both madness and spiritual condemnation. Lee's ambivalence here regarding traditional family values is noteworthy.

Boyz N the Hood and *Jungle Fever,* in fact, demonize black female sexuality as a threat to black male heterosexual identity, and yet both films are extremely appealing and seductive. *Boyz N the Hood,* at the narrative level, and *Jungle Fever,* at the visual level, successfully employ mass cultural codes to entertain us, so that it becomes possible, as a black feminist viewer, to enjoy one's own symbolic decimation. The only possible corrective here, it seems to me, has to come from theoretical analysis. Whose theory this will be is, of course, much more problematic to decide.

1. "Boyz in the (Holly)Wood," a cover article in the *New York Times Magazine*, Sunday, July 14, 1991, illustrates the invisibility of black women filmmakers.

2. Shahrazad Ali, *The Blackman's Guide to Understanding the Blackwoman* (Philadelphia, Pa.: Civilized Publications, 1989).

Houston A. Baker, Jr.

"You Cain't Trus' It":
Experts Witnessing in the Case of Rap

Preface: I am not gay, but I have many gay friends; whom I love and support, and have watched the expressive cultural works of gay and lesbian creators. In 1972, the late professor Don Howard (who died of AIDS about three years ago) came to me, as a black man, then in my late twenties, on the program committee of the Modern Language Association [MLA]. Don, who was about ten years older than I was, made this request:

"A group of people in the MLA have asked me to come to you to discover how we can find a way to be represented. Of course I don't know why they chose me. *They* are gay and lesbian. I don't know why I have been chosen to do this. But we know that you're a black man on the program committee, and we'd like for you to take the idea in. What do you think?"

I said, "I think it's a good idea."

I took it to the program committee, and certain men on the committee (who have subsequently outed themselves) attacked me: "This is not analytical enough, is it?" they asked. "Isn't this a space that we don't have enough scholarship on? Are you sure that we should be doing this?" I think they took that stance as a way of allaying the anxiety of people on the program committee they knew would not allow this idea to go through unless it was entirely argued out.

Now, I tell that anecdote because it seems to me that, if one wants to look back to our history, we find, in the fifties, sixties, and seventies, black men— and you can code that sign as you will—were put in that position. They were told, "You should be first to get bitten by the police dogs. You should sit at lunch counters and get your heads beat." And when we moved north: "You should be the cadre that apes and emulates the paramilitary, parapolice forces of this country. When moral egregiousness leaps across the landscape like roaring fire, you should be there in the gap, brother, wearing combat boots, with your rifle on your shoulder, protecting your woman, your children," and so on.

We were told this by white people, we were told this by black people. The "we" is very pleonastic—code the sign "black men" as you will. But the incumbencies of the landscape of the fifties, sixties, and seventies put that sign right up in the forefront to take the heat.

And a lot of people said, "I don't know why they chose me to come and ask you this." A lot of people said, "When you finish with this, maybe you black men could come and look at our cause too, brother, and carry that for us." And globally people said, "Jesus, you all are *doing it*. It's true that Clark and Hampton (and all those other Panthers that Angela could tell you about) are dead or in prison, that those black people are scarred for life down there in the South, it's true, but, black men, keep on doing it."

Now, historically, as far as I am concerned, that was an interesting load, burden, positionality for black men to carry transnationally. I think they made a lot of mistakes under that sign. I think a lot of *bad* stuff went down under that sign. I think a lot of people committed all kinds of transgressions and just plain old nonsense under the sign "black men." They got into believing their fantasies. On the other hand, my friends, there would not be this conference today, there would not be African American studies, there would not be black academics, there would not be transnational black cultural studies today without "black men," unless, in some strange James Joycean mode you, like Stephen Dedalus, walking along that beach pondering the "ineluctable modality of the visible," can close your eyes and make history disappear. Now if you can't do that, I say you have got to deal with the sign "black men," in all its mistakes, in all its essentialism.

And this is my word on essentialism: David Duke's constituency has no doubt about its essentialism. Seventy-five percent of Louisiana's white males voted because they were white male. And they can code that sign for you if you want to travel down there and ask them. And a greater percentage of that state, essentially speaking, because they were *black*—not because they carried a whole lot of multiple, multiplying, ambiguous multiplicities in their head, but because they knew that though their minds might be somewhere else, their black asses were not—voted *black,* essentially *black.* So, essentially, they voted against

David Duke.

Now, if you want to talk about the politics of all this, I say, if the answer is—
"We new cultural studies scholars are thinking about these matters because
they're so complex. Get back to us on political strategies in a few years after
we've worked this through"—your thinking might be written on toilet paper
from concentration camps. I personally go with the kind of common-sense essentialism that black Louisiana showed.

Am I suffering from an acute case of forty-something peevishness? Have I
reached the almost-fifty plateau where academic debates surrounding such popular cultural sites as rap music, MTV, nation-conscious T-shirts, high-tops,
fades, and kufi hats seem to infuriate me? Are such debates destined always to
be replete with smug apologetics? Perhaps my dissatisfaction with academic debates over popular culture is merely a function of a certain atavistic, some may
even say adolescent, proclivity for popular culture that haunts my mental life
like some troublesome ghost. Or perhaps, just perhaps, I was too dauntingly
educated in scholarly listening and writing at Howard University to suffer such
smug apologetics. Now, I ask these questions and pose these answers as a way of
getting a handle on my response to two essays I read in the *Boston Review*
(December 1991): one entitled "Beyond Racism and Misogyny: Black
Feminism and 2-Live Crew" by Kimberlé Crenshaw; and the other, "The
Intelligent Forty-Year-Old's Guide to Rap" by Mark Zanger. I came to both
essays with an open mind and read them, as well as the enthusiastic response to
Crenshaw by Henry Louis Gates in a single sitting. When I had finished the essays, I was energetically out of my seat, and my mind was decidedly closed
against what seemed to me a drearily conventional mode of response by adult
scholars to popular cultural forms.

The conventional response I have in mind seems to reflect what I call a "start
in the middle of the game approach." Let me explain. A media-reported controversy or a dinner-party conversation or a tragic public event, such as the
Central Park jogger episode, occurs and calls attention to one or an array of
popular cultural forms. I think most grown-ups, if it is at all possible, ignore
the popular cultural form, the controversy, the public event, and everything
else beyond their bedroom and kitchen walls and making money. But if the
adults are academics, they will tell you that their obliviousness is a function of

too many committee assignments or their residence in the long, dark tunnel of the tenure process. They will insist that they never have time to raise their heads above mere iambic pentameter or the middle style of publishable prose. But if the triggering event that brings the popular cultural form to attention will not go away, or if it is taken up by a media network—and media networks seem to work in only two modalities these days: wedge issues and controversial infotainment—then even the most oblivious adults seem compelled to write something, anything, to take action, any action, vis-à-vis the popular cultural form in question.

The essays in the *Boston Review* seem to demonstrate the typology I have in mind. Let me run quickly through this typology. Though 2-Live Crew's lyrics and productions "in themselves and for themselves" cannot be considered innocuous in any way, the Crew is controversial for one reason only: the networks, media networks, in a mode that I call "instant expertism," have made them so. Now, if I understand Crenshaw's argument correctly, it is an argument about "intersectionality." Crenshaw debates whether she should judge 2-Live Crew as a black or as a woman. Now, I suggest that kind of judgment is like deciding whether one should vote for George Bush because one is white or a man. In other words, the intersectionality, which is simply a dualism here, forecloses the possibility of what any one of us might encounter in our everyday travels anywhere—and that is a black Vietnamese American, Ivy League-aspiring, basketball-playing, sushi-eating woman. Now, what then privileges, in such multiplicity, the simple duality of black or woman? Where is the carnivalesque site of the griotic tradition of African-American culture—a space occupied mainly by women? Where is the voodoo priestess who stands, not at an intersection, but literally and figuratively at the beginning and the ending of all roads that lead anywhere, mediating the marriage of heaven and hell, life and death? And why does a simple intersectionality prevent an academic scholar from seeing that the simple one-liner, "Ain't I a woman?" can be an encyclopedia for cultural studies? Harriet Tubman and Sojourner Truth did not have trouble being both and much, much else, right?

I think that what privileges this mode is the necessity for an instant expertism, which is to say, Crenshaw has written interestingly, eloquently and, I think, persuasively on this intersectionality in the discourse of black women and the law. I don't think it can be instantly applied to 2-Live Crew. The ques-

Luther Campbell, leader of the rap group 2-Live Crew, before opening arguments in the group's obscenity trial in Fort Lauderdale, Florida, October 16, 1990.

tion I have is, why on any grounds would one sanction the 2-Live Crew? They are vile, juvenile, puerile, misogynistic guys who are out there to bank beaucoup "dead presidents." All they think about is keys and G's and being as nasty as they want to be.

Well, that's fine. I got nothing against that. But my son taught me a saying a few years ago: "If you take the bait, you bear the weight." Now you may get very rich, but you may also, as with Wall Streeters Ivan Boesky and Michael Milken, get arrested. And when you do, you can't say, "Why persecuteth thou me? Everybody's doing it. Broward County even had a topless donut shop, so why you messin' with us, man? It's racism!" I submit to you that such a calling of "foul," while pointing to the *community standard,* makes no sense at all. Your injunction certainly cannot be a messianic, "Why persecuteth thou me?" It's gotta be, *à la* Kurtz in *The Heart of Darkness,* "Exterminate them all, including me."

I am saying there is absolutely no reason for a noble, shocked defense of 2-Live Crew within the popular culture forum of rap music—a forum that has raps dedicated to the education of black children and white children; that says, "Be a father to your child;" that strongly advocates the rights of women; that is perhaps one of the only sites available to young people in this society that says, "This is what policing and surveillance are about. These are your rights in a free society;" that has so many positive sites that these, in combination with video imaging of MTV and BET, become transnational informative youth cultural sites.

Nobody is going to tell me that the only place I can go to reference that form is 2-Live Crew. Nobody is going to tell me that I have to say, "No Nick Navarro, no Gonzalez, no. Stay away from those people."

I think the police should have arrested the 2-Live Crew, and I think those who came and stood gawking in front of the blonde aerobicist Madonna, if they were going to carry out their job, should have arrested her, too, just like Bobby Brown was arrested in Columbus, Georgia.

I don't want to sound horribly moralistic here—and the answer comes back, "Hah, you stand little chance of that now" (as an audience response).

I mean, I think Tipper Gore should not be heeded by anyone under 135 years old; I believe the people at the Parents Music Resource Center should be locked in an elevator playing nothing but a continuous loop of the politics, history, sociology, and music of popular culture. I am a card-carrying member of Right to Rock.

On the other hand, we always know that at the sites of the popular and expressive, black people have been told what they *must* like. Recall with me that scene in *Uncle Tom's Cabin* when Simon Legree is carrying a coffle of black bondspeople into hell. When they begin singing, he says, "Shut up you old cuss, do you think I want to hear any of your old Methodism? Give us a lively tune. Get rowdy now." Ralph Ellison comes to mind: "Get hot, boy, get hot!"

So, I understand that there is no innocent sexuality, innocent as in puppy love or as in non-overdetermined by market conditions. I understand that, but I also understand that one has to know the history of the form, one has to understand the spaces of the popular, one cannot constitute oneself as an instant expert and send or sing just anything that comes down the line because you have been asked to do so.

I was asked to travel to a country that was considered a very dangerous "investment climate." (That means that people are getting killed regularly and for no apparent reason.) And so I asked my son, who expressed great concern about this, "What do you think, Mark, what should I do?" He said, "Well, what would you say, if you got killed, about why you went?" I said, "I guess what I'd say up in heaven or down in hell is, 'They invited me.' " He said, "Dad, that's dumb."

In a word, all instant experts on popular cultural forms always seem to need to get their stuff far, far more together before they take the stand. After all, everybody knows that when people speak about a unique popular cultural form that *they have not bothered to fully inform themselves about,* we simply cain't trus' it. Public Enemy has the final word, then, on instant experts, no matter whether they are black or white.

Robert Reid Pharr I have a question for Houston Baker, and then I'd like to follow up with Marlon Riggs. Houston, you opened your talk by saying, "I am not gay, but I have many gay friends." You didn't say, "I am heterosexual," but, "I'm not gay." And I wondered whether or not one of the assumptions behind that statement was that if you'd said, "I am gay; I am speaking with a gay voice," that it would have lent some tenor of authenticity to what you were going to say. I wanted Marlon to follow up on that because, with that question in mind, I had a fair amount of skepticism about the eager response of the audience to your talk, given that, before you said anything, you were identified as a queen, an unleashed queen. Indeed, it seems to me that we know several people's sexuality on the panel. We know that Marlon is a queen, that Lisa Kennedy is a girl who likes girls a lot,* and that Houston is a person who is not gay, but no one felt it was necessary to identify as heterosexual.

Houston Baker I am heterosexual. And that was not an easy positionality or identity to arrive at, but I arrived at it in the way that presumably all of us in this room are in the process of arriving at or have arrived at identity. As I understand Hegel, et al., it's by negation. Cornel West reminds us, under a pragmatic banner, that wherever one sets down philosophically in African, West African, East African traditions, one does it by negation. It's a dialectic. You decide what you are not, rather than leaping out of the womb saying, "I am this"—which is, as I understand it from the gay artists I have had the great pleasure of watching at work, much of the pain. Part of the pain is that people are always trying to force you to be something else, saying that you must affirm that you are the following sorts of things. And the battle is very much about saying: "I am not this. I am not that. I am not the other thing. You cannot do this to me. I will find my own ground of affirmation."

---

*Refers to unpublished remarks that do not appear in the current collection.

140   Gordon Parks, *Black Children with White Doll*, 1942.

I think that part of my own struggle in this respect has to do with some of the things that Lisa Kennedy talked about.* Insofar as Lisa had the great courage to come forward and talk about that family matter, and insofar as I have a soon-to-be twenty-one-year-old, let me share with you just a bit of information. My father, who I think came through without the kind of strong family support that I'd like to think that my wife, son, and I have moved to now, had real problems with identity. We had battles. And I understand a certain problematic, because my older brother was the one I let fight those battles. He stood up and said, "You cannot do this to me. You cannot compel my definition. You cannot force me down. You cannot repress me. I will speak. I will speak out of who I am." My father was really upset by this because he thought authority consisted very much in silencing. As a middle child, I remember hiding behind that "manliness" of my older brother. I was the good boy, hence passive, hence my father was very worried about what I might be—so that, even though he and my older brother fought like hell, it was a battle about identity in which I got situated.

What came out of that was a certain code of black fathering in this country—which I think has not been written on and needs to be written on—in terms of fathers and sons. That is, a cycle of violence that gets set in motion because its the only code that you know for dealing with questions of identity where sons are concerned—particularly if you are in a segregated Louisville, Kentucky, where the wrong word at the wrong time can set off economies of violence that we so well understand, having seen Clarence Thomas and Anita Hill do it on TV for four days. One begins, it seems to me, where one is.

A lot of this came out of the 1960s, a time when one really was privileged to have people bringing one forward. If you want to talk about a sense of outing— I did a Ph.D. in British Victorian literature and thought that I was going to write the definitive, to be sure, biography of Oscar Wilde (because I worked on "The Decadence") and that I would die with a copy of *Sybylline Leaves* stretched across my chest like Tennyson, moonlight flooding into some chamber of some Ivy League school. I was outed as black by a group of committed black people, men and women. There was a strong sense of identity as a heterosexual black male. It comforted, strengthened, and helped me, helped my son, helped my wife, helped our family unit through the years. And all I'd like to say is that the sixties were a great time to deal with identity politics. I wish you had all been there.

Marlon Riggs Some of us were.

I'm not sure where to go from there because I think the questioner has raised some interesting issues that audience members need to interrogate themselves about. There does seem to me a degree of not reconciling certain tensions that are here—the need to disclose what one is not, and yet not really deal with the definitions that hide behind the disclosure. I guess, particularly since last night—with the question that was asked Henry Louis Gates about his investment in *Looking for Langston*—it has become clear to me that the languages we are using to talk about these issues of sexuality are different, and the assumptions behind these languages are different as well. So that, for this person to say, "I am not gay," means something very definite whereas, for me, it really means nothing. Because I can tell you, and I think every queen in this room knows this, there are many men with rings on their fingers and wives and children at home who will go down and turn cheek without a word, and enjoy it. And they would not call themselves gay. So, for me, there's still a great degree of ambiguity in these identities, and the questions that need to be asked really have to go beyond the simple "Are you gay?" or "Are you het?" or "Are you bi?" What is the behavior? Then let's move into conceptualizing it.

Wellington Love My question is still somewhat tied to what Houston Baker said. I guess maybe I should say I'm not straight. You made this connection between saying, first of all, that black men have been traditionally sent out as guinea pigs, and I just want to clarify, before I ask my question, if you said that you were asked to be a spokesman for a gay/lesbian audience. Is that true?

Houston Baker For a group that was very interested in forming a caucus within the Modern Language Association of America.

Wellington Love So, as someone who is not gay, you didn't feel that your experience was adequate to represent them, or was your response homophobic as a straight black man?

Houston Baker I would leave that to a very wide jury to decide. What I did was to take the request as an earnest one for diversity, plurality, and representation for something people genuinely felt was absent. I took it as my responsibility to carry the request before the program committee of the Modern Language Association, and the forum was approved. I suggested, in fact, that Christopher Isherwood would make a fine keynote speaker. Christoper Isherwood was invited, the forum was held, the caucus was launched, the caucus is now a division of the Modern Language Association, and I'm the president. And we will have more.

Wellington Love I misinterpreted.

Houston Baker You did. But it's okay. It always happens. You see, what you can't do, for several reasons, is box me in here. What I want you to understand is that I represented a group because I felt it was an absence; it constituted a caucus; it became a division; it has grown very strong; it has many, many forums and programs in the MLA. There will be more during the next year because I am president and will make sure that there are more.

Kinshasha Conwill I feel compelled to say that it would be unfortunate for the many people in here—whom I am sure do not know who Houston Baker is, do not know very much about black popular culture, or black culture period, who are kibitzers, who are people who are on some level novices, minimally, at understanding the depth of this, and who are novices at understanding the depth of this man's contribution—I think it would be unfortunate for African-American people to use a forum like this to one-up each other in some kind of pseudohistoricism, because the real thing is that some incredibly brilliant people from all across the spectrum have been speaking here today and yesterday, and will I'm sure tomorrow. I hope that really becomes the point. True, generational and other differences exist, and I don't mind controversy—I live with it every day because the Studio Museum in Harlem lives with it every day. So, you know, if this is a forum and one has to show that you're brave, then fine, we can do that, but I just hope we will not lose the brilliance of all the panelists and get sidetracked from the issues.

I have a question for the panel, as well, about the role of the critic and the relationship between the critic and the producer of cultural expressions. I'm thinking of some of the things that were raised around the issue of what an audience expects and what a critic expects of the audience. I'd like to have these critics, cultural producers, or cultural workers talk about the relationship the critic has to the audience. Do you see yourselves as defining culture? Do you see yourselves as describing culture? Do you see yourselves as teachers of an audience? If no one else is interested, I'd like Judith Wilson to answer since she's an art historian. The visual arts need a little play here, and I don't mean that film isn't a visual art, but I'm referring to painting, sculpture, and all of that.

Judith Wilson Kinshasha, I wish I knew. You've asked me the ultimate question. I don't know who my audience is at this point. In many ways, I feel like what goes on with the so-called fine arts, in terms of black participation, is so marginalized and so dispersed that I genuinely have no sense of who I am writing to anymore. On individual occasions, yes, but as a whole, absolutely not. And what has brought it home to me is having some of my colleagues say to me recently, "Well, why did you quit writing?" And saying to myself, "But I've been publishing more in the past five years than I ever have before." So I can't answer. I wish I could.

Houston Baker Kinshasha, thank you for that. I'd just like to try the notion that seems to have emerged out of, as you quite rightly point out, the brilliance of this conference—a kind of scripting of prose of some sort or another. With bell hooks somewhere between prose and poetry and epic recitation, and Cornel West with his homiletic def-ness, dopeness, and flyness in combination with philosophical hermeneutic excellence, it is hard to say precisely what one means by scripting prose, but it does seem to me that all of us are at the site of, or trying to find a site of, popular vernacular speaking culture. That is to say, bell hooks and Cornel West and other people didn't get up and simply do what I call my rendition of the high academic stutter, stoop, bowing of head and pipe. You know, where you get before your audience and take off your glasses and say, "Uh, uh, uh, I wanted to speak with you today." No one can hear.

Forty-five minutes later, the person raises his head and says, "Thank you very much." I think many of us stopped doing that some ten years ago. It was partially an impulse of the black performers we were seeing who called themselves poets and critics and culture workers, like Baraka and Sonia Sanchez. I mean, who can get up now saying they're doing the entire tradition of black poetry and say, "April is the cruellest month, breeding/Lilacs out of the dead..." You got to move. You got to bust a move, it seems to me.

Much of the work that we produce is intended for at least a multiple audience. You want to be sure it can go in *Diacritics* or *Cultural Critique,* if you want to send it there (with modifications on the Toshiba), *and* that you can get up and perform it, as Marlon did. Do you think you could really read this and come out the same way you came out of what Marlon did as a performer? I think we've got more than one audience in mind.

Jacquie Jones I'd like to say one thing about the criticism issue. At *Black Film Review,* we are very involved in this question of who we're writing to and why we're writing. And one thing about film, in particular, is that the role of the critic changes depending on what we're talking about. After all, what the critic should do for *Boyz N the Hood* and what the critic should do for *Daughters of the Dust,* for example, are in my opinion two separate things. It has to do with where the work is placed and what it actually needs to get to an audience and to be received by an audience.

Thomas Harris This is the panel on gender and sexuality, and I'm just not hearing that much about sexuality. It's really important, especially at this time with AIDS, for us to gather and start talking about sexuality—about the relations between black men and black women, between black men and black men, between black women and black women. Marlon's the only one who has discussed AIDS, but it's touching all of us. bell hooks has talked about the ways we look for release that make having safe sex very difficult for us—very difficult for me as a black gay man, very difficult, across gender lines, for black women to tell men to put on condoms. We are not talking about that, and that's something we need to discuss.

146   Still from *Cycles*, directed by Zeinabu Davis, 1989.

Jacquie Jones In some ways, we *are* talking about it when we talk about the different kinds of inequalities in terms of the way men and women perceive each other. Personally, I have thought a lot about sexuality and where it should be situated when we define ourselves. One thing I realized was that if I'm saying, in essence, my reflection, or what's reflected back to me about who I'm supposed to be, is not who I am, is incomplete, is not even a whole person, then to engage in a discussion about sexuality is not right. I mean, you can't have sex with someone who is not a person. Sexuality gets caught in a very strange place it seems to me—which is why I thought the gender thing had to come first.

Thomas Harris Well, I think it's about a certain amount of risk. And we are all responsible for taking that risk. I keep coming back to this: thirty percent of the people who are HIV positive or have AIDS are black people. And that's a reality that isn't being addressed in the media, it's not being addressed on this panel, and I think we have to start dealing with it.

Bérénice Reynaud I wanted to say that I liked Houston Baker's presentation, but I think he made a little slip of the tongue, which I wanted to analyze. You got us to laugh when you said that when this woman was questioning whether she should react to 2-Live Crew as a black or as a woman (I haven't read that article so I don't know if it's good or bad), it was the same thing as wondering if you should vote for George Bush if you were white and a man. Structurally, it's not the same thing. What you should have said is, "Is it correct to vote for George Bush if you're white and a woman?" And then nobody would have laughed. Because it's a question for any woman to consider—white, black, or Asian—whether it's in her interest to vote for George Bush, knowing his sexual politics.

I also wanted to say something about what Jacquie and Lisa brought to the panel that hasn't really been addressed. They remarked that, as women, they've felt displaced in looking at films like *Boyz N the Hood*. Now, as a white woman, looking at such films as *Fatal Attraction,* I feel displaced by the existence of this character, created by a man, played by Glenn Close. This is not me, and I think any woman listening to the lyrics of 2-Live Crew feels displaced, and, without undermining what you said, I think this film was not addressed in your talk.

Houston Baker Well, one of the reasons that I did not engage in the Freudian gesture of slip-of-the-tongue (it's really very carefully crafted prose) is because if you look at the voting statistics on George Bush's popularity, he is, or was in the last election, more popular among white women than among white men. What I wanted to say, therefore, is that it's necessary, if you want to start from a positionality of abjection, to take the point statistically where you have the greatest abjection in the choices that are made along an essentialist axis. That's why I used it. It's just a matter of reading who voted for him.

Tiffany Patterson Coming back to the issue of HIV. Though it's a luxury to talk about whether or not you feel displaced by 2-Live Crew, it's not a luxury to talk about black people dying from AIDS. They're dying. And, of the thirty percent that Thomas talked about, a disproportionate number are black women. I'm not going to elaborate. I just wanted to bring it back on the table so that maybe we can talk about it. I think it's an important point, and it should not be skirted.

Lisa Kennedy I think that Thomas brought up a very good point. When we were talking about gender, I know I didn't do quite the job I should have in talking about exclusion, but that was why I chose the subject I did. I think that's why everyone talked a little bit about gender and talked about what their sexuality was or wasn't. And in the process of doing that, we also excluded people who are HIV positive (except for Marlon, who spoke). But, you know, my brother passed away two weeks ago from AIDS. It's not always about exclusion. To be on this panel and suddenly feel accused—as if you let people down because you talked about certain things in a certain way. You know, I was in that package that Marlon was talking about. I am always out in my writing, except this one time, and suddenly, it's as if the *Village Voice* has never run an article about people of color and their sexuality. I think this is a real challenge. It's true that we didn't include being HIV positive, but, in a way, I think we also did. I think we set a foundation for talking about exclusion, and because we're also talking about popular culture and images, we could assume a certain kind of naiveté: "Well, they don't talk about it, so the panel didn't have to." There's a way in which you made a really good point, Thomas, which was also extra-panel. And that's fine, but I don't feel like I want to bear the responsibility—or that any of us should—for not speaking to this. Because we tried to, even if it wasn't in a clear way. That may be the problem, but I'm not going to say that we didn't speak to it on some level.

The Urban Context

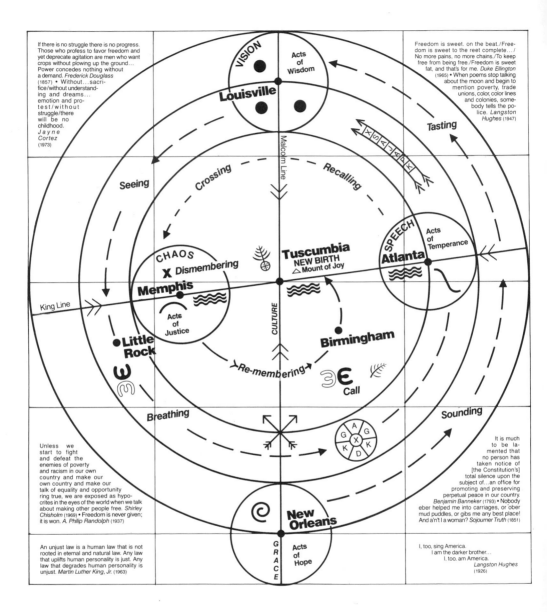

The following text appears within the diagram:

If there is no struggle there is no progress. Those who profess to favor freedom and yet deprecate agitation are men who want crops without plowing up the ground... Power concedes nothing without a demand. *Frederick Douglass* (1857) • Without...sacrifice/without understanding and dreams... emotion and protest/without struggle/there will be no childhood. *Jayne Cortez* (1973)

Freedom is sweet. on the beat./Freedom is sweet to the reet complete.../ No more pains, no more chains,/To keep free from being free. *Duke Ellington* (1965) • When poems stop talking about the moon and begin to mention poverty, trade unions, color, color lines and colonies, somebody tells the police. *Langston Hughes* (1947)

VISION

Acts of Wisdom

Louisville

Malcolm Line

Seeing Crossing Recalling Tasting

CHAOS
X Dismembering

Tuscumbia
NEW BIRTH
△ Mount of Joy

SPEECH
Atlanta

Acts of Temperance

Memphis

Acts of Justice

CULTURE

King Line

Little Rock

Birmingham

Re-membering

Call

Breathing Sounding

Unless we start to fight and defeat the enemies of poverty and racism in our own country and make our own country and make our talk of equality and opportunity ring true, we are exposed as hypocrites in the eyes of the world when we talk about making other people free. *Shirley Chisholm* (1969) • Freedom is never given; it is won. *A. Philip Randolph* (1937)

It is much to be lamented that no person has taken notice of [the Constitution's] total silence upon the subject of...an office for promoting and preserving perpetual peace in our country. *Benjamin Banneker* (1793) • Nobody eber helped me into carriages, or 'ober mud puddles, or gibs me any best place! And a'n't I a woman? *Sojourner Truth* (1851)

G R A C E

New Orleans

Acts of Hope

An unjust law is a human law that is not rooted in eternal and natural law. Any law that uplifts human personality is just. Any law that degrades human personality is unjust. *Martin Luther King, Jr.* (1963)

I, too, sing America. I am the darker brother... I, too, am America. *Langston Hughes* (1926)

Houston Conwill, sculptor, Joseph De Pace, architect, and Estella Conwill Majozo, poet, *The New Cakewalk Humanifesto: A Cultural Libation*, 1989.

John Jeffries

Toward a Redefinition of the Urban:
The Collision of Culture

Before I proceed, I'd like to offer a few qualifying remarks to frame my presentation. I consider myself a social scientist. There are even times when I voluntarily self-identify as such. And I am familiar with social science's failure to capture and keep the interest of those who are not already predisposed to that interest. That's one reason my social science orientation is far from conventional. In fact, both inside and outside of social science circles, I, along with other social scientists like Julianne Malveaux, am often described as a renegade. (The tone of these descriptions is not unlike those we've all heard families use when referring to a relative who is a bit impish or out of the ordinary, but of whom the family is nonetheless proud.) We are considered renegades because we respect the importance and function of analysis, but, at the same time, are diligently critical of the methodologies and epistemologies that underlie the social sciences and the conclusions reached when they are routinely employed.

An important dimension of the critique we bring to bear on conventional analysis, and the criticism that critique engenders, is a thoughtful recognition of the influence of culture. Of particular interest to me is the extent to which social science itself is conducted and interpreted as a cultural practice. At this stage, I believe we're far beyond simplistic appeals and one-dimensional attempts to "bring culture into the analysis." For me, the point of departure is the fusion of analytic social science with the identity and construction of that which we deem cultural. To that end, I'll introduce four specific themes that, in my opinion, inform contemporary considerations of black popular culture in the urban context.

The first suggests that any articulation of Western, and, in particular, American, culture (popular or otherwise) must make reference to the social construction of race as an analytic concept. More specifically, what I have in mind is the social construction of race that takes place in the United States during the eighteenth and nineteenth centuries.

Second, and very briefly, at the risk of invoking an unpopular vocabulary in these postmodern times, I'd like to suggest that when assessing urban culture in general, and U.S. twentieth-century black urban culture in particular, it is absolutely "essential" that consideration be given to the Enlightenment's "dark side."

The third theme builds on insights that have been pointedly brought to our attention in this conference by Stuart Hall concerning, as he so eloquently put it, the "repertoires of black popular culture." Following Stuart's lead—in a manner akin, I hope, to the way a very young Miles followed the leads of Dizzy and Bird on the bandstand in the late 1940s—I'd like to emphasize the significance of the place, defined both in geographic and political economy terms, in which these "repertoires of black culture" are born and remixed: the city.

The last theme sketches what I refer to as the parameters associated with authenticity and resistance when we identify urban black popular culture in the United States.

On the Social Construction of Race

During the eighteenth and nineteenth centuries, the United States of America was a major contributor to the social construction of race as a Western analytic concept. The point here is not that the word "race" is written or spoken for the very first time in Western history, by virtue of its employment in the lexicon of the United States, but that the birth of the United States as a nation-state breathes life into the term in two uniquely American, and ultimately profound, ways.

By the middle of the eighteenth century, the momentum generated by the colonies' political revolt from Mother England forced the designated spokesmen of the American Revolution to address, at least rhetorically, the subject of how the new nation would reconcile its philosophical embrace of democracy, liberty, and equality in light of its pragmatic reliance on the enslavement of Africans. Although I would argue that racial (as we understand the term today) justifications of American slavery are most accurately traced to nineteenth-century (not eighteenth-century) conventions, the notions of liberty, equality, and the inalienable rights of men—principles on which the new nation was founded—required further explanation, given the undeniable presence of African slaves and "freemen" prior to and after American independence.

By the last quarter of the eighteenth century, those universal principles were invoked with frequently ambiguous allusions to a necessary and "reasoned" differentiation among those who would populate the New World and nation. From the vantage point of Puritan colonial culture, it was not very difficult to perceive the physical characteristics of the Africans living in eighteenth-century North America, the overwhelming majority of whom were slaves, as different from the physical characteristics of the recently arrived Europeans who populated the colonies. As a consequence, the physical characteristics of Africans in North America, and their typical status as slaves in the eighteenth-century New World, made them increasingly conspicuous as support for a revolutionary independent nation grew.

Within the context of founding a new government, the nation's forefathers, in an effort to show that the principles of liberty and democracy were capable of tolerating a range of beliefs, continued to differentiate philosophically and politically among those who would ultimately reside in the New World. Both the Bill of Rights and the U. S. Constitution, as well as the debates from which they surface, are concrete testimonies to this process of differentiation. The differentiation between "us and them" and the Enlightenment differentiation among "us" were products of the revolutionary fervor of the time.

Implementing the blueprints for a revolutionary nation of "equals," founded on liberty and the sanctity of individual freedom, required a rhetorical smoothing over of the increasingly conspicuous presence of enslaved Africans; it also laid the intellectual groundwork for the social construction of race as an analytic category in the nineteenth century.

The second uniquely American contribution to the social construction of race was also tied to the United States's struggle for national identity, roughly a half century after the revolution.

At the beginning of the nineteenth century, the United States was very much preoccupied with distinguishing itself, culturally, from Europe. Although the United States was politically independent, the conventional wisdom on the European continent at the time was that America had not made, and probably would never make, any meaningful or longstanding contributions to Western culture. As a nation made up of outlaws, America was not intellectually or artistically capable of doing so.

During the course of America's defensive and insecure responses to these scathing criticisms, no single topic consumed the nation's political and economic braintrusts more than slavery. At issue was slavery's economic and political feasibility and its growth (or overflow, depending on the interests you held) into the western territories. As irony would have it, the increase in the number of independent pirates involved in the African slave trade displaced the seemingly more genteel trading companies involved in the seventeenth and eighteenth centuries, and as a consequence, European nation-states declared the slave trade illegal. This change in international law curtailed the supply of African slaves at a time when hotly contested debates concerning an increased demand for slave labor were commonplace within the United States.

In the face of an undeniably shrinking international supply, questions concerning who would serve as slaves in the expanding plantations of the American South received a great deal of attention. Once again, the presence of African slaves in the U.S. was pushed into the limelight. Through the hegemonic influence of science, and its nineteenth-century preoccupation with established modes of inquiry developed in physics and biology, the "American School" of "craniometry" (the measuring of human skulls for the purposes of classifying the human species) gained worldwide notoriety. This new branch of science "objectively" differentiated among human beings based on characteristics that were empirically verifiable and subject to quantification and measurement. In the eyes of the world's scientific community, the American School of craniometry firmly established the concept of race. The extent to which this American cultural feat served to earn the accolades of Europe cannot be overstated.

As we all know, the American School concluded that Africans were an inferior human species. That classification "logically" justified their social status as slaves. Even nineteenth-century anti-slavery and abolitionist rhetoric conceded African inferiority. Therefore, it is important for us to understand that the scientific construction of race (with which we are all too familiar and comfortable for reasons I'll allude to in a minute) is itself a social construction, in two senses: first, because the impetus for the verification of the term "race" cannot be divorced from debates concerning the future of African slavery in the United States. Second, the presumed "scientific verification" of the term by the

American School led to the popular and regular use of the word within the United States and across the globe. The analytic construct "race" was reified by American culture, popular and otherwise.

Even after later methods of "scientific" inquiry unequivocally discredited the methods and conclusions of the nineteenth-century American School, the reified notion of race as a verifiable analytic construct remained deeply ingrained in U.S. (and Western) culture. As a result, race, and its twentieth-century counterpart, ethnicity, became "real" scientific concepts that continue to haunt our discussions of the social and the cultural.

And nowhere is the conceptual tar baby "race" more pronounced than in our discussions of contemporary urban culture.

The Enlightenment and the City

Two intellectual thrusts associated with the Enlightenment movement greatly improved the image of the city: one, the emphasis on the inherent capacity of any individual to reason his (and I use that pronoun advisedly) way through a task, including the quest for personal fortune; and two, democracy's insistence that all citizens have the opportunity to pursue any goal within reason.

If pre-Enlightenment thought was dominated by characterizations of the city as a sinful, amoral place where only the ungodly resided, the "Age of Enlightenment" countered with descriptions of the urban as the quintessential hot bed of "high" culture. But the city was also a place where other-than-high culture existed and was respectfully tolerated. By the late nineteenth century, cities were perceived and promoted as "sophisticated" places. Individuals (and families) willingly gravitated to these places because life could be truly lived there. Given the abundant opportunities, life in the city was "what you made it."

It was also understood, however, that urban life implied risks. There were no guarantees. And it was precisely the sense of "fair play" that fueled this romantic, and fundamentally humanist, view of the city. Progress (personal and societal) was there for the asking. No place epitomized this more than the cultured, bourgeois city.

But as Cornel West has so insightfully pointed out, the liberating and democratic rhetoric of the Enlightenment cannot be separated from the human degradation and oppression of people of color, women, and the large numbers of individuals whose lives were tied to wages. (These categories are obviously not mutually exclusive.) As a consequence, an underside has also been associated with urban life. From the vantage point of ninteenth-century political economy, it would be misleading to simplistically attribute these "darker elements" of the romantic, bourgeois city to the residual dogma of the Church—which continued to characterize cities as ungodly places.

In the American case, southern cities during the Reconstruction era, New York, Chicago, and Boston in the early twentieth century, and the cities of the Jim Crow South (just to name a few) are historical testimony to the perverse spatial offspring conceived and nurtured by the marriage of laissez-faire capitalism and those democratic principles that valorize the individual. Consider the behaviors and conditions routinely rationalized in the name of profit, personal financial gain, or, what came to be synonymous—"the hustle and bustle of the city": income generated by deliberately preying on and/or betraying family members, friends, and strangers; the unfettered destruction of the natural landscape and the pollution of the air and water; the construction and corruption of local law based on innumerable forms of privilege; high concentrations of abject poverty and unprecedented personal wealth; the intractable commodification of space (distinct from land); and the constant redefinition of ultimately contradictory and conflicting designations of the public and private spheres.

I'm not suggesting that these behaviors and conditions were exclusively urban phenomena. However, by the beginning of the twentieth century, no American city was free of any of these influences. In fact, urban culture exposed these influences as it perpetuated the more romantic, progressive image of itself. It is against this backdrop that black popular culture in the urban context, during the first half of the twentieth century, must be situated and interpreted.

The "Repertoires" of Urban Black Popular Culture

Stuart Hall spoke of three elements in the "repertoires of black popular culture." The first concerned style. For the mainstream culture and its critics, style is merely a veneer, a coating that is not particularly interesting. In stark contrast, for black popular culture, style is the subject matter at hand. The second referenced black popular culture's deep-rooted attachment to music, in contrast to mainstream culture's logocentric fascination with the written word. And the third concerned black popular culture's deliberate use of the body as a canvas.

I'd like to add a fourth element. The place where new dimensions of black popular culture are often born is also significant. And that place is "the city."

In black popular culture, the city is hip. It's the locale of cool. In order to be "with it," you must be in the city, or at minimum, urban culture must be transplanted, simulated, or replicated outside of the city wherever possible. The city is where black popular styles are born—especially clothing and hairstyles. Black music, although it often has roots in traditions that are distinctly rural, is always radically transformed and remixed by black urban dwellers. Out of black popular culture come new words, and new meanings and connotations are given to the routinely employed mainstream vocabulary. The language of black popular culture not only more fully describes the emotions and circumstances black urban residents encounter, it also defines what is contemporary. The language is spoken for the black popular ear. According to black popular culture and the contemporary vernacular, the city (today) is dope 'cause it still got the juice.

One of the most illustrative examples of this idea of the hip city in black popular culture appears in several of Chester Himes's Coffin Eddie and Gravedigger Jones detective novels. The two that are probably best known, because of their conversions to the movie screen, are *Cotton Comes to Harlem* and *A Rage in Harlem*. Both are set in the quintessential black urban place, Harlem, New York, and are based on the following storyline: some black folks from the "country" end up in Harlem with something hidden (a large sum of money in a cotton bale in the former, and gold in the latter), and the chaos that results exposes Harlem residents, black and white, as not so hip after all. The two black detectives, Coffin Eddie and Gravedigger Jones, represent urban black men who, by virtue of their place of residence and savvy, will not be outdone. They use their wits, and they fail or succeed, without caring about or soliciting the aid of whites.

While adding the significance of the city to considerations of black popular culture, I'd like, however, to qualify, and offer a critique of, that addition. The active ingredients of the critique are mired in the social construction of race and its injection into American popular culture in general, and urban culture in particular.

Redefining the Urban

As a group, blacks in the diaspora have realized few, if any, of the progressive ideals associated with life in the bourgeois modern city. But not for lack of trying. For blacks in America, the social construction of race has served as a major obstacle to enjoying the "good life" in the city.

As a result, urban black popular culture has pursued many avenues to ease the pain associated with the elusive urban good life, and it has created its own profound and sometimes feeble semblances of the good life—some at the expense of other black people in the same boat.

Principal among those urban bourgeois ideals was the widely held notion that if you lived in a city, you were free to be as anonymous as you desired. Many people moved to cities precisely because they wanted to become more anonymous than sparsely populated other-than-urban places allowed. They wanted to distance themselves, physically and emotionally, from those parochial influences they believed were "holding them back."

Unfortunately, blacks (individually and collectively) have rarely found "the city" to be a place of refuge from those restraining influences for two primary and interconnected reasons: (1) the parochial influences blacks are most interested in escaping are either unambiguously racist or infected with racist overtones and, therefore, are as prevalent in urban areas as they are in rural areas; and (2) American culture, popular and otherwise, treats blacks as though they are both invisible and highly conspicuous at the same time. Blacks are ignored while their status as inferior others dictates that their behavior is heavily and constantly scrutinized.

The Jim Crow South brutally prohibited blacks from participating in and partaking of the "public sphere" in southern cities. Blacks who migrated from the South to cities in northeastern and midwestern states over the course of the twentieth century met with social and economic hostility. Those who were fortunate enough to land industrial jobs in those cities often worked under life-threatening conditions for wages that were considerably lower than those received by their white counterparts. Those employed outside the industrial sector earned income by providing the same services they had been forced to provide for whites in the South. The architecture of density and urban sprawl, designed to accommodate economic growth and decline, dictated that the living conditions most urban residents were forced into were also tenuous and life-threatening.

By the twentieth century, most American cities were sustained by some form of nascent, actual, decaying, or residual capitalist economic activity. Individual, family, and/or household dependence on wages became so pronounced that one's material life in the city could never be taken for granted. This was especially true for blacks. The social and cultural codes associated with race dictated that blacks were conspicuous wherever they migrated or settled. Consequently, a great many income-generating occupations were simply not available to the descendents of slaves living in twentieth-century American urban places. And in addition to or instead of typical wage work, many urban residents acquired income from the varied opportunities crime in the city provided. (For the record, what constitutes a crime is, in my opinion, socially, not universally, determined.)

As capital's rampant commodification of virtually all things and services would have it, the great migration to and from cities supported one of the most prevalent urban income-generating activities practiced in cities—the confidence scam. Based on gaining the confidence and trust of others, urban "con" artists relieved people of their financial resources with reckless abandon, infinite wit, and sometimes, unspeakable physical violence.

As I mentioned earlier, I'm not suggesting that the con game is an exclusively urban phenomenon. Its proliferation in twentieth-century American cities, however, developed into a cultural practice that moved freely across legal and extralegal boundaries. In fact, large personal fortunes generated from highly organized confidence and protection schemes that began inside urban neighborhoods were accumulated and used to finance existing and start-up "legitimate" capitalist enterprises.

In urban black popular culture, there is nothing hipper than a "con." But it's ironic that the practice and execution of the con is often revered as an art form in black popular culture because blacks and other recent arrivals to American cities were the victims of these schemes; over time, black men and women perpetrated new and modified forms of the trade for the explicit purpose of fleecing other blacks (as well as whites).

At the risk of understatement, the con game, as an income-generating activity, became an American urban cultural practice to which urban black popular

●

culture greatly contributed. It was also organically linked to the bourgeois, romantic vision of the city as a place filled with opportunities—opportunities there for the taking as well as opportunities to take anyone who exposed their vulnerability.

In a similar manner, the social construction and popular use of race, which by definition dehumanizes the black subject, led to the migration of large numbers of black subjects from places that were routinely associated with black degradation (that is, the Jim Crow South and "the country") to cities, where they could take advantage of opportunities that would ultimately help them reaffirm their humanity.

Unfortunately, the definition of what it means to be human in the twentieth century cannot be divorced from infectious notions of the commodity-consuming, wealth-accumulating individual. Or, to state the paradox conversely, the absence or lack of sufficient income acquired to purchase socially necessary (that is, life-reproducing) commodities (food, clothing, and shelter) severely compromises any attempts made by black men and women to reaffirm their humanity.

In defense of itself, urban black popular culture has taken refuge in its "blackness" in an attempt to reaffirm the humanity of black subjects. What I'm suggesting is that urban black popular culture has attempted to do this in the face of three formidable cultural dominants: the degradation of Africans and "blackness" intrinsic to the very conception of what a race is; the human degradation associated with capitalist economic activity and commodification; and the cultural degradation represented by the schizophrenic progressive/decaying modern city.

Postscript

The question of whether or not urban black popular culture will be required to continue its reaffirmation of black humanity in the coming century is not simply a rhetorical one. And although it's highly likely that will indeed be the case, it cannot be predetermined.

However, from my vantage point, the cultural signifiers that black popular culture employs to do so may already be overdetermined—overdetermined in the sense that the significance of place, and the presumed authenticity associated with the signifier "black," are both being displaced.

Modern notions of "place" have been effectively eroded by elaborate systems of transportation (in the early twentieth century) and the instantaneous retrieval, manipulation, and transmission of information (in the latter part of the twentieth century)—both constructed for the realization of profit. The resultant global interdependence and flexibility have resulted in a kind of profit-seeking fragmentation that severely implicates modern definitions of the social significance of "places," especially those represented in culturally "authentic" terms.

Nonetheless, contemporary references to Afrocentrism and "black business/buy black" social policy, in particular those versions that remain infected by homophobia, misogyny, greed, and (ironically enough) "scientifically" supported theses of "racial purity," are significant elements of late-twentieth-century urban black popular culture.

Lewis Mumford wrote: "Human life swings between two poles: movement and settlement." But, as displacement becomes the rule rather than the exception, capital's commodification of culture and space has rendered that balance suspect. Late-twentieth-century cities have been transformed into vast depositories for the culturally hybrid. We are all living in capitalist economic spheres that are simultaneously severely fragmented and constantly overlapping. We are also living within and producing cultural spheres that are perversely plural (not to be confused with democratic), deeply xenophobic, "hyper-real" (distinct from authentic), and yet every now and then profoundly liberating.

These other-than-modern, "postmodern," and socially constructed pairings give rise to a constant collision of human beings engaged in cultural (and economic) practice—it is these collisions and their hybrid by-products that dictate a redefinition of the urban. For urban black popular culture, there is no hip way to escape these collisions and the resultant call for redefinition.

Sherley Anne Williams

Two Words on Music: Black Community

In one of those ironic twists that seem so characteristic of African-American history, disco and rap, although they ultimately draw from different sources, share the same root and moment of creation—the style of DJing pioneered in the early seventies in New York City dance clubs that sought to keep the groove going record after record in one seamless, endless, and in the case of disco, ultimately boring, song. Disco club jocks, working between two turntables, matched the tempos of one record to the next, cueing the beginning of the second record to blend with the ending of the first. The white patrons of those trendy midtown clubs, where the rhythmic music that became known as disco was spawned, were more often preoccupied with styles of dress than modes of dance. And the recordings designed for that club scene rapidly devolved into a "genre" defined largely by the number of drum and bass beats that could be squeezed into a minute.[1]

Black vocal music was so thoroughly integrated into disco that one could even talk about the black "domination" of disco—Black diva Donna Summer was considered its queen—without straining credibility. Yet disco, by the very nature of its production—composed in the studio by engineers and producers combining various prerecorded tracks to make a record—was incongruent with spontaneity, improvisation, and participatory re-creation, the values that have traditionally defined black expressive culture. For the first time in its long history on this continent, black popular music was in danger of being completely absorbed by the mainstream it had previously defied.

On the other hand (and at the other end of the economic scale), in the Bronx and other inner-city black areas, itinerant street jocks, working house parties in the winter and block parties in the summer, concerned themselves with "the break"—the instrumental interlude, often dominated by drums or a funky bass, between the lyric's end and its reprise—which could be isolated and replayed. Playing copies of one record on twin turntables, the street jocks cut back and forth between the same few bars, extending the break into an instrumental. Soon—in a virtuoso show of manual dexterity, a mocking parody of the advanced multitrack technology that had first created these records— they were scratching, repeating beats, breaks, words, and phrases on the same record, and mixing beats and breaks from different records. And I was initially drawn to rap because I was tickled by the way these young people got around— in a way that was itself technically brilliant—the expensive electronic gadgetry that could have locked them away from the cutting-edge music of their generation.

Rap, then, was anti-disco. It replaced the plush, multitrack orchestral phrasings of disco—which could be produced only in the studio—with more or less spontaneously combined "break beats," appropriated from a combination of records in various musical genres, using minimal technology. It could, therefore, be created by almost any Negro off the street who had, not so much the equipment, but the dexterity, the imagination, and, most of all, the ability to read the scene, the people, the mood, the moment, and, drawing on a range of musical genres, play to it. Like ragtime and jazz, rap was not, initially, a lyrical music. It began as "instrumental" dance music. The MCs, who in the wake of the wildly successful "Rappers Delight" (the first commercial rap record) became "rappers" themselves, were added to the mix after the DJs had created the musical form (the beats over which the MCs rapped). Only in what one might call the degeneracy of the present era did the MCs become the stars of the genre.

Originally, rappers rapped about the DJs and the words were almost incidental to the groove or beat. Aggressive, self-aggrandizing boasts about the rapper's own prowess were added, in the tradition of the badman street toasts, together with new sayings going the rounds in the streets. These tributes, boasts, and slogans were unified by internal rhymes—the virtuoso single-sound free-rhyming that Stephen Henderson first identified as a hallmark of black vernacular style.[2] These improvised street boasts and rhymes, freed of melody because they, like the toasts that fathered them, were chanted rather than sung, communicated in more detail, and with a greater directness, than conventional song forms and displaced the romantic idealism and upwardly mobile ethic of such anthems of the disco era as "Staying Alive" and "Good Times."

Boastful as the blues, and even more bare of figurative language, the new

genre was built on the black verbal traditions of formulaic, in-group word-play learned in childhood and adolescence (by males *and* females) and never really forgotten. Rappers created their own raps, thus doubly controlling their material in a way that is rare among pop vocal artists, who, almost always, even when they have chosen the titles themselves, are singing someone else's songs. Rap became an enabling lyricism for a host of new-style troubadours (and some no-talent white people without much rhythm). Its chanted lyricism sidestepped what had always been a stumbling block to the total cannibalization of black music—black vocal techniques and voice textures. Almost anybody could be coached into talking their way through some semblance of rhythm—hence, The Beastie Boys, Vanilla Ice, Young Black Teenagers, Third Base, and other lesser known "crossover" groups.

I have given this rather long and, for this audience, perhaps, redundant history of rap music because I want to emphasize the fact that rap is homemade, what we might, in another era, have called "mammy-made"—except that by the time rap hit the Anglo-American mainstream, "yo mamma" would have "knock[ed] you out" for talking like many of the most popular rappers do in front of her. Now, the best rap is still characterized by funky beats and positive messages. The shocking themes and images of a violent and decaying inner city of such rap classics as Grandmaster Flash and the Furious Five's "The Message" and Public Enemy's "Fight the Power" helped to move the genre beyond boasting, bragging personality commercials.

But precisely because rap is as black as the blues, as jazz, as R&B and because, until quite recently, its production, distribution, and promotion, as well as its composition and direction, were under black control—in a way that these other genres of black music have never been, not even in the golden era of independent producers in the early fifties—black people have to ask ourselves why so much of it has become so vehemently misogynistic, violent, and sexually explicit, so soaked in black self-hatred? Why, given the way we are so ready to jump on Hollywood, the Man, the Media, and black women writers for negative and distorted portrayals of black people, have black academics, critics, and intellectuals been so willing to talk about the brilliant and innovative form of rap? Proclaiming rap's connection to traditional wells of black creativity and thus viewing even its most pornographic levels as "art," intellectuals have been slow to analyze and critique rap's content. We have, by and large, refused to call that content, where appropriate, pathological, anti-social, and anti-community. And by our silence, we have allowed what used to be permissible only in the locker room or at stag parties, among consenting adults, to become the norm among our children.

I started out talking about rap because black people coined the genre, but I don't exempt songs by both male and female vocalists—Baby Face, Keith Sweat, Salt-n-Pepa, and others—from the list of what has not just strained the bounds of "good taste" (always an elastic term in the black community anyway), but has also gone beyond the bounds of what used to be common sense. I am not naive enough to see popular music as the sole culprit in the dissolution of black communities—which have always been under siege and direct assault—but, unlike a lot of what threatens us, black popular music is something over which we have some direct control and influence. The sexuality promoted in such lyrics as "Do Me, Baby," "Try Me," and "Push It, Baby" is a particularly pernicious ethic to push in this age of AIDS. It feeds into and intensifies the syndrome of early and promiscuous sex that has resulted in more than a quarter of all babies born in the black community being born to unwed mothers, most of whom are under the age of eighteen.

Epidemic violence, not just the publicized drive-by shooting, but the everyday ass-kickings and knifings that occur so routinely among our young people that many of them—even the ones who are not involved in gangs—feel the need to go out armed as a matter of self-defense, is sanctioned by its visualization in the wasteland of TV and by its whisperings through the earphones on our children's ears. Black population growth, given our high infant mortality rate, on the one hand, our homicide rates—on the other, and the terrifying statistics on the spread of the HIV virus among us—is at or very near zero. (We would know this if the government dared release the true statistics.) I am not promoting legalized censorship of the kind some Florida counties have tried to perpetrate. I'm talking about the need for some self-examination and self-discipline, about the need for education on the distinction between the rock (and I'm not talking about rock 'n' roll, either) and what lives under it—and ought to die when it's exposed to the light of day. In the same way that technology has presented the legal and medical professions with situations for which they have no ethical and moral guidelines or precedents, drugs and integration have presented black communities with situations that we don't have the institutions to cope with. While the concept of law and the practice of medicine will no doubt survive contemporary debates, it's really questionable if black communities will.

Providentially, or so it seemed then, just as I began formulating the issues I raise here about the consequences for black communities of valorizing the underside of human experience in too much contemporary black music, I happened to catch an infotainment show on late night TV about rap music and its values. The show pitted members of Bytches with Problems and a member of The Gheto Boys against noted psychiatrist Dr. Alvin Poussaint and a member of one of the more politically progressive rap groups. Poussaint tried to mount a vigorous assault against the extreme emphasis in much rap music on violence, promiscuity, and misogyny.

It will probably come as no surprise to this audience that Poussaint was soundly dissed by the Bytches, who said, first of all, you didn't always feel like "Hold[ing] On" (signifying, of course, on En Vogue's hit record), especially when you had just been two-timed and quit by some low-life who talked about you and yo mamma, too. As a massafac, you wanted to make it real plain that the little catgut hanging between his legs didn't mean a thang to a real woman like yourself, and if he looked closely, he just might see that *he* hadn't gotten away intact. Your bad moufing him was, in fact, a way of making yourself feel better, just as he'd made himself feel better by murder-moufing you.

Certainly, I could understand where the sisters were coming from, but even though these are sentiments that I have, upon occasion perhaps, expressed myself, I don't want to hear them blasted over the airwaves at all times of the day and night. And I'm sure Dr. Poussaint knew where they were coming from, too. He objected to the explicit language in which rap too often phrases such feelings, but he didn't do so as vociferously as he might have, had his opponents been his peers, or had the forum in which they disagreed been more suited to serious discussion. He also objected to their assumptions that he did not live in a black community and that he disparaged rap without having listened to it. Still, they continued in their belief that he didn't know the reality they lived and sang about, and they dismissed him accordingly.

It was probably a unique experience for this celebrated psychiatrist. He was disrespected, by black people, for being precisely what he, and they, had worked so laboriously to have him become—a certified professional, a Harvard professor, the expert consultant on black health and experience. Lest I be

accused of speaking from the same "rarified" air or, worse yet, of talking like
nothing but a parent, let me confess that while I *own* very few rap releases (I
refuse to pay money to be insulted and offended, and if what one hears on the
air is "mainstream," that is, watered-down rap, I have no desire to find the cutting edge), I *live* in the inner city—or, as I've always called it, home. And yes, I
am a mother, and I feel some responsibility to "mother," *nurture,* not only my
son and his children, but the children of our communities, as well. And it is
precisely because I live in the ghetto, and am trying to raise children there, that
I am so alarmed about too much of what's happening in black popular music
today and the consequences of our silence about it.

One of the things black people have always held against whites is "bad science," their habit of putting theory and "scientific investigation" before people,
before any obligation to community, of using "for the good of humanity" to justify voyeuristic curiosity or the advancement of their own careers. As intellectuals, we're in danger of going the way of white people, acting as though
our research has no consequences for the black community because (a) we ourselves no longer live in black communities, (b) the people about whom we
write will not read what we have written, or (c) that the only impact of our research is on the white scholarly community: it will make them love us more.

Black people, as intellectuals and activists, seldom disagree nowadays unless
we feel personally attacked. Then, we go for the jugular—accusing each other
of ignorance, anti-intellectualism, moralistic preaching, or of being anti-
black—any time questions are raised about the effects, methods, or purposes
of our research and scholarly writing. As a result, dissent and debate are almost
totally absent from our public discourse—except as character assassination.
Our activists and strategists haven't thought a new thought in years because
whenever someone questions or dissents (offers a new idea), they are shouted
down and silenced or ignored. So the children of the ghetto, noting all we have
(and haven't) done for them since we've been grown, listen only to each other,
and have such contempt for us they hardly listen to a word we say (and barely
understand what they do hear). In fact, they seem to feel they can do what we
do without having done what we did.

The political climate in which I wrote this paper is far different from the one
in which it will now be read. Ice-T had not been assaulted by a Texas police

group because of the persona in one of his adolescent raps, nor had Sister Souljah been mugged by democratic presidential nominee Bill Clinton for remarks quoted out of context in the *Washington Post*. The Supreme Court had not then affirmed, as it has now, the license taken by white hate groups to harass and intimidate blacks and others as a constitutional right. Even the president and vice president have gotten into the act, posturing about Ice-T's "Cop Killer" (as if boycotting Time Warner would reduce the national debt). These events make it more difficult, and dangerous, to critique any aspect of rap. No doubt, some will accuse me of taking sides with the president and like-minded jerks, which I would really resent. Rappers' fantasies about killing white people, in general, or policemen, in particular, are no more than the letting off of steam about the almost unbearable racist pressure under which most of us live; *these fantasies are not the ones that are acted upon.* Black male homicide rates are not the highest in the country because these young men decided to take out a cop or some white person. Those rates are created by black men offing each other. No, it's the so-called fantasies about pulling "a trigger on some nigger" that concern me, the ones about the "gang-banging 'ho" and the "ghetto bitch" the rapper feels perfectly justified in "stickin dick" to that frighten me. These are the realities I see enacted in the streets in my part of the city.

Some may ask, as did one listener after hearing this presentation, how I can condemn one of the few things of value that unempowered young black people have managed to create for themselves. Well, I haven't "condemned" rap; I've questioned the content of some rap songs. To question my motivation in those terms implies that rap is above criticism, particularly by black people, and is just another way of avoiding open, and serious, discussion about the meaning and implication of rap's themes. That may work and even be appropriate with Clinton and the police; it must not work among black communities. Like I said, the monkey live here. Rap is a statement in the tradition of black expressive culture, and this critique is a response to that statement, a necessary comment upon it. And, as in a classic blues verse, the meaning of both statement and response must be taken into account if the song is to move toward any successful resolution.

Moreover, our silence about the negative aspects of rap is exemplary of another, equally significant silence about the performance, or lack of performance, of black elected officials, black organizations, and the few institutions that remain to us. It's not enough to blame it all on racism and let it go at that. We've been subject to racism in this country for more than three hundred years; it hindered but could not stop us. I am among those who won't let racism, or phony appeals to its specter, stop us from the discussions we so urgently need now.

Theories of popular culture ain't doing my neighborhood no good. What trickles down to the kids on my block is that what they're doing must be all right because it is celebrated, not just in their own songs, but in white people's stories, rapped about by some heavy-weight dudes and sisters at colleges and conferences, in books they can't even *read,* the shit so deep. And so some brother feels free to kick another sister's butt, jump into her ass, as they say, drop another baby (because that's the only "art" they know), off another brother 'cause "Hey, everybody's doing it. That's reality." But "reality" is also us and what we make it or change it to be. If these children could create an industry where there was none, surely we can give them some hope in their future that doesn't depend on their participation in the destruction of their own communities in order to make it in the white world.

1. This sketch of rap's development follows the history so lucidly detailed in David Toop, *The Rap Attack: African Jive to New York Hip Hop* (Boston: South End Press, 1984).

2. Stephen Henderson, *Understanding the New Black Poetry; Black Speech and Black Music as Poetic References* (New York: William Morrow & Co., 1973).

Kofi Natambu

Nostalgia for the Present:
Cultural Resistance in Detroit 1977–1987

What I am going to discuss is the relationship between the general political economy governing the metropolitan Detroit community and the largely African-American cultural formations that have emerged there since the late 1970s. Within that context, my remarks will be limited to an analysis of how these cultural expressions (music, art, literature, and critical theory) were, in effect, an insurgent political resistance to the dismantling of the city's economic and social infrastructure. This steady dismantling has taken a heavy toll on the human and material resources of Detroit since 1973—the pivotal year of the so-called energy crisis, the Watergate scandal, and the election of the first black mayor in the history of the city, Coleman A. Young.

I'll focus on four major cultural formations (or, more accurately, three groups and one individual) from the period 1977–1987, fusing a description of my own experience in black working-class and academic cultural activity with what was occurring in these four sites. In this way, I hope to provide a perspective on the wide spectrum of cultural expressions that have dominated alternative, oppositional, and "radical" discourse on Detroit's urban identity since the economic disintegration that began after such cataclysmic national and international events as the "oil crisis" (1973), the defeat of the United States in Vietnam (1975), and the rise of the political right wing on the jingoistic coattails of Reaganism after the 1980 national election. Compounding all of this for the city of Detroit has been Japan's rise to international domination of the automobile industry during the past fifteen years, with the corresponding collapse of that industry in the United States as demonstrated by the rapidly declining sales, prestige, and reputation of the Big Three automakers—General Motors,

Ford, Chrysler—all headquartered in Detroit during this period.

Contributing to this dreary picture: the subsequent rise in unemployment (reaching a depression level of twenty percent in the black community); the largely passive retreat of the once powerful and progressive labor movement (particularly the United Automobile Workers (UAW) and the American Federation of State, County, and Municipal Employees (AFSMCE) unions) in its feeble political response to the conservatives in both national political parties; the large-scale economic and social abandonment of the city by corporations in both the manufacturing and retail sectors through "runaway shop" policies of transferring plants, equipment, and consumer outlets to national and interna-tional sites of cheap labor (absent of unions) like the southern United States and Korea; and the massive "white flight" to the suburbs by middle-class residents and companies. Added to this disruptive mix is the tremendous increase in racial conflict and hostility between the predominantly black city of Detroit (now seventy percent of its population) and its metropolitan suburbs, which re-semble nothing so much as funkmeister George Clinton's model of a "chocolate city and its vanilla suburbs." However, given the incredible tension that persists between the city and its mall-driven neighbors (fueled by the pervasive ex-ploitation of the city's resources by these wealthier former residents), it would be even more accurate to describe it in grim, familiar terms as a blacktown sur-rounded by a white noose.

The circumstances in Detroit have been made more volatile by the anta-gonistic relationship between the suburban residents and a mayor with deep roots in both black and labor movements. Mayor Young has the (some say dubi-ous) honor of being not only the first black mayor in the city's history but also the one with the longest term of service (eighteen years and counting). His feisty, often abrasive personal style is vociferously opposed by a highly con-tentious group of white politicians, journalists, and developers. And there are regular citizens, from the city and its suburbs (some of whom are from the black middle class), who simply despise the mayor and everything he represents as a human being and political force.

It is within this festering historical context that one must try to make sense of Detroit's utterly unique, and yet utterly typical, status as an urban indus-trial/postindustrial center. Its dire situation portends the future of the rest of the nation's cities. That an understanding of what is happening in my hometown is so important to the rest of the country will be the major subtext of my discussion. I hope such a realization will be the beginning of an ongoing dialogue with other urban centers struggling to define the role of cultural activity in their communities.

Detroit, I Do Mind Dying: Cultural Politics and the Urban Crisis, 1977–1982
In the spring of 1977, I returned to my hometown of Detroit after spending two lonely years in graduate school in the barren and racist wilds of Cambridge and Boston, Massachusetts. To say I was ecstatic upon returning is to understate it by half. After growing up in a nearly all-black, working-class environment, which was nothing if not proudly self-sufficient in terms of culture, I was used to, and took for granted, Detroit's legacy of independent, sophisticated black political engagement. After 1965, white flight and continual black migration to the city led to a dramatic shift in the population—from sixty percent white to sixty percent black in just ten years. This meant that people of my generation (I was born in 1950) spent most of their teenage years, and all of their early adulthood, in a city that was not only the fifth largest in the nation, but also one dominated (at least in physical terms) by a strong and cohesive black working class and the largest black middle class in the country. We had also inherited a long history of independent black radicalism, in both its Marxist and nationalist dimensions, going back to the momentous labor struggles (and the rise of the Nation of Islam) during the 1930s.

Such legendary black labor activists and leaders as Buddy Battle, Nelson "Jack" Edwards, Erma Henderson, Horace Sheffield, Tom Turner, and John Conyers, Sr. had as much to do with the actual founding and building of the powerful labor movements of the AFL and CIO (which merged in 1955) as any white man. I was also used to the fact that blacks could and should be elected to national political office. After all, both Charles C. Diggs (son of a well-to-do black funeral director) and John Conyers, Jr. had been elected to Congress as early as 1961 and 1964, respectively. To this day, Detroit is the only city where both congressional representatives are black, and, of course, John Conyers is still one of them.

I also knew about, and followed closely, the exploits of such inspirational figures as George Crockett, an outstanding radical trial attorney (later, judge and congressman) sentenced, under the notorious Smith Act, to a year in prison for defending the legal rights of Communists at the height of the McCarthy years. Finally, we were all greatly aware of Coleman Alexander Young, a child of the black working class who, after organizing workers in both the Ford automobile plants and the U.S. Post Office, was summarily labeled a subversive and fired from both jobs during this same period. In 1952, Young confronted the witch-hunting House UnAmerican Activities Committee (HUAC) with an impassioned speech in which he denounced the committee's existence in Paul Robeson–like fashion.

During the mid and late 1960s, the emergence of such legendary radical organizations as the Marxist League of Revolutionary Black Workers and the nationalist Republic of New Africa led to national reputations for activists such as the late Kenny Cockrel (who was elected to the Detroit City Council in 1977 and was gearing up for a run for the mayor's office when he died at the age of fifty in 1989). As a student member of the League in 1969 and 1970, I was inspired by these activists' example and wanted to emulate their intense organizational and aesthetic style.

In contrast to that period, the late 1970s represented the rather stagnant cultural and political scene that characterized the somnolent Carter years. Toward the goal of shaking up that stagnation on the local level, I, along with a group of five artists in the areas of music, dance, visual art, and multimedia performance, co-founded a nonprofit community arts organization called Go-for-What-You-Know, Inc. (The title, of course, was taken from the well-known black popular expression of the late 1960s). During the first five years of the group's existence, we sponsored and organized multimedia art performances, music and literary workshops, and a regular weekly radio program called "Sound Projections" on Detroit public radio (WDET-FM), featuring jazz, blues, R&B, and rap, as well as interviews, live performances, readings, and social commentary. We also organized a regular series of lectures and readings by artists and scholars in the city.

Our most ambitious activity was the founding of a quarterly literary maga-zine called *Solid Ground: A New World Journal,* which we began in the spring of 1981. During the six-year history of the magazine, we published 12 issues and one major anthology of essays, cultural criticism, fiction, reviews, and poetry, covering five years of writing about politics, literature, art, dance, music, and history. *Solid Ground* was the culmination of a three-year struggle to create an intellectual and cultural organ that would truly engage, critique, and challenge the official pieties of cultural Reaganism and conventional modernist aesthetics in Detroit and the national culture at large. In fact, *Solid Ground* provided a public forum for a creative and critical alternative to the reactionary social and cultural policies and practices that attempted to destroy all vestiges of radicalism during the notoriously backward 1980s.

Our purpose, as outlined in our first issue, was to "focus on contemporary American and world literature and art from a multiracial, multicultural perspective, and to encourage original, innovative writing that is truly concerned with 'radical' ideas about society and culture, especially as they relate to the rest of the world." In the quixotic tone of that first editorial, we said we also wanted to rely on our own experience as the basis for theoretical and strategic models for change and not be imprisoned by, or dependent on, theories from the past.

Nearly all of our writers came from the Detroit area, though there were occasional articles by such important figures as the late C. L. R. James, to whom we dedicated a special issue in 1984. In the period from 1981 to 1987, we featured more than sixty writers, many of whom have gone on to even greater success as scholars and activists, including such black and Latino working-class intellectuals as Tyrone Williams, Rayfield Waller, Leonard Langston, Leslie A. Reese, Nubia Kai, Schaarazetta Natelege, Larry Gabriel, Kaleema Hasan, Sadiq Muhammad, Stella Crews, Bill Harris, Lolita Hernandez, Ron Allen, José Garza, Geoffrey Jacques, and Faruq Z. Bey.

We saw our activity, and the magazine itself, as an independent response to the exclusive and pretentious white avant garde, which, in our view, failed miserably, as did the general political Left, to recognize, acknowledge, support, or include the different critical perspectives and theoretical positions of African Americans. We also differed with the views of some African-American scholars and critics on the question of canon formation and the role of academia in cultural studies and activism.

In relation to Detroit, we consistently opposed much of the official dogma of the city's political administration and its corporate sponsors on important questions regarding "race," class, and the economy. Because so many of our regular contributors were not only writers, but also working people within the larger community, we felt strongly that we should take principled positions on major ideological and political issues that deeply affected the city. Needless to say, given the global nature of the capitalist economy (of which Detroit remains an integral part), this necessitated our bringing critical theories to bear on the concrete international ramifications of these new postindustrial cultural formations.

In an important ten-page essay/review of our 1985 publication *Nostalgia for the Present: An Anthology of Writings (From Detroit)*, a 210-page collection of the "best" writing in *Solid Ground* from 1981 to 1985, we were gratified to see our views vindicated by cultural critic Barbara Harlow.[1] Harlow clearly understood what we were trying to do and, through her sharp insight, taught us many things about our own practice.

In the words of Cornel West, the activity of *Solid Ground* was conceived and was perceived as "insurgent creative activity on the margins of the mainstream, ensconced within bludgeoning new infrastructures." The focus of all the writing in the anthology is an oppositional critique of the various cultural industries in music, literature, multimedia, and film that attempt to manipulate and circumscribe new conceptual ideas and structures. Thus, much of the critical theory is tied to specific analyses of how these institutional strictures have played a role in the cultural mediation of these aesthetic forms. As Harlow makes clear in her essay:

> Indeed, to refer only to mass culture and high art, one of the conceits exploded by Rayfield Waller, is to remain intransigently within the terms defined by the cultural establishment. The writers in *Nostalgia for the Present* contend for another, oppositional alternative to the dichotomy presented by Patrick Brantlinger, for example, in his recent study *Bread and Circuses: Theories of Mass Culture as Social Decay*. Whereas Brantlinger distinguishes between contemporary critiques of mass culture as either "positive classicism," looking to the past for an ideal culture, or "negative classicism," comparisons of modern society with Roman imperial decadence, politically informed cultural projects such as those that find expression in *Nostalgia for the Present* suggest a more contestatory practice. The basis of such a practice is neither elegiac nor apocalyptic, but oppositional, with the "nostalgia" rooted in the material conditions of the historical present.

The Lines Series at the Detroit Institute of Arts, 1980–1990

In November 1980, poet, critic, and educator George Tysh began what became, in my view, the most important reading series in the United States. Called *Lines: New Writing at the Detroit Institute of Arts*, this series featured more than three hundred writers in ten years of programming. The list constitutes a literal "who's who in American writing" over the past thirty years. Significantly, more than seventy-five of these writers from across the country were black, brown, red, or yellow. Of that number, fifty were African Americans, a phenomenal sum, especially when you consider the abysmal record of representing African-American voices in nearly every other series of this kind in the nation. The extraordinary quality of this series served as a lightning rod for the entire cultural community of Detroit during a time of concerted assault on the arts, orchestrated by the national right wing.

The *Lines* series included both writers of national stature and major voices within the city of Detroit. Speakers included such novelists, poets, critics, and essayists as Samuel Delaney, Henry Louis Gates, Jr., Jayne Cortez, Valerie Smith, Houston A. Baker, Jr., Alice Walker, Ishmael Reed, Ntozake Shange, Al Young, Quincy Troupe, Amiri Baraka, Gloria Naylor, Charles Johnson, Erica Hunt, Nate Mackey, Terry McMillan, Lorenzo Thomas, Clarence Major, June Jordan, and Sonia Sanchez. *Lines* also provided the local community with a consistent public forum for the critical examination of ideas and cultural practices through seminars, workshops, and symposia run by, and featuring, Detroit writers, critics, scholars, and poets. There were regular academic and popular programs, not only in literature and critical theory, but also in art, multimedia, music, and film. Artists and theorists featured included John Cage, William Burroughs, Linda Williams, Kathy Acker, Victor Hernandez Cruz, Ron Mann, Lizzie Borden, Pedro Pietri, Jessica Hagedorn, Bob Holman, Erroll Mars, and Gayatri Spivak.

The exciting and inspiring characteristic of George Tysh's visionary programming was that it was resolutely multicultural and multiracial. There were African-American, Latino, Asian-American, Native-American and Arab-American writers, critics, artists, and scholars, as well as artists and writers from China, Japan, India, and Africa. *Lines* and its offshoots were also heavily involved in the community, offering lectures, panel discussions, concerts, performance art, and classes to a wide spectrum of metropolitan Detroit.

Attendance and participation of people of color was always high, and there was a great deal of cross-cultural communication and interaction. Diverse, controversial, and unorthodox views were always welcome, even encouraged. As a teacher in the various workshops and seminars for the period 1983–1987, I can vouch for the tremendous enthusiasm and support for these activities.

The entire *Lines* series (some four hundred cassette tapes, and many original brochures, flyers, posters, and promotional materials) will be leased, on a long-term basis, to the Contemporary Art and Poetics Archives at San Francisco State University.

Creative Arts Collective, 1979–1990

The Creative Arts Collective was formed in the spring of 1979 by two Detroit jazz musicians, Spencer Barefield and Anthony Holland, and the legendary multi-instrumentalist and composer Roscoe Mitchell, from the Art Ensemble of Chicago. Originally conceived as a workshop for Detroit-area musicians and composers interested in new music/avant-garde experimental work, it quickly evolved into a varied program of concerts, workshops, and collaborations with painters, writers, video artists, and dancers. It also became a regular outlet for young musicians and composers to showcase their work.

Soon, CAC was collaborating with an extraordinary Detroit ensemble, Griot Galaxy, which had been appearing, to standing-room-only crowds, at various Detroit clubs, bars, and concert stages since 1976. Led by local legend Faruq Z. Bey on tenor and soprano saxophones, Griot featured former Chicagoan Tani Tabbal on drums, percussion, and tabla, and Detroiter Jaribu Shahid on bass. Saxophonist David McMurray (a member of the Detroit-based pop-funk band Was Not Was) also played with the ensemble.

By the fall of 1979, CAC and its ten-member group of local musicians were sponsoring highly popular concerts of black avant-garde music at the Detroit Institute of Arts. These performances featured many great names in contemporary black creative music, including Lester Bowie, Henry Threadgill, Arthur Blythe, Richard Davis, Anthony Braxton, Muhal Richard Abrams, Roscoe Mitchell, the Art Ensemble of Chicago, AIR, and the World Saxophone Quartet. CAC also included original music and performances by more than fifty Detroit musicians in concerts ranging from solo saxophone to orchestral events. By 1981, CAC and Griot Galaxy were being offered major recording

Tyree Guyton at work on "The Heidelberg Project," in Detroit, 1986.

From "The Heidelberg Project," in Detroit, 1986.

contracts by American and European companies, which led to a series of records, under the CAC banner, and three Griot Galaxy recordings, which received rave reviews in the national music press, including two five-star write-ups in *Downbeat* in 1982 and 1984.

The critical praise lavished on the CAC led to a number of art awards, nationally and from the state of Michigan, and a series of grants from both the state and local arts councils, as well as substantial support from the National Endowment for the Arts (NEA). Performances took place monthly over a ten-year period, finally ending in the spring of 1990 because of severe funding cuts, cuts that have taken such a devastating toll on art in the United States since 1984. Despite these political and economic problems, CAC managed to educate more than two hundred young people in its music workshops, and thousands more attended CAC concert performances at the Detroit Institute of Arts over the years. All in all, more than one hundred Detroit musicians participated directly in the CAC programming, including such internationally renowned Detroit musicians as Marcus Belgrave, Kenn Cox, Kirk Lightsey, Harold McKinney, Phil Lasley, Kenny Garrett, Pheeroan Ak Laff, and Geri Allen, all of whom were featured in Detroit settings with their peers.

Tyree Guyton: The Struggle for Public Art, 1986–1991

In 1986, a thirty-one year old black Detroit painter, sculptor, and environmental landscape artist, Tyree Guyton, began what soon became an internationally acclaimed public art production known as "The Heidelberg Project." This massive, postindustrial art landscape encompassed three city blocks on Detroit's east side. Guyton had grown up there in a working-class neighborhood, which, by the late 1970s, had become ravaged by poverty, drugs, and street crime. Determined to continue living in the area, Guyton, with the dedicated assistance of his wife Karen, and his now ninety-three-year-old grandfather and mentor, Sam Mackey,[2] began to transform the very geography of the area by creating a veritable "art park." This park featured houses made over into gigantic sculptures festooned with "found" objects such as bicycles, suitcases, tires, street signs, cast-off TV sets, radios (some of which actually worked), shoes, old clothing, and a thousand other items. One stunning two-story house was literally covered from top to bottom with plastic doll limbs (heads, arms, legs, torsos, and feet), which Guyton said "represented the beauty and ugliness of living in the city today with all its homelessness, drugs, and children struggling to free themselves." In fact, "The Heidelberg Project" (so named because it began on the very street where Guyton and his family live and work their magic) was conceived from the very beginning as a public commentary on so-cial, economic, and political conditions within the city. The artistic spirituality and the depth of emotion that saturate all of Guyton's work are also present in his personality, which is focused, tough, soft-spoken, eloquent. Guyton's own words explain his project:

> We were talking about how people don't take the time to really see, and that's what I see in my work—I've learned to listen, and pay attention. Like grandpop was saying, I think that a piece of art should talk about something, it should talk about some life, it should express something, it should have a meaning. And, at the same time, I think you're supposed to bring that work of art to life, and that's what I try to put in it. I try to take things that people throw away—they say it's useless now—but to me, I can do something with it. It's like it's talking to me. And a lot of times I tell people, you know, "I hear that piece," and people think you're a little cuckoo. But it's not that— you have learned to listen. I mean, that piece, or that element, or whatever, it's got a life, and you learn to listen to it...You're letting it say things, you know, and you're just listening...it's so beautiful, I mean the music that I hear from this work.
>
> The project over here on Heidelberg, I did that because I felt that it needed to be done—because the house next door was speaking to me. Then the whole area started to—to sing to me. I just wanted to answer, you know, and I felt that I did. And even today, it's still telling me to do things. See, I grew up on the street here, Heidelberg Street, and I have seen war in the area, growing up. And what I decided to do, once I got grown, is that I wanted to talk about this here, I wanted to talk about this love that I really didn't see growing up...When I try to do the work, I try to bring that work alive. I mean I want that work to say something, you know, whatever I might be thinking at that moment. We've had people from as far away as Japan and Malaysia to come on over to see it—people from Zimbabwe, people from Kenya, Paris, London, Italy, all over the world. They come to look at this and talk with us about it. And bringing something different to the neighbor-

hood has truly been a blessing for the neighbors, because the people who were not speaking and the people that didn't associate with each other, they came together, you know, and the people in the area, they tell family members and friends from the west side, and the north end, and they bring them over to see it. We had some people in the neighborhood to come over and give me a donation, to keep it up! We had a woman in the next block to come over and say "Can you put a piece over here?" And having the kids in the community to come over and paint, you know, to sign the street, to be a part of it—to bring stuff. We've had little kids to bring some of their old toys over here and donate to us and say "Can you put this on the house for us?"

The whole idea of taking a neighborhood that's basically been discarded, and picking it up, and cleaning it off, and then starting from that, and bringing in other stuff that's been discarded in other parts of the city, and putting it all together, and painting it, or whatever—and then you got something that's better than what they had to begin with. It's incredible!

In the summertime we go sit outside and just look around—you don't have to go anywhere, you can just come out here and sit and look, and really enjoy yourself. Not only do we have the art out here, but at times you could come down the street and hear jazz playing—always had some music playing coming from the back of the house, and then at night we would cut the TV set on that's on the top of the Fun House next door, and people really get a kick out of that.

Even today I can still hear the Heidelberg Project talking to me—it changes all the time, it keeps growing—and I feel that the project itself is growing too, like the Fun House or some of the other large sculptures are growing. Heidelberg Street at the heart of the project, between Ellery and Mt. Elliott. The project covers two blocks—it covers Heidelberg between Mt. Elliott and Ellery and also Elba between Ellery and Mt. Elliott. So both of those blocks we decided to utilize and make them into works of art. We wanted to let people know what was happening over here, so we put that sign up on Mt. Elliott and started calling it The Heidelberg Project...

The preceding remarks, taken from a December 1988 interview with Guyton conducted by Detroit writer and poet John Sinclair (then editor of the *City Arts Quarterly,* sponsored by the Detroit Council of the Arts), turned out to be not only a very informative general statement on the aesthetic and social objectives of "The Heidelberg Project," but also an eerie counterpoint to the tragic series of events that have taken place since the triumphant summer of 1990, when Guyton's work was given a critically acclaimed one-man exhibition at the Detroit Institute of Arts Museum.

Postscript

The rise to national power of a highly racist and sexist right-wing coalition has played a major role in the systematic dismantling of the cultural work presented here. In 1990, George Tysh's budget was cut so severely that he was forced to end his *Lines* series, as well as all but one of the regular seminar classes that he and various writers from the city taught. All lectures and performances by guest artists were also eliminated. On December 4, 1991, major budgetary cuts at the Detroit Institute of Arts led to the dismissal of more than one hundred employees, including Mr. Tysh. This was part of an ongoing economic gutting of the city by Republican governor John Engler, a forty-two-year-old draconian politician who, since he became head of the state government in January 1991, has eliminated all general assistance in the state (to some 100,000 welfare recipients, many of whom are disabled); axed the Michigan Council for the Arts; eliminated most state monies for Medicare, Medicaid, and allotments for the homeless; and put the internationally prestigious Detroit Institute of Arts on a half-day schedule by eliminating $16 million in state funds from its budget. Even the Detroit Public Library is seriously threatened by Englernomics. In late spring 1991, all of Creative Art Collective's budget was cut by the state council and the Detroit Institute of Arts because of budgetary problems. I don't have to tell you what happened to their NEA funding, do I?

In 1987, I left Detroit to live in New York. Money was very scarce. I had to abandon my original idea of continuing the publication of *Solid Ground*. In early 1991, I was informed that the grant I had received in late 1990 has been cut sixty percent by Engler, thereby effectively delaying the journal's return.

As for Tyree Guyton and "The Heidelberg Project," there has been a series of demolitions by the city government—beginning with "The Baby Dollhouse" in 1989. On November 26, 1991, city bulldozers, accompanied by five Detroit police cars, engaged in a sneak attack at 5 AM. They informed Tyree that he had fifteen minutes to recover whatever materials he wanted to salvage from his

artwork. Essentially, one whole block of art was leveled, with the encouragement of a local citizens group that had petitioned the city to destroy the work
because they considered it a public eyesore. These, and related events, finally
led to formal charges against Guyton, for creating a public nuisance with his
"Shoe Project." The Shoe Project included littering the streets of three city
blocks with old shoes so that automobile traffic could run over them. Guyton
did this as a public protest against the abandonment of the poor, and as a comment on the reactionary nature of the city's response, not only to his work, but
to the general needs of the community. In January 1992, he was told to pay a
small fine and won a victory (of sorts) when a judge declared his work was indeed "art," and not "junk."

Even though Guyton's work has been lauded by critics throughout the world
and has appeared in magazines like *People, Art News,* and *Newsweek,* much of the
Heidelberg Project has now been destroyed. He even made an appearance on
"The Oprah Winfrey Show" to discuss opposition to his work. Although currently discouraged by the city's brutal response, Guyton has, as always,
remained dedicated to continuing his work in the face of those determined to
dictate the terms of art. Despite these and other negative turns of events, the
struggle for a truly radical and transformative culture continues in the beleaguered city of Detroit.

*For Samuel "Grandpa" Mackey (July 29, 1897–June 29, 1992) whose artistry and wise
counsel continues to serve as an inspiration.*

1. Barbara Harlow, "Cultural Resistance in
Detroit," *Black American Literature Forum* 20,
no. 3 (Fall 1986), 317–326.
2. Sam "Grandpa" Mackey died June 29,
1992 at the age of ninety-four. Mentor to and
confidante of his grandson Tyree Guyton, his
paintings are on display in museums in Paris
and Lausanne.

Hazel V. Carby

The Multicultural Wars

As a black intellectual, I am both intrigued and horrified by the contradictory nature of the black presence in North American universities. We are, as students, as teachers, and as cultural producers, simultaneously visibly present in, and starkly absent from, university life. Although it costs approximately $20,000 a year to attend Yale and approximately $50,000 a year to reside in a New York jail, black males are being incarcerated at unprecedented rates. The press and the culture industry, having "discovered" the black woman writer for the first time in the seventies, are now finding it increasingly profitable to market narratives of the lives of successful black men. Articles about black males who have "made it" are no longer found only in the entertainment or sports sections of national newspapers: musicians and basketball stars have been joined by film directors and academics in the pages of our Sunday magazines.

In particular, the very existence of black male professors seems to fascinate the *New York Times*. On April 1, 1990, the *Times* ran a cover story entitled "Henry Louis Gates, Jr.: Black Studies' New Star." Stanley Fish, chair of the English Department at Duke University, patronizingly described Professor Gates's professional success as "entrepreneurial P. T. Barnumism." Adam Begley, the author of the story, concludes that with "a phone in his Mercedes-Benz, a literary agent in New York and an impressive network of contacts in the academy, publishing and the arts, [Professor Gates] seems more like a mogul than a scholar."[1] The *Times* article is, at best, ambivalent toward its black subject and frequently adopts such an incisive tone of ridicule that one wonders if the newspaper's editorial staff consciously decided to create an April 1 cartoon of black studies as a ship of fools. A much more serious, considered, and sober article about Cornel West appeared in the same magazine, describing him as "Princeton's Public Intellectual."[2]

The Merit of Afrocentric Education. Photograph by Chester Higgins, Jr.

In stark contrast to the attention paid to individual black professors is the glaring absence of any equivalent publicity about the paltry presence of non-white ladder faculty in universities: 4.1 percent are Black, 3.8 percent are Asian, 1.3 percent are Latino, and 0.4 percent are Native American.[3] Derrick Bell, a professor at the Harvard Law School, has argued that

A widespread assumption exists that there is an irreconcilable conflict between achieving diversity in law school faculties and maintaining academic excellence...It serves as the primary reason why most college and university faculties across the nation remain all-white and mostly-male almost four

decades after the law barred them from continuing their long-practiced policies of excluding minorities and women because of their race and sex
without regard to their academic qualifications.[4]

These "contentions" Bell maintains "are simultaneously racially insulting and
arrogantly wrong": They are insulting because they insinuate that the old rules
of racial segregation rightly correlated color with intellectual inferiority. They
are arrogant in that they assume that all of those with upper-class–based qualifications are by definition exemplary scholars and teachers.[5]

Bell continues by stressing that "minorities who achieve are deemed exceptions," whereas those "who fail are deemed painful proof that we must adhere
to hiring standards that subsidize the well-placed members of our society while
penalizing those, white as well as black, from disadvantaged backgrounds."[6]
That more than ninety percent of all faculty members across the nation are
white is a scandal but is not, apparently, a cause for journalistic outrage or
newspaper headlines.

The percentage of black students in college populations has steadily de-
creased throughout the last decade, as has the number of B.A.s awarded to
black students, even though the absolute number of bachelor's degrees awarded
has been increasing nationally. In graduate schools, the proportion of American
graduate students who are black is decreasing and the proportion of doctorates
awarded to black people is also in significant decline. The number of tenured
black professors has increased slightly, but the number of untenured black appointees is decreasing.[7] Clearly, if the black student population continues to
decline at the undergraduate and graduate levels, the current black intellectual
presence in academia, small as it is, will not be reproduced.

During the past two years, debate about the inclusion of people from a variety of ethnic, national, and class backgrounds as appropriate subjects for
educational study and research has become focused on what is now commonly
referred to as the multicultural curriculum. Multiculturalism appears as a controversial issue at all levels of the national educational system; the debate is not
confined to universities. Despite the apparent uniformity of the issues being
fought over in these multicultural wars of position, there are, in fact, significantly different interests in play and at stake as these battles take place
regionally and in the public and private spheres of education. However, it is im-

portant to recognize that even though this debate is differently inflected at different levels, all aspects constitute a debate about contemporary meanings of race in North America. Indeed, I would argue that multiculturalism is one of the current code words for race—a code just as effective as the word "drugs" or the phrase "inner-city violence" at creating a common-sense awareness that race is, indeed, the subject being evoked.

Since the fall of 1990, we have witnessed a barrage of journalistic attacks on the concept of multiculturalism and attempts to institute multicultural curricula. These reports have either implicitly or explicitly acknowledged multiculturalism as a discourse about race, and many have frequently asserted that there are close and disturbing links between multiculturalism, affirmative action, and threats to freedom of speech guaranteed by the first amendment.

In common-sense terms, affirmative action is no longer referenced by the media as a necessary corrective social policy but as a social problem that itself needs correction. The press's perceptions of the threats to freedom of speech and expression have shaped a moral panic about allegedly terroristic attempts to institute "politically correct" thought and behavior. Indeed, this danger is thought to be so real that it has elicited condemnation from President Bush himself. It is as if the historical contradictions between the original Constitution, which sanctioned slavery, and the fourteenth and fifteenth amendments, have returned to haunt us yet again—only to be dispelled by a form of executive exorcism.

The fundamental contradictions of a society structured by racial inequality from its founding moment have been shaped in the 1990s by an administration in Washington that is not only unsympathetic toward any demands for civil rights but also blatantly antagonistic to such demands. If we also consider the moral panics about affirmative action, antisexist and antiracist codes of behavior, and multiculturalism in the pages of numerous journals like *Time, Newsweek,* the *Atlantic Quarterly,* the *New Republic,* the *Chronicle of Higher Education,* the *Boston Globe,* and the *New York Times,* it would appear as if liberal, as well as conservative, opposition to increasing cultural and ethnic diversity in higher education is becoming entrenched.[8]

For those of us who recognize the need for transformations in our educational systems and in the ways in which we organize fields of knowledge, it is frequently dismaying to consider what is sometimes thought to constitute

change in educational policy and practice. Departments and programs in many
private universities, for example, will proudly point to an "integrated" curriculum while being unable to point to an integrated student body—except in the
photographs in their student handbooks, photographs that contrive to demonstrate "diversity" by self-consciously including the pitiful handful of black/
Latino/Asian/Chicano/and perhaps even fewer American Indian students on
campus. As Nicolaus Mills has argued in his survey of 1990 college publications, the contemporary college view book presents an idealized world in
which the dominant code word is "diversity."[9]

> "Diversity is the hallmark of the Harvard/Radcliffe experience," the first
> sentence in the Harvard University register declares. "Diversity is the virtual
> core of University life," the University of Michigan bulletin announces.
> "Diversity is rooted deeply in the liberal arts tradition and is key to our edu-
> cational philosophy," Connecticut College insists. "Duke's 5,800
> undergraduates come from regions which are truly diverse," the Duke
> University bulletin declares. "Stanford values a class that is both ethnically
> and economically diverse," the Stanford University bulletin notes. Brown
> University says, "When asked to describe the undergraduate life at The
> College—and particularly their first strongest impression of Brown as fresh-
> men—students consistently bring up the same topic: the diversity of the
> student body."[10]

In this context, Mills concludes, diversity means that "a college is doing its best
to abolish the idea that it caters to middle-class whites."[11]

The various cultural and political presences of black women in universities
provide particularly good examples of the contradictions embedded in the various curricular practices that occur under the aegis of "diversity." On many
campuses, coalitions of marginalized and nonmarginalized women, students,
and professors have formed alliances to ensure the inclusion of the histories of
black women, and other previously excluded categories of women, in the university curriculum. But the result has been a patchwork of success and
spectacular failure. Clearly, the syllabi of some courses, particularly within
women's studies and African-American studies programs, have been transformed, and the demand for the establishment of programs in ethnic studies is
both vocal and assertive. However, changes too frequently amount only to the

inclusion of one or two new books in an already established syllabus rather than a reconsideration of the basic conceptual structure of a course.

Within women's studies programs, and within some literature departments, black women writers have been used and, I would argue, abused as cultural and political icons. In spite of the fact that the writing of black women is extraordinarily diverse, complex, and multifaceted, feminist theory has frequently used and abused this material to produce an essential black female subject for its own consumption, a black female subject that represents a single dimension—either the long-suffering or the triumphantly noble aspect of a black community throughout history. Because this black female subject has to carry the burden of representing what is otherwise significantly absent in the curriculum, issues of complexity disappear under the pressure of the demand to give meaning to blackness.

Certainly, we can see how the black female subject has become very profitable for the culture industry. The Harper Collins reprinting of all the previously published books of Zora Neale Hurston, for example, has been an extraordinarily profitable publishing enterprise based primarily on sales within an academic market. [12] We need to ask why black women, or other women who are non-white, are needed as cultural and political icons by the white middle class at this particular moment? What cultural and political need is being expressed, and what role is the black female subject being reduced to play? I would argue that it is necessary to recognize the contradictions between elevating the black female subject to the status of major text within multiculturalism and failing to lead students toward an integrated society, between making the black female a subject in the classroom and failing to integrate university student and faculty bodies on a national scale. Instead of recognizing these contradictions, the black female subject is frequently the means by which many middle-class white students and faculty cleanse their souls and rid themselves of the guilt of living in a society that is still rigidly segregated. Black cultural texts have become fictional substitutes for the lack of any sustained social or political relationships with black people in a society that has retained many of its historical practices of apartheid in housing and schooling.

The cultural, political, and social complexity of black people is consistently denied in those strands of feminist and multicultural theory that emphasize "difference" and use it to mark social, cultural, and political differences as if they were unbridgeable human divisions.[13] This theoretical emphasis on the recognition of difference, of otherness, requires us to ask, different from and for whom? In practice, in the classroom, black texts have been used to focus on the complexity of response in the (white) reader/student's construction of self in relation to a (black) perceived "other." In the motivation of that response, the text has been reduced to a tool. The theoretical paradigm of difference is obsessed with the construction of identities rather than relations of power and domination[14] and, in practice, concentrates on the effect of this difference on a (white) norm. Proponents of multiculturalism and feminist theorists have to interrogate some of their basic and unspoken assumptions: to what extent are fantasized black female and male subjects invented, primarily, to make the white middle class feel better about itself? And at what point do theories of "difference," as they inform academic practices, become totally compatible with, rather than a threat to, the rigid frameworks of segregation and ghettoization at work throughout our society?

We need to recognize that we live in a society in which systems of dominance and subordination are structured through processes of racialization that continuously interact with all other forces of socialization. Theoretically, we should be arguing that everyone in this social order has been constructed in our political imagination as a racialized subject. In this sense, it is important to think about the invention of the category of whiteness as well as that of blackness and, consequently, to make visible what is rendered invisible when viewed as the normative state of existence: the (white) point in space from which we tend to identify difference.

If, instead, we situated all North American peoples as racialized subjects of our political imagination, we would see that processes of racialization are determining to all our work. But processes of racialization, when they are mentioned at all in multicultural debate, are discussed as if they were the sole concern of those particular groups perceived to be racialized subjects. Because the politics of difference work with concepts of individual identity, rather than structures of inequality and exploitation, processes of racialization are marginalized and given symbolic and political meaning only when the subjects are black.

My argument for the centrality of the concept of race is not the same as the assertion, from within the politics of difference, that everyone has an ethnicity. I am not arguing for pluralistic research paradigms or for a politics of pluralism, the result of much work on ethnicity. But, I am arguing for an educational politics that would reveal the structures of power relations at work in the racialization of our social order.

As a final exercise in thinking about the ways the black female subject has been addressed and, to a great extent, invented within the curricular practices designed to increase "diversity," I would like to question the marginalization of the concept of race in the phrase "women of color." This phrase carries a series of complex meanings. Historically, it has its origin in the need of subordinated, marginalized, and exploited groups of women to find common ground with each other, and in the assertion of their desire to establish a system of alliances as "women of color." But what happens when this phrase is then taken up and inserted into the language of difference and diversity? Does "women of color" have other meanings inflected by theories of difference and diversity? I know we are all supposed to be familiar with who is being evoked by this term, but do we honestly think that some people lack color? Do white women and men have no color? What does it mean socially, politically, and culturally not to have color? Are those without color not implicated in a society structured in dominance by race? Are those without color outside of the hierarchy of social relations and not racialized? Are only the so-called colored to be the subjects of a specialized discourse of difference? And, most important, do existing power relations remain intact and unchallenged by this discourse?

We need to ask ourselves some serious questions about our culture and our politics. Is the emphasis on cultural diversity making invisible the politics of race in this increasingly segregated nation, and is the language of cultural diversity a convenient substitute for the political action needed to desegregate? In considering a response, we would be wise to remember Malcolm X's words: "There is nothing that the white man will do to bring about true, sincere citizenship or civil rights recognition for black people in this country... They will always talk it but they won't practice it."[15]

While the attention of faculty and administrators has been directed toward increasing the representation of different social groups in the curriculum or the college handbook, few alliances have been forged with forces across this society that will significantly halt and reverse the declining numbers of black, working-class, and poor people among university student bodies and faculty.

From one perspective, academic language in the decade of the eighties appeared to be at odds with the growing conservatism of the Reagan years. It seemed, at times, as if life in the academy was dominated by questions about the monolithic (and mono-ethnic) nature of courses in Western civilization; about texts that constituted all white and male literary and historical "canons"; and about issues of "diversity" and "difference." Students on campuses all over the country formed movements that condemned apartheid in South Africa and vigorously worked to persuade university administrations to divest their economic holdings in that country. However, we have to confront the fact that the white middle and upper classes in this country, from which these students predominantly come, have, simultaneously, sustained and supported apartheid-like structures that maintain segregation in housing and education in the United States. Comparisons with South African apartheid are a part of the language of black American daily life: the Bronx becomes "New York's Johannesburg"; Chicago is called "Joberg by the Lake"; and the *Minneapolis Star Tribune* is known by black politicians as the "Johannesburg Times."[16]

In Connecticut, the state where I live and work, the state constitution provides for free public elementary and secondary schools and specifically states that "No person shall be subjected to Segregation or Discrimination because of Religion, Race, Color, Ancestry or National Origin."[17] According to a recent report, there are 450,000 children at school in Connecticut, and one out of every four is non-white. But eight out of ten so-called minority students "are concentrated in ten percent of the school districts. By the year 2000, minority enrollments in Hartford, Bridgeport, and New Haven public schools will be approaching one hundred percent."[18]

Such systems of segregation ensure that the black working class and the urban poor will not encroach on the privileged territory of the white middle and upper classes or into the institutions that are the gatekeepers and providers of legitimated access to power, universities included. The integration that has occurred has been primarily on the grounds of class assimilation, and affirmative action has become an important mechanism for advancing a very limited number of black people into the middle class. The admissions practices at Harvard University, discussed in a recent report on affirmative action, are a good example: Harvard has sought to avoid the problem [of attrition] by ensuring that most of its black students come from middle-class families and predominantly white schools. As an admissions officer explained, "It is right for

Harvard and better for the students, because there is better adjustment and less desperate alienation."[19]

Because entry into the professions is a major port of entry into the middle class, universities have been important and contested sites within which to accomplish the transformation of the previously outcast into an acceptable body for integration. The social and political consciousness of the undergraduate population currently enrolled in universities has been formed entirely during the Reagan and Bush years, and the disparity between the groups which have benefited from, and those that have been radically disadvantaged by, the social policies of conservatism is stark. Public systems of education in particular regions have had to respond rather differently from overwhelmingly white private or public universities to questions of diversity and difference.

The New York City educational system, for example, has a population of students, in some schools and colleges, where the so-called minority groups are overwhelmingly in the majority and where issues of difference and diversity are not theoretical playthings at odds with the context in which teaching occurs. New York public schools, which seem to have the most radically diverse and transformed curriculum in the country, find that this curriculum is now under vigorous attack by the New York regents. At the same time, it is precisely the state and city educational systems that have a majority population of black and Hispanic students that are disastrously underfunded. The withdrawal of federal financing and, now, the drastic decline in state and city financing will soon decimate what is left of the promise of the city's schools and colleges.

Meanwhile, in the universities with money, the National Association of Scholars, its friends and allies, and the media campaign against curricular reform have had significant effects in shifting the general climate against educational reform and against affirmative action. Not the least of these effects is the example of the $20 million donation to Yale University for the promotion of scholarship in Western civilization, a donation that was only one of four equivalent donations from the same family within one year. No equivalent donation has ever been made to institute courses in non-Western civilizations that I have been able to find, but I can imagine the difference to the New Haven public school system an injection of $80 million might make.[20] In the public sphere, the most recent presidential educational initiative seeks to replace federal funding of the public schools with corporate funding. One has to ask, will this mean corporate control of the curriculum as well?

In the post–civil rights era, then, one has to wonder at the massive resources being mobilized in opposition to programs or courses that focus on non-white or ethnically diverse topics and issues. One wonders, too, about the strength of the opposition to affirmative action, when social mobility has been gained by so few black people, and black entry into the so-called mainstream has been on the grounds of middle-class acceptability and not the end of segregation. Perhaps it is not too cynical to speculate that the South African government has learned a significant lesson by watching the example of the United States in the last two decades: some of the most important aspects of an apartheid system can be retained without having to maintain rigid apartheid legislation. It is in this social, political, and economic context that I feel it is appropriate and im-portant to question the disparity between the vigor of debates about the inclusion of black subjects on a syllabus and the almost total silence about, and utter disregard for, the material conditions of most black people.

From the vantage point of the academy, it is obvious that the publishing ex-plosion of the fiction of black women has been a major influence in the development of the multicultural curriculum, and I have tried to point to the ways in which the texts of black women and men sit uneasily in a discourse that seems to act as a substitute for the political activity of desegregation. But it is also evident that in white suburban libraries, bookstores, and supermarkets an ever-increasing number of narratives of black lives are easily available. The re-tention of segregated neighborhoods and public schools and the apartheid-like structures of black inner-city versus white suburban life mean that those who read these texts lack the opportunity to grow up in any equitable way with each other.

Indeed, those same readers are part of the white suburban constituency that refuses to support the building of affordable housing in its affluent suburbs, aggressively opposes the bussing of children from the inner city into its neigh-borhood schools, and would fight to the death to prevent its children from being bussed into the urban blight that is the norm for black children. For white suburbia, as well as for white middle-class students in universities, these texts are becoming a way of gaining knowledge of the "other," a knowledge that appears to satisfy and replace the desire to challenge existing frameworks of segregation. Have we, as a society, successfully eliminated the need for achieving integration through political agitation for civil rights and opted instead for knowing each other through cultural texts?

1. Adam Begley, "Henry Louis Gates, Jr.: Black Studies' New Star," *New York Times Magazine,* April 1, 1990, 24–27.

2. Robert S. Boynton, "Princeton's Public Intellectual," *New York Times Magazine,* September 15, 1991, 39, 43, 45, 49.

3. These figures are from the American Council on Education, Office of Minority Concerns, "Seventh Annual Status Report on Minorities in Higher Education," Table 13, as quoted in "Recruitment and Retention of Minority Group Members on the Faculty at Yale," the report of a committee chaired by Judith Rodin, Yale University, 1. In the National Research Council's report *A Common Destiny,* the outlook for black faculty is gloomy: "Figures for 1977–1983 show a drop of 6.2 percent in the number of full-time black faculty at public four-year institutions and of 11.3 percent at private institutions. Black under-representation is greatest at elite universities and at two-year colleges. There is little prospect for growth in black representation in light of the declines in both the percentage of blacks going on to college and the percentage pursuing graduate and professional degrees." Gerald David Jaynes and Robin M. Williams, eds., *A Common Destiny: Blacks and American Society,* National Research Council, (Washington, D. C.: National Academy Press, 1989), 375.

4. Derrick Bell, "Why We Need More Black Professors in Law School," *Boston Sunday Globe,* April 29, 1991, A1.

5. Ibid.

6. Ibid.

7. "Recruitment and Retention of Minority Group Members on the Faculty at Yale," 1.

8. A number of articles in the national and local press have been extremely critical of what is called the "hegemony of the politically correct" and described attempts to transform the canon as "liberal fascism" or terrorism. See, for example, *New York Times,* October 28, 1990, 1, 4; *New York Times,* December 9, 1990, 5; *Chronicle of Higher Education,* November 28, 1990, A5. An issue of *Newsweek* even went so far as to inscribe the words "Thought Police" on stone on its cover: December 24, 1990, 48–55. In contrast, the *Boston Globe Magazine* ran a much more sympathetic account of multiculturalism as a phenomenon of the "melting pot," entitled "The New World." However, it concluded with a negative article on multicultural education, "Too Many Have Let Enthusiasm Outrun Reason," by Kenneth Jackson: October 13, 1991, 27–32.

9. Nicolaus Mills, "The Endless Autumn," *The Nation,* April 16, 1990, 529–531.

10. Ibid.

11. Ibid.

12. Presumably influenced by the possibility of sharing some of the massive profits realized by the publishing industry through marketing the black female subject, film distribution companies have recently begun to vigorously market films about black women to university professors for course use. See Hazel V. Carby, "In Body and Spirit: Representing Black Women Musicians," *Black Music Research Journal* 11 (Fall 1991), 177–192.

13. I would like to thank Paul Gilroy for the many conversations we have had on this issue. His influence upon my thinking has been profound.

14. See Elizabeth Weed, "Introduction: Terms of Reference" in *Coming to Terms: Feminism, Theory, Politics,* ed. Elizabeth Weed

(London: Routledge, 1989), xvii.

15. Video interview with Malcolm X from *A Fan* (1989), an installation by David Hammons at the New Museum, as quoted in Maurice Berger, "Are Art Museums Racist?" *Art in America* (September 1990), 69–77.

16. John Matisonn, reporting for National Public Radio's "All Things Considered, Weekend Edition," February 2, 1991, Transcript, 21.

17. Constitution of the State of Connecticut, 1965, as quoted on the PBS special "Schools in Black and White," produced and written by Vivian Eison and Andrea Haas Hubbell, broadcast September 4, 1991.

18. Ibid.

19. Andrew Hacker, "Affirmative Action: The New Look," *The New York Review,* October 12, 1989, 64.

20. Giving this extraordinary amount of money, $80 million, to an already well-endowed institution needs to be measured against initiatives to support inner-city schools by using black churches as sites for supplemental educational classes and activities. The Association for the Advancement of Science has spent $800,000 over a period of four years for educational programs in eight hundred churches in seventeen cities. The largest donation by a private foundation for church-based educational programs seems to be $2.3 million spread among nine cities from the Carnegie Foundation. See the *New York Times,* August 7, 1991, A1.

Julianne Malveaux

Popular Culture and the Economics of Alienation

Listening to my colleagues talk about their reactions to popular culture, I feel a connection, yet a distance, from their words. I am reminded that I am a social scientist, that I view the world in a way different from the way artists do. I see popular culture as the creative manifestation of that which is happening in the economy. The riveting rhythm of the raps is a reflection, from where I sit, of the awful economic oscillations we are experiencing today. High unemployment rates lead to alienation, to people who are angry and hostile and who express that in their art. Economic uncertainty leads to cynicism, as well. And we see that, hear it, in music, in dance, and on posters. When we talk about popular culture, we come to this from very different places, different disciplinary focuses.

At this moment, the single most powerful aspect of the economy is the way urban areas have been disconnected from funding streams. Cities are getting less money from the federal government, and consequently, they are cutting budgets for health, for social services, and for the arts. Mayors say they have no money to deal with a growing set of needs. And, though their constituencies grouse at their spending patterns, they are not simply "pleading poor." In the urban continuum, we are fighting (in San Francisco, where I come from) to fund HIV services at the same time we're fighting just to inoculate the homeless against the flu virus. People are asking how we prioritize. This is, ultimately, political. If you care about HIV, if you care about the kind of popular culture or other culture that will be funded, if you care about the dissemination of culture, then you need to care about who occupies 1600 Pennsylvania Avenue. You need to care about getting fools out of the White House, out of the Senate, out of the Congress. You need to care enough, be politically involved enough to write letters—daily, weekly—to elected officials, telling them about the programs you think need to be funded.

This is important. Congressional representatives say that for every letter they get, they assume there are a thousand people who aren't writing. In 1988, *Essence* did a survey, and fewer than one percent of the respondents said they had ever written a television station, a radio station, or a manufacturer with an opinion or complaint. At the same time, the ultra-Right floods the media and manufacturers with letters. If Doogie Howser uses a condom, they protest. If the word "abortion" is mentioned, they protest. We complain, here, to each other. But we do not protest.

And the economics of advertising show that the Left buys as much as the Right. If the conservatives boycott Procter & Gamble, then so can we. But they won't know it unless we say something. We are allowing people on the Right to set an artistic agenda by using economic pressure simply because we don't speak up.

And all of this is happening in the midst of competing paradigms. On one hand, with the Berlin wall crumbling, with the Soviet Union collapsing, capitalism is affirmed. On the other hand, there are clear and obvious problems with unrestricted and unfettered capitalism. Neoconservatives talk about the triumph of the individual, but they are really interested in the triumph of profit and capitalism, and we have failed to develop a paradigm that illustrates the weakness in their thinking. Radical economists have failed, in general, to offer alternatives to unfettered capitalism, or even ways to think about how our economy works.

Let me offer a way of looking at capitalism. Let's think of it as a wolf. And let's think of the government as the dentist. Now the wolf is large, ugly, brutal, but if the wolf goes to the dentist, it can be made kinder and gentler (or, alternatively, leaner and meaner). You want the wolf to go to the dentist, but you want the dentist to have the right things in mind. When the wolf went to the dentist under some administrations, the wolf's teeth dulled a bit, so the most wanton effects of capitalism were minimized and we had active social programs. But when the wolf goes to a Reagan-Bush dentist, its teeth are sharpened, social programs are decimated, and the savings and loan industry is looted. The wolf is literally savaging us.

Lorna Simpson, *Untitled*, 1989. An illuminated bus shelter in San Francisco from a project for Art Against AIDS.

I don't mean to be simplistic, but I think this wolf analogy is useful in the absence of an alternative paradigm. What I know is that we need a better dentist for the wolf. When the Reagan-Bush dentist started sharpening the wolf's teeth, these are the words they began to use: deregulation, risk, market forces. You hear them all the time. Government's role, of course, is to be a modifying force when capitalism gets crazy. And capitalism has now gotten crazy; it is lunatic; it needs to be committed, but the dentist isn't even ready to do anything with the wolf. We are living in an economy that has alienated many of us. And that alienation has had cultural outcomes.

The results of economic alienation have been a particular kind of in-your-face culture that speaks to that alienation, as well as a disengagement and lack of involvement among a number of other people. Ninety-seven million Americans, the majority, do not vote, in other words, just don't care, do not think that they can make a difference. If you get a political movement as bold as David Duke's, of course, people will come out. But it was amazing to me that even four percent of African Americans voted for Duke. These folks had been so seriously colonized they were asking for tickets back onto the plantation, much like the slaves that failed to respond to the Emancipation Proclamation.

We will not often find symbols as virulent as a David Duke with pictures of him selling Nazi literature out of his legislative office. But if you decompose something that David Duke said, you'll find in him the governor of California. Pete Wilson said, "We are tired of all these immigrants in California. If we could just get rid of the immigrants, we would have a better quality of life." What immigrants? Who is he talking about? Just a year before he had a conference on trade with the Pacific Rim, charged people $3,200 to come to it and then said, "We'd love to do trade with Japan." Now the immigrants are coming to get us. Well, we know what immigrants he means, and we know what color those immigrants are. Decompose David Duke.

I call Duke a son-of-a-Bush because, if you think about it, you'll find elements of George Bush in David Duke. We will not often get a David Duke, but among these other folks, many of whom are white male, we'll find the same thing.

Let me deal with the symbolism "white male" brings to the table in the urban continuum. Because white men are feeling defensive these days. Everybody picks on them, they say. And you can say white male, white male, with a vocal inflection that makes it sound like a swear word. But let's deal with the income issues. Among wage and salary workers who have incomes over $50,000, there are 8.6 million white males. That represents eleven percent of all white males. In contrast, there are 1.5 million white women (1.8 percent of white women), 229,000—big jump—black men (2.3 percent of black men), and a paltry 89,000 black women (.7 percent of all black women) who make more than $50,000. At a time when we have lack and people are talking about changing configurations, you see who is holding on and why. Consequently, the shorthand "white male" is a very useful shorthand. It is a shorthand reflected in the economics of who has and who does not.

The economics of alienation is about haves and have nots, about a wolf that is leashed or unleashed, about the different dentists the wolf has had. Unregulated capitalism, the unleashed wolf, has decimated our labor market. And that's important because that's where so many of us get our identities. The question "What do you do?" is now a cocktail party staple, but more than that, our work is our means of gaining self-esteem. As Albert Camus said, "Without work all life is rotten." High unemployment rates have reduced millions of Americans to rotten lives.

In the African-American community, we used to say there was always work at the post office, but that is no longer the case. Forty-five thousand people will be laid off from the postal service by 1993. But the post office is not the only place where we'll see these layoffs. You cannot pick up a newspaper without reading about layoffs. IBM, who says, "We never lay off," is laying off. The concept of job security is gone. The core work force is shrinking, and the peripheral or contingent work force is growing. Some contingent workers are well paid, but they are still contingent. Here's an example: John Doggett, the witness for Clarence Thomas in the Senate Judiciary Committee hearings, said he was an international business consultant. In other words, he was a black man with some frequent flyer miles and a business card. And by testifying, he got what was essentially a fifteen-minute free commercial for his business. (Or was it "bidness"?)

Contingent workers don't have health care, don't have pensions, and don't have other benefits. Self-employment is growing incredibly rapidly—many of us choose self-employment so that we can live the way we want to live—but that has long-term implications for the way we plug back into society. It has implications for our health and for our old age, among other things. Meanwhile, we have a president who vetoed the family and medical leave act. Employment in small businesses is growing more rapidly than employment in large businesses, but small businesses are not penalized for discrimination. Employers with fewer than fifteen employees do not have to follow safety and health laws, equal employment opportunity laws, or labor standards laws.

Historically, unionization has been the only protection that many African-American people have had. African-American men in unions earn about fifty percent more than African-American men who are not in unions. For women, the difference is about thirty percent. But the level of unionization is dropping, and fewer and fewer workers are protected by unions. In addition, a structural shift from manufacturing to service employment has created lower-paying jobs.

In the eighties, families in the top fifth of income earnings saw their incomes rise by thirty percent; everybody else saw their incomes drop. This whole notion of deregulation has meant that we have no safety or health in this country. Think of the Imperial Foods fire in Hamlet, North Carolina, where twenty-five women perished, leaving forty-two children without mothers. A disproportionate number of those people were African American. None of them made more than five dollars an hour. This is George Bush's American dream, and this is how you get to the point where 97 million people say, "I cannot change anything about this politics and policy, so I'm not going to vote." The climate is depressing, especially the erosion in our notion of security. All of our financial institutions have also been questioned—not only the savings and loan institutions and banking, but now the insurance companies.

Is there any hope on the horizon? Economists say there is for the top twenty percent of income earners. You measurably improve your chances in life if you go to college, yet, we know that the proportion of African Americans going to college is dropping and that the availability of financial aid is shrinking. Schools will give you $20,000 worth of loans, but no grants. Students are having to borrow more money than their families can earn in a year. Despite the end of the cold war, there is plenty of money for bombs, but not for books.

Why? Because we're funding a massive military-industrial complex; because as soon as the wall started crumbling in Berlin, we found somebody else to mess with in the Persian Gulf. And we will find somebody to mess with again and again to prop up this military-industrial complex.

And we will continue to use the words of alienation against women, and against African-American women, in particular. The welfare mother has suddenly become the most hated person in the country. Since everybody feels like bashing on the welfare mother, let me just say: being on welfare is hard work. It is hard work for a woman to raise two children on less than seven hundred dollars a month. We find ways to pay people when we want to. We've propped up certain individuals with legislative agreements that say "You will be the exclusive contractor for this particular product," but we can't prop up children. Now, that is rhetoric. I would absolutely admit that's rhetoric. Economist Thomas Sowell has written, mocking the liberal rhetoric, "How come you can send a man to the moon, but you can't feed people?" He says it is useless, but I find it useful, because it is a rhetoric that addresses the politics and economics of alienation.

The rhetoric is about priorities, about who funds urban art and other things we care about. The federal government has cut in half the money it sends to cities, and they want to cut it more. What does this mean in the context of competition for urban funds? What gets cut first?

Some of that cut affects not only arts and culture or health and HIV research and care but also institutions at a time when our country is becoming deinstitutionalized. You see people who have been going to a community center for ten years—that's where they hang out—but now there's no community center. You have set them loose from an institution. And we've done that massively.

Forty percent of all African-American families, and about twenty-five percent of all white ones, survive off poverty—not on poverty, but just above the poverty line, because women are working. That means children have decimated institutions in terms of their own families. You're talking about crumbling public institutions. Issues of safety and security are intertwined, and people are not finding safety, are not finding security, are cocooning—and what do people do when they go inward like that?

On one hand, we have a lot of urban conflict—which is a function of everyone feeling there's not a piece of the pie for them. The easy scapegoats are African Americans, because we're visible. It's a Black Thing, You Gotta Understand. When somebody turns on the TV and sees a black woman reading the news, that person figures African Americans have all the jobs. That is *one* job. Who is pointing the camera? Who's the producer? Who's making the decisions? And all the way down the line. But, instead, we get this rhetoric: "Well, I think they should be able to compete with the rest of us."

There has never been any competition except the competition of the wealthy to keep all the wealth. Let's be very real about that.

We also see the alienation of white youth. But I say, *a skinhead is nothing but a white boy without a job.* Absent his beliefs, absent his fear, he is as unemployed as a boy in the 'hood. Lock that boy in a room and make him grow hair, first of all. Give him some skills. He won't have time to run around making hate phone calls and spouting nonsense. He will look for work.

The alienation comes from white youth, the alienation comes from black youth, and so you get this in your face—as Ice Cube said, "Yeah, I want to kill this one, Yeah, I want to do this. . ." He is saying what we all feel. Where is there space for us in this economy? Where is there space for us in this society? Can you value my life? A Korean woman—and this is not race-bashing—got off with five-hundred hours of community service for killing a fifteen-year-old black girl. Community service! Give me a break. And Los Angeles is about to pop right now.

But we are behaving as guests of the black middle class. Black intelligentsia and black artists, I think, aren't especially honest. We behave like guests at the table. We don't say what we need to say. We are sitting there so happy to be at the table that we don't want to say, "What about all the other folks standing at the wayside," see? We built that table, our ancestors served meals at that table. And now this table—it's called society—is locking people out. As long as we have a table that people are looking at, where some are eating and others are not, we're going to have an in-your-face kind of popular culture that speaks of this alienation.

The other issue, in terms of the intertwining of safety and security, is the extent to which television now becomes the educator of choice. Fifty-seven percent of all Americans told pollsters they were afraid to leave their houses at night. Regardless of race. People are staying inside because they're afraid of what's outside, and that means that television has just that much more influence. That's why we have to put this focus on television and look at the economics of both public television (where we're getting very little) and locally produced television (where more and more cities are saying they're not going to produce public affairs programs). So, how do you learn what's happening?

You watch "Oprah" and find out that somebody raped somebody twenty years ago. This becomes what binds us together as a culture. And that's frightening. But it pays. How do we turn it around? I will leave you Cornel West, who always talks about how we renew. But I think we need to combine culture with politics, move people to get involved, put the wolf in a chair, get a reasonable dentist, and turn the rascals out.

Remarks from December 7, 1991. A more extended discussion can be found in Julianne Malveaux, "The Parity Imperative: Civil Rights, Economic Justice, and the New American Dilemma," in *The State of Black America,* ed. William A. Tidwell (New York: National Urban League, 1992).

Barbara Omolade I want to take a few minutes to describe some of the work that I have been doing, because I think there's an absent voice here; that is the voice of African-American working women. I work with women who work in the public sector and are single parents in the African-American communities around New York City. In examining the personal lives of these women, one of the questions I have is about the alienation that this current group of African-American women feels from traditional cultures (which have been very much honored in feminist writings) and about their attempts to survive in the very, very harsh times you've just heard described. The question is: what is the relationship between leisure time and cultural development or appreciation? Because the women that I work with—and the women that I think I have also had the privilege (in many ways, the dubious privilege) of being a part of in terms of my own experiences—are not listening tonight to a discussion about culture; they are cooking, cleaning, raising children, trying to get ready so that they can go to work on Monday. The question is: where is the space in our popular culture, and in our theories about culture, for African-American working-class women?

Julianne Malveaux I think your question, Barbara, is very provocative in terms of the realities that African-American women, especially single mothers and working-class women, face in urban areas where services and programs are being decimated. As you and John Jeffries were talking, I was thinking about the impact of the high and low culture discussion. In listening to this and thinking about the demographic changes that are happening, I was noticing how, despite what happens, we find that our museums and our ballet will always be funded, our symphony will always be funded. You can go on down a list of what will always be funded and what will not be. As cities turn more colored—not only black, but more diverse in general because all cities have been magnets for

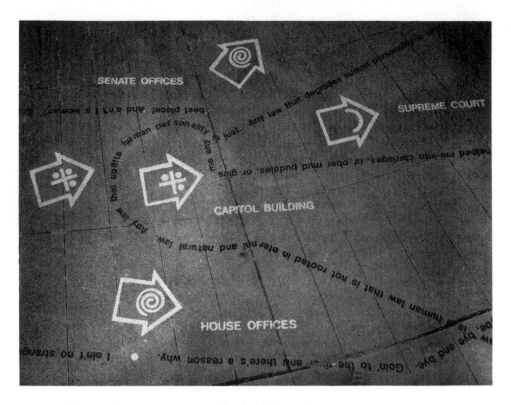

Houston Conwill, *Markings on the Sand* (detail), 1989

people who are immigrants and, in many ways, others—we must think about how we get control of these budgets. How do we take some of high art's money to give to low art—I don't like that word "low" actually—*our* art?

When we place these art issues in a sociopolitical context and suggest that women can make a difference in allocation decisions, we also suggest that they can take on another burden, another involvement, that they can add another burden to backs which can't (supposedly) break. In placing issues of art allocation in the political context, we ask people to come out, walk a precinct, do some calling. And of course that involvement is important. But equally important is the notion that these women have limits, that they are supposed to be challenged by art, not challenged to obtain it. Given paid work, household work, child care, and other requirements, asking urban women to do one more thing borders on the impossible. But we keep doing it when we raise questions about who gets arts funding.

When we look at urban budgets or come up against something like the Bass family giving $80 million to Yale, as Hazel Carby mentioned, we should be clear to recognize that privilege is being reinforced. Bass gives money to fund western culture, but who gives money for "expansion" arts. If we are being fair about this, it is clear that Bass funds ought to free up other funds at Yale. This is really about the allocation of resources and remembering that the composition of our cultural audience is shifting. Bass funds should be about opening doors, not reinforcing the barricades that keep people out.

Public television raises the question of who is the public. Most programming falls into the pale male talking-head stereotype. Despite the fact that an African-American woman is in charge of programming at the Public Broadcasting Service, some people have brought her things that have been described as "too black."

A woman named Dell Marie Cobb has a fantastic program in Chicago called "Street Life." It's a news magazine–type program where all the correspondents are African American. This show is enthusiastically received in Chicago, but not nationally. If four black people talking news is too black, can we dismiss the McLaughlin Group on the basis that four white people talking news are too white?

What are we producing, and for whom? What does that mean about what we think of "high" art and "low" art? We have to answer these questions in the context of public sector dollars, public broadcasting, state funding for the arts, and urban arts initiatives. The task for cultural workers and for political activists is to make sure that all kinds of art is shown in all kinds of places. This may mean staging a play in a public-housing project, or mounting an exhibit in a community center, not an art gallery. It means planting white hyacinths in places we have become accustomed to neglecting. If the purpose of art in society is to nurture and to challenge, then there must be some place for art in places where urban women, African-American women work, live, and congregate.

Question The problem of talking about where the faces of African-American women are in culture is already evident here, where the majority of people are white. This is a conference on black popular culture, but we barely have enough black people who know about this thing, or have been reached out to, in order to listen and voice our concerns. Maybe that's just a sign of the way things are

Bill Sanders, from "Demolished by Neglect," a project organized by the Urban Center for Photography, a coalition of photographers in Detroit. The photographer placed photomurals of a child doing drugs in the back door of a crack house as a reminder of young victims of the drug dealer's trade.

today and where we need to go, but to me, it's a rather frightening concept that there just aren't enough of us doing this. And we're keeping it among ourselves.

Valerie Smith I have a question about the relationship between cultural critics, intellectuals, or whatever you want to call us, and the work that we're doing on topics that have to do with the urban context. It seems to me that around issues such as domestic violence, for example, and even to some degree, albeit inadequately, around issues of sexuality, I always feel there is a framework. But when I want to talk about issues of substance abuse, I find that I don't have a way into talking about these kinds of questions. I was listening to this panel on the urban context, in particular, to see how people would enter into that conversation. I know Julianne Malveaux addressed it to some degree, but I wondered if the panelists could discuss some ways cultural critics could begin to talk about how issues relating to substance abuse figure into circumstances among African Americans in the urban context. And, for me, this also raises a question about where my first question comes from. I'm concerned about a kind of parasitic quality that plagues my own work: In looking for a way to talk about these kinds of issues, what is the payoff for me? What is the payoff for the population affected by the issues that are so puzzling to me?

John Jeffries That's an interesting question. In this redefinition of what the urban is, one of the things that I am suggesting is that we have to be careful about what the redefinition entails, but, at the same time, we really have to go about the job of redefining. In thinking about what the urban is, for example, we have some preconceptions. And on the East Coast, we'll have to reveal our East Coast biases. For those of us who live on the East Coast, especially considering the way L. A., with its urban conflict and gangs, has been described to us in the newspapers, some of the images that were most shocking in *Boyz N the Hood* were the shots of the low-density housing. Many of us in East Coast audiences either subconsciously or unconsciously asked, "Where's the city?"

Now, that kind of question reveals a kind of regionalism. But, what's more important are the film's two powerful answers to that question. One was, "It's a violent place." Helicopters, police violence, or boyz against boyz violence— therefore, it must be an urban place. That clears it up for us. The other answer came in the specific depictions of black women—female-headed households, bodies booming, children out on the street, single women who have difficulties—"Oh yeah, that's urban." Unfortunately, our understanding of the urban is complicated by ideas and images about density, about what a lot of people being in a small place implies. And these generalizations come from the Enlightenment influence.

I referred to the schizophrenia that African Americans in particular experience. On the one hand, cities are positive because they are the places, literally—and feminist theory is quite direct about this—where what's public and what's private is open to contestation. The urban is the place where anything goes, and black folks take that as positive. Hence, the urban is the place of hip, and even, in the anti-intellectual parts of it, stupid hip—like hip-cubed or something. Now, on the other hand, notions of the urban which imply that the "place" cannot be transformed are problematic. Although cities are places where lots of things are tolerated, our interpretation of what's positive and negative in cities is often ambiguous. To the extent that artists are involved in observing activity and behavior through lenses that other people don't always have access to, substance abuse, for example, is an example of a positive and negative urban activity in which black folks are involved—which, for me, makes it legitimate subject matter.

One of the reasons, again, that urbanness and substance abuse come together, and are legitimated, is because—and here's where capitalist cultural imperialism comes in—the people that are involved in it conceive of it as a business activity. They say, "Hey, it's not personal. Nothing but business. I got to do you because you're going to do me." It's all about collecting dead presidents and the magnitude associated with doing that. And the reason we feel okay and uneasy about that at the same time is because of the business end of the activity. The violence is legitimated because, "Well, we don't have access to jobs, the labor market sucks, and what really matters is the bottom line—money." We hear, and often employ, those kinds of rationalizations. For people who are artists, then, it seems to me that anything within the urban center is worth looking at through a variety of lenses because it is always, in fact, hybrid social activity. There is no pure way to think about these things. The whole notion of a search for authenticity, I would argue, is suspect.

In the late sixties, one of the most popular films was *Panic in Needle Park*. It was about junkies talking about junkies. Al Pacino, the lead in the film, was not a junkie in his personal life, but what made the film "real" was the urban footage that was shot for the film. What I'm suggesting is, jump in, tell us what you see. We may not like it, but we need to have other kinds of less than "authentic" views about this thing called urban. Because what we're being told is urban is precisely what needs to be transformed.

One more thing. Urban planners now use a method they call "behavioral mapping." They use it to get a feel for the functionality of a place, to determine how people interact in specific surroundings. For example, a planner will sit in the corner of an emergency room and watch and take notes. Just sitting there, without actually interacting, taking the *time* to absorb the personality of a place, helps them to make better decisions about creating other spaces and improving existing ones. What I am suggesting is that artists and social scientists could learn from each other about the means of observation and representation. It is this kind of dialogue that is important here.

Question I'm from Toronto, Canada, and I'd like to address Sherley Anne Williams on the issue of rap music. I work at a radio station there—a community radio station—and I've been involved with rap music for a number of years. One of our most popular programs is a rap show that has been on the air for years and years. It has done a lot for the local black community, particularly for black youth. I thought your talk was important because we need to be talking about rap music in public spaces like this, but I want to take issue with some of the points you made.

If I did not know what I know about rap music as a whole, I wouldn't know that there is much good about it. You have to have a deep understanding of the American music industry. American music dominates the whole music industry, in Canada as elsewhere. In Toronto, just as in the United States, we have two different kinds of rap scenes: the commercial scene, which promotes a certain kind of rap and hip hop; and the street scene, in which there are a number of different things happening all the time. A certain amount of rap is extremely conscious and positive, but it doesn't get promoted, except on the community radio stations, which don't get any respect in these kinds of gatherings. It's important to say that because there's an activist media community that isn't visible here.

Anyway, a young rapper from Toronto went to L. A. to work on a record deal with a major American label. His raps range from the sexist and misogynist stuff to the more conscious stuff, and he's grappling with the issue of sexism and trying to bring that out in his rap. They went through his songs. They ditched all the conscious stuff and said, "We want more 'bitches' and we want more 'ho's'." I think that's an issue that should be dealt with more directly by academics. I've used a lot of academic work in my own radio program to back up a lot of what I have to say. So, I'm not saying this to attack you, but I feel it's something that needs to be addressed.

Sherley Anne Williams Certainly, from your tone of voice and also from the content of what you said, I don't really feel attacked in any way. Having said that, let me say again that I think the best rap is characterized by what are positive messages, or innocuous messages and funky beats. It is, after all, music; it's not something that can take the kind of political load that a lot of people have tried to give it. Part of the difficulty is that you have these destructive and pernicious lyrics that are not emanating from a fully articulated or even conscious intellectual or ideological stance but still have political and social repercussions. Black people are under attack from so many sides that even questions can seem like another attack. I recognize what you say, but I also feel that we have to be, where necessary, very clear about what some of these lyrics are saying.

Question This is an open question. To what extent would it be possible for us to move urban life and urban understanding away from commodities? In different ways, everybody on the panel has talked about a certain sense of frustration with the way in which people, social ills, cultural products, and artistic endeavors all become products to be consumed. I think the cynicism and the inhumanity involved with that is obvious. Yet, for us to address that, there must be some sort of organizational structure that doesn't simply involve criticism, or criticism of criticism, but some kind of organized movement that will actually try to reorient people's vision away from commodification, away from the taking and buying and selling of goods and toward a more humane exchange.

What can we do to move in that direction and away from the kind of capitalist dispossession and inhumanity we have now?

Barbara Omolade I don't think you can talk about economic transformation unless you're talking about a revolutionary political movement. You can't do it through culture, and you can't do it through academic work. As a kind of middle ground, though, John Jeffries and I just came from the Paulo Freire Conference. It's a conference about critical pedagogy, and it seems to me that those of us who are multiculturalists or teachers at the college level, and certainly the people who teach in the public schools and public high schools, have a tremendous responsibility, if we are somewhat conscious, to try to integrate into those educational studies a vision of a new kind of society. The role of culture and cultural workers can help facilitate that process. I always think you have to take it back to people in the community—and I include schools as a community space—to really begin to talk about how we can transform. To me, that can't be answered by a panel. It really is a *process* that is ultimately going to be political and revolutionary.

John Jeffries Forgive me for sounding like a teacher, but I have a very important point of clarification. You cannot think of commodity or exchange and capitalism as synonymous. What is difficult and oppressive is capitalism. Commodities, when exchanged, may be just fine. It is capitalism that dictates the way in which those things are commodified, the way they are exchanged, the value that they hold, and what that implies about their distribution. That's what is problematic. So, if you want to think about your question, we ought to be thinking about the particular economic system that dictates how we get not only those material things we need for physical reproduction, but also those material things we need for our cultural reproduction. And part of the problem is not that we have to commodify or exchange them, but, quite the contrary, that they are commodified and exchanged under a capitalist economic system. That's what makes it difficult. That's what makes it hard for us to think about what it is we would do next. So, if you pose your question again, I would decouple those things to help all of us think about what it is we are actually attempting to do.

Discussion

Kofi Natambu One of the definitions of urban, if I may extrapolate on that, is a site where there is a war going on, and where there has been a war going on forever, over the future identity of the United States. When we talk about political economy and the world capitalist economic system that rules us all, what we're really talking about—when we talk about all these racial and sexual identities and the conflicts and problems between classes and between men and women—is the urban as a site for the attempted resolution of those questions.

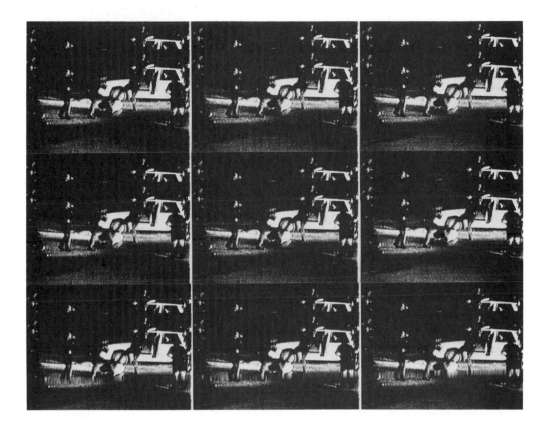

Danny Tisdale, *Rodney King Police Beating 1991, Disaster Series*, 1992.

The Production of Black Popular Culture

Tricia Rose

Black Texts/Black Contexts

When we speak about the production of Black popular culture, we need to keep at least two kinds of questions in the foreground: the first has to do with Black aesthetics, style, and articulation, and the hybridization of Black practices; and the second involves the historical context for the creation, dissemination, and reception of Black popular forms. Now, this may seem kind of obvious. I hope it does, because what often happens instead is that people attend to one or the other, focus so much on one that they can't explain what's taking place at the other site. The tendency, therefore, is to look at these factors in isolation.

Without historical contextualization, aesthetics are naturalized, and certain cultural practices are made to appear essential to a given group of people. On the other hand, without aesthetic considerations, Black cultural practices are reduced to extensions of sociohistorical circumstances. Rap music, for example, has been explained in ways that reflect the gap between these two kinds of questions. We understand urban America as the reason we have rap music, or we see rap merely as an extension of Black oral traditions that sort of floated over time and dropped somewhere on Southern Boulevard in the Bronx. It is really important, instead, to hold *both* these kinds of questions and investigations, the aesthetic and the cultural, in tension.

I'm going to give two examples from my own research that demonstrate why maintaining a balance between addressing questions of style and understanding the significance of the social contexts for stylization is so important. One example centers around technology in rap, the other around sexism and rap lyrics; in both cases, I want to look at gender and at the social contexts for production and reception.

Obviously, digital technology has been critical to the ways in which rap music has developed. It has revised Black aesthetics such that processes of intertextuality, versioning, the cut and the break, and percussive pleasure are very different now. Consequently, rap has changed the way technology functions: rap producers use sampling machines in ways that have revised their "normal" uses. New machines are now designed to accommodate the kinds of bleed factors that many rap producers use, and rappers are thinking about intertextuality with the digital technology in the front of their minds and at their fingertips. These things take place simultaneously: technological development creates new recording possibilities; and rap artists find new ways of making the technology respond to Black stylistic priorities. Increased access to recording facilities and multitrack production means you don't have to be a millionaire to do certain kinds of recording and composing and that you can copy your tapes in mass quantities and get paid (in full).

But who has access to this technology? All the usual suspects—culture industries, technofreaks, and middle-class "boy toy" consumers—continue to have access to new technologies, and young Black males have more access now than ever before. But this access has not been afforded to Black women; there are almost no Black women rap producers. My interviews with rap producers indicate that this is true because of the ways in which public space gets territorialized as a privileged site of production for men. Even male rap producers with either very strong feminist friends or some sort of feminist ideology themselves have found that the men just don't feel comfortable if there are women interns around in the studio. They can't say all the things they would normally say because they might offend these women. And even when these women say, "It doesn't matter. You can say whatever you want to me, I want to learn this stuff," eventually the male creative process is challenged.

Now, this gender dynamic is not a given, but it is one of the contexts that needs to be talked about in relation to technology and access to it. That there are so few women rap producers is not just a matter of access to the technology; it's also about the social site in which that technology is deployed and the different aspects of cultural capital created there. In other words, cultural capital is not only about the development of technology, but also about social sites and how ideas are shared in them. This involves power relationships, gender, race, and class, and the shifting relations between them.

The access to and use of advances in technology also depend on where and how we actually participate in reception and production. Today we not only get

Still from *Young Soul Rebels*, directed by Isaac Julien, 1991.

sounds sliding by—huge, amazing sounds on jeeps and boomin' systems—but we also get home video and the walkpeople (walkmen and walkwomen). The sounds we hear are often linked to the mode of sound reception most suited to the social terrain. For example, as Chuck D. has suggested, the music that comes out of New York is often produced with the walkpeople's earphone acoustics in mind, whereas, the more auto-based cities of Miami and Los Angeles produce music that reflects automobile cultures and acoustics.

The second example I want to draw on to illuminate the tension between aesthetics and sociohistorical contexts is the interpretation of rap's sexism and misogyny. Sherley Anne Williams's talk about rap grossly misunderstood the context within which rap develops and, unintentionally perhaps, located sexism in rap as an anticommunity symptom of a postindustrial urban nightmare rather than a manifestation of a long-standing set of gender relations.* If any of us heard a toast or prison boast from a hundred years ago, it would make our hair either curl or straighten, respectively. And many of those early toasts would

*References are to Sherley Anne Williams's talk at the conference and not the version presented in this collection.

make the 2-Live Crew sit their whiney asses down in a minute because they do not have the final word on sexism. It is critical to understand that male rappers did not invent sexism. Black practices have been openly sexist for a long time, and in this regard they keep solid company with many other highly revered dominant Western practices. Today's rappers are not alone in their symbolic objectification of Black women. They have lots of real live, and substantially more powerful, company, none of whom rap or make records.

The problem is: one, that technology brings these vernacular practices, the practices most vulnerable to middle-class outrage, into spaces where they might never have been heard twenty-five years ago; and two, rappers are vulnerable, highly visible cultural workers, which leaves them open to increased sanctions. But sexism, at the level of the toast and the boast, is only a subset of structurally sanctioned sexism. In that way, all manner of cultural practices and discourses that do not challenge the structures upon which these ideas are based wind up confirming them. Why, then, is the concern over rap lyrics so incredibly intense, particularly from Black middle-class guardians? Why not the same level of moral outrage over the life options that Black folks face in this country? It seems to me we need a censorship committee against poverty, sexism, and racism.

To acknowledge the history of sexism is not to say that sexist articulations do not change over time. The toasts of a hundred years ago are not the same as rap lyrics today. Again, what I am trying to talk about is the way aesthetic practices and historical conditions must stay joined in our analysis. The tenor and focus of the attacks on Black women in rap lyrics speak to contemporary heterosexual Black male anxieties. Black male anxieties regarding Black women and their newfound sexual freedoms, as well as Black male fears of vulnerability are cast in distinctly late-twentieth-century language describing the transformation of courtship rituals, marriage, economic equality, and commitment. Sexism in rap is not a direct outgrowth of the process of deindustrialization and the assault on Black America. The history of sexism is longer and much more complex than that. Nor is rap responsible for harassment and violence against women. If this were so, how would we explain the history of abuses against women. The blues? Rock 'n' roll? Better yet, how would we explain the sexism of Clarence Thomas and the entire U.S. Senate? Maybe they're closet rap fans...

More often than not, rap lyrics articulate a wide range of ideas about contemporary life in urban America, usually rearticulating already existing ideas about Black identity, community, and the class and gender frictions which lie just beneath the surface. For this reason, I'm quite disappointed that a conference on Black popular culture did not devote a panel exclusively to rap so that rap's articulations, its emergence from disco culture, its technological revisions, and its incorporation and containment could be more fully explored. Many of the ideas expressed in rap are the most disturbing, powerful, and important to have emerged from any cultural workers in quite some time. And this is a great deal more than I can say for most politicians, and others who enter the arena of public discourse. At least rappers got style.

Ada Gay Griffin

Seizing the Moving Image:

Reflections of a Black Independent Producer

I am the executive director of Third World Newsreel, one of the oldest media centers in the United States dedicated to supporting the production and dissemination of alternative media, that is, independent film and video by Africans, Asians, Latinos, Arabs, Pacific Islanders, and Native peoples throughout the world.

Third World Newsreel has embodied, since its inception, what has become a very unpopular perspective—the multicultural. It is unrelenting in its prioritization of perspectives and in the involvement of third-world peoples in shaping the utility of the moving image. Third World Newsreel has a distribution service, two production workshops, a film archive, sponsors touring exhibitions of third-world cinema and video programs, and provides production facilities and technical support to independent producers. We produce about two third-world productions each year in house.

Given my position in this kind of organization, one of about a dozen or so that exist in this country—the numbers are growing, but media centers dedicated to a multicultural perspective remain exceedingly fragile institutions, underfinanced and overextended—you might imagine that I have a position on Black culture as it relates to independent film and video production. And I do.

Before I say what it is, let me say that it occurred to me, when I saw the poster for this conference (of Anita Hill and Clarence Thomas), that I'd been thinking about lynching for the last couple of months or so. It reminded me that one moment in my early defining of who I was and exploring my history and culture was organized around the image of a Black person being lynched. That kind of phenomenon was often explained to me as a reaction by white people to their fear and ignorance of Black people. And it occurs to me, when I think about that explanation and how often it is used to describe the reactions of white supremacists to black people, that much of the time the fact of lynching, of being dehumanized in any way on the basis of race, is not explained in terms of the terror the subject of that racism experiences.

The fundamental aspects of Black cultural production and Black culture itself are underlined by a certain terror that is constantly in our consciousness. Having an independent thought is a question of survival. And our cultural survival consists primarily of what we do minute by minute when we are not selling our labor and souls on the market. Black culture is the product of an ongoing struggle between the extremes of defiance and assimilation, of resistance and complacency. Those aspects of our culture and history that come most often to our attention, usually because they have been popularized by or expropriated by the dominant society, tend to line up along the side of assimilation and, as a consequence, are available as vehicles for our oppression.

Many aspects of mainstream culture—which virtually everyone assumes originates in some mythological, perfect Europe—are actually products of Black struggle, such as universal literacy. Public education, for example, did not exist as an institution in this country until it was demanded and fought for by former slaves. Although most of us are aware of the influence of jazz and hip hop and, of late, Malcolm X (now twenty-five years gone, he is cool for our children to learn about), Assata Shakur, who's very much alive and in danger, is not cool to learn about. What are the origins of a worldview that determines Black heroes to be dead and living revolutionaries to be dead wrong? For most of us, the reality of our history and culture as Africans in America has come to us through a conscious and necessary pursuit, a decision to ask and answer difficult questions about a community comprising different and often seemingly contradictory parts. What do we share? In what ways is a Black community in the United States singular and distinct? Well, we share a common heritage that began in Africa, ancestors who experienced middle passage, chattel slavery, and Jim Crow. We all live daily, minute by minute, with the reality of racist oppression, whether we admit it or not, and each of us experiences discrimination and bigotry because of our race.

The reality of being an African American in the United States, or in any other community on the two American continents, is more and more anything

230 Still from *Dreaming Rivers*, directed by Martina Atille and Sankofa, 1988.

but a singular identity or experience. Our people's culture—which is both self-determined and imposed by an institutionalized oppression imitating colonialism—is made up of the particularities and interactions of many communities and identities. But it is also true that our shared historical oppression, our current condition, and our vision as a people link us to each other. For those of us who seek to position ourselves in the continuing struggle for the liberation of all Black people, our cultural legacy is to create work that reflects and embodies that struggle and propels it forward. So, as a cultural worker, as an independent producer, and as a filmmaker, it has been necessary for me to develop a working definition of Black cinema, in general, and of filmmaking by Black women, in particular. And I must constantly investigate the conditions and possibilities for producing oppositional work and having it seen.

Black films, Black videos, and Black media are those productions directed by Black artists on subjects and forms that reference the Black experience and imagination. They are productions in which the artistic vision is controlled by a person of African descent. They are not productions by Asians, of that diaspora, who identify themselves politically as Black, nor are they productions by white directors based on adaptations of Black plays, Black novels, or even scripts written by people of African descent. They are not productions in which Black crews or even Black actors are primarily or exclusively used. Why is it important to make this distinction? For the same reason it has been important in other areas of the arts, particularly literature and fine art, but also music. Ultimately, it is about power over the image.

The moving-image medium, now one hundred years old, is currently the primary apparatus for the communication of information, ideas, and history in this country. The issue of the consumption of media is becoming inconsequential next to that of the ownership of production, and now distribution—soon to be almost exclusively carried out by telephone wire. To make significant changes in what is presented in theaters and on TV, we need to support the alternatives to the media readily available in these forms.

As consumers of Black film, it has become fashionable to ask the question, "Where are the Black women filmmakers?" This question is finally being asked by Black feminists. I have to say that there are several Black women who have either recently completed, or are in the process of making, their first feature films. Examples are Julie Dash and her film *Daughters of the Dust,* Neema Barnett (who just signed a deal with a major studio in Los Angeles to produce a feature film), and Ayoka Chenzira (who is seeking completion money for her first feature film). At least a dozen other Black women directors have produced feature films that have not received commercial financing or theatrical distribution. And, of course, Euzanne Palcy, the Martiniquian filmmaker, proved she is a highly competent and political filmmaker with *A Dry White Season.*

But what makes pursuit of the reality of Black women's filmmaking possible? Although I cannot speak for all Black women filmmakers, I think it is the material evidence that an alternative filmic vision is possible. For me, it was seeing films by Sarah Gomez, Haile Gerima, and Third World Newsreel in the late seventies. I distinctly remember the first time I met a Black woman filmmaker—and this story points to what has become the lie of drawing a straightforward gender analysis in terms of examining Black film production. It was in 1980, and I remember driving several miles to the University of Pittsburgh to see a film called *The Cruz Brothers and Miss Malloy,* which was to be followed by a discussion with the filmmaker, Kathleen Collins.

The film is about the relationship of an aging white woman to two Puerto Rican teenagers who become her groundskeepers on an estate in upstate New York. After the film was shown, there were two questions posed to Collins. The first was a question I also wanted to ask: "This film didn't have any Black characters. Do you plan to make any films with Black characters in them?" Her response was, yes, she certainly intended to do that. But she went on to say that she did not define herself as a Black filmmaker or as a woman filmmaker, but simply as a filmmaker who could make films about anything she wanted to, and she refused to be labelled by any term. As a twenty-four-year-old Black woman, I was pretty crushed by that response. And it's a response I am still trying to learn from.

As I said before, we do not all approach the process of making films in the same way. I began to make films by watching independent and third-world cinema a long time ago. I also studied Black women's literature, theater, and political science, and attended some of the first Black feminist studies courses ever presented in this country. This experience helped develop the perspective that has enabled me to believe I can make a film about Audre Lorde—and I'm engaged in the process of making that film, a documentary that explores her life and legacy. This film charts her life, as she describes herself, as a Black/lesbian/mother/poet/warrior who proposes, in her actions and her words, the acknowledgment and respect of racial, cultural, sexual, and gender differences as prerequisites for overcoming shared oppression.

I am in the sixth year of making this film, which is not unusual for Black women filmmakers, or independent filmmakers for that matter. I'm working with Michelle Parkerson, who is herself a Black feminist, a lesbian, a poet, and a proud dread woman, who has worked in film and television for two decades. Like dozens of other Black women filmmakers, we cannot finish our film until we raise the money to complete it. In other words, we began it, and we produce it as we go along raising the funds. This hasn't been easy for us, presumably because Audre is a lesbian and because we are Black women. The point is: in raising funds for this film, every cent, with the exception of $150, has come from individuals who are either women of color or lesbians or both, or from foundations where the program director has been a woman of color or a lesbian or both. And this is not because we haven't tried to get money from other places. And I think this situation quite obviously reflects the prevailing conditions faced by Black women when we want to tell our stories on film.

Thomas Allen Harris

About Face:

The Evolution of a Black Producer

I am an activist, an advocate, and a cultural warrior who is continually exploring, searching for new and different media venues in which to work effectively.
Over the past four years, I have been developing my critical process and applying it to my work as a producer of videos and films, as well as public affairs
programs for public television. As a staff producer/journalist for two New
York City public television shows, "The Eleventh Hour" and "Thirteen Live," I
produced public affairs programs that provided forums on local and national
issues: black and Latino veterans from World War II, Korea, and Vietnam discussing the Gulf War; black, white, and lesbian feminists on women and the
war; black men and black families; and adolescents and AIDS. In these programs,
I presented perspectives from various communities generally marginalized from
and silenced in mainstream media. My programs attempted to reflect the different communities constituting New York City, including community activists,
critics, students, lesbians and gays, and people with AIDS [PWAs], in addition
to the usual fare of elected officials, bureaucrats, and other "experts."

Although the programs were well received (judging by the audience response and two Emmy nominations), they often drew criticism from the show's
executive producers, who accused me of activism (as opposed to journalism).
Their position was that, though there is no such thing as "absolute objectivity,"
we as journalists must make every attempt to appear neutral (in the guise of
maintaining balance). Ultimately, this meant trying not to betray that we actually did have a point of view. I, on the other hand, was aware that every step of
the media-generating process is subject to what Stuart Hall calls the "common
sense" of the producer. That is to say, the process is subject to the producer's

Still from *Race Against Prime Time*, produced and directed by David Schulman, 1985.

values, prejudices, and personal investments. It became clear to me that journalism's adherence to "objectivity" was simply another way to obscure its interests and its power.

The programs I produced came out of my experiences as a black gay male raised in a working-class community in the Bronx, who has also lived and traveled abroad in Africa and Europe for four years. It was in the process of attempting to hold true to these experiences that I became increasingly aware of my relationship to, and my personal investment in, the subject matter I approached. I was interested in disclosing this investment in ways that were critical, self-reflexive, and accessible. The challenge was to accomplish this within a corporate broadcast media structure. My executive producers responded to my programs by telling me with a chuckle: "You don't need to produce a mini–United Nations each week."

A program entitled "The Changing Face of the AIDS Epidemic" provoked particularly harsh criticism. This program had a roundtable format with a host and four guests: a black female doctor who worked principally within black and Latino communities, a white male doctor whose patients were generally middle-class gay men, and two PWAs—Norma, a Latina AIDS activist, grandmother, and former IV drug user, and a white gay professional who had been living with AIDS more than six years.

The program was very successful because it differentiated along the socioeconomic tiers of the AIDS epidemic and among the axes of gender, race, and class. It not only fleshed out different perspectives on AIDS in an engaging manner, but also allowed people from different communities to enter into dialogue with one another.

After the program, my executives castigated me by calling the program a failure. *They* did not understand Norma and told me I showed poor judgment in booking this inarticulate woman. Norma did not speak like the college-educated white gay man sitting next to her, nor did her life experience coincide with his. She had a mild accent and spoke like most of her education came from the street. Prior to booking her, however, we had several long telephone conversations and understood each other perfectly.

I informed my executives that not only did I understand Norma, but I also considered her to be a wise and courageous woman. The program would have been a failure without her. Their response was that our audience wouldn't, as they hadn't, understand Norma and would find her contribution nothing but annoying. This seemed all the more absurd considering I had been hired for the perspective I would bring to the show. Their attack on my judgment was an attack on the experience and background that enabled Norma and I to communicate and empathize with one another. It is no surprise, then, that public television fails miserably in its reputed attempts to attract black, Latino, and Asian viewing audiences in a city where these constitute the majority.

How does one get around white middle-class heterosexual biases working within broadcast media?

As a response to multicultural pressures, public television has made cursory efforts to compensate for white middle-class heterosexual biases by hiring token producers of color. Real changes, however, can occur only when there is diversity at the level of creative decision-making that reflects the populations being served (or not served). Tokenist inclusion is more often than not accompanied by a relative lack of power (for the token, of course) and much frustration. As the only black staff producer who was also a member of many different communities—from independent media to the arts and lesbian and gay communities—I was constantly banging my head up against calls for "balance." This left little room for complexity or a plurality of voices that might deconstruct monolithic notions of identity even within ethnic, sexual, gender, and economic groupings.

I have often wondered how different my experience would have been if I had worked for a black executive producer or for a black producing entity. In thinking about this question, I recalled that at New York City's public television station, WNET, two of the top executives are black men, and, in fact, the programming czar of Public Broadcasting Service is a black woman. Yet, black producers have to fight to do black shows. On programs that are not exclusively produced by blacks, there are other kinds of problems. "Edge," for example—a nationally aired arts magazine show produced jointly by PBS and the British Broadcasting Corporation, reputedly about American popular culture—had only one staff producer of color, a black woman. At the time she left the show, not one of her segments had ever made the air. Yet, the person who okayed the "Edge" series is a black woman.

Another example: The first person to censor Marlon Riggs's experimental documentary about black gay men, *Tongues Untied,* was a black executive of a major public television station in Boston. Ironically, he objected to Riggs's representation of black men.

Is it enough to have a black person in a position of power?

To paraphrase Isaac Julien, "Black is no longer enough for me. I want to know what your politics are." So, I'm not satisfied with the token or symbolic inclusion of blacks as an answer to the problem of black people being able to articulate our concerns. Black perspectives on public TV, on public affairs programs, on television in general, are fragmented and discontinuous precisely because of these very acts of tokenism. In fact, for the past twenty years, the Right has used tokenism to dismantle affirmative action and other legal gains of the sixties. And this continues today, as evidenced by the confirmation of

Clarence Thomas to the Supreme Court and the appointment of the various black officials who have been responsible for dismantling not only affirmative action policies, but also funding for education, health, and welfare.

At this point, whenever I see one or a few of us anywhere, I'm on my guard because it means that person, or those few people, are the gatekeepers. And I want to address this issue specifically in relation to this conference—the organizers and the panelists, myself included.

The politics of location: Black popular culture at the Dia Center for the Arts—Is it an accident? Does it matter?

I find it ironic that Clarence Thomas and Anita Hill are on the poster for this conference because it underscores for me the parallel between the Thomas hearings before Congress and this conference being held at Dia. Both Thomas and Hill were keenly aware that the buck stopped at Congress—the entity that would decide their legitimacy and authenticity—and they directed their performances accordingly.

Holding this conference here at Dia legitimizes it in very tangible ways: money, visibility, and prestige. But as I stand here at the podium looking out at the audience, this space, Dia, seems to be a very white space—physically and psychically. Some of the audience members are funders of the arts or deans of academic institutions—white people with money and power and jobs to offer. They are here to learn, but what will they do with that knowledge? Are they going to fund our projects? Will they use the knowledge garnered here in ways that are productive to our communities? How is black popular culture defined in this context? As black critics, intellectuals, and producers, we must articulate our relationship with this audience and this space as we engage in this performance we are calling the Black Popular Culture conference.

I do not acknowledge whiteness here to warn black folks to be careful with our "dirty laundry." On the contrary, it is precisely those difficult, deeply personal, and funky areas that must be addressed to truly claim this space as our own. We must privilege the contradictions, the ambivalences, the fluidity, and the complexity of black diasporic culture in the modern world.

Here at the Black Popular Culture conference, we are not discussing the pressing issues facing our communities today: the violent sexism pitting black women and men against one another, black sexualities and AIDS, unemployment and drug cultures, self-hatred, and the lack of self-respect underlying black on black violence, including the rampant abuse of addictive substances. What is our own relationship to these issues? How do these inform our work? How do/can we create opportunities for us as critics, intellectuals, and producers to impact on popular culture, white or black?

One of the high points of the conference was when we began to enter into dialogue during the sexuality panel discussion. In the middle of a heated discussion involving Houston Baker, Marlon Riggs, and several audience members who were interrogating Baker about his having opened his presentation with the statement "I am not gay," Kinshasha Conwill, director of the Studio Museum in Harlem (the co-sponsor of the conference) stood up and presented closure on the discussion.

We must begin to allow for the contradictions in our dialogues and in our identities. We must disrupt our privileged position of sitting at the table while our sisters, mothers, brothers, and children are not even getting our crumbs. So instead of presenting closure when a panel discussion begins to get hot, I think we need to open up and let the panel run wild if it needs to.

I decided to leave public television when I found there was no opportunity to make real change. I felt I had accomplished all that I could there, and I had been selected to become a critical studies fellow at the Whitney Independent Study Program, where I hoped to explore theory as a way of engaging critical questions around authorship and audience. As a producer who places himself as a subject in his work, I'm interested in the significance of the author in relation to works by people of color and gays and lesbians. However, at the Whitney, I quickly realized that, within an institution that privileged whiteness and heterosexuality and was invested in archaic strategies of the Left, many of my questions would have to be answered through the process of my own work.

My first videotape, *Splash,* began as a experimental documentary about a black woman, hair, and conventions of beauty and desire. As I began to delve deeper into the project and immersed myself in the works of Isaac Julien, Marlon Riggs, bell hooks, Stuart Hall, Toni Morrison, and Alice Miller, as well as my brother, Lyle Ashton Harris, I began to understand that my interest in this project was about my own ambivalence around issues of ethnicity, gender, representation, and desire, issues I was exploring indirectly through this black woman.

In the beginning, when little Tommy was a little boy, he was fascinated with little girls. He loved their pretty pink dresses, their stockings, and their hair—tied up in pretty pink ribbons. In fact, Tommy loved little girls so much that he wanted to be one. And oh how flagrantly he played with the little girls, trying on their clothes, playing with their dolls, and playing with their hair. He longed for long hair like a girl should have, so that they could play with his.

And then, little Tommy wanted to be pretty, too, and everyone knew that only little girls with their long straight hair, and rosy pink cheeks that matched the pretty pink pink ribbons tying up their long blond hair, that only these girls could be pretty little girls.

But Little Tommy's Daddy, Big Tommy, was big and strong. He didn't want little Tommy to be no sissy boy. So he took little Tommy to see a psychologist, who told little Tommy to draw a picture of a little boy and a little girl.

And then he told Big Tommy that little Tommy was normal, very very normal. But big Tommy didn't believe him. And he said no more playing with the pretty little girls or their pretty little dolls. And little Tommy was sad. But Daddy said: "Now, that's just too damn bad!"

This was about the time Little Tommy realized that he liked little boys and their little tiny toys. But one day a friend of Mother's came and told a story about a man who took another man home to bed. But—by the morning he was dead! Mother didn't say anything. But she looked at Little Tommy and told him to leave the room. Too late, Tommy had already promised himself never ever to have a date.

So every night, when he closed his eyes, little Tommy transformed into a shiny sparkling pretty little girl, nice, fresh, and new. And then Little Tommy could have a boyfriend or two. Boyfriends he could like and would like him, too. Boyfriends who were nice and fresh and said: "I think you're cute. Will you go out with me?"

Just like the notes the little girls passed little Tommy in school, which said: "I think you're cute. Will you go out with me?"

Just like the notes little Tommy passed the little girls in school, which read: "I think you're cute. Will you go out with me?"

And so each night in Tommy's dreams when the rosy girl kissed the rosy boy goodnight, Tommy knew that one day there'd be a price he'd have to pay.

—Thomas Allen Harris, *Splash.*

For me, talking about desire, and ambivalence along the lines of race and gender, meant moving past the fear of daring to be different, daring to speak the unspoken. It was an act of personal liberation. As a black gay man, I continually resisted the narrow definitions of masculinity imposed on me, first by my father, an ex-marine, and later, by other men who uncritically embraced skewed notions of "masculinity" and "manhood." My act of resistance, my struggle to survive, necessitated freeing myself of the gender prison imposed by my father, a prison that manifested itself in his inability to nurture his sons (despite his love) except with blows and brutality.

This oppression, which began at home, was not exclusively about gender conformity. It encompassed issues of self-hatred that had been passed down for generations. "I'll kill you boy!" followed by a hug was a common way my father expressed his love for and pride in me. I know my father's pain and his beauty, his isolation and self-hatred, his self-respect and self-rejection, his love and his anger. And as his son, I have inherited them all.

My second videotape, *Black Body,* is an attempt to come to terms with these contradictions (inherent in the experience of blackness and maleness) by exploring this psychic legacy of African diasporic people through the ambivalence black people demonstrate toward their bodies—both individually and collectively. I am particularly interested in exploring the ways the body internalizes oppression; how is the body used as an agent of resistance or of relief?

My third and most challenging project, currently in production, is an experimental documentary that looks at African-American families through the interior worlds of three groups of black lesbian and gay male siblings (including my brother and myself). This tape, entitled *All in the Family,* will attempt to challenge "popular" yet narrow constructions of family through its presentation of black lesbian and gay male siblings who are creating spaces of difference within the larger African-American family framework.

A collaboration among three sets of black lesbian/gay siblings—three lesbian sisters, a gay brother and lesbian sister, and two gay brothers—this project disrupts notions of authorship through its use of the camera. The siblings operate and rotate the camera themselves. They conduct the interviews and dialogue with each other. The camera becomes not simply a documentary tool, but a tool for conscious meditation and interaction. The siblings are also collaborating on the writing of dramatic re-creations and reconstructions. These will be used to challenge the "realness" of their interactions, to examine the relationships between past and present, fantasy and real, truth and memory.

As a member of several different communities, I have had the opportunity to see my own work play to a variety of different audiences who have responded in markedly different ways. Principally my work has been shown at lesbian/gay film festivals and other white independent media venues, largely because of homophobia and heterosexism within our own black communities. However, the work resonates most with black audiences, regardless of sexual identity, and the response I have received from these audiences has been the most productive and supportive. As a community, we have to begin to build broader definitions of ourselves. We must take responsibility for critically nurturing our own individual and collective bodies.

I am grateful to Lyle Ashton Harris, Dawn Suggs, and Raul Ferrera-Balanquet, without whose contributions this essay would not have been possible.

Greg Tate

Preface to a One-Hundred-and-Eighty Volume Patricide Note: Yet Another Few Thousand Words on the Death of Miles Davis and the Problem of the Black Male Genius

The day after Miles died, the trio had a concert. I realized, when we played that night, we had been getting closer to that sixties rhythm-section sound Miles is responsible for. Kicking the beat around and kicking bebop on a little trip, it made me want to try and define what it is that we've lost.

> It is pure intent. Miles was a resonance. And when he died, we lost that resonance for all the young players who were playing in that room. The materials of the walls just changed.
> —*Keith Jarrett*

With all respect to John Coltrane or Bob Marley or Jimi Hendrix, they became immortals because they died. Miles was immortal before he died. I have a video of Muhammad Ali's first fight with Joe Frazier in Madison Square Garden. Everybody was looking at Miles when he came in. I mean everybody, including Muhammad Ali and Joe Frazier. He was that powerful.

> —*Carlos Santana*

In the fifties, Miles and Max Roach were speaking like men, acting like men. I saw them and said, "That's the life I want to live." Miles showed you how to carry yourself. He inspired people to think beyond what they thought they were capable of.

The time I'm talking about, from 1957 on, this is before the Civil Rights Movement of the sixties, before anyone knew about King or Muhammad Ali or Malcolm X. Miles was the person people of my generation looked to for those things. So when the sixties came, I didn't need anybody to tell me, "We shall overcome." I was already living it.

> —*Tony Williams*

Like the death of James Baldwin, that of Miles Davis returns us to a state of innocence and incoherence where certain narratives of Black modernity, identity, and continuity are concerned. We see clearly how these individuals have functioned as speculative models of a Blackness conceived as the source of opposition, affirmation, and countersupremacy. We also recognize how these individuals contributed myths of struggle, conquest, and wartime conduct against the ongoing project of African dehumanization.

When Keith Jarrett speaks of Miles as a resonance, he must mean Davis was the sounding board off of which other musicians bounced their most exploratory ideas. In this sense, Miles's demise signals the end of a certain heroic master narrative of Black male artistry. It also reacquaints us with the sorry state of artistic and intellectual ambition in contemporary Black culture. Miles was a holdover from a time when Black intellectual and artistic achievement was a major currency through which racial progress could be bought and symbolically sold—on a rarified, individual basis—a time distinct from the postnationalist present where Black representation is a market force capable of raking in corporate profits without being allied to our agendas of social advancement and reform.

Among Black musics, jazz and hip hop have the effect of making the Black-identified imagination unsatisfied with white supremacist definitions of modernity. From the beginning of his career, Davis functioned as the classical twentieth-century mock modernist—one whose practice foregrounded his theory and forwarded the possibilities of the medium. Operating out of both Black cultural nationalist and twentieth-century modernist impulses, Davis embodied the belief that the democratic expansion of Black rights cannot but entail the discomforting inclusion of militant Black cultural differences. The agility with which he lobbed his balls back and forth through the lofty airs of modernist aesthetics and over the muddy waters of American race politics is inspirational.

Miles's work helped make it impossible to conceive of a modernism that was not Black-derived, not Black-identified and directed in some way, not already subsumed by Black production. As Tony Williams commented, Miles's career functioned as a paradigm for how Black people wanted to position themselves in relation to the American experience. The question of what positions we want to take up in the post-American century just around the bend is still waiting for its prophets and, of course, its profiteers.

Miles's legacy challenges other Black cultural nationalists to recognize the affirmation of Black cultural differences as merely a starting point for self-development, not as an endgame to be punted about the end zone of white supremacy.

Davis's death is not so much an occasion for despair as an occasion to despair over the absence or invisibility of daunting intellectual, spiritual, and artistic models along the transcendental horizon of Black culture as we now know it. Ironically, this is a despair we can wallow in and rejoice over if it provokes us to fashion a Black consciousness movement more intrigued by evolutionary possibility than by the erection of a smug countersupremacist stance. The power of a Miles Davis was that he always seemed to be waving back from the other side of Black culture's transcendable horizon, from the post-liberated side of Black potentiality. That other shore was not emblematic of emancipation. What was over there was freedom from fear of a Black romantic imagination. At the end of the day, the seductiveness of artists like Davis isn't from awe at their skill. It's the dangerous visions they unleash in others that make them truly arresting and irresistible, their power as dreamers to decolonize their audience's dream spaces. Or to unlock their nightmares.

I could speak once again here of Miles as a misogynist monster, as I did in my *Village Voice* memorial. (There, I said Miles may have swung like a champion, but where his relationships with women were concerned, he went out like a roach.) Instead, I'll share a letter I received, after the publication of that piece, from a sister I know who was in a relationship with Miles just prior to his return to active performing in 1981. You should know that she had been pursuing litigation against Miles for violence he had done to her. Excuse me if this letter sounds self-serving.

Dear Greg:

Your much deserved praise of the music man and how he touched your life moved me deeply. Miles lives, not only in his musical legacy, but in those of us who suffered his madness and live with the nightmare still. Thanks for adding our voices to your memorial.

I'm going to leave you with an excerpt from a science fiction novel I'm working on. It's called *Altered Space, Race Mutation Theory*. To me, it's an example of how you make use of something I think Miles gave us—I call it VWA, vulnerability with attitude.

Dracula think he be cool. Dracula takes a drag on a fag, sucking his own blood with a smoking nicotine solo. The fangs are fake and the cloak is a rental but he actually believes he'll hit the stage tonight and cut a fearsome figure. A wallflower vampire nursing a nosebleed who can't even net the butterflies doing blue angel turns in the wild blah yonder of his stomach. He considers this chilling hard. The Robo Coptic Boys want to know which schmuck pulled the nails out of the coffin for him. And what paper bag test did he pass to even get the gig. Who was setting him up to be embarrassed like that. If he didn't look so foolish maybe they'd pull him aside, have mercy on his soul, drop a dime on a brother, pull a brother's coattail and whatnot. But ain't nothing no self-respecting Black man can do for no rocky horror reject like this 'un here. The Robo Coptic Boys Doo Wop and Dark Magus got a gig of their own to consider, later, uptown, in Seventh Heaven. Usually a two-man team, one on trumpet, one on turntables and cooking pots, their sound all tinkling brass and blang-clang boomerangs in the night. Tonight they'll be joined by D. J. Sphinx for a special evening of scratchnoise and be-atific bursts of blissed-out melody. In the interim, though, they've found a new fool they'd like to laugh at. They figure they've smirked evil in Drac's direction long enough, devoted as many rounds of derision as need be to cracking up all of his face. Now it's time to get loud and niggerish. Like, okay, doo double-U riddle me this, What the fuck does singing got in common with sucking blood? I don't get it. You don't get it, I get it simple. Let me science you. Now singing is to sucking blood as singing is to seduction, which is to say, if a singer can charm you out of your pants then why not out of some blood? Singers can make you give up the ghost as quick as a blood-sucking motherfucker, right? Give up the boots, too. Plus I've heard it feels good to have your blood sucked and like Bill Withers sang if it feels this good being used, then keep on using me 'til you use me up.

Drac is trying not to listen carefully, trying to look like he's beyond anger, or even caring. But he's awestruck by how quickly the pitter of their patter falls from the lips, game-set-match. If he really was Drac, he'd be invulnerable to such naked eyeballing. He'd pull their tongues out of their throats. X marks the spots that can't be X-rayed. He knows when he hits the stage the Robo Coptics will be way upfront all but tearin' down his pants before the crowd. The worst of it wasn't the prospect of that so much as the realization that he needed to move his bowels badly and that they were flanking the doors to the bathroom. And if that's not enough, up strolls the bandleader Taurus who has barely done more than grunt at him through the entire grueling emergency two-day rehearsal he put in on his behalf. When Taurus figures out who was snatching so much sarcasm out of the Robo Coptics, he'll sheepishly bond with them because what else can he do, shaking his head, curling his lip? Drac knows that standing before the gateway to his intestine's salvation will be three men who have publicly fouled on him and dared him to do anything about it. In recognizing his position he knows the only way to regain his dignity is to bludgeon the three of them beyond recognition, here and now, to take, say, that fireman's axe over there and hack their faces apart, to send their hands screaming to their heads scraping about for noses that are no more and lips that are blubber on the floor. He knows he has the rage, but wonders about his speed and surgical skill for the task at hand. It'll be the last thing they'd expect from him so he knows he has the element of surprise, but does he possess the lightning reflexes? As he debates with his bodily powers over the likelihood of his imaginary massacre becoming a living colour horror show, up rolls who but the wife with the twins in tow. And when she asks him why is he standing there looking like a fool and whips her breasts out of her blouse and declares her titties don't make no more milk, the threesome lose it, totally lose it, and fall into the toilet resounding its walls with the sort of gut-bursting, gutterminded guffaws that could only be beaten back into their throats by an airless vacuum. Like Dracula imagines how sweet it would be if you could blow the back wall out of that toilet and instead of Second Avenue being on the other side, there was deep space, a vacuum arrived to do violence to Dracula's detractor, sweep them way on out there, to where known space ends and infinity begins. Yes, boy, look at them go, rolling and tumbling over stars like intergalactic sagebrush before being freeze-dried and blown apart from within and there goes my wife Drussilla with them jesus what a sight that is to behold. This vision is as clear to Drac as any one of the Ten Commandments but especially the one that goes Thou Shall Not Fuck with Me in the Shadow of the Valley of Death, or That's Your Monkey Ass.

Arthur Jafa

When I was thinking about what I wanted to do at this conference, the first thing I thought about was giving my talk with my back to the audience as a sort of allusion to Miles Davis, you know, postural semantics and all. But then I had this dream, which I'm going to tell you about.

I was in Clarksdale, Mississippi, where I grew up. I was in my bedroom, the room I remember growing up in, sitting and listening to music—the kind of music my mom used to call psychological music. You know, jazz, rock, reggae, anything that was strange (to her). And I was sitting in the room with The Alien—I don't know how many of you saw the movie *The Alien*—and we were just chilling, you know, just grooving, like me and my friends did when we were growing up. And my mom pops her head in the room occasionally like she did when I was with my friends and smiles and sort of steps back out. And my father creeps in without saying anything and turns down the volume on the music. Eventually, my friend The Alien gets up and splits. And then my father comes in and says, "Who was that big-headed nigger you were in here with?"

I don't want to be a big-headed nigger, so I'm not going to do this with my back to the audience. But, I am going to use digressions like Marlon Riggs did in his talk. One thing that's been interesting for me to see so far in this conference is the anxiety around what I would call the performative. The very first night Stuart Hall stood up and gave his talk, and I felt a little bit like that guy in the Memorex commercial. I thought, damn, he's relentless. I mean, I turned to the people next to me and said it was like listening to John Coltrane—it just didn't stop. And then after that Cornel West came out and did his thing, you know, "Give me an Amen!" He doesn't say it, but you know what he wants. Then bell hooks came on, and she did her thing, and Marlon did his incredible thing. And then there was Hazel Carby. She was interesting. She was the only person who got the "oooh" effect. She got this effect when she was pointing out the relationship between certain male academics and Zora Neale Hurston.

My primary interest is in Black film. When I first got into film at Howard University, the people who were there—Haile Gerima, Alonzo Crawford, Abiyi Ford—were very much concerned with questions around Black cinema and with defining what it was. At that time, they would have probably defined Black film as something like "We're against Hollywood," which is interesting because that definition allows you to get to certain kinds of places, and it's clear. But eventually I started to ask myself, well, is that enough? It seems they had put us in this binary opposition with Hollywood that can be kind of limited. I thought we had to ask more sophisticated questions about what Black cinema was and, in fact, could be.

One of the first things I asked was, well, if this work is supposed to be Black film, why does it use what is essentially strictly classical Hollywood spatial continuity? You know, was it significant that you respected all of the 180-, 360-degree rules around spatial organization? Was that arbitrary?

They would show the work of Oscar Micheaux, whom anyone who's interested in Black cinema, or American cinema, for that matter, should be familiar with. (I find it incredible that Black filmmakers don't know Oscar Micheaux. That's kind of like being a jazzman and not knowing Louis Armstrong.) And they would always present Oscar Micheaux's work as an example of what not to do. I got this a lot: it was incompetently realized; its class and color politics were all messed up. But I felt like they never really looked deeply into his work and saw what was worth studying.

David Bordwell and Kristin Thompson did a very interesting analysis of Ozu, the master Japanese filmmaker. They demonstrated that the spatial paradigm Ozu employed wasn't a deficient control of a Hollywood spatial paradigm, but that, in fact, it was an alternative paradigm—which oftentimes ran parallel to the Hollywood one, but just as often would transgress it.[1] Donald Ritchie, who is considered an early expert on Ozu, would say, "This is a guy who's considered one of the most controlled formal filmmakers in the world, but he got sloppy at those moments." Right.

But what was interesting about Bordwell's and Thompson's analysis was that it provided an entree into analyzing Black film. And I started to look at Micheaux's work and said, wow, this is not an accident; this is consistent over the course of his career (and I think he made more than thirty-eight feature films). It just got badder and badder and badder.

I'm going to do a little jump right here.

I had read the anti-essentialist position in that last cinema issue of *Screen*,[2] and I said, wow, I really don't agree with some of the things that the anti-essentialists are saying. I mean, I had a hard time understanding (and perhaps it was my misunderstanding) what they were trying to say. So I said, well, I must be an essentialist. And then I read what the essentialists were saying, what they were supposed to be saying, and I said, well, maybe I'm just an "anti-anti-essentialist." What I've come to now is what a friend told me when I asked how she would describe me. She called me a "materialist retentionist" (something like that).

What that means is that I have a belief in certain levels of cultural retention. People carry culture on various levels, down to the deepest level, which I would call a kind of core stability. Nam Jun Paik, the godfather of video art, has this great quote: "The culture that's going to survive in the future is the culture that you can carry around in your head." The middle passage is such a clear example of this, because you see Black American culture particularly developed around those areas we could carry around in our heads—our oratorical prowess, dance, music, those kinds of things. There are other things not so easy to carry. Architecture, for example. When we got here, we didn't have an opportunity to make many buildings. Not right off, at least. So I have this notion of core stability and how that informs what we do, of cultural sophistication and how we apply that to the task of constructing Black cinema.

I like to think about films and the kinds of things that are possible. For example, I want to do Martin Luther King's life in the style of *In the Realm of the Senses* (Nagisa Oshima's amazing hard-core feature). I want to do Malcolm X's life as a series of moments—Malcolm arriving home at two o'clock in the morning and looking in at his little girls asleep. I like the stories that Bruce Perry tells in his biography of Malcolm X—like when he says that Malcolm X was, in fact, in love with another Betty. And in his anxiety about whether Betty was actually going to accept his proposal of marriage, he asked Betty Shabazz to marry him instead. A few weeks later, he ran into the first Betty's brother, and was being congratulated by him, you know, "Congratulations on your marriage, brother Malcolm. But why didn't you ever call our sister back? She's

been waiting for you. She wanted to accept the proposal." And Malcolm X broke down and started crying.[3] That's the Malcolm X I want to see. And I would like to know what kind of version of Little Richard's life Andrei Tarkovsky would do.

I think understanding culture and having a sophisticated understanding of applying culture to the construction of Black cinema means we have to understand how culture gets played out in various arenas. And we have to be able to look at these arenas to see how Black people have intervened to transform them into spaces where we can most express our desires. A classic example, of course, is basketball. Like the question that went around for a long time (before Michael Jordan made it irrelevant) about who was the best basketball player, Magic Johnson or Larry Bird. That depends on what you mean by best, obviously. If you use a rational Western evaluation of what's best, then you come up with the statistical, which means who can put the most balls in the hoop, right? And by that definition, certainly Larry Bird can be measured with the best there's ever been. Bird can put the ball in the hoop. Anybody that tells you he can't has got a serious racial anxiety thing happening. But then you have to ask yourself, if Black people enter into this game, which was invented by Dr. Hans Nasmith (and we know he certainly didn't create it with Black folks in mind), how has it been transformed? And how many levels does that play itself out on? I mean, is it just that we function as players, or have we affected other aspects of the game? And if you ask yourself these kinds of questions, then the question of who's the best basketball player becomes irrelevant. What you're going to end up with is Larry Bird coming down the floor, going up for a shot. Two points. He comes down again. Two points. Then maybe he'll shoot one of those long ones he's good for. Three points, you know. But then Michael Jordan will come down, spinning acrobatically in apparent defiance of all known laws of gravity. Ten points.

Black pleasure (not joy)—what are its parameters, what are its primal sites, how does Black popular culture or Black culture in general address Black pleasure? How does it generate Black pleasure? How do those strategies in Black music play out the rupture and repair of African-American life on the structural level? How do they play out the sense of the lost and the found? How are Black people preoccupied with polyventiality (a term of mine)? "Polyventiality" just means multiple tones, multiple rhythms, multiple perspectives, multiple meanings, multiplicity. Why do we find these particular things pleasurable? How do African retentions coalesce with the experiential sites in the New World, with new modes of cultural stability? What does Wesley Brown's "tragic magic" mean when he says, "I played in a Bar Mitzvah band. And it was a great job until I got hit by that tragic magic, and I start playing a little bit before the beat, a little bit behind the beat. I couldn't help myself. I lost the job." This whole question of addressing Black pleasure is a critical thing.

I've heard people talk about issues of representation and the content of culture. But I'm trying to figure out how to make Black films that have the power to allow the enunciative desires of people of African descent to manifest themselves. What kinds of things do we do? How can we interrogate the medium to find a way Black movement in itself could carry, for example, the weight of sheer tonality in Black song? And I'm not talking about the lyrics that Aretha Franklin sang. I'm talking about *how she sang them.* How do we make Black music or Black images vibrate in accordance with certain frequential values that exist in Black music? How can we analyze the tone, not the sequence of notes that Coltrane hit, *but the tone itself,* and synchronize Black visual movement with that? I mean, is this just a theoretical possibility, or is this actually something we can do?

I'm developing an idea that I call Black visual intonation (BVI). What it consists of is the use of irregular, nontempered (nonmetronomic) camera rates and frame replication to prompt filmic movement to function in a manner that approximates Black vocal intonation. See, the inherent power of cinematic movement is largely dependent on subtle or gross disjunctions between the rate and regularity at which a scene is recorded and the rate and regularity at which it is played back. Nonmetronomic camera rates, such as those employed by silent filmmakers, are transfixing precisely because they are irregular. The hand-cranked camera, for example, is a more appropriate instrument with which to create movement that replicates the tendency in Black music to "worry the note"—to treat notes as indeterminate, inherently unstable sonic frequencies rather than the standard Western treatment of notes as fixed phenomena. Utilizing what I term alignment patterns, which are simply a series of fixed frame replication patterns (and I have 372 at this point), the visual equivalencies of vibrato, rhythmic patterns, slurred or bent notes, and other musical effects are possible in film. You could do samba beats, reggae beats, all kinds of things. This is just a beginning for trying to talk about certain possibilities in Black cinema.

1. David Bordwell and Kristin Thompson, "Space and Narrative in the Films of Ozu," *Screen* 17, no. 2 (Summer 1976), 41–73.
2. *Screen* 29, no. 4 (Fall 1988).

3. Bruce Perry, *Malcolm: The Life of a Man Who Changed Black America* (Barrytown, N.Y.: Station Hill Press, 1991). Distributed by The Talman Co.

Isaac Julien

Black Is, Black Ain't:
Notes on De-Essentializing Black Identities

In his essay "Change the Joke and Slip the Yoke," Ralph Ellison discusses his re-action to Stanley Edgar Hyman's essay on the Negro American's relation to the folk tradition:

> On his side of the joke the Negro looks at the white man and finds it difficult to believe that the "grays"—a Negro term for white people—can be so absurdly self-deluded over the true interrelatedness of blackness and whiteness. [1]

If we apply the above statement to the scopic imperatives that mark both the contours of Michael Jackson's ghostlike black face and the bodies of the all-white Young Black Teenagers rap group, we can share Ellison's joke. Sometimes, he continues, "it is for the sheer joy of the joke...to challenge those who presume, across the psychological distance created by race manners, to know his identity." [2]

Ellison's essay testifies to the constructedness of black and white identities and thus begins the work of de-essentializing them. In *Invisible Man,* Ellison's preacher defines the blackness that is recreated in the vernacular signifying tra-ditions of the church sermon, where being black is an open-ended identity. The call and response dialectic is present in the sermon's oratorical exchange be-tween the preacher and his congregation, as the fluid continuum of blackness is made and remade:

> "Brothers and sisters, my text this morning is the 'Blackness of Blackness.'" And a congregation of voices answered: "That blackness is most black, brother, most black..."

BLACK MAN HOLDING WATERMELON

Carrie Mae Weems, *Black Man with Watermelon*, 1986.

"In the beginning…"

"At the very start," they cried.

"…there was blackness…"

"Preach it…"

"…and the sun…"

"The sun, Lawd…"

"…was bloody red…"

"Red…"

"Now black is…" the preacher shouted.

"Bloody…"

"I said black is…"

"Preach it, brother…"

"…an' black ain't…"[3]

But black popular culture has changed, and although the church remains the cultural backbone of black communities, queerness is still not read outwardly. In "Towards a Black Gay Aesthetic,"[4] Charles Nero discusses a short story by Craig G. Harris that takes place at the funeral of the character Jeff's lover, who has died from complications from AIDS. Both the family and the church, two major institutions in African-American communities, are allied against Jeff. In other words, there is an active censorial practice at work in the church that is also reproduced in homophobic black popular culture.

Nero's inquiry into black popular culture challenges the more fixed idea of blackness currently politically fashionable. Black romanticism is high on the political agenda of people like Louis Farrakhan and the Nation of Islam and various rap groups prioritizing their very narrow versions of black masculinity. It mythologizes the past as it erases memory.

In the game of naming and renaming the end of the "essential black subject" who has come out of "the age of innocence" (Stuart Hall's much quoted phrase), black popular culture figures try to fix it in rap, as Ice-T has recently:

I knew this guy that was never that fly, couldn't act cool, even when he tried. When we played rough, he always cried. When he told stories, he always lied. A black brother who was missin' the cool part. He had the color but was missing the true heart.[5]

Now I'm a write this song, though the radio won't play this, but I got freedom of speech, so I'm a say it. She want to be les, he want to be gay, but
that's your business, have it your way. I'm a straight up nigger.[6]

In the *New York Times,* Jon Pareles writes of rap artist Ice Cube:

On the life side Ice Cube is serious. Clearly influenced by Louis Farrakhan's
Nation of Islam, which he encloses in liner notes, Ice Cube favors black separatism although he doesn't want any black nation to include homosexuals,
"true niggers aren't gay or yuppies." In his opposition to miscegenation, he
probably has a lot in common with the campaign of David Duke and his notion of racial purity.[7]

The rise of rap as signifier of hetero black masculinity in black studio films,
notably *New Jack City* and *Boyz N the Hood* (the two are interconnected in that
central protagonists Ice Cube and Ice-T are the black commodity fetishes that
guarantee box-office sales), has made it difficult for more complex representations of blackness in popular cinema. Even Afrocentrism's privileging of a new
black aesthetic is not dialogic enough to think through the "hybridity of ethnicity," let alone liberated enough to include "queerness" in its "blackness." In the
debris of this postmodern moment, the rise of essentialist black thinking is in
part a reaction to a decade of Reagan-Bush-Thatcherite policies. And in the response to the AIDS crisis, the rise of Queer Nationhood lends itself to a similar
form of identity politics in aligning itself with an anti-heterosexual essentialism.

In the project of demarginalizing and recentering black literary figures, I
have been particularly inspired by Henry Louis Gates, Jr., Houston A. Baker,
Jr., bell hooks, Gayatri Spivak, Paul Gilroy, Stuart Hall, Homi K. Bhabha,
Kobena Mercer, Cornel West, and Kwame Anthony Appiah. Their writings,
along with Essex Hemphill's powerful poetry, formed the background to the
making of my film *Looking for Langston*. I wanted to readdress the debate around
race and representation and the queerness in blackness from a diasporic perspective. But making *Looking for Langston* was extremely difficult, and trying to
get it shown in the United States proved to be extremely problematic. Bad
Object-Choices, editors of a volume on queer film and video, summarize the
position succinctly:

Around the time that Helms's amendment was signed into law, Isaac Julien's film *Looking for Langston* (1988) was screened at the New York Film Festival...Before the festival showing, the audience was informed that owing to a copyright dispute the film's sound would be blocked out in two archival sequences of Langston Hughes reciting his poetry. They were not informed, however, that the version they would see had already been altered in response to censorship: still more of Hughes's poetry had been replaced on the soundtrack by Julien in response to an injunction sought by the Hughes estate to prevent showing the film. Although the estate's legal claim was indeed one of copyright infringement, its wish to censor lay elsewhere: it objected to Julien's association of Hughes with homoeroticism.[8]

Langston Hughes's queerness was a widely kept secret. The repicturing of an iconic figure like Hughes trespassed across the essentialist battle lines of blackness. As D. A. Miller points out, secrecy can function as the subjective practice in which the oppositions of private/public and inside/out are established:

> The phenomenon of the open secret does not, as one might think, bring about the collapse of those binarisms and their ideological effects, but rather attests to their fantasmatic recovery.[9]

As Stuart Hall has suggested, the partnership between the past and the present is an imaginary reconstruction.[10] This relationship lends itself to film in particular. For me, it was the construction of race, memory, and desire, the closet in black popular culture, that needed to be explored filmically.

Desire is always the axis along which different forms of cultural policing take place. And desire across racial and sexual lines was the site for constructing my film *Young Soul Rebels*. The crossing of these lines causes anxiety, undermines the binary notions of self/other, black/white, straight/queer. This anxiety in relation to sexuality and race can be located in the history of black criticism as well; there is the example of W.E.B. Du Bois's reaction to Claude McKay's 1920 novel *Home to Harlem*. McKay, who was gay and Jamaican, wrote about nightlife in Harlem and described the gay and lesbian bars.

> Claude McKay's *Home to Harlem* for the most part nauseates me, and after the dirtier parts of its filth I feel distinctly like taking a bath...McKay has set out to cater for [the] prurient demand on the part of white folks.[11]

The practice among black academics and intellectuals of ignoring gays and lesbians in almost every articulation of matters of race and culture runs a direct line from Du Bois to the late George Bass, former secretary to Langston Hughes and executor of the Hughes estate, who tried to prevent any discussion of Hughes's sexuality.

The establishment of icons in a black literary canon has had the unfortunate effect of setting a neoconservative, populist agenda for the discussion of black popular culture. A similar conservatism has affected the kinds of black films that are currently fashionable, for instance, the wave of new mainstream black gangster films. As Philip Dodd maintains in an essay on these films:

> The race to the popular could of course have other consequences. The emergence of a popular black gangster idiom in films like *New Jack City* and *Boyz N the Hood* may mean that other new black filmmakers [as well as older ones like Charles Burnett and Julie Dash] with a more complex aesthetic will be judged against the popular.[12]

Mark Winokur continues the argument: "It is the contemporary gangster film that best embodies the ambivalence of filmmakers towards ethnicity and race."[13]

Young Soul Rebels, though made against the grain of black popular cinema, could be misinterpreted as such because of the box-office success of films like *Boyz N the Hood* and *New Jack City.* In constructing *Young Soul Rebels* as a narrative, I committed the major avant-garde sin of trying to tell a story. If the genre is not strictly adhered to, it's because I'm more interested in ideas, distanciation, decor. *Young Soul Rebels* does not meet the demand for a documentary guarantee as do the black U.S. gangster films. In the end, as Paul Gilroy has suggested to me, *Young Soul Rebels* is an allegory of empire.

Barry Walters, however, in his review of *Young Soul Rebels* in the *San Francisco Examiner,* said the world doesn't need another film about a "creepy closet case who preys on other gays."[14] Well, actually the world is full of such closet cases. And I want to raise ambivalent questions about the sexual and racial violence that stems from repressed desires of the other within ourselves, or, as in the case of Ken, anxieties toward the other that turn the subject into an object across both racial and sexual lines. When looking at *Young Soul Rebels,* such critics look for gay characters who have a positive image—a positive white gay image. But what is a positive image? As Parveen Adams has stated:

After all, what would happen if we demanded positive images?...It would be as if some images are in deficit of what we want to identify with as adequate representations...the imaginary capture by a positive world in which identity is a *prêt à porter*.[15]

The project of producing positive images is an impossible one. Though it may have the best intentions of redressing imbalances in the field of representation, it is bound to fail as it will never be able to address questions of ambivalence or transgression. In making *Young Soul Rebels*, it seemed important not to fulfill those transcendent duties that require the black or queer, or black queer, filmmaker to represent a specific community of interest—since these categorical imperatives always overshadow questions of doubt, skepticism, or transgression. Identity politics in its positive-images variant is always purchased in the field of representation at the price of the repression of the other.

If there is a criticism of *Young Soul Rebels* to be made, it is not in connection to the threat of Ken the "gay killer," but to the quasi-utopian representation of Caz and Chris. Maybe there is some wish fulfillment in my depiction of the world of Caz and Chris; Ken, then, would represent a necessary dystopia for the positive-images brigade. Barry Walters goes on to say: "This is a film about racial and sexual togetherness that just *happens* to revolve around a budding Jeffrey Dahmer [the psychotic white gay killer who murdered several black gay men he picked up in Chicago]."[16]

Walters's reference to Ken the Killer is hyperbolic, but in *Young Soul Rebels*, we have the invasion of a positive (gay) world in which identity is not *prêt à porter*. Ken suffers from castration anxiety, and as an intentionally underdeveloped character, he plays hide-and-seek with his own identity. Unable to come to terms with his own desire (for black men), he disavows and punishes. Ken, in other words, guarantees that the film is not politically correct. But I am interested in these kinds of transgressions that cut across the neoconservative demand for positive images.

Racial anxiety is projected onto black subjects in the scopic register. It is the repressed desire for this other that surfaces as violence. In *Young Soul Rebels*, I try to expose this double repression: the other is both gay and black. If we must use the language of positive and negative images, at least *Young Soul Rebels* is a film that uses such images dialectically. In the film's first frames, I raise the is-

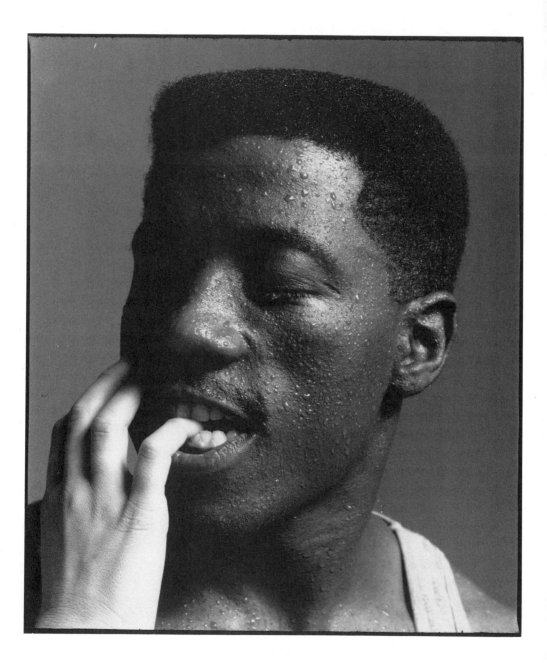

262   Wesley Snipes and Annabella Sciorra in *Jungle Fever*, directed by Spike Lee, 1991.

sues of homosexuality and pathology, but I deliberately do not develop the generic and narrative expectations this "negative" conjunction might receive in dominant narrative cinema.

Young Soul Rebels could also be read as a critique of another pathology, recently represented in Spike Lee's film *Jungle Fever*. In fact, *Young Soul Rebels* could be read as the antidote to *Jungle Fever* in terms of its presentation of non-pathological interracial relationships. Crossing racial lines usually results in punishment. In the case of *Young Soul Rebels,* the gay characters transgress racial lines at the margins—in outdoor sites of nighttime pleasure and danger in the park. In *Jungle Fever,* it's the black middle-class family that is threatened. And it is of paramount importance that it is saved from the so-called pollutions of drugs and interracial relationships.[17] (Spike Lee's opposition to miscegenation probably has a lot in common with David Duke's notion of racial purity.) The notion of a black essence, central to any discourse of Afrocentrism, I am of course contesting. As the preacher's sermon goes, "Black is, Black ain't."

1. Ralph Ellison, *Shadow and Act* (1953; New York: Vintage, 1972), 55.

2. Ibid.

3. Ralph Ellison, *Invisible Man* (1947; New York: Vintage, 1972), 9–10.

4. Charles I. Nero, "Towards a Black Gay Aesthetic," in *Brother to Brother,* ed. Essex Hemphill and Joseph Beam (Boston: Alyson Publications, 1991), 229–252.

5. Ice-T, "Bitches 2," *Original Gangster.* Sire Records, 1991. CD/Cassette.

6. Ice-T, "Straight Up Nigga," *Original Gangster.* Sire Records, 1991. CD/Cassette.

7. Jon Pareles, "Pop View: Should Ice Cube's Voice Be Chilled?" *New York Times,* Sunday, December 8, 1991, Sec. 2: Arts & Leisure, 30.

8. Bad Object-Choices, *How Do I Look?* (Seattle, Wash.: Bay Press, 1991), 17.

9. From D. A. Miller, *The Novel and the Police,* cited in *Epistemology of the Closet,* ed. Eve Kosofsky Sedgwick (Berkeley: University of California Press, 1990), 67.

10. Stuart Hall, "Cultural Identity and Cinematic Representation," *Framework* 36, 70.

11. W. E. B. Du Bois, cited in Nero, 236.

12. Philip Dodd, "Popular Rules," in *Sight and Sound* 1, no.7 (1991), 3.

13. Mark Winokur, "Eating Children Is Wrong," *Sight and Sound* 1, no. 7 (1991), 10.

14. Barry Walters, " 'Young Soul Rebels' With a Cause," *San Francisco Examiner,* December 5, 1991, D8.

15. Parveen Adams, "The Art of Analysis," *October* 58 (Fall 1991), 92–93.

16. Walters, " 'Young Soul Rebels' With a Cause," D8.

17. See Paul Gilroy, "Spiking the Argument," *Sight and Sound* 1, no. 7 (1991), 29–30.

Judith Wilson This is only a footnote. A point was made in one of the presentations that African-American culture is what we carry in our heads. I think that's very interesting, but I just happened to finish reading a piece in this week's *Village Voice* about a recent conference on African-American architecture and, in fact, a great deal of antebellum architecture was constructed by slaves.

Greg Tate I wanted to direct a question to Ada Gay Griffin because she talked about being crushed by Kathleen Collins's identification of herself as a sort of raceless, sexless filmmaker. I just wondered, after you overcame being crushed by that position, what is your own identification? How do you identify yourself as a filmmaker, and how do you deal with those issues in terms of your practice?

Ada Gay Griffin As I said, I am still learning from her comment. What was important for me to understand was that Kathleen was part of the first of three waves of contemporary black women filmmakers. The first wave consists primarily of people who were not formally trained as filmmakers. In other words, they didn't go to film school or art school or study film, per se, and there wasn't really a community of black women filmmakers to support them. They were the vanguard, so to speak. Kathleen Collins and Jackie Shearer and Madeline Anderson, along with a number of other black women filmmakers from the United States, were pioneers in terms of their decision to make films. The next wave was the group of women who went to film school and had a more nurturing environment (although not so much as the men who were their peers did) in which to make films and build careers. The third wave is sort of a hodgepodge of everybody—many of whom are still making films from the first two waves—people who are very eclectically trained and have a whole number of different visions. I would consider myself in this third wave of black women filmmakers, and I definitely, like all of these women, including Kathleen, identify and try to know as many of these black women filmmakers as possible. We all know each other, have studied with each other, and see each other quite often.

Question I'm very interested in what A. J. [Arthur Jafa] was talking about at the end of his presentation. I'm wondering if you could elaborate, A. J., on how the analysis of tone and black visual movement connects to the subject of African retentions.

Arthur Jafa A lot of this is somewhat theoretical for me at this point. Last year, I got a pretty good grant from NYSCA [New York State Council on the Arts], which has allowed me to buy a computer and some other things. So, I'm just starting to test these hypotheses. But it has a lot to do with privileging music, trying to understand how music affects black people—not that it doesn't affect everyone, but how it has particular resonances for black people—and trying to imagine the possibility of certain tonal frequencies being translated into a filmic arena.

Ultimately, what happens when I talk about having 372 alignment patterns, or various ways in which you can process visual movement, is that your nervous system will have to decide whether these patterns, in fact, work or not. In the way we generally understand it now, when we say a film was successful, we talk about the text of the narrative. You know, we say, "That was a good film," which means that we can synopsize the narrative. But how do we start to think about movement as also being able to carry a certain amount of expressivity?

For example, if you look at the various black musics around the world—not to be essentialist about it, but there's a certain classical tendency now in black musics to treat tones as mobile phenomena. In the traditional Western paradigm, tones are fixed frequencies in space. There are diatonic scales, and they fracture the sonic spectrum in a certain way; whereas, in most black musics, and in many non-Western musics, and now, in fact, in a lot of contemporary Western music, tones are mobile—in other words, you'd never have what you'd call a pure A. If you take, for instance, the creation of jazz, the apparatus developed in response to a set of expressive needs. It's about efficiency: you can hit this key, and you're going to get a specific tonality. And it's always a pure tonality, right? But black musicians would sit at that piano coming from an African heritage where there's a much broader range of certain kinds of tonal formations. There were certain resonances—like what we call the blue note— that would strike a particular chord for black people and provoke a particular response for which there was no point of entree on the piano. So, they started hitting two keys, mis-hitting keys (like Monk did), flubbing notes to fight the equipment.

We have to be able to go into the apparatus, interrogate it on every level, break it down, sometimes very hypothetically and retroactively at this point in the camera's development, almost as in science fiction and say, "What if we had put the apparatus that we understand as cinema in Africa five hundred years ago? What would we have now?" If you take a hand-cranked camera—which as I've said is a more appropriate tool with which to realize motion that has a certain level of plasticity (much like a talking drum)—how can we go back and say, "Wow, why was that ever abandoned?"

We can understand industrial development in its most simple articulation in the Western prerogative, which moved inexorably toward a certain metronomic, or standardized, reality. "And how," as Ishmael Reed once said, "can a metronome know the thunder or summon a god?" I think that's critical to understand in order to make the apparatus more responsive to our expressive needs. And we can do this on every level—it's camera placement, it's everything. We can decode it, break it down, and put it back together in our own image.

Bérénice Reynaud This is not really a question, but a continuation of the discussion Greg Tate and Ada Gay Griffin were having. I was preparing a talk on similar issues, and I went through some of my documentation and pulled a quote by Julie Dash that gives a bit more matter to what you said. Julie was talking about taking her film *Illusions* (1988) to Europe, and it was shown around with Kathleen Collins's *Losing Ground*. She was stirred by the reaction of white critics who would say these black women are not being depicted realistically (they dress well, they're not victims, they're not ghettoized, they're not miserable). *Losing Ground* was made just after Collins filmed *The Cruz Brothers and Miss Malloy,* which I think was the first picture made by a black woman in America, and so that opens up difficult problems of accountability. I feel Kathleen Collins's answer—that is, her refusal to be defined by any label—is a question of her generation. It might have been difficult to have defined oneself then as a black female filmmaker. Maybe this is something you yourself could also comment on. When you have so very few women, black men, or black gay men, how do you deal with the issue of accountability and representability?

Ada Gay Griffin What you're saying is absolutely correct in the sense that different generations see their position in relationship to the power base, or what they perceive as the controlling apparatus, differently. Now, black women producers are much more comfortable stating who they are and what their agendas are. I don't know if that's what you're getting at, but sure, that's a perfectly reasonable assumption to make about what Kathleen was saying. I interpret it more as a matter of saying that we (as A. J. was pointing out before) have to do our work as best we can. That we are black or women is incidental to the work that we're trying to do and the stories we're trying to tell. But it's still important. And it was important to me as a young woman in 1979 who was dying to make films and dying to have somebody out there who was also doing it. Because I don't like to do things first. I want to have some indication that there's somebody else out there to hold my hand, or be with. So, Collins's statement was crucial.

Arthur Jafa Just a quick response to Bérénice's question. I think a lot of this has to do with identification. The reason I identify myself as a black filmmaker is because I meet with resistance along those particular parameters. I'm trying to make space for black people to be comfortable with the idea of being themselves in any context. But, at the same time, I love the Sex Pistols, for example, and there's no way I'm going to factor that out of the totality of who I am. This is why Miles is such an incredible model (if you look at his life and certain kinds of aesthetic choices he made). You have to get to a point where you are confident enough with the idea that your cultural base, whatever it might be, is strong enough that it can subsume whatever it takes in, where you know that it will eventually be integrated into this field that I would call blackness.

Isaac Julien I also think these questions of authorship, of the burden of representation, and of refusing representativeness come about, obviously, because the naming of race occurs only when it is a black filmmaker or if someone declares their ethnic identity. In Sankofa [the British film collective], we have always said we speak *from* experiences rather than *for* experiences. One has to have some means of diffusing the expectations. At the same time, one has to have some sort of dialogic relationship to communities of interest.

Discussion

Question As a member of the audience, I, as a black woman, want to see myself and my culture reflected in film. So, whether or not someone wants to be labeled black or not is irrelevant to me. I'd like to have black women reflected in our society and to see us on the screen representing part of that society.

Thomas Harris I'd like to pick up on that because of the work I've been doing over the last five years producing television. Your name doesn't connote your race or your sexual orientation, so, as a black gay producer on public television, it was very important for me to represent a diverse (there that word is again) number of communities around different issues—not only along the lines of black and gay identities, but the communities within those communities. Again, I have to reference Isaac Julien's films and Marlon Riggs's films. Yes, it's important for me that they are black gay filmmakers. But what is more important to me is the power of the imagery they create and the messages they articulate. For me, this politics of representation is about what you're saying and what you're doing.

Pearl Bowser In reference to Kathleen Collins and her film *The Cruz Brothers and Miss Malloy,* Collins did say, in an interview that she had made a film about a subject that was not necessarily out of her own culture but that what she had wanted was to explore a particular format. She was using an intellectual approach to cinema. The short stories she had read excited her as a filmmaker, and she wanted to explore something very specific in focusing on these particular short stories.

I also have a question in connection to what A. J., and perhaps the rest of the panel, has been alluding to. When you look at American culture, you realize that there's very much blackness in American culture. And though it's important for us, in this political atmosphere, to identify ourselves and tell our own stories on screen each time we have a camera in our hands, do we not have the right—not the privilege, but the right—to focus, from our own aesthetic point of view, on the larger society that we live in?

Arthur Jafa I'm glad you asked that because—just as nobody would think it was weird if Bob Marley sang about John Brown—we, as individuals, have the freedom to address whatever we want to address. We certainly have the right. I do, at least. But we do need to understand that there is a range of ways we can approach and address whatever issues might be in the world.

Greg Tate It's times like these I wish I had Cornel West's powers as a dialectician, because a lot of things have been going through my head—particularly from the moment Ada was speaking about Kathleen Collins and the whole issue of a generational response to certain historical conditions of your identity. In that particular generation of black artists that Kathleen Collins came out of, people—like a Bill Gunn, a Ralph Ellison, or a Miles Davis—were identified as being special, exceptional Negroes (as the term goes). They were targeted or stigmatized or identified as being special, as being rare. And I thought Kathleen Collins's definition of herself as a raceless, sexless artist was a response to, a critical response to, the condition of being an exceptional Negro.

If you look at the back covers of all the black novels we've read, particularly if you get some of the first editions, and see some of the responses to them, there is a critical trope: "The best novel ever written by an American Negro." In reaction to that, you see those artists trying to speak through and affirm a tradition and a people, trying to take on the burden of being a representative of the people. They're combating this critical apparatus that, on the one hand, wants to use them *against* the cultural, communal, collective mass from which they come, that says, "You are better than those you came from." On the other hand, this critical apparatus wants to make you feel as if you're not quite as good as the white masters. I think, psychologically, a Kathleen Collins response is a reaction to that.

Now, when you have artists who emerge after a period of collective political awakening, out of a struggle that has what Cornel West calls a great amount of moral credibility, it becomes, in fact, a badge of honor to affirm yourself as a certain kind of ethnicity or sexuality, and so forth. That becomes part of your attack on those powers of oppression. Whether you then begin to take that affirmation and that base—a sense of solidity around identity—and launch it into new forays in terms of your work, and in terms of your critique of your tradition, is a more complicated issue. This is what I was alluding to when I talked about the fear of black romantic imagination.

When I think about Miles's music that is most important to me, it's probably the most abstract. In the critical response to jazz, there are all these clichés about what tones and resonances mean. There are these ideas that if you play a certain series of notes, if you play something that expresses a certain kind of emotionality, then your work has a certain authenticity or validity. But when you think about a work of Miles's band in the sixties like "Nefertiti," you can't really attach any emotional values—in the clichéd kind of way—to that music. There's a formal play going on among those musicians that is totally dialogic, totally conversational. It's the result of people developing an abstract language in music, but it also has parallels—when you think about that particular group of musicians—in the kinds of lives they want to live and the kinds of things they talk about philosophically in their work.

Wayne Shorter, for example, is an amazing philosopher. I said to him once, "In your music, there's this incredible attention to detail that I consider almost sculptural." And he said,

> Well, that comes from the idea that you can have a penny without a million dollars, but you can't have a million dollars without a penny. When I listen to music, I listen to see if the penny's in there. If the penny's not in there, it ain't happening.

That's what I'm talking about. You can't attach a clichéd notion of racial consciousness to that idea. That has to do with someone who is able to work within a solidified cultural aesthetic frame and then begin to think—in some very rarified ways—about processes, procedures, and operations in their work.

Lisa Kennedy introduced a phrase that I like a lot: "the black familiar." It encapsulates the notion that there's a cultural base, an incredible body of knowledge and information which, if you want to function at all as a black thinker or writer or artist, you have to have at least passing familiarity with. If you come up in a certain black communal context, there are a lot of experiences and emotional responses, vernaculars, and so forth that you have access to.

bell hooks I've been thinking about something that I don't feel we've effectively addressed, and that is whether, in fact, a lot of Afrocentrism—the sense of separatism coming forth in black popular culture—isn't a concrete response to the fear of erasure. To what extent does the de-essentialization of blackness change the nature of black popular culture?

Isaac Julien In terms of thinking through identity and hybridity, the notions of ethnicity and blackness always seem to be fairly fixed. There's a lot of taken-for-grantedness, even in the discussions here, of a unitary blackness that, to be honest, I think is a fiction. If we're going to discuss questions of de-essentializing blackness, what I mean by that is talking about blackness as something that has more scope, that has a wider frame of reference than this narrowing down to very specific reactions.

I've been thinking a lot about the resurgence of this binaristic thinking that makes people feel safe in their separate groups. There are exclusions that occur because of that, and I think Kathleen Collins is one of them. I think her film *Losing Ground,* for example, was an extremely interesting film. However, it was totally dismissed by the avant garde here in the United States. Only a few critics wrote about it—Clyde Taylor and a few others. When she came to London, we had a screening of her film, and I was surprised because her work had difficulty functioning in this narrow way of talking about black culture, and black cinema, in particular.

Thomas Harris When I think about your question, bell, I think about recent events. I should say, first of all, what I am trying to do in my videotape is deal with black masculinity as something that is not as narrow as it is presented to be in black popular culture. It's important to open up that space. I'm thinking of Lisa Jones's article in the *Village Voice* about black women—which asked where their voice was as far as opposition to Clarence Thomas—and Greg Tate's support of black women filmmakers. These voices move in the direction of opening up spaces where black isn't just black macho men. I'm just wondering what kinds of interventions will take place or if these interventions are going to create a dialogue. I've been thinking about music videos, and I'm thinking about looking for a black gay rapper, getting a rap together, and putting it on MTV. You know, that's an in-your-face kind of thing. I think it's about opening up those spaces.

Ada Gay Griffin I don't think we can really talk about essentialism or separatism until we're in the game. It's like talking about something that doesn't even yet exist. Already we're starting to criticize black women's film when that history is only twenty years old. We only have a hundred films to talk about. It's important that we talk about this work now, since we have the great opportunity to discuss it at this early stage, but we can't set up rules about what women can and cannot talk about when the game is just beginning. I feel like the rules change every time I get there, you know what I mean? Now I have to hear, "You threaten me! I feel hurt because you black women want to be alone!" How can I accept that my experience is somehow threatening, that my need to be with others like myself—whom I have been isolated from—is somehow threatening to another group that has greater power than my group?

Greg Tate As Isaac said, the notion of a fixed blackness is a fiction. But so-called black essentialism is a fiction as well. It's a position you take up against reactionary positions within black popular culture. bell asked how black popular culture would change if it was de-essentialized, but there's such a small amount of work that could be called expressively separatist, or even culturally nationalist. There are certain champions who, in interviews, express those kinds of positions, but at the same time they're collecting checks from Columbia Records, Universal Pictures, and on down the line. It's a question of just how separatist they want to be, whatever game it is they're talking.

bell hooks I think people are misunderstanding my question. I see what is taking place here as a kind of trivialization of the fact that the emphasis on separatism isn't always knee-jerk essentialism. People do feel threatened. I'm not just thinking about the producers of popular culture, but about the audiences who receive popular culture—most of the members of which we know are not present here. If we're going to talk about expanding, as I would advocate, our senses of blackness, how would we see this expansion intersecting with the real political threat to the masses of underclass black people who receive something that nourishes them from the very black popular culture that has been the subject of critique here? If we're going to trash it, I want to know what we're going to replace it with.

Arthur Jafa That's the critical question, bell. It struck me the other day when Cornel West was doing a breakdown on the meaning of religion. He said *religere* means "to bind."* Clearly, people who adopt the kind of position I've adopted—when I called it anti–anti-essentialist—understand the impulse be-

*Refers to unpublished remarks that do not appear in the current collection.

hind de-essentializing blackness. Even when it's something as silly as my going around with a list of words I've never heard black people say in a film. Like, I've never heard a black man say "sorbet" in a movie. On the most trivial level, that's about de-essentializing blackness. It's about opening up spaces around black men. I liked one of my best friends from the first time I met him because he was the only black man I knew who would use the word "exquisite." It's about consolidating blackness and, at the same time, opening up the space we can be black inside of.

Culture is really about, as Cornel said of religion, creating sustaining narratives that make meaning of the absurdity of black life in America and in the world. We have to sustain one another, and then, at a proper time, open up these spaces for dialogues. But we can't go into the street when the Klan attacks us and say, "Well, I'm black and from the South, and you're black from the city." They'll just, like you said, bell, exterminate us all. We always have to maintain that tension between making spaces for our specific individuality and binding together.

Thomas Harris I recently saw a film by Daresha Kyi, a black woman filmmaker. In the film, a woman returns home to her family, and finds her father is an alcoholic. They play cards, the father gets drunk, she leaves with her boyfriend, and she and her boyfriend have an argument back at his house. She finds out that her boyfriend's father is an alcoholic as well. He is angry, and she responds to his anger by saying, "We can unite in our pain. We can talk about it." And even though he says he doesn't want to talk about it, she approaches him and hugs him. For me—and a lot of this has to do with reading your work, bell—it's about talking about the pain, coming together, and opening up. It's not enough to come together because we're black. What about the class differences? What about what we're protecting? There are black people who have a lot at stake in the status quo even though they might not say they do. What about coalitions across class lines? I feel empathy toward my sisters, particularly my lesbian sisters, as well as toward my gay brothers. Cornel West talks about coalition building, but I think we need to open ourselves up and find a way to talk about pain. Ice Cube has one way, but there are other ways of talking about it.

Black Cowboys. Photograph by Keith Williams.

Isaac Julien Basically, in the work that I do, I try to produce a critical self-reflexive response. I think blackness is a term used—in the way that terms like "the black community" or "black folk" are usually bandied about—to exclude others who are part of that community. The "black" in black popular culture is really monopolizing that term. To create a more pluralistic interreaction in terms of difference, both sexual and racial, one has to start with de-essentializing the notion of the black subject because it's very fixed at this moment, especially in the domain of the cinema.

Greg Tate I don't think we're talking about displacement. I think we're talking about enhancement, about creating room for more critical thought and opening people up to the idea of a critical response to what they consume. I'm always worried about the leveling of effect, about not allowing for the multiplicity in responses from an audience simply because a particular artist may, in an interview or even in the work, express very sexist or homophobic notions. In terms of what an audience receives from that work, there's something else going on. I don't think anyone, even someone who is self-defined as an anti-essentialist, wants to give up a certain kind of romance we have with being black, with being part of a black collectivity, and with identifying ourselves as black in the world. These are all parts of what gives meaning and sustains us as black folks. We are really talking about making the culture itself less reactionary. And the real question is, how do we do that in a way that makes people listen in the same way they will to a dope track?

Arthur Jafa Right. Black pleasure.

Do the Right Thing:

Postnationalism and Essentialism

Hamhocks. Photograph by Coreen Simpson.

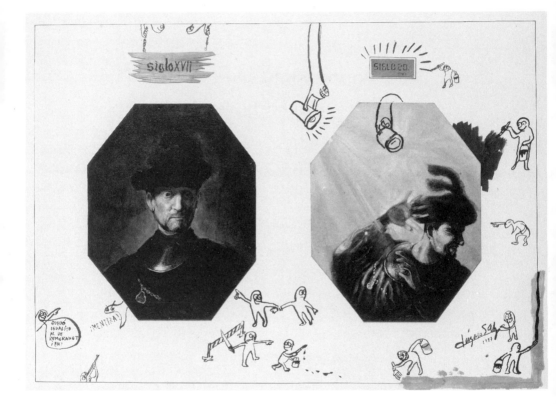

278 Lázaro Saavedra González, *"Mesa Sueca" (Smorgasboard)*, detail.

Coco Fusco

Pan-American Postnationalism:
Another World Order

In Cuba, where the black people in my family spent a couple of centuries before coming to the United States, there is a popular refrain from the Abakua religion: "*Chivo que rompe tambor, con su pellejo paga,*" which literally translates as "the goat who breaks the drum will have to pay with his skin." But it can also mean that the troublemaker turns him or herself into the instrument, in order to continue the music. I keep thinking about that refrain as I listen to how and why black vernacular cultures have so many explanations for the critical positions black people adopt within identity and community. Black popular cultures, especially musical cultures, have generated an abundance of archetypes that embrace dissonance and contend with internal difference; these, I take to be semantic residues of histories of contradiction and conflict. Maybe one of these days our intellectual debates will catch up with our popular cultural ability to engage with dissent, without the defensiveness that continuously rears its head in other spheres.

In the course of this conference, it has become increasingly apparent to me that "doing the right thing" could easily have been the title of the entire event. Postnationalism, essentialism, and black cultural criticism, rather than simply being the topics of this panel, are, in actuality, the terms that have been defined and redefined throughout the last three days of discussion. Clearly, all of us who have engaged in the racial and cultural "wars of position" have our none too savory recollections of the punitive injunctions against artists and intellectuals (especially feminists, gays, and lesbians) who have "done the wrong thing," so to speak. And clearly, the notions of identity, culture, and community invoked by such gestures can feel like a burden, if not a muzzle. And yet, our continued

280   Wall calling for a popular democratic government. From the photo essay *Nicaragua*, by Susan Meiselas, 19

engagement with these ideas, would indicate that we are not ready to give them up—for such divestment still appears too similar to the racial violence that has robbed black peoples of the right, first to be considered human beings, and then to have access to political power. For black peoples, at this historical moment, the postmodern fetishizing of the exchange of cultural property seems less like emancipation and more like intensified alienation.

In this country, the black cultural critic's ethical responsibility to do the right thing frequently generates public displays of anxiety (Did I do the right thing?), opportunism (Only I can do it), and theatrical exercises in defensive authoritativeness (Only I can tell you how to do it). These positions point to a paradox at the heart of nationalist and essentialist ideas of identity—for while they invoke an absolute, preexisting blackness, they also characterize it as performative. To *be* black, we must understand, doesn't just mean to do the *right* thing, but also to *do* it. And yet, the complete transfer of identity from essence to action, from innate property to consumable or reproducible activity, without any ethical referent or political grounding, is a form of cultural politics few blacks would benefit from, given the political and economic inequalities that continue to divide American society along racial lines. As we have argued these issues, it has been apparent throughout that this particular group of black cultural critics does not think of culture and identity without asking about politics— that is, about relations of power—and about ethics—that is, about responsibility. We cannot confuse the appearance of access created by the commodification of ethnicity and, as Hazel Carby noted, the celebration of diversity, with the decentralization of wealth and the democratization of political power that have yet to take place in this country.

I see some very good signs in these debates. The ease and vitality of the dialogue between black American and black British cultural critics and media artists is, for me, a cause for joy (a word for Cornel West), a reason to reflect for a moment on the past, and a source of hope. Joy, because among other things it signals the waning of the isolationist view of culture characteristic of postwar American thought. That distinctly American chauvinism (which is a kind of nationalism in patriotic disguise) was not entirely absent from many of the initial responses in this country to the black British cultural renaissance of the 1980s, as some might recall.

At the time, I was motivated to take on the work as a cultural critic because I thought contending with different black cultures outside the United States would help to make more space for the differences within and among black cultures at home. I also thought it would eventually curtail the impulse on the part of blacks and whites to treat any one individual or diasporic culture as a prototype of blackness. At the time, it seemed of particular political importance to insist that this encounter be orchestrated by and between black people (with a glance to their cultural politics), to avoid retracing "intercultural" patterns established by modernism, surrealism, and ethnography, which had positioned white avant gardes, for decades, as the gatekeepers of otherness and arbiters of aesthetic value. It was a difference that made a difference, not because of some kind of romantic essentialism about black unity, but because of a strategic need to distinguish between ideology and politics, between multicultural rhetoric and desegregation in American culture. And like all the other goats in this room who have beat their drums too loudly, I paid the price for having done so. But, if I had to, I would do it again.

I now reflect on this because I continue to believe that doing cultural criticism necessarily involves interpreting and contributing to such transformations as these. And, finally, I hope that the de-essentializing logic of this postnationalist dialogue will eventually lead to another—one that will eliminate, or at least diminish, the linguistic and historical barriers which have impeded black critical dialogue between the Anglo-American and Latin American worlds. We are living in a moment in which these populations are coming together with greater frequency and in increasing numbers. In addition, as American mass culture deepens its entrenchment in the South, the experience of "blackness" in Latin America becomes increasingly influenced, if not dominated by, mainstream media's versions of black American popular culture.

The dialogue I am hoping for will not only require getting around accents and the differences between internal and external migrations. It also means breaking down the jingoistic English-only barriers that essentialize language as if it were some kind of impenetrable, irreducible difference. It calls for the refusal to lapse into the bad habits which have enabled the U.S. government and the American media to turn hundreds of ethnic groups into one—Hispanic, Latino, you name it—and systematically promote its misinterpretation as a racial term, for the benefit of a segregationist system that sees only in black and white, no matter what the other's color is. It also involves comprehending how the respective colonialisms of the North and the South engendered different social constructions of race, despite shared legacies of slavery, the sexual exploitation of black and indigenous women by white men, and segregationist legislation.

In the North, a combination of prolonged legal and social segregation and a deeply embedded ideology of essentialist separatism, supported by the pragmatist stronghold on American philosophy, has continuously deferred recognition and affirmation of this country's and its people's racial and cultural hybridity. In the South, at least two centuries of ideological celebration of hybridity (the many discourses of *mestizaje*) often brings Latin American intellectuals to reject binary understandings of race. Latino cultural critics tend to insist on the historical difference of a more variegated racial classification system, claiming that class counts more than race, that Latinos have always had a higher rate of interracial unions and a progressive, nationalist, anti-colonialist tradition, which is, at least in theory, integrationist. Although it is true that the independence struggles and nationalist discourses of the Spanish Caribbean stipulated racial equality whereas the American Revolution did not, it is also true that no multiracial Latin American society has eliminated racial inequity. What is often left out of these equations are the similarities between northern and southern segregationist legislation, social practices, and economic hierarchies. What is also occluded is the political manipulation of hybridity, by Latin American official cultures in the nineteenth century, which encouraged miscegenation (without legitimating interracial marriage) as a strategy for diminishing the threat of black political power. And finally, in the twentieth century, this rhetoric has been used both to mask racialized economic disparities and to fuel the popular conception that blackness is something Latinos get rid of with socialization, interracial sex, and hair straightener.

I hear echoes of that strategy in the deployment of contemporary multicultural rhetoric in this country—an official celebration designed to contend with white fears of a growing non-white population and to hide increasing economic polarization. And, as U.S. late capitalism begins to resemble late feudalism, I perceive greater and greater similarities between the deplorable living conditions and excessive policing of people of color in the South and that in the North. The national and linguistic differences between them don't really make that much of a difference anymore.

The black British–black American dialogue has helped to highlight the historical contradictions that forged an oppositional relationship between race and nationality in the Anglophone contexts. It has extended a debate on black hybridity, both racial and cultural, that had already been broadened by the feminisms of such writers as Michele Wallace and Angela Davis. And I firmly believe that this debate can be enhanced only if recast as a pan-American dialogue, taking into account the complementary discourses on race and nation in Latin America that began five hundred years ago and have informed revolutionary political movements and cultural syncretism in the region's multiracial societies.

While the advanced technologies of contemporary societies have facilitated popular cultural dialogue between geographically disparate black populations, it is also true that the concurrent postwar immigrations of black Americans, Afro-Caribbeans, Puerto Ricans, Dominicans, and Cubans to the inner cities of the United States are creating the conditions for the production of hybrid black/latino, english/spanish/spanglish cultures. Not even the social engineering that demands conveniently absolutist, but pseudoscientific, distinctions between black Americans and Caribbean Latinos can completely suppress the history of over a century of cultural and political dialogue between jazz musicians and *soneros,* between Cuban revolutionaries and civil rights leaders, between Young Lords and Black Panthers. Those dialogues resonate in the exchanges between black and Latino rappers who hail from the barrios of New York, Los Angeles, São Paulo, and San Juan, and in the formation of pan-Caribbean syncretism in Brooklyn and the Bronx. Those interactions are transforming what was once a largely Caribbean phenomenon into the seeds of America's cultural present and future.

Manthia Diawara

Afro-Kitsch

My title comes from Donald John Cosentino, who wrote an article on Afro-kitsch, applying it to African art.[1] I am using it in respect to African-American art and, specifically, in respect to the discourses of Afrocentricity and the kind of work I do myself—literary theory and film theory.

The word "kitsch" is often applied to objects that mark signs of indeterminacy. You know, we say things like, "Is it art or is it kitsch?" Kitsch connotes the banal, the inauthentic, the cheap imitation. Kitsch art is often accused of cutting loose old forms from their social networks and redeploying them in utterly new contexts. And kitsch art functions to reinforce identification and to promote consumption of the object thus put forth; it requires an unmediated emotional response. Finally, kitsch art is said to be a murderer of authentic art.

Now, this definition seems untenable today—as we are well aware of the poststructuralist celebration of difference, hybridity, creolization, and the carnivalesque. Questions of textuality are no longer so simple. In fact, the definition of kitsch art, which I have adopted here from Herman Bloch, seems conservative today. It positions the high and rarified over the low and popular. But I want to retain kitsch, nonetheless, in order to address such related matters as national style, mass conversion, and nostalgia. I am concerned that forums such as these have become sites of temporary feel-good, spaces for mass conversions that cover our wounds without healing them, or redeeming us. Revolutionary traditions are invoked only to be coopted in these cathartic moments. And generic pan-African symbols increasingly seem the preferred style for that mode of uplifting.

Spike Lee's *Do the Right Thing* is a good example of the ambivalent situation for which kitsch art is known. In 1989, the year *Do the Right Thing* was made, there was a ban on realism. Hollywood produced mostly sequels and remakes.

We had one more Indiana Jones, Star Trek, and Superman. And amid this nostalgia for old glory, the attempt to recover what America "used to be," *Do the Right Thing* seemed authentic. After all, the Reagan-Bush administration was returning us to glorious America, and this was not so glorious for black people.

But by what means do we measure *Do the Right Thing*'s authenticity? Wahneema Lubiano reminds us that the authenticity of the representation of the black community in films such as *Do the Right Thing* depends more on films by other black directors than on some essentialist notion of the black community.[2] *Do the Right Thing* produced mass identification in at least three directions (and this is why it's kitsch): black neonationalists saw it as an emblem of their cause; whites identified negatively in the form of their denial; and feminists re-created a martyrdom in its discourse. Is it art or is it kitsch?

As if that was not enough, John Sayles created his version of *Do the Right Thing* in *City of Hope*. And there we have it—repetitions, sequels, imitations. Certainly, if Spike Lee can speak for black people, John Sayles can speak for white and black liberals. Is it art, or is it kitsch? Art or racism?

I turn now to James Brown to further address the murkiness of kitsch art. I am concerned here with the new in kitsch. In other words, can kitsch make new? And can a new discourse be cutting edge, grounded in the material conditions of a people, combining politics and culture in order to liberate us? I'm going to give the authentic me at this point.

In 1965, Radio Mali advertised a concert by Junior Wells and his All-Star Band at the Omnisport in Bamako. The ads promised the Chicago group would electrify the audience with tunes from such stars as Otis Redding, Wilson Pickett, and James Brown. I was very excited because I had records by Junior Walker, and to me, at that time, with my limited English, Junior Wells and Junior Walker were one and the same. (That still happens to me, by the way.) It was a little disappointing that we couldn't have James Brown in person. I had heard that Anglophone countries like Ghana, Liberia, and Nigeria were luckier. They could see James Brown on television, and they even had concerts with Tyrone Davis, Aretha Franklin, and Wilson Pickett.

Sure enough, the concert was electrifying. Junior Wells and his All-Star Band played "My Girl," "I've Been Loving You Too Long," "It's A Man's World," "There Was a Time," "I Can't Stand Myself," "Papa's Got a Brand New Bag," "Respect," "Midnight Hour," and, of course, "Say It Loud (I'm Black and I'm

Proud)." During the break, some of us were allowed to talk with the musicians and to ask for autographs. The translator for us was a white guy from the United States Information Services. I remember distinguishing myself by going past the translator and asking one of the musicians the following question: "What is your name?" His eyes lit up, and he told me his name and asked for mine. I said, "My name is Manthia, but my friends call me J. B." He said something about James Brown, and I said something else. By that time, everybody else was quiet, watching us. I had only two years of junior high school English and the three-month summer vacations I had spent in Liberia to assist me. I got the nickname J. B. from my James Brown records.

The next day the news traveled all over Bamako that I spoke English like an American. This was tremendous in a Francophone country where one acquired subjecthood through recourse to *Francité* (thinking through French grammar and logic). Our master thinker was Jean-Paul Sartre. We were also living in awe, a form of silence, thinking that to be Francophone subjects, we had to master *Francité* like Léopold Senghor, who spoke French better than French people. Considered as one who spoke English like Americans and who had a fluent conversation with star musicians, I was acquiring a new type of subjecthood that put me perhaps above my comrades who knew by heart their *Les Chemins de la Liberté* by Sartre. I was on the cutting edge—the front line of the revolution.

You see, for me, then, and for many of my friends, to be liberated was to be exposed to more R&B songs and to be *au courant* of the latest exploits of Muhammad Ali, George Jackson, Angela Davis, Malcolm X, and Martin Luther King, Jr. These were becoming an alternative cultural capital for the African youth—imparting to us new structures of feeling and enabling us to subvert the hegemony of *Francité* after independence.

I want to use this personal anecdote to make a few comments about the discourse of blackness and of Afrocentricity—which I call the "kitsch of blackness"—hence, Afro-kitsch. I have placed the music of James Brown and others at the cutting edge to make some remarks about the academic front line.

Words and phrases such as "revolution," "subversion," and "transformation of society" are no longer permitted in Marxist theory, feminist theory, or deconstruction. (And I name only these because I work inside of them). In my opinion, feminism lost the cutting edge when it turned its back on the subversion of patriarchal systems and concentrated, instead, on the empowerment of a few women. One can appropriately label the present state of feminism as "essentialist," because it no longer looks for the social constructions that oppress women. It has become a grand narrative with a beginning, a middle, and an end. Marxism, too, lost the cutting edge when its best theorist abandoned the revolution and was co-opted by structuralist analyses of hegemonic texts. And finally, deconstruction reached a dead end when it ran out of texts to deconstruct and became a theory about difference with a capital "D." As Stuart Hall said, some differences might not make any difference at all.

One might say that James Brown lost the cutting edge when he was co-opted by disco music in the seventies. We had to look to George Clinton and the Parliament Funkadelic to determine whether or not James Brown had eluded co-optation. Deconstructivists, feminists, and Marxists no longer have texts with which to theorize their subversive views; they have turned their backs on the material conditions of their discourses. They turn to themselves, cite themselves, and repeat themselves. Meanwhile, like every bourgeoisie, their rank and file keeps growing and their critique of the system grows less and less subversive. It is this intellectual self-fashioning and self-promotion, in the name of a theory that bears the appearance of subversion (and yet only shapes the career of the theorist), that led me to entitle my talk "Afro-kitsch."

Afrocentrists, having learned the rules of the game from feminists, Marxists, and deconstructivists, have turned their backs to texts. And by "texts," I mean the lived experiences of black people in New York, Detroit, Lagos, and Dakar. Afrocentrists have recreated Egypt, the old African city, but their discourses, unlike James Brown's music in the sixties, do not serve the homeless in Philadelphia, let alone inspire revolution in South Africa. And I submit that until Afrocentricity learns the language of black people in Detroit, Lingala in Zaire, and Bambara in Mali, and grounds itself in the material conditions of the people in question, it is nothing but a kitsch of blackness. It is nothing but an imitation of a discourse of liberation. Afrocentric academics fix blackness by reducing it to Egypt and *kente* cloths. Hence, like Judaism, Christianity, and Islam, Afrocentrism has become a religion, a camp movement, where one can find refuge from the material realities of being black in Washington, D. C., London, or Nairobi.

By placing James Brown on the cutting edge, and life on the front line, as Eddie Grant would say, I want to bring black cultural practitioners' attention to the precarious situation of kitsch theory. James Brown always risked the danger of co-optation, and once he was co-opted, he became a kitsch of himself, a cheap imitation. Feminism, deconstruction, and Afrocentricity are at the same impasse that James Brown met. They imitate themselves and refuse to look at new texts of oppression. They elevate intra-class rivalries to the rank of oppression against the homeless and the wretched of the earth. They co-opt oppression for themselves. One should not become as comfortable in blackness, or in feminism, as the happy man or women of religion. Blackness and feminism are not a discovery of a truth that lives with one ever after.

Elsewhere, I have defined blackness as a modernist metadiscourse on the condition of black peoples in the West and in areas under Western domination. Blackness is a compelling performance against the logic of slavery and colonialism by those people whose destinies have been inextricably linked to the advancement of the West, and who, therefore, have to learn the expressive techniques of modernity—writing, music, Christianity, industrialization—in order to become uncolonizable. Blackness, in the last instance, is a reflexive discourse, what W.E.B. Du Bois would have called "an afterthought of modernity," a critical theory on the cutting edge of modernity and modernism, a frontline discourse. Blackness is not removed from the material base of politics and theory. It always seeks to liberate spaces, to subvert orthodoxies, to give voice to the oppressed.

When blackness is conceived as a humanist metadiscourse on the condition of black peoples in the West and in areas under Western domination, it becomes easier to see how people in Africa appropriate its Western modes—*négritude*, black consciousness—to sing their right to independence. The formulation of blackness in the West also empowers them with Africanism: African tradition, history, language, and nomenclature. Blackness and Africanism depend on each other, feed on each other, though they are not always interchangeable.

Blackness, as a modernist metadiscourse on the West imbued with revolutionary potential, is always enabling as a model to other repressed discourses like feminism, gay and lesbian rights, and minority cultures in totalitarian systems. The Chinese students and workers in Tiananmen Square sang "We Shall

Overcome"—a black song signaling a challenge to the logic of authoritarianism through Christianity. Blackness itself is challenged in the hands of its postcolonial and postmodern subjects. By focusing on such zones of ambivalence as identity formation, sexual politics, and hybridization, the postmodern subjects of blackness attempt to prevent it from falling into the same essentialist trap as whiteness.

1. Donald John Cosentino, "Afrokitsch" in *Africa Explores: Twentieth Century African Art*, ed. Susan Vogel (New York: Center for African Art, 1991), 240–255.
2. Wahneema Lubiano, "But Compared to What? Reading Realism, Representation, and Essentialism in *School Daze, Do the Right Thing*, and the Spike Lee Discourse," *Black American Literature Forum* 25, no.2 (Summer 1991), 253.

Manning Marable

Race, Identity, and Political Culture

The fundamental rules regulating race relations have changed since the Civil Rights Movement. No longer do we witness the "white" and "colored" signs on the doors of restaurants, restrooms, schools, and motels. No longer do we deny African Americans the right to vote. But the passage of legislation does not represent the fundamental empowerment of the oppressed. Instead, we bear witness to a more insidious and complex structure of domination. Race continues to be a decisive variable in the national structure of power, privilege, and class exploitation. It permeates the political culture and distorts electoral outcomes.

Briefly, I would like to explore three sets of interrelated questions within the rubric of race and American political culture. First, how does race continue to structure the character of American politics? What is the essence of the "race card" in the presidential election of 1992? How does race assume a central position in the dynamics of electoral politics and both political parties? Second, how has this reconstitution of race manifested itself within African-American political culture? Let us reexamine the Anita Hill–Clarence Thomas controversy in this light. I will argue that one of the factors that led many African Americans to support then Supreme Court justice nominee Clarence Thomas was the impasse within the political ideology of "liberal integrationism," and within it, the concept of "symbolic representation." The basic assumptions and tactics that guided the African-American middle class for several generations no longer reflect the actual economic, social, and political conditions challenging the Black community. And third, what elements of African-American nationalism and the cultural politics of Black history are relevant to a renaissance of the Black freedom struggle today? I believe it is possible to take the progressive kernels out of the concept of Black nationalism and liberal integrationism, moving toward a new definition of "Blackness," one that can be used in the struggle to create a more democratic, multicultural America.

Despite the passage of desegregation laws and the granting of democratic rights to African Americans nearly a generation ago, "race" continues to be the most influential factor in American politics. Graphic illustration of the centrality of race in the electoral system was provided by the November 1991 gubernatorial election in Louisiana. African Americans came to the polls in record numbers to block the election of neo-Nazi and former Ku Klux Klan leader David Duke—who had campaigned for the governorship on a thinly veiled program of white supremacy. However, if Black voters had stayed home, Louisiana's white electorate would have elevated Duke into the governor's mansion. According to voter surveys, about fifty-five percent of all whites supported Duke over three-term former governor Edwin Edwards. And Duke's greatest concentration of support was registered among whites who had suffered most in the state's economic recession. Sixty-eight percent of all whites with a high school education or less, sixty-nine percent of the white "born-again Christians," and sixty-three percent of all whites with family incomes between $15,000 and $30,000 favored Duke. Conversely, only thirty percent of whites who annually earn more than $75,000 voted for the former Klansman. This illustrates just how highly effective race can be in mobilizing white working-class discontent.

Both the Democrats and the Republicans are aware that race will be the crucial factor in determining the 1992 presidential race. The Democratic candidates go into the election as distinct long-shots for at least two reasons. First, despite Bush's decline in popularity, incumbent presidents of either party rarely lose. The only incumbent presidents defeated seeking re-election since World War I have been Herbert Hoover and Gerald Ford, the victims of the Great Depression and the Watergate scandal, respectively.

Second, Republicans have received a majority of whites' votes in every presidential election except one since 1948. No matter who the Democrats nominate for the presidency, the candidate will have the same difficult task: pulling together northern white ethnics and many white workers from the South while courting African-American and Latino voters. The only recent Democratic candidate to have achieved such a coalition was Jimmy Carter in 1976, and even Carter failed to gain a majority of the white vote nationally.

The Republicans and Bush have already begun to respond by playing the race card: the deliberate manipulation of racial prejudices for partisan political purposes. By first vetoing and later signing a weakened civil rights bill, Bush postured in the shadow of Duke. Bush's counsel, C. Boyden Gray, attempted to force the president to sign a policy statement that would have ended the use of racial preferences in federal government hiring policies. Although Gray's statement was repudiated, the controversy it provoked among civil rights and congressional leaders illustrated once again that Bush has absolutely no principled commitment to the fight against discrimination.

Bush calculates that if two-thirds of all white Americans support him in 1992 (exactly the same percentage of whites who backed Reagan eight years before), he will win the White House without a single Black or Latino vote. By pandering to white racism, Bush solidifies his support among fearful, frustrated whites. Millions of jobless, discouraged whites are searching for simplistic answers to explain their poverty and economic marginality. By playing this race card, an environment is created in which thousands of minorities may lose their jobs or fall victim to racist harassment. But Bush couldn't care less.

Bush's only worry about the race card is his competition from the right wing within his own party. By running for the Republican nomination for president, reactionary journalist Patrick Buchanan pressured Bush to assume more conservative policy positions. Duke even suggested that he and Buchanan run as a conservative "tag team" to challenge Bush. But all speculation concerning the demise of Duke as a national presence because of his recent electoral loss in Louisiana is highly exaggerated. Duke flourishes because Bush has prepared the ideological and cultural terrain by pandering to racism. In political terms, Duke is Bush's "illegitimate son" and "heir." Duke is the child the president desperately desires to disown, but Duke's political features of hatred and hostility to civil rights bear too striking a resemblance to those of his "father."

Duke's emergence and Bush's cynical manipulation of racist symbols are only part of the contemporary burden of race. In very different ways, the continuing reality of race as a political factor affects African-American political behavior and expectations. The best recent illustration of this problem was the controversy over the appointment of Clarence Thomas to the Supreme Court. The vast majority of African Americans realized that Thomas, a Black conservative and former Reagan administration official, was a bitter opponent of affirmative action and civil rights. Hostility increased when Thomas's former assistant, University of Oklahoma law professor Anita Hill, gave persuasive testimony before the Senate Judiciary Committee that indicated that Thomas had committed acts of gross sexual harassment. Despite such evidence, millions of African Americans supported Thomas's elevation to the Supreme Court. How do we explain their behavior?

My own impression is that most African Americans rationalized their support for Thomas in distinctly "racial" terms—"He may be an apologist for Reaganism, but at least he's Black." If Bush was going to replace the liberal jurist Thurgood Marshall with a conservative, shouldn't he be "one of us"? This was the reason that Jesse Jackson, who expresses himself on virtually every political issue, was silent on Thomas. The problem with this argument is that there are two very different types of Blackness, and Thomas was the beneficiary of African-American confusion on this issue.

Race is essentially a group identity imposed on individuals by others. During Jim Crow segregation, a person's color told us much about his or her background, kinships, social behavior, culture, and politics. We were isolated as a group from the "mainstream" of American society by the walls of legal racism. But in the post–civil rights era, this is no longer true. Blackness, in purely racial terms, only means belonging to a group of people who have in common a certain skin color and other physical features. In this limited sense, both Thomas and I are "Black." But today, this racial identity doesn't tell us anything significant about a person's political beliefs, voting behavior, or cultural values.

Blackness, or African-American identity, is much more than race. It is also the traditions, rituals, values, and belief systems of African-American people. It is our culture, history, music, art, and literature. Blackness is our sense of ethnic consciousness and pride in our heritage of resistance against racism. This African-American identity is not something our oppressors forced upon us. It is a cultural and ethnic awareness we have collectively constructed for ourselves over hundreds of years. This identity is a cultural umbilical cord connecting us with Africa.

When African Americans think about Blackness, we usually are referring to both definitions simultaneously—racial identity, a category the Europeans created and deliberately imposed on us for the purpose of domination, and Black cultural identity, which we constantly reinvent and construct for ourselves. But for many white Americans, their understanding of Blackness is basically one definition only, racial identity. They have little awareness or comprehension of African-American history, politics, religion, or culture. Blackness to them is skin color and a person's physical features, period.

These divergent definitions of Black identity are at the root of the contemporary dilemma of African-American political culture. Throughout the twentieth century, the bulk of the Black middle-class leadership has espoused an ideology of liberal integrationism, grounded in faulty racial assumptions. Liberal integrationism, in brief, is a strategy of political action that calls for the deconstruction of institutional racism through liberal reforms within the government and the assimilation of Blacks as individuals within all levels of the work force, culture, and society. This approach to political change is based on what I term "symbolic representation"—that is, a belief that if an African American receives a prominent appointment in the government, the private sector, or the media, that Black people as a group are symbolically empowered. This was essentially the argument by many Black liberals who defended the nomination of Republican conservative Clarence Thomas to the Supreme Court. Despite his reactionary ideology, it was argued, Thomas is nevertheless racially Black; "he shares our experiences of oppression and will sympathize with our concerns once he's appointed to a lifetime job."

This thesis of liberal integrationism was largely true during the era of Jim Crow segregation. Black professionals were connected with Black working-class and poor people by enumerable linkages. Black doctors depended upon Black patients; Black college professors taught in historically Black colleges; Black lawyers usually had Black clients, maintained their offices in Black neighborhoods, and lived next to other Black people. The police didn't inquire about an African American's socioeconomic background or level of educational attainment if she/he was in violation of Jim Crow laws. But in the post–civil rights era, the structures of accountability for the Black professional middle class have begun to erode. A new type of African-American leadership emerged inside the public and private sectors; this leadership lives outside the Black community and has little personal contact with other African Americans. Symbolic representation no longer works with bureaucrats and politicians who like Clarence Thomas, feel no sense of allegiance to the Black freedom struggle.

Liberal integrationism's chief economic assumptions were those of expansive, liberal capitalism and Keynesianism. Two generations ago, when the NAACP and the Black liberal political leadership were integrated into the New Deal coalition as junior partners, the economic basis of unity was liberal capitalism—the belief that the economic "pie" could expand indefinitely. Today's Black leadership in the Democratic Party holds many of the same economic assumptions, despite the radical transformation, deindustrialization, and destruction of the U.S. political economy in the past thirty years. The dire economic conditions of African Americans cannot be addressed by liberal reforms or by tinkering at the margins of a system in the midst of structural crisis. Poverty in the Black community won't be significantly reduced by minority economic set-asides, urban "enterprise zones," or by neo–Booker T. Washington–style Black Capitalism.

Since the 1960s, the vast majority of Black liberal integrationist leaders have defined politics almost solely as electoralism. Electing more African Americans to Congress, state legislatures, and city councils is perceived as increasing the political power of Blacks as a group. There are at least two major problems with this notion of politics. As previously mentioned, symbolic representation works to empower a constituency only when institutions of structural accountability—that is, those with the power to reward and to punish—exist between leaders and those they supposedly represent. Moreover, African-American leaders currently minimize tactics that a generation ago were at the heart of the Black freedom movement—sit-ins, teach-ins, selective buying campaigns or boycotts, civil disobedience, strikes, and demonstrations of all types. It is significant to note that neither Martin Luther King, Jr., Malcolm X, Paul Robeson, Fannie Lou Hamer, nor A. Philip Randolph were elected officials or drew their political authority from the electoral arena. King's chief political practice was going to jail to assert his political and moral beliefs. Somehow, Black leadership today has forgotten the tactics and lessons of the past and invested heavily in an electoral process that was never really designed to articulate Black grievances or demands.

Finally, liberal integrationism has at its core a blind loyalty to the Democratic Party. Since the Walter White regime at the NAACP fifty years ago, the bulk of the national Black leadership has perceived itself as an essential part of the political coalition behind national Democratic Party candidates for the presidency

298   Howard Beach, July 21, 1987.

Annapolis, Maryland, March 2, 1964.

and Congress. Even Jesse Jackson's break from this mainstream position, challenging Walter Mondale and Michael Dukakis inside the Democratic presidential primaries in the 1980s, was, in retrospect, a maneuver to articulate Black grievances inside the framework of the existing system. It is always difficult, if not perilous, to read Jackson's mind, but I believe that the "Country Preacher" never really intended to break with the Democratic Party or launch an independent liberal-left challenge to the two-party system. Mentally, emotionally, and ideologically, most Black leaders are committed to the Democratic Party—even if their constituents increasingly are not.

How do we revive the sense of militancy, activism, and independence within African-American politics as we enter the twenty-first century? What is required is not a full-blown ideology or a political dogma, but a creative, flexible approach and critical perspective on politics based on contemporary realities and the new conditions confronting African Americans today. Organizationally, we need several new kinds of institutions to help rebuild the Black freedom movement. First, and perhaps foremost, we need a new "Student Nonviolent Coordinating Committee," a youth-oriented formation that taps the energies and abilities of the hip-hop generation. A militant Black youth movement, directed and led by young people themselves, could target the issue of Black-on-Black violence in a more effective manner. It could help develop leadership skills among young people, acquainting them with the whole range of political interventions and tactics, such as economic boycotts and civil disobedience.

Second, we need a progressive political forum or activist/theoretical center bringing together progressive intellectuals, legislative aides, and community organizers to articulate a progressive public policy agenda that breaks from the strategy of traditional liberal integrationism. It must serve as a creative vehicle for debate and dialogue, constructing the public policies and tactics that can foster a new spirit of activism. It could serve as a pressure group on public policy, creating the influence necessary for greater accountability among traditional Black leaders. The center could hold regular public forums covered by the national media on crucial economic, social, and political issues or respond to crises as they erupt.

If such a center existed, several recent political events could have had very different outcomes. In the winter of 1989, for example, Jesse Jackson made a deliberate decision to demobilize the Rainbow Coalition and to cut off any avenues toward independent politics at the local level. This decision demoralized thousands of young activists throughout the country. If a progressive Black policy center had existed, with real connections to dozens of grass-roots, labor, women's, and youth organizations across the country, pressure could have been put on Jackson to reverse his decision. In the fall of 1991, there was no coherent, collective Black progressive voice heard nationally on the Anita Hill–Clarence Thomas debate. Without such pressure from Black progressives, African-American formations such as the Southern Christian Leadership Conference and the Urban League either endorsed Thomas or equivocated in their public stance.

But the central tragedy of Thomas's elevation to the Supreme Court is that his powerful image as a negative, racial role model for millions of African-American young people will be constantly reinforced every time we see the Supreme Court on television. His victory, and our failure to develop new structures of Black resistance in the post–civil rights era, reinforce tendencies toward compromise, political pessimism, and accommodation. Today, there is an entire generation of African Americans who were born after the struggles of the desegregation movement. They never witnessed the sit-ins, freedom rides, or desegregation boycotts. They never took part in Black Power demonstrations. Many of these African Americans, particularly in the upper-middle class, grew up in the white suburbs, attended white schools, and now are employed in predominately white businesses. They frequently don't attend Black churches or belong to Black social organizations. They have little personal contact or experience with the harsh problems of the inner city. One can argue that these individuals are certainly "Black" in racial terms, as defined by white society, but their "Blackness," as far as cultural connections and social experiences are concerned, is limited at best.

So, what should we conclude from these connections between race, ethnic identity, and political culture? The current political crisis of the 1990s forces African Americans toward a new historical conjuncture—the end of a set of familiar racial assumptions and realities and the beginning of a new configuration of race, politics, and power within American society. The political vision that guided the Black freedom struggle from Frederick Douglass to Martin Luther King, Jr. rested with two goals: first, the dismantling of racism within the legal, economic, and social apparatus and the granting of democratic rights to

African-American people; and second, the empowerment of the Black community in the context of culture, social relations, and daily life. This is what W. E. B. Du Bois meant, in *The Souls of Black Folk,* by the phrase "Of Our Spiritual Strivings." This is our sense of culture and beauty, our music, dance, and artistic sensibility, our quest for human dignity in our relations with whites. The struggle for freedom has always been a search for authentic identity, a sense of "being-for-ourselves," and not for others.

The contemporary challenge is to transcend these historical boundaries, drawing strength and recognition from our past traditions and struggles for identity and democratic rights while charting a new strategy and new organizations for collective resistance. We need to construct a new, dynamic culture of politics to inspire a new generation of African Americans—drawing, in part, from elements in the Black nationalist and liberal integrationist traditions but expressing this new vision of social and political transformation in strategic challenges to the system of white power and corporate privilege.

Such a break with the past, in order to advance to the next stage of the struggle for Black freedom, will require a new articulation of Blackness. In Europe, and particularly in England, "Blackness" is defined not in racial or ethnic/cultural terms but as a political category for the mobilization of several different ethnic groups including Indians, Pakistanis, Indonesians, West Indians, and others. We must find new room in our identity as people of color to include all other oppressed national minorities—Chicanos, Puerto Ricans, Asian/Pacific Americans, Native Americans, and other people of African descent. We must find the common ground we share with oppressed people who are not national minorities—working-class people, the physically challenged, the homeless, the unemployed, and those Americans who suffer discrimination because they are lesbian or gay. I believe that a new multicultural America is possible, that a renaissance of Black militancy will occur in concert with new levels of activism from the constituencies mentioned above. But it is possible only if we have the courage to challenge and to overturn our own historical assumptions about race, power, and ourselves. Only then will we find the new directions necessary to challenge the system, to "fight the power," with an approach toward political culture that can truly liberate all of us.

Paul Gilroy

It's a Family Affair

The complicated phenomena we struggle to name as black nationalism, cultural nationalism, and neonationalism have now been so reconfigured that our essentially nineteenth-century, or maybe even eighteenth-century, understanding of them has to be abandoned. Everywhere, as a result of both internal and external pressures, the integrity of the nation-state, as the primary focus of economic, political, and cultural action, has been compromised. The impact of this on nationalist ideologies (black and otherwise) is particularly important and needs to be taken into account. I am not satisfied with just pinning the prefix "neo" onto nationalism and feeling that we've done the job of analyzing it. If we are to distinguish the contemporary discourses of black nationalism from the black nationalisms of the past, we have to examine the novel modes of information and cultural production in which they circulate.

Perhaps the easiest place to begin is to think about the changes in information and communication technologies that have taken all nationalisms away from their historic association with the technology of print culture. This is one way of conceptualizing the changed notions of space and time we associate with the impact of the postmodern and the postindustrial on black cultures. If we are to think of ourselves as diaspora people, how do we then understand the notion of space? How do we adjust our understanding of the relationship between spatialization and identity formation in order to deal with these techno-cultural changes? One thing we might do is take a cue from Manuel Castells,[1] who describes the shift from an understanding of space based on notions of place and fixity to an understanding of place based on flows. Or, what another exiled Englishman, Iain Chambers, introduces in his very suggestive distinction between roots and routes.[2] (I don't think this pun has quite the same force in American versions of English). If we're going to pick up the vernacular

Still from *Young Soul Rebels*, directed by Isaac Julien, 1991.

ball and run with it, then maybe the notion of the crossroads—as a special location where unforeseen, magical things happen—might be an appropriate conceptual vehicle for rethinking this dialectical tension between cultural roots and cultural routes, between the space marked out by places and the space constituted by flows. The crossroads has a nicely Africalogical sound to it too: a point at which the flows of black popular cultures productively intersect.

These issues point to the way we will have to refine the theorizing of the African diaspora if it is to fit our changed transnational and intercultural circumstances. Though the current popularity of Afrocentrism points to other possibilities, we might consider experimenting, at least, with giving up the idea that our culture needs to be centered anywhere except where we are when we launch our inquiries into it. Certainly, we will have to find a better way to deal with the obvious differences between and within black cultures— differences that live on under the signs of their disappearances, constituting boundaries that stubbornly refuse to be erased.

I wish I had five bucks for every time I've heard the trope of the family wheeled out to do the job of recentering things when the debates of the last few days promised to question the spurious integrity of ideal racial culture. The trope of the family is especially significant right now when the idea of belonging to a nation is only infrequently invoked to legitimate the essence of today's black political discourses. Certainly in England, and probably in the United States, as well, there are a number of other legitimation strategies, but the invocation of "race" as family is everywhere. Its dominance troubles me because, at the moment, in the black English constituency out of which I speak, the trope of the family is not at the center of our discussion of what a black politics could or should be. And I'll return to that point later.

Afrocentricity names itself "systematic nationalism" (that's what Molefi Kete Asante calls it)[3], but it is stubbornly focused around the reconstitution of individual consciousness rather than around the reconstruction of the black nation in exile or elsewhere. The civic, nation-building activity that defined the Spartan-style aspirations of black nationalism in the nineteenth century has been displaced in favor of the almost aesthetic cultivation of a stable, pure, racial self. The "ism" in that nationalism is often lacking, too; it is no longer constructed as a coherent political ideology. It appears more usually as a set of therapies—tactics in the never-ending struggle for psychological and cultural survival. In some nonspecific way, then, a new idea of Africanness, conveniently disassociated from the politics of contemporary Africa, operates transnationally and interculturally through the symbolic projection of "race" as kinship. It is now more often a matter of style, perspective, or survivalist technique than a question of citizenship, rights, or fixed contractual obligations (the things that defined nationality in earlier periods).

Indeed, though contemporary nationalism draws creatively on the traces of romantic theories of national belonging and national identity, derived from the ethnic metaphysics of eighteenth-century Europe, Afrocentric thinking attempts to construct a sense of black particularity *outside* of a notion of a national identity. Its founding problem lies in the effort to figure sameness across national boundaries and between nation-states. The first sentence of Asante's "Nia—The Way" can be used to illustrate this: "This is the way that came to Molefe in America."[4] But the text's elisions of African-American particulars into African universals belie this modesty. Look also at the moment in the same text where the author struggles with the fact that only thirty-seven percent of the blacks who live in the Western hemisphere live in the United States. Forty percent, he muses to himself, live in Brazil. What do we do about that? Where are their inputs into Africalogical theory?

The understanding of blackness that emerges routinely these days gets projected, then, onto a very different symbolic landscape than it did in either nineteenth-century black nationalism, in Garveyism, or in the nationalism of the Black Power period. The new popular pantheon of black heroes is apparently a diasporic one—Marcus, Malcolm, Martin, Marley, Mandela, and *Me!* The narcissistic momentum of that masculine list is another symptom of a cultural implosion that must work against the logic of national identity. The flow is always inward, never outward; the truth of racialized being is sought, not in the world, but in the psyche. I know that the moment of epistemological narcissism is necessary in building movements that actually move, but doesn't it abandon the world of public politics, leaving us with a form of therapy that has little to offer beleaguered communities?

Some of the rhetoric of nationalism, however, does remain. It's there in the service of groups like the Five Percent Nation and the Nation of Islam. But for them it legitimates an ideology of separation that applies as viciously within the race as it does between blacks and whites. If there is still a coherent nationalism in play though—and I say this from my own perch in London—I want to suggest that it is the nationalism of black Americans. This nationalism is a powerful subtext in the discourse of Afrocentricity, but it has evolved from an earlier period in black U.S. history. It is a very particular way of looking at the world that, far more than it expresses any exilic consciousness of Africa, betrays a distinctively American understanding of ethnicity and cultural difference. The family is the approved, natural site where ethnicity and racial culture are reproduced. In this authoritarian pastoral patriarchy, women are identified as the agents and means of this reproductive process.

This is where the question of the family begins to bite: representations of the family in contemporary black nationalism, transcoded—maybe wrongly—from London, appear to mark the site of what can, at the least, be called an ambivalent relationship to America. So, recognizing this, I don't want to call it Afrocentrism any more. I want to call it Americocentrism. And I want to suggest that it has evolved in a very uneasy mode of coexistence with the pan-African political discourses that gave birth to it. Of course, the identification with Africa, on which that Americocentrism is premised, is necessarily partial and highly selective. Contemporary Africa, as I have said, appears nowhere. The newly invented criteria for judging racial authenticity are supplied instead by restored access to original African forms and codes. It is significant, however—and this is where the trope of the family begins to look like a disaster for black feminism—that those definitions of authenticity are disproportionately defined by ideas about nurturance, about family, about fixed gender roles, and generational responsibilities. What is authentic is also frequently defined by ideas about sexuality and patterns of interaction between men and women that are taken to be expressive of essential, that is, racial, difference. This authenticity is inseparable from talk about the conduct and management of bitter gender-based conflicts, which is now recognized as essential to familial, racial, and communal health. Each of these—the familial, the racial, the communal—leads seamlessly into the next. Where was that heavy chain of signifiers forged? Whose shackles will it make? How does that conjunction reveal the impact, not just of an unchanged Africa, but of a contemporary America?

Now, the changed status of nationality in black political discourse can also be felt in the way the opposition between the local and the global has been reinscribed in our culture and in our consciousness. Today, we are told that the boys, and the girls, are from the 'hood—not from the race, and certainly not from the nation. It's important that the 'hood stands in opposition to foreign things—if you remember John Singleton's film—in opposition to the destructive encroachments of Seoul-to-Seoul Realty or the idea of turning the ghetto into black Korea. (Does Singleton's choice of that proper name for the Korean menace signal a rebuke to Soul II Soul?)

From London, the untranslatability of the term "'hood" troubled me. I thought it marked a significant shift away from the notion of the ghetto, which is eminently exportable, and which carries its own very interesting intercultural history that we should be able to play with. But, if the 'hood is the essence of where blackness can now be found, which 'hood are we talking about? How do we weigh the achievements of one 'hood against the achievements of another? How is black life in one 'hood connected to life in others? Can there be a blackness that connects, articulates, synchronizes experiences and histories across the diaspora space? Or is it only the sign of Larry Fishburne's patriarchal power that holds these different local forms of blackness together?

This matters not just because images of black sociality not derived from the family seem to have disappeared from our political cultures, but also because, if Tim Dog is to be believed, Compton is as foreign to some blacks in New York as Kingston, London, Havana, Lagos, Aswan, or Capetown—possibly even more so. His popular outrage against West Coast Jheri curls and whack lyrics registers (as does his claim that all that gang shit is for dumb motherfuckers) disappointment and frustration that the idea of a homogeneous national community has become impossible and unthinkable. Maybe this is what happens when one 'hood speaks to another.

> Ah, shit. Motherfucker step to the ring and cheer.
> The Tim Dog is here.
> Let's get right down to the nitty gritty.
> And talk about a bullshit city.
> Talking about niggers from Compton.
> They're no comp and they truly ain't stompin'.
> Tim Dog, a black man's task,
> I'm so bad, I wear Superman's mask.

All you suckers that rip from the West Coast,
I'll dis' and spray your ass like a roach.
You think you're cool with your curls and your shades,
…and you'll be yelling outrage.
A hard brother that lives in New York.
We suckas are hard, and we don't have to score.
Shut your mouth, or we come out stompin'.
And yo Easy, fuck Compton.[5]

Now, I don't pretend to understand everything Tim Dog's performance means here in the United States, but in London it has a very particular meaning. This has to do with a bewilderment about some of the self-destructive and sibling-cidal patterns of sociality that have been a feature of black U.S. inner-urban life. The same tension between the local and the global—implosion at one end, dissemination at the other—is, again, part of the story. Of course, when these things come down the transnational wire to us in Europe and to black folks in other parts of the world, they become metaphysical statements about what blackness is. And we have to deal with them on that basis.

Obviously, there are other voices, and there are other subject positions. In fact, one of the things I find troubling in debates about rap is that I don't think anyone actually knows what the totality of its hypercreativity looks like. I am a compulsive consumer (user, actually) of that culture, but I can't keep up with the volume of hip-hop product anymore. I don't know if anyone can. There is simply too much of it to be assimilated, and the kinds of judgments we make have to take that volume into account. It's a flood—it's not a flow, it's a flood, actually—and just bobbing up and down in the water is not enough.

But when we come back to the family, the idea of hip hop as a dissident, critical space looks more questionable. Ironically, it is precisely where the motivation is constructive that the pastoral patriarchy of race as family gets reproduced. Another voice I want to present answers, in a sense, the calculated nihilism of Tim Dog. It's an attempt, by KRS 1 (Chris Parker), to locate the politics of race in what he describes as the opposition between civilization and technology—an interesting opposition because of its desire to hold onto the narrative of civilization and make it part of a grand narrative of black development. But this attempt is notable not just for its humanism—humanity versus technology—but for the extraordinary emphasis that falls on the family. I wonder how much the trope of the family allows him to hold the very diverse forces of this new racialized humanism together.

> Be a Man, not a sucker.
> And don't disrespect your baby's mother.
> When the pressure's on, don't run for cover.
> We gotta move on and be strong for one another.
> You can't just be a lover, build the nation.
> We gotta start with better relations.
> 'Cause the family is the foundation.
> We're here to heal, and we're here for the duration.
> Multi-educating.
> Definitely develop your African mind because we are all family. And once we see that we are all brothers and sisters no matter what, we go far beyond the nuclear family—from an Afrocentric point of view.[6]

I don't want to be forced into the position of having to point out that it may not help to collapse our intraracial differences into the image of ourselves as brothers and sisters any more than I want to be forced into the position of saying that we don't all recognize our own images in the faces of Clarence Thomas and Anita Hill (which adorn the posters for this event) but that is some of what this Americocentric obsession with family brings to mind. I recognize that the discourse of racial siblinghood is a democratic one. I know it emerged from the communitarian radicalism of the church and that, as W.E.B. Du Bois pointed out long ago in *The Souls of Black Folk,* this happened in a period before the slaves enjoyed the benefits of nuclear family life. The political language of brotherhood and sisterhood can be used in ways that accentuate an image of community composed of those with whom we disagree. From this perspective, the differences we still experience, in spite of white supremacy's centripetal effects, might be seen as a precious and potentially productive resource. However, at the moment, the wind is blowing in another direction.

Obviously, not all of this popular culture wants to bury its differences in images of an organic, natural, racial family. And I have been especially engaged by the voices within hip-hop culture that have sought other strategies for living with difference and building on the hybrid qualities of the form itself to affirm the value of mixing and what might be called creolization. There are some absorbing poetic attempts to explore the consequences of a new political ontology and a new historicity. I am excited, for example, by Rakim's repeated suggestion that "it ain't where you're from, it's where you're at." It grants a priority to the present, emphasizing a view of identity as an ongoing process of self-making at a time when myths of origins hold so much appeal. Sometimes that kind of idea is strongest where the Caribbean styles and forms, very often dominated by Pan-African motifs, are most developed. Caribbean popular cultures have their own rather more mediated and syncretized relationships to Africa. But it's also important to remember that reggae has constructed its own romance of racial nihilism in gun culture, misogyny, and machismo.

Rebel MC's "Wickedest Sound" comes from London and points to a different notion of authenticity.[7] Its racial witness is produced out of semiotic play rather than ethnic fixity, and a different understanding of tradition emerges out of the capacity to combine the different voices, styles, and motifs drawn from all kinds of sources in a montage of blackness(es). This version of the idea of authenticity, premised on a notion of flows, is also alive in diaspora culture. It's dear to me because it appeared within the version of hip-hop culture that we have produced in London. There are, of course, African-American traces here struggling to be heard among the Caribbean samples, but, happily, the trope of race as family is nowhere in sight.

Against this playful, vibrant, postracial utopia—which argues that there is no betrayal in the acknowledgment of a white listening public—an Americo-centric, postnationalist essence of blackness has been constructed through the dubious appeal to family.

There have been other periods in black political history where the image of race as family has been prominent. The nineteenth-century ideas of a nationality exclusively concerned with male soldier-citizens were produced in a period when an anti-imperialist or an anti-racist political project among diaspora blacks was unthinkable. We would do well to reconsider them now. Because they haunt us. In *Africa or America*, Alexander Crummell drew his theory of nationality and racial personality from the work of Lord Beaconsfield (Benjamin Disraeli):

> Races, like families, are organisms and the ordinance of God. And race feeling, like family feeling, is of divine origin. The extinction of race feeling is just as possible as the extinction of family feeling. Indeed, race is family. The principle of continuity is as masterful in races as it is in families, as it is in nations.[8]

This discourse of race as community, as family, has been born again in contemporary attempts to interpret the crisis of black politics and social life as a crisis solely of black masculinity. The family is not just the site of cultural reproduction; it is also identified as the mechanism for reproducing the cultural dysfunction that disables the race as a whole. And since the race is nothing more than an accumulation of families, the crisis of black masculinity can be fixed. It is to be repaired by instituting appropriate forms of masculinity and male authority, intervening in the family to rebuild the race.

Even hip-hop culture—the dissonant soundtrack of racial dissidence—has become complicit with this analysis. It's interesting, in thinking about the changing resonance of the word "nation" in black culture, that reports say Michael Jackson wants to call his new record company Nation Records. (One of the extraordinary things about the Jacksons is that they have turned their dysfunctionality as a black family into such an interesting marketing strategy.) Images of the black family complement the family tropes of the cultural forms themselves. These images are all around us in the selling of black popular culture. They are so visible in the marketing of Spike Lee and his projects that they point to the value of reading his oeuvre as a succession of Oedipal crises.

On the strange kind of cultural loop I live, I saw Marlon Riggs's powerful film *Tongues Untied* for the second time on the same night I first saw *Boyz N the Hood*. (We get these things in a different sequence than in the States). Listening to that authoritative voice saying that black men loving black men was *the* revolutionary act—not *a* revolutionary act but *the* revolutionary act—the force of that definite article set me to thinking about *Boyz N the Hood*. I know there are differences between these two projects. I have an idea of where some of them dwell. But aren't there also similarities and convergences in the way that love between men is the common focus of these "texts"?[9]

Let me say why I think the prominence of the family is a problem. Spreading the Oedipal narrative around a bit can probably produce some interesting effects, but this bears repeating: the trope of the family is central to the means whereby the crisis we are living—of black social and political life—gets represented as the crisis of black masculinity. That trope of the family is there, also, in the way conflict, within and between our communities, gets resolved through the mystic reconstruction of the ideal heterosexual family. This is the oldest conservative device in the book of modern culture. Once again, *Boyz N the Hood* is the most obvious illustration of an authentically black and supposedly radical product that is complacently comfortable working within those deeply conservative codes. In Isaac Julien's recent film *Young Soul Rebels,* the fragile image of nonfamilial community that appears has been much criticized. It's the point at which the film ends and a kind of surrogate, joyfully disorganic, and synthetic kin group constitutes itself slowly and tentatively—in and around desire, through music, affirmation, celebration, and play.

Lest this look like a binary split between conservative, familial Americana and the truly transgressive counterculture of black Britons, I want to amplify what I take to be a similar note of disorganicity in the way that kinship can be represented. It is drawn from an American hip-hop record popular on both sides of the Atlantic right now—a tune called "Be a Father to Your Child" by Ed O. G. and Da Bulldogs.[10] It's been very popular in London, partly because of the sample it uses—a seventies black nationalist love song called "Searching" from Roy Ayers—which gets transposed into a different conceptual key by this contemporary appropriation. Two things interest me about this cut. First of all, the object of desire in the original version of the tune was gendered female; it is about searching for the love of a black woman. In the Ed O. G. version, the object of desire is ungendered. I found the opening up of that signifier suggestive. It means that when Ed O. G. talks about familial obligation, he's not saying be a father to your son—he's saying be a father to your child.

Second, and more important, Ed O. G. makes the pragmatic *functionality* of family the decisive issue, not the biological payback involved in family life. If you are responsible for producing a child with someone, he says, and that child is being supported by somebody else who is prepared to father it effectively when you fail, then back off and let him get on with it—even if that person is not the biological parent. That small gesture is something I want to celebrate. I think it shows—though I don't want to sound prescriptive about this—that the struggle over the meaning of family is alive within the culture, that a critical perspective on these complex questions isn't something that needs to be imported into that vernacular from outside by people like us. We don't play that role.

> Hey yo, be a father.
> It's not, Why bother?, son.
> A boy can make 'em, but a man can raise 'em.
> And if you did it, admit it. Then stick with it.
> Don't say it ain't yours, 'cause all women are not whores.
> Ninety percent represent a woman that is faithful.
> Ladies can I hear it?
> *Thank you.*
> When a girl gets pregnant, her man is gonna run around,
> dissin' her for now, but when it's born he wants to come around
> talkin' that I'm sorry for what I did.
> And all of a sudden, he now wants to see his kid.
> She had to bear it by herself and take care of it by herself.
> And givin her some money for milk don't really help.
> Half of the fathers and sons and daughters don't even want to take 'em.
> But it's so easy for them to make 'em.
> It's true, if it weren't for you, the child wouldn't exist.
> Afterwards, he's your responsibility, so don't resist.
> Be a father to your child...
> See, I hate when a brother makes a child and then denies it.
> Thinkin' that money is the answer, so he buys it
> a whole bunch of gifts and a lot of presents.
> It's not the presents, it's your presence and the essence
> of bein' there and showin' the baby that you care.
> Stop sittin' like a chair and havin' your baby wondering
> where you are or who you are.
> Who you are is daddy.
> Don't act like you ain't 'cause that really makes me mad, G,
> to see a mother and a baby suffer.
> I had enough o' brothers who don't love the
> fact that a baby brings joy into your life.

You can still be called daddy if the mother's not your wife.
Don't be scared, be prepared.
'Cause love is gonna getcha.
It'll always be your child, even if she ain't witcha.
So, don't front on your child when it's your own,
'cause if you front now then you'll regret it when it's grown.
Be a father to your child...
Put yourself in his position and see what you've done.
But just keep in mind that you're somebody's son.
How would you like it if your father was a stranger,
and then tried to come into your life and tried to change the
way that your mother raised ya.
Now wouldn't that amaze ya?
To be or not to be.
That is the question.
When you're wrong, you're wrong.
It's time to make a correction.
Harrassin' the mother for bein' with another man.
But if the brother man can do it better than you can, *let 'im.*
Don't sweat 'im, dude.
Let him do the job that you couldn't do...[11]

I'll end by saying that even the best of this familialization of politics is still a problem. I don't want to lose sight of that. I want to have it both ways: I want to be able to valorize what we can recover; and I want to be able to cite the disastrous consequences that follow when the family supplies not just the only symbols of political agency we can find in the culture, but the only object upon which that agency can be seen to operate as well. Let's remind ourselves that there are other possibilities. Historically, black political culture's most powerful notions of agency have been figured through the sacred. They can also get figured through the profane, and there, a different idea of worldly redemption can be observed. Both of these possibilities come together for me in the traditions of musical performance that culminate in hip hop. In them, we find what I call the ethics of antiphony—a kind of ideal communicative moment in the relationship between the performer and the crowd that surpasses anything the structures of the family can provide.

1. Manuel Castells, *The Informational City* (Oxford: Basil Blackwell, 1991).

2. This distinction has also been employed in similar ways by Dick Hebdige and James Clifford. See Iain Chambers, *Border Dialogues* (New York: Routledge, 1990).

3. Molefi Kete Asante, *Afrocentricity* (Trenton, N.J.: Africa World Press, 1988).

4. Ibid.

5. Tim Dog, *Fuck Compton* [EP], Columbia Records, 1991. CD/Cassette.

6. H.E.A.L. [Human Education Against Lies], KRS 1, "Family Got to Get Busy," *Civilization Against Technology,* Elektra/Asylum Records, 1991. CD/Cassette.

7. Rebel MC, "Wickedest Sound," *Black Meaning Good,* Desire Records LUVCD12.

8. Alexander Crummell, *Africa or America* (Springfield, Mass.: Willey and Co., 1891), 46.

9. I use the word "texts" in quotation marks because I don't think any analysis that appropriates these cultural forms exclusively as texts will ever be adequate.

10. Ed O.G. & Da Bulldogs, *Life Of A Kid In The Ghetto,* Mercury Records, 1991. CD/Cassette.

11. Ibid.

Angela Y. Davis

Black Nationalism:
The Sixties and the Nineties

Initially, I had planned to discuss masculinist dimensions of Black nationalism and cultural challenges to male supremacy in the work of the Blueswomen, since my current work revolves around ways of retrieving possible cultural histories of African-American women. But my preliminary reflections on the kindred character of Black nationalism(s) and ideologies of male dominance during the sixties led me to consider an autobiographical approach. Therefore, I will attempt to revisit my own experience with the nationalisms of the sixties and to suggest ways in which contemporary Black popular culture may have been unduly influenced by some of the more unfortunate ideological convergences of that era.

I begin with some thoughts on the impact of Malcolm X's nationalist oratory on my own political awakening, which I would later think of in terms similar to Frantz Fanon's description of the coming to consciousness of the colonized in *The Wretched of the Earth*.

I remember the moment when I first felt the stirrings of "nationalism" in my—as I might have articulated it then—"Negro Soul." This *prise de conscience* occurred during a lecture delivered by Malcolm X at Brandeis University, where I was one of five or six Black undergraduates enrolled. I might have said that I felt "empowered" by Malcolm's words—except that the notion of power had not yet been understood in a way that separated the exercise of power from the subjective emotions occasioned by an awareness of the possibility of exercising it. But I recall that I felt extremely good—I could even say I experienced that joy that Cornel West talked about—momentarily surrounded by, feeling nurtured and caressed by Black people who, as I recall, seemed to have no par-

THE VIOLENT END OF THE   MAN CALLED MALCOLM X

ticular identity other than that they were Black.

This invitation to join an empowering, but abstract community of Black people—this naive nationalist consciousness—was extended to me in a virtually all-white setting. It was a strange, but quite logical, reversal. Having grown up in one of the most segregated cities in the South, I had never personally known a white person in my hometown. The only one with whom I remember having any contact was the Jewish man who owned the grocery store in our neighborhood. White people lived across the street from my family's house, but we litcrally lived on the border separating Black from white and could not cross the street on which our house was located. Because of the mandatory character of the Black community in which I grew up, I came to experience it as somewhat suffocating and desperately sought a way out.

Now, finally, on the other side of this feeling evoked in me by the offensive nationalist rhetoric of Malcolm X—offensive, both because he offended the white people in attendance and because he was ideologically on the offensive— I was able to construct a psychological space within which I could "feel good about myself." I could celebrate my body (especially my nappy hair, which I always attacked with a hot comb in ritualistic seclusion), my musical proclivities, and my suppressed speech patterns, among other things. But I shared these feelings with no one. It was a secret thing—like a collective, fictive playmate. This thing distanced me from the white people around me while simultaneously rendering controllable the distance I had always felt from them. It also meant that I did not have to defer to the mandatoriness of my Negro community back home. As a matter of fact, as a result of this experience into which Malcolm's words launched me, I felt a strengthening of the ties with the community of my birth.

This nationalist appeal of the early Malcolm X, however, did not move me to activism—although I had been something of an activist since the age of thirteen. I didn't particularly feel the need to *do* anything. It ended for me where it began—in changing the structure of my feeling. Don't get me wrong. I really needed that. I needed it at least as much as I would later need the appeal of the image of the leather-jacketed, black-bereted warriors standing with guns at the entrance to the California legislature. (I saw that image in a German newspaper while studying with Theodor Adorno in Frankfurt.) That image, which would eventually become so problematic for me, called me home. And it directed me into an organizing frenzy in the streets of South Central Los Angeles.

In a sense, the feeling that Malcolm had conjured in me could finally acquire a mode of expression—collective, activist, and, I hoped, transformative. Except that once I arrived in Southern California—with contacts I had gotten from Stokely Carmichael, whom I met, along with Michael X, in London at a "Dialectics of Liberation" conference—my inquiries and enthusiasm were interpreted as a desire to infiltrate local Black organizations. After all, I had just gotten off the boat from Europe. I had to be CIA or something. But, eventually, I did embark upon an exploration of some of the nationalisms of the era. I found out, during my initial contacts, that Ron Karenga's group was too misogynist (although I would not have used that word then). Another organization I found too middle class and elitist. Yet another fell apart because we, women, refused to be pushed to the back of the bus. And even though we may have considered the feminism of that period white, middle class, and utterly irrelevant, we also found compulsory male leadership utterly unacceptable.

Today, I realize that there is no simple or unitary way to look at expressions of Black nationalism or essentialism in contemporary cultural forms. As my own political consciousness evolved in the sixties, I found myself in a politically oppositional stance to what some of us then called "narrow nationalism." As a Marxist, I found issues of class and internationalism as necessary to my philosophical orientation as inclusion in a community of historically oppressed people of African descent. But, at the same time, I needed to say "Black is beautiful" as much as any of the intransigent anti-white nationalists. I needed to explore my African ancestry, to don African garb, and to wear my hair natural as much as the blinder-wearing male supremacist cultural nationalists. (And, by the way, I had no idea my own "natural" would achieve its somewhat legendary status; I was simply emulating other sisters.)

My relationship to the particular nationalism I embraced was rooted in political practice. The vortex of my practice was always the progressive, politicized Black community—though I frequently questioned my place as a Black woman in that community, even in the absence of a vocabulary with which to pose the relevant questions. Within the Communist Party, "Black" was my point of reference—which did not prevent me from identifying with the multiracial working class and its historical agency. I am not suggesting that the negotiation of that relationship was not fraught with many difficulties, but I do know that I

Angela Davis in 1972.

probably would not have joined the Communist Party at that time if I had not been able to enter the Party through an all-Black collective in Los Angeles called the Che-Lumumba Club.

The sisters who were my closest comrades, in SNCC, in the Black Panther Party, in the Communist Party, fought tenaciously—and we sometimes fought tenaciously among ourselves—for our right to fight. And we were sometimes assisted in this by sympathetic men in these organizations. We may not have been able to talk about gendered racism, "sexuality" may have still meant sexiness, homophobia, as a word, may not yet have existed, but our practice, I can say in retrospect, was located on a continuum that groped and zigzagged its way toward this moment of deliberation on the pitfalls of nationalism and essentialism.

I revisit my own history here to situate myself, in this current exploration of postnationalism, as a revolutionary activist during an era when nationalist and essentialist ideas about Black people and the Black struggle in the United States crystallized in such a way as to render them capable of surviving in the historical consciousness of people of African descent throughout the diaspora, but especially in the collective imagination of large numbers of African-American youth today. Perhaps we might make a similar observation about the Garveyism of the 1920s, but, among other things, the undeveloped state of—and forced exclusion from—both media technology and popular historical consciousness prevented us from later being inspired in the same way as by those slogans and images of the late sixties.

Today, of course, young people are explicitly inspired by what they know about Malcolm X and the Black Panther Party. And I find myself in a somewhat problematic position because my own image appears now and then in visual evocations of this nationalist impulse that fuel the advocacy of revolutionary change in contemporary hip-hop culture. These days, young people who were not even born when I was arrested often approach me with expressions of awe and disbelief. On the one hand, it is inspiring to discover a measure of historical awareness that, in our youth, my generation often lacked. But it is also unsettling. Because I know that almost inevitably my image is associated with a certain representation of Black nationalism that privileges those particular nationalisms with which some of us were locked in constant battle.

What I am trying to suggest is that contemporary representations of nationalism in African-American and diasporic popular culture are far too frequently reifications of a very complex and contradictory project that had emancipatory moments leading beyond itself. For example, my own first major activist effort as a budding "nationalist" was the construction of an alliance with Chicano students and progressive white students in San Diego for the purpose of demanding the creation of a college we called Lumumba-Zapata. It is the only college in the University of California, San Diego system that is identified today by its number—Third College—rather than by a name.

A further example: Look at the issue of the Black Panther Party newspaper in the spring of 1970 in which Huey Newton wrote an article urging an end to verbal gay bashing, urging an examination of Black male sexuality, and calling for an alliance with the developing gay liberation movement. This article was written in the aftermath of Jean Genet's sojourn with the Black Panther Party, and Genet's *Un Captif Amoureux* reveals suppressed moments of the history of sixties nationalism.[1]

Such moments as these have been all but eradicated in popular representations today of the Black movement of the late sixties and early seventies. And I resent that the legacy I consider my own—one I also helped to construct—has been rendered invisible. Young people with "nationalist" proclivities ought, at least, have the opportunity to choose which tradition of nationalism they will embrace. How will they position themselves en masse in defense of women's rights and in defense of gay rights if they are not aware of the historical precedents for such positionings?

With respect to the exclusion of such progressive moments in the sixties' history of Black nationalism, the mass media is not the sole culprit. We also have to look at the institutions that package this history before it is disseminated by the media—including some of the academic sites occupied by obsolete and inveterate nationalists. Furthermore, we need to look at who packages the practice. The only existing mass Black organization that can claim the so-called authority of having been there during the formative period of contemporary Black nationalism, and therefore, of carrying forth Malcolm X's legacy is the Nation of Islam. Who is working with gang members in South Central Los Angeles today? Who is trying, on an ongoing basis, to end the violence and to bring warring gangs together in dialogue? Why is the rap artist, Paris, who calls himself the Black Panther of Rap, a member of the Nation of Islam? Why is Ice Cube studying with the Nation? Impulses toward collective political practice are being absorbed, in this instance, by a movement that accords nationalism the status of a religion.

As enthusiastic as we might be about the capacity of hip-hop culture to encourage oppositional consciousness among today's young people, it sometimes advocates a nationalism with such strong misogynist overtones that it militates against the very revolutionary practice it appears to promote. Where is the door—or even the window—opening onto a conception of political practice?

Where cultural representations do not reach out beyond themselves, there is the danger that they will function as surrogates for activism, that they will constitute both the beginning and end of political practice. I always go back to Marx's eleventh Feuerbach Thesis because, as Cornel would say, it brings me joy: "Philosophers have interpreted the world in various ways. The point, however, is to change it."

1. Jean Genet, *Un Captif Amoureux* (Paris: Gallimard, 1986); translated as *Prisoner of Love* (London: Pan Books, 1989).

Question This question is for Professor Marable. I'm one of those persons you talked about who was born after the Civil Rights Movement. You noted the difference between race and ethnicity, but then you found it problematic that, for Clarence Thomas, his race doesn't equal his ethnicity. I'm wondering if you could explore that further. If there is a difference between race and ethnicity, why, then, is Thomas problematic?

Manning Marable Race is generally, in my mind, something that has been imposed on us. Ethnicity and culture are things we create for ourselves. In other words, the notion of race is historically new. Culture and ethnicity have been around ever since human beings have been in social groups. That's the basic difference. But most bloods don't make a distinction. They see Thomas as black—meaning that he's going to operate ethnically, politically, and culturally in a certain way. He *is* black, in the sense that he belongs to a racial category constructed by other folks and imposed on us—the power and privilege relationship of exploitation rooted to a capitalist political economy—but that has nothing to do with the politics of his practice.

Joe Wood I wanted to ask Angela about contemporary expressions of nationalism. You said that kids of this generation are often awed by seeing you. I was wondering if you think the images of nationalism today privilege death and, also, what you think about the thesis that Cornel West has been fancying about nihilism. Do you think these cultural expressions are nihilistic, or that some of them are?

Angela Davis That is a very complex question. Cornel seemed to be referring to Ice Cube during his presentation.* I recently conducted a two-hour videotaped interview with Ice Cube at the request of his publicist. I began the conversation by telling him how difficult it was to agree to engage him in dialogue because I found his sexist vocabulary so offensive—the "bitches" and

*Refers to unpublished remarks that do not appear in the current collection.

326 Lyle Ashton Harris, *Miss America* from the series "Reflections of a Past Life Through Glass," 1987/88.

" 'ho's" violate both my ears and my sense of historical struggle around representations of women. I did find the discussion insightful, however, and would
hesitate to call his work nihilistic. There seems to be something creative and
transformative struggling to express itself in Ice Cube's work, but it gets caught
up in a web of narrow, sixties-style nationalism and the notions of male dominance that have been promoted by this nationalism.

Looking at hip-hop culture from a feminist perspective, I feel compelled to
invoke the women rappers who situate themselves in opposition to the crude
male dominance of rappers like Ice Cube and Too Short, not to speak of the
commercially promoted 2-Live Crew. I am convinced there's a common
ground for intergenerational dialogue with young African Americans in the
context of hip hop.

Many of the rappers call upon a market-mediated historical memory of the
black movement of the sixties and seventies. The image of an armed Black man
is considered the "essence" of revolutionary commitment today. As dismayed as
I may feel about this simplistic, phallocentric image, I remember my own responses to romanticized images of brothers (and sometimes sisters) with guns.
And, in actuality, it was empowering to go to target practice and shoot—or
break down a weapon—as well, or better, than a man. I can relate to the young
people who passionately want to do something today, but are misdirected in a
way that leads Cornel to describe their political impulses as nihilistic. I think
that it is something more than a spiritual deficiency that leads to what he calls
nihilism. This is why I decided to attempt some form of communication with
Ice Cube.

I'll say one other thing. I have been teaching a course on women's cultural
awareness at the San Francisco County Jail for the last year. It helps to keep me
connected. I need this kind of connection because it compels me to look at issues that may very well make a difference, issues that might not occur to me
otherwise.

Thomas Harris Picking up on what you just said, I find that there are some divisions in black communities along class lines that aren't always articulated. I
was speaking to a friend the other day—an older woman who's writing a book
about half of her family who passed and the pain of this for her mother and
herself. And I was just thinking about the *ideological* passing of the black middle

class and wondering about what kind of communication we can have. Another way to get at this might be to ask, why do I feel more comfortable coming here to this conference than going and trying to do something like what you're doing at the jail?

Angela Davis The issue of difference within the black community—which we have been exploring throughout the weekend—has to be addressed in a way that does not minimize the complex ways in which African Americans are situated and the way they politically position themselves in relation to race, class, gender, and sexuality. The televised confrontation between Clarence Thomas and Anita Hill symbolically represented the passing of a conception of community with which many of us have lived. I experienced it both as a loss and as an emancipation. I used to be able to talk about "my people." I grew up in a Southern black community where we always protected each other, no matter what. Community was racially all-embracing. This is why my mother, who politically identified with Anita Hill, also felt compelled to embrace and protect Clarence Thomas. That she now finds herself in an untenable situation is a consequence of the historical obsolescence of the particular sense of community we once found so necessary.

This particular sense of community is also called into question by the emergence of a contemporary consciousness of biraciality, or multiraciality, which has not yet been addressed here. It was previously the case that if one parent was black—generally the father—the child was also black. It was rarely possible for a white woman with a black child, regardless of whether the father was present, to rear her child anywhere other than in the black community. Current discussions on issues around biraciality or multiple heritage have begun to problematize the notion of "race" as an unreflected basis for community building. When, for example, the Black/African Student Organization at the University of California, Santa Cruz decided to conduct a series of forums on diversity, the first one revolved around cultural and racial diversity within the black community.

Eddie Glaude I wanted to ask a question because I'm one of those younger cats on the scene. To what extent does the generational gaze Professor Davis mentioned represent a monologic consequence—that is, a selective reflection upon historical processes of overcoming that constitute one of those overdeterminations Stuart Hall talked about—which evidences itself at different sites including that of nationalism? What I mean is: although there are selective appropriations of the nationalist tradition that we find commodified and sold on the streets of Harlem or Philadelphia, there's something else that contributes to that selective reflection on the historical process. It's not just younger cats saying "Malcolm means this, Martin means that." And I want us to isolate that, too.

Angela Davis What is the something else you're thinking about?

Eddie Glaude I would argue there's a history of certain representational traditions that comes down. It evidences itself even in your generation vis-à-vis how you looked at, for example, the NAACP. This history represents a romantic construction of community. It gives us a sense of community, a sense of self, that enables us to navigate the hostility in which we find ourselves. I'm trying to say that it's not as if we're doing something totally out of the ordinary. It just so happens that we've chosen the nationalist tradition at this particular juncture. And I want us to look at this process in a more nuanced way.

Angela Davis I absolutely agree with you. Look at the debate around pan-Africanism, for example, which influenced the direction of black nationalism during the late sixties and early seventies. The opposing positions established within the debate did not take into consideration the anti-imperialist context within which Du Bois—the so-called father of Pan-Africanism—elaborated his conception of the relation between African and diasporic populations. These kinds of distinctions are not always made. As a "communist" during this period of late capitalism, even though I may not now be a member of a "communist party," I believe that issues of revolutionary transformation, strategies for moving toward democratic socialism are as much a part of our political agenda as nationalism.

Crystal Zook I wanted to add to some of the intergenerational dialogue Angela was talking about. I'm a Ph.D. candidate in the program where she was just hired. In Santa Cruz, there's a certain context that I think needs to be spoken to here. I—as a biracial person—am being told, predominantly by white academics—Angela is the first person of color to teach in this program—that I am not really black. And I'm writing a dissertation on the resurgence of nationalist thought in black contemporary culture. Experiences like that are some of the kinds of responses that push us, this generation, further toward nationalism—which might be seen as narrow by a lot of people.

What I want to ask is, in what ways can we use some of the strategic nationalism or strategic essentialism people have been talking about? What I really want are concrete examples. I think this conference is a concrete example, and what I want is more of that because we're dealing with these day-to-day situations that push us toward this more militant edge. The young people who've grown up in the Reagan-Bush years have needed this more than ever before. A certain kind of alienation exists that is new. And when I look around campuses, I see more and more people like me—my father was white and my mother is black, so that's the reverse situation, but I see so many more of us now because we came out of the sixties. How do we handle this push? Especially people like me who feel we need that nationalist edge because it's a home. It's a kind of home, in the same sense that family is, and it's pretty much all we have right now.

Paul Gilroy It might be a home, but it's probably the easiest home you can find. Remember, I come from a place where the race-class interface is completely different, where the link between blackness and poverty is a much more immediate one, where we don't have blue-vein clubs, and we haven't had 150 years of independent black education and all these other autonomous institutions of a black middle class. I don't actually think there is a black middle class in Britain yet. There are a few people, but it's not a class in the sense of its being self-conscious—a class in itself, a class for itself. Not yet. It's a not-yet-class. It might be a class at some stage, but there are a lot of us who are working against that.

I think it's very interesting, if you make the shift from thinking about nationalism to thinking about nationalisms, to look at the social basis of the different forms of nationalism we encounter. One of the things we find is that the intensity of nationalist ideology is strongest among that not-yet-class because it's that not-yet-class that fights with whites for the few professional opportunities around. And when you're speaking of the black poor (not just in London, but in the rest of the country as well), the blackest neighborhoods are thirty-to-forty-percent white, and that means that race and class look a different way. So I would look at that nationalism as something that is specific to the experience of that group, as a way that group, that not-yet-class, resolves its deeply problematic and conflictual relationship with the black poor.

Wahneema Lubiano In the spirit of Angela Davis's enhancing of the record by certain kinds of reminders, I thought, given the enthusiastic response to Paul Gilroy's talk, that it's probably ironic, but not surprising, that your critique of black nationalist tropes of the family might do the work that feminist critiques seem not to have been able to do. And when I say feminist, I mean black and non-black, lesbian and straight. The reason I find it ironic is that, given the way the trope works, there's a particular part of the family that always saves another particular part of the family. I'm still ready to warm my hands at the fire of anybody's critique of the family, especially because of the way the family sweepstakes came down heavily in the Clarence Thomas—Anita Hill confrontation. However, I want to remind us of a legacy, to use Angela Davis's word, of another kind of discourse. And I invoke the feminist discourse precisely because the feminist discourse gets demonized when it makes itself available in, for example, the work of African-American women writers. Their critique of the family trope gets called anti-black, but maybe yours will be more successful.

Paul Gilroy I just want to be clear about what I said and what I didn't say. For me, there is a promise in that notion of family which maybe—we can struggle over it—in this new democratic politics which we're trying to construct, we can make over. But it has to be somehow disorganically figured. People will want to call themselves brother and sister, and I didn't mean to dis' that because I know it carries the ambiguity of a democratic tradition of struggle, particularly in the States. I don't want to trivialize that for a second. I'm saying that I would like us to try and be more imaginative about it or, at the very least, to think before we invoke it.

Michele Wallace

Afterword: "Why Are There No Great Black Artists?" The Problem of Visuality in African-American Culture

From the outset, the Black Popular Culture conference exceeded my wildest expectations. During the three days of the conference, I was stunned, awed, and amazed by the output of such a fascinating array of minds. But perhaps the most surprising and welcome gift of all was Manning Marable's discussion of the political content of the conference poster, which juxtaposed images of now Supreme Court Justice Clarence Thomas and University of Oklahoma professor Anita Hill. Since the poster had initially been viewed as problematic by the staff of the Studio Museum in Harlem, it had not been displayed during the first evening of the conference, which was held there.

From the earliest planning stages, it had always been my hope that the conference poster would refer to recent popular cultural events. But there was no way I could have anticipated such a mass cultural event as the Hill-Thomas hearings. For weeks, images of Thomas and Hill flooded our newspapers, magazines, and television screens. Moreover, for many feminists, myself included, the Hill-Thomas confrontation became a watershed event for its conjunction of issues of politics, race, and gender.

When Anita Hill accused Clarence Thomas, Supreme Court judge nominee and former head of the Equal Employment Opportunity Commission, of sexual harassment, Thomas responded by accusing the United States Senate and the press of engaging in the high-tech lynching of an uppity black. The newsprint, news magazine, and video representations of the faces of either Hill or Thomas, or both in combination, rapidly came to signify a complicated nexus of the histories of slavery, lynching, sexual harassment and sexual abuse, the Supreme Court and Senate, black conservatism and black politics in general, and African-American culture in the public imagination.

Hill and Thomas are conservatives, and as such, the hearings featured a long line of their conservative supporters, demonstrating the resourcefulness and strength of middle-class blacks on the Right.[1] Because both Hill and Thomas are from poor, rural backgrounds, are dark-skinned, and have obviously black facial features, there were no grounds upon which to accuse either of being less than authentically black. Yet their graphic and highly publicized argument with one another immediately caused a crisis of interpretation in the black community; the threat of a woman who had broken the unwritten law of gender was seen as more of a problem than Thomas's right-wing politics on the Supreme Court. Hill was automatically interpreted by an alarming number of black women as scheming and conniving for no other reason than that she was a black middle-class woman with an education and a career, and because she had complained of sexual harassment on the job.

It was my suggestion to the designer, Bethany Johns, that we juxtapose newspaper images of Hill and Thomas in the poster because of the way in which their confrontation had come to represent multiple issues having to do with the hybridity of black popular culture. Featuring the two of them together was meant to pose symbolically the various contested narratives of black culture/popular culture/U. S. mass culture the conference was designed to explore: the debates of black feminist discourses versus black male authority in black struggles, black republicanism and conservatism versus blacks on the Left, black nationalism versus black popular culture, black crossover appeal in mass culture versus black-centered popular culture. Also, I was fascinated by the automatic volatility of situations in which race collides with gender in visual representation.

I would suggest that some of the anger the Hill-Thomas hearings aroused had to do with many viewers feeling overwhelmed by the visualizations of TV. Although the most sensitive matters discussed were not visualized—such as the pubic hair on the Coke can—the threat that they might be was perhaps looming, given the presence of the medium of television. To picture Hill and Thomas in our conference poster would indeed be a picture that would invoke a thousand (million?) words.

In fact, since the conference I've been imagining the image in the context of Barbara Kruger's work, which has never featured a black image. The text would read, "Mommy and Daddy are fighting"—speaking to another set of psychological tensions provoked in the black community (perhaps the very thing the Studio Museum was uneasy about) in response to Anita Hill's charge of sexual harassment. According to the official version in black political thought, black males and females are never supposed to disagree, even, or perhaps especially, in the context of the family. This is partly why the myth of the Huxtable family in "The Cosby Show" has so much power for black television audiences. The psychoanalytic paradigm in which the family romance describes the struggle within the family for sexual identity is supposed to have little or no relevance in a black context, and yet the very denial of it gives it an added explosive power.

That the juxtaposition of Hill and Thomas in the poster proved to be a problem reveals something about the problem of visuality in African-American culture. I would like to propose that vision, visuality, and visibility are part of a problematic in African-American discourse, and that problematic has much to do with related issues of gender, sexuality, postmodernism, and popular culture. The problem takes many forms—from the resistance to using Hill and Thomas as an image for a black popular culture conference to the problem of a white-dominated art world that does not usually conceptualize blacks as visual producers.

In the context of mass culture, the image of the black is larger than life. Historically, the body and the face of the black have posed no obstacle whatsoever to an unrelenting and generally contemptuous objectification. And yet, until recently, there has been no position within or outside American visual culture from which one could conceptualize the African American as a subject. The prominence of black directors in film finally threatens to change that picture. But the difficulty of the project for black film has to do precisely with the history of a mostly invisible black visuality.

In 1971, art historian Linda Nochlin wrote an essay titled "Why Are There No Great Women Artists?"[2] thus founding, in one extraordinary stroke, the discourse (dare I call it a movement?) of feminist art history. Of course, we are immediately suspicious of this simplistic narrative. There were, in fact, a lot of other struggles going on, including the political struggles among women and blacks; and within those struggles, there were a lot of art historians and critics and, most of all, there were a lot of artists. Such moments as Nochlin's article are anchored in multiple historical conjunctions and cultural formations. For

Judge Clarence Thomas and Anita F. Hill testifying before the Senate Judiciary Committee, October 1991. ▶

instance, Lucy Lippard, who was and continues to be a major agent for feminist activism in the art world, was also writing art criticism at the same time. But what really fascinates me about the Nochlin article, to which I expect to return again and again in the work I am doing on visuality in African-American culture, is the profoundly positive and constructive effect of what many unbelievers then perceived as a negative gesture.

Indeed, I have already seen the fruits of my own negative gesture in naming this paper "Why Are There No Great Black Artists?" In her review of the conference, Daniela Salvioni remarked that she couldn't figure out why I would want to entitle my closing remarks "Why Are There No *Famous* Black Artists"[3]—"especially given the recent surge of black visual artists in the mainstream art world—among others, Adrian Piper, David Hammons, Cheri Samba, Renée Green, Frédéric Bruly Bouabré, and Glenn Ligon...a reorientation of the central question posited by Nochlin—a baffling denial not only at the end of an otherwise Herculean accomplishment, but also at a time when the art world appears to be committed to recasting, extending, and developing the networks and principles by which it has always defined its parameters."[4]

Salvioni's article appears in an issue of *Parkett* devoted to David Hammons and Mike Kelley. That Hammons, who is black, recently won a MacArthur and was included in the exhibition "Dislocations" at the Museum of Modern Art [MoMA] is perhaps what Salvioni means by suggesting that the art world is demonstrating a new commitment to extending its parameters. But Kirk Varnedoe, director of painting and sculpture at MoMA still feels the works of female and/or black artists are of insufficient quality. The principal engineer of the "High & Low" exhibition at the MoMA, he managed to refer extensively to American popular culture without ever mentioning or invoking the image of blacks, much less referring to blacks as visual producers.

And do we need to be reminded of the records of the Guggenheim, the Whitney, even Dia, and the figures Howardena Pindell compiled in "Art (World) & Racism," in regard to exhibiting and collecting the works of black artists?[5]

Even as a short list of names—Piper, Hammons, Martin Puryear, Jean Michel Basquiat—appear to Salvioni to be redefining the parameters of white art world acceptance, it would be futile to attempt a list of white male artists (who continue to epitomize what constitutes the center) that wouldn't cover several pages. Indeed, Salvioni's substitution of "famous" for "great" in her recapitulation of my talk's title is a telling mistake. "Famous" suggests the judgments and trends of the moment—which have always been promiscuous in their instrumentalization of black artists—whereas "great" usually refers to more lasting cultural processes as they have been codified in art history and museums for centuries. Fame may or may not lead to greatness. If you're black, and you're not a musician (music is the one area in which blacks are allowed "greatness"), it almost certainly will not.

When the article by Nochlin first came out, I, too, was among the unbelievers, one of those who were profoundly suspicious of the negativity of Nochlin's proposition. I was nineteen years old, and I was seriously thinking about majoring in art history at the City College of New York. I was taking art history courses and already occasionally writing art criticism. Under the influence of my mother—who was an artist involved with the Art Workers Coalition, Art Strike, and an organization she founded called WSABAL (Women Students and Artists for Black Art Liberation)—I was participating in the artworld Left as a black feminist activist. At the time, it never occurred to me even to think about being an art historian. I was going to be an art critic, a black Lucy Lippard who could effect the here and the now as I saw it, the situation in the streets. But first, I had to get through these art history courses.

These were my identities, feminist, black, art critic, writer, left activist. Although I insisted at the time that all these things were connected, they were not—not in or through me and not in the world. And because of that, I couldn't deal with those art history courses. It has taken me decades to understand how difficult it would have been to do what I was trying to do then—become an art critic.

For me, the purpose of this conference was to nurture critical practice among African-American intellectuals. As an African-American intellectual, I know how difficult it has been and continues to be to engage in critical cultural practices. The purpose of this conference was to move the center of African-American cultural discourse beyond literary criticism into other politically significant precincts such as popular culture. In the process of planning this conference, I anticipated that black visual art, art criticism, and artists would be neglected (even though the conference would be given by two fine art institutions). And so, I named my talk "Why Are There No Great Black Artists?" to address this lack and to specifically challenge the wisdom of excluding regimes of visuality from discussions of black popular culture.

Now, as I said, I was one of the unbelievers in response to Nochlin's article. What the hell did she mean there were no great women artists? For starters, my mother was a great woman artist and, moreover, there were lots of other great women artists I knew about. That there were more great men than great women had to do with how women had been unfairly disadvantaged historically. It was wrong, I thought, to rub salt in the wounds. But, as I was to subsequently discover over a period of twenty years, Nochlin was engaging in an institutional critique. She was addressing the problem of the institutionalization of rock-solid (as solid as the statue of Teddy Roosevelt with his Indian and his African in front of the Museum of Natural History) social, cultural, and economic boundaries around Western conceptions of genius, individual talent, art, creativity, the artist, the master, and culture. Nochlin's article was about women letting go of an old, defeatist, masochistic, soul-killing paradigm.

Her article shared a parallel conceptual framework with other initiatives taking place around gender issues across a variety of discourses in the social sciences, the humanities, and the other arts. This moment founded a new kind of feminist scholarship and criticism and, indeed, a new "kind of woman." Feminist scholars went from chasing windmills to modeling the kinds of foundations of thought upon which alternative institutions and alternative critical practices are built.

Now the problem with all of this, as we well know, was that it proved to be a very white middle-class affair; and even for those who were white and middle-class, this feminist scholarship was and is still experienced as alienating and too abstract (although, if you return to Nochlin's article, it is devastatingly clear). A lot of people had a problem with the careerism of those who followed in the footsteps of such innovators of feminist criticism as Nochlin. But the most radical elements of that very institutionalization have not managed to graduate from their rather tenuous foothold on the margins of the art world and the academic establishment.

But I wish to retrieve a moment from Nochlin's article for further use. Throughout, as Nochlin grapples with the historical problem of the woman artist and, even more importantly, the visual problem of the representation of women in art, she adds to her formulations again and again the words,

"and black artists, too."

Of course, the key problematic among feminist theorists of color in our debates around identity and "otherness" has been this notion of "and blacks, too." The insight of the most recent generation of feminists of color has been that blacks (or black women or women of color or black men) cannot be tacked onto formulations about gender without engaging in a form of conceptual violence. In no theoretically useful way whatsoever are blacks *like* women.

However, what Nochlin writes about the inaccessibility of the institutionalization and construction of greatness is absolutely and frighteningly true for black artists, too. Indeed, black artists in the U. S. context have been subject to an even more absolute and devastating restriction upon their right to genius, individual talent, and Matthew Arnold's celebrated "sweetness and light."

One of the major focuses of Nochlin's article is the status of the female body in the proliferation of the nude in Western art. As is well known, the white woman is objectified with great frequency and loving and lavish attention. But as Judith Wilson discussed at the conference, black nudes are virtually nonexistent in the work of black artists of the nineteenth century, and in the twentieth century, they continue to be rare. Black artists were, no doubt, responding to the extraordinary contempt and loathing surrounding the black body in European and American eighteenth- and nineteenth-century thought and visual culture. The question of the black nude is, then, one of the subjects for which the formulation "and blacks, too" would be totally inappropriate.

The problem here has to do with the always volatile combination of race, gender, and sexuality. Whereas the sensuous white female nude, painstakingly objectified for the pleasure of the white male spectator, is not only a commonplace but, indeed, a cliché of white western imagery in fine art, the black female nude is disproportionately rare, especially in the conceptualizations of black artists.[6] White artists rarely depicted black nudes because of their lack of faith in black humanity, and black artists, in their turn, did the same, perhaps in response to the stereotypical emphasis on an allegedly animalistic hypersexuality.

"There are no women equivalents for Michelangelo or Rembrandt, Delacroix or Cezanne, Picasso or Matisse, or even, in very recent times, for de Kooning or Warhol, any more than there are black American equivalents for the same," Nochlin wrote.[7] The question most characteristic of hegemonic discourse—if you are just as good, where are your Beethoven, your Bach, your

Titian, your Rembrandt?—is also the characteristic question in a black context. According to Paul Gilroy, long before "scientific racism gained its intellectual grip," Hegel "denied blacks the ability to appreciate the necessary mystery involved in the creation of truly symbolic art." [8]

Interestingly enough, however, the "Why are there no great black artists" mindset (and I mean in regard to visual artists) has not really been formally challenged by critical practices. And herein, I am expanding the category of visual art to include a much greater array of the visual work in a technological society: advertising, as well as commercial photography, design, architecture, fashion, film, and TV, in addition to the more elevated forms of fine art— painting, sculpture, and conceptual art. There has not been nearly the focus on reconceptualizing aesthetic criteria that there has been on refuting scientific rationalizations of racism. Basically, this means what we've tried to do is tie down one of the two fists (science and aesthetics) in a combination punch. It should come as no surprise that racism succeeds again and again in freeing the other fist.

For those who can't fathom the relationship between the judgments and practices of the art world and the art market, I am here to tell you that the relationship of this formation in corporate capitalism, which has global manifestations, is that of two peas in a pod. Coming back for a moment to the issue of the institutionalization of visual regimes, I see "Why are there no great black artists?" as a crucial question. It is key, first of all, to providing the support to artists—in so-called black communities, outside of black communities, and around the world—that they need to continue their very critical work of disproving the lie of black invisibility, on the one hand, and lack of vision, on the other. I do not mean this self-indulgently. This is not merely about entertainment or pleasure, although these concerns are crucial as well.

From what I heard said sometimes about the visual arts during the conference, I think many black intellectuals don't know who black artists are. I sensed a contempt for the visual art institutions in which the conference was held, especially the Studio Museum, where the audience was forced to share the space with current exhibitions. This was so because the Studio Museum is a black institution; unlike Dia, it doesn't have enough money to have a separate auditorium. Quite a lot of black visual artists were present at the conference; I recognized Camille Billops, Mel Edwards, Lorraine O'Grady, Renée Green,

Lorna Simpson, Faith Ringgold, and Seitu Jones, to name a few. Black artists can be very quiet. I learned a new respect for the quiet ones; it is precisely the ones who are most quiet that we need to pay attention to.

These people—black visual artists—make things and make visions. Their job, their goal is to re-envision vision. What have they ever done to deserve our contempt? I think we need to begin to understand how regimes of visuality enforce racism, how they literally hold it in place.

In black communities and in white communities and in all the colored communities in between, I am interested in the potential for a revolution in vision. The relationship of the problems of visuality (who produces and reproduces vision) to popular culture and material culture and, ultimately, history is vital. We are in danger of getting wasted by ghosts, by what the black film historian Thomas Cripps calls "black shadows on the silver screen,"[9] by effusions and visual traces that haunt us because we refuse to study them, to look them in the eye. Many of us who come out of a black analytical tradition are in a world of darkness in regard to these matters.

Parallel to the visual void in black discourse, and intersecting with it, is the gap around the psychoanalytic. Besides Frantz Fanon, another African-American interpreter of Freud and the psychoanalytic is Ralph Ellison in *Invisible Man*. We need to look for others. This gap brings us to the verge of another crisis, a crisis of mind. As we all know, the mind, even the black mind, is not made up of just literacy and intellect. It has not finished its work or fulfilled itself even if it can sing like Mahalia Jackson or dance like John Bumbles. It goes on fucking us up and throwing us back, and it must be listened to. For me, the crucial aspect of African-American nihilism that can be concretely addressed is that which we might identify as psychoanalytically derived, if such a dimension were conceivable in a black context.

Take, for instance, the very compelling scenario that unfolded at the conference, in which Houston Baker provocatively began his presentation by stating that he was not gay. Ostensibly he was responding to Henry Louis Gates's remarks about viewing *Looking for Langston*, remarks in which Gates suggested that he and Baker experienced homoerotic pleasure.

More to the point for me, when Baker, who could be described as the dean of African-American literary criticism, announced that he was not gay, it was as if the entire conference reformulated itself around him. In emotional terms, I would describe it as the moment the father said he was not gay, which every son in the room had to challenge. His remarks caused an extraordinary amount of consternation. The debate that ensued between him and young male members of the audience proceeded to completely preoccupy this panel, which was ostensibly about gender *and* sexuality and, as such, would have ordinarily been expected to focus on matters having to do with black women as well.

One of the goals of this conference was to achieve a gender balance in which the black feminist voice would be at least as strong as the male voice, but that didn't quite come off. Usefully, Lisa Kennedy suggested the discussion had gotten bogged down in Oedipal reenactments and that such reenactments were characteristic in African-American cultural discourse.* Paul Gilroy went on to rebuke African-American theorists for their presumably wrongheaded preoccupation with the family paradigm. But I don't think we have a chance of comprehending our own irrationality outside of the framework of the family romance.

One more thing. There is by now too vast an array of compelling narratives in which African-American music is the founding discourse of the African-American experience. Indeed, African music is the founding discourse of the diaspora, and that is probably as it should be. But, for my part, I am at war with music, to the extent that it completely defines the parameters of intellectual discourse in the African-American community. For me, the self-limiting paradigm is not the family but musical production.

The morning of the final day of the conference, Gene, my husband, flicked on the television just in time to hear the words of a Cable News Network commentator announcing Kimberly Bergalis's death: "Kimberly Bergalis, who gave AIDS a human face." This seemed to me an extraordinary visual formulation: a white middle-class woman infected with HIV by her dentist. And, of course, it implied that all the faces of people of color and gays with AIDS are not human.

Throughout this conference, the specter of AIDS and the threat it poses to all constructive intellectual activity on the Left haunted us. Despite the emotions this problem arouses, I think we owe it to ourselves to analyze the visual constructions of AIDS that render our visions both invisible and impossible. Mourning the dead, while deeply necessary (and I do mean to suggest that the hoopla over Baker's announcement was a kind of mourning), doesn't rid us of

---

*Refers to unpublished remarks that do not appear in the current collection.　　**345**

the necessity for analyzing the past, doing something to shape the present, and anticipating the future.

I would like especially to thank Phil Mariani for the initial idea of giving this conference at Dia and for her absolutely crucial contribution, as co-organizer, to its execution. I've always suspected that she was a heroic individual, but this conference proved it beyond a doubt. I would like to thank David Sternbach, Brian Wallis, Maud Lavin, Cornel West, Stuart Hall, bell hooks, and Lisa Kennedy for their encouragement and support and for their help in the formulation of black popular culture as a discourse. Most of all, I would like to thank Coco Fusco who first introduced me to Ada Gay Griffin, Isaac Julien, and black film circles in general, and who recommended me for inclusion in the 1988 Birmingham Film Festival where I first met Stuart Hall. And, finally, I would like to thank Gina Dent, who made this volume possible.

1. Since the revision of this essay, Toni Morrison's excellent collection *Race-ing Justice, Engendering Power: Essays on Anita Hill, Clarence Thomas and the Construction of Social Reality* has appeared and provides a provocative and informative addendum to our discussions of Anita Hill. This volume accounts, in part, for the shift in our conception of Anita Hill as conservative, a shift which is also confirmed by her recent organization of and participation in a conference entitled "Race, Gender and Power in America," Georgetown University Law Center, October 16, 1992. Other engaging work on these topics includes bell hooks's "A Feminist Challenge: Must We Call Every Woman Sister," in *Black Looks: Race and Representation*; The Black Scholar's *Court of Appeal: The Black Community Speaks Out on the Racial and Sexual Politics of Thomas vs. Hill*; and the depiction of Anita Hill by black artist Willie Birch in his recent exhibition in SoHo, New York.

2. Linda Nochlin, "Why Are There No Great Women Artists?" *Art News* 69 (January 1971); reprinted in Nochlin, *Women, Art, and Power* (New York: Harper & Row, 1988), 145–178.

3. Daniela Salvioni, *Parkett* 31 (1992), 136–139. [My emphasis].

4. Ibid., 139.

5. Howardena Pindell, "Art (World) & Racism," *Third Text* 3/4 (Spring–Summer 1988), 157–190.

6. See Lorraine O'Grady, "Olympia's Maid: Reclaiming Black Female Subjectivity," *Afterimage* 20, no. 1 (Summer 1992), 14, 15, 19.

7. Nochlin, "Why Are There No Great Women Artists?" 150.

8. Paul Gilroy, "Art of Darkness: Black Art and the Problems of Belonging to England," *Third Text* 10 (Spring 1990), 47.

9. Thomas Cripps, *Black Shadows on the Silver Screen* (documentary), 55 min. 1976. Produced by Post Newsweek Stations. Distributed by Lucerne Media.

Bibliography of Related Sources

Popular Culture: Theory and Criticism

Cultural Studies
Film, Television, and Media—
  History and Criticism
Literary Criticism
Religion

Anderson, Talmadge. *Black Studies: Theory, Method, and Cultural Perspectives.* Pullman: Washington State University Press, 1990.

Baker, Houston A. *Afro-American Poetics: Revisions of Harlem and the Black Aesthetic.* Madison: University of Wisconsin Press, 1988.

———. *Blues, Ideology, and Afro-American Literature: A Vernacular Theory.* Chicago: University of Chicago Press, 1984.

———. *Modernism and the Harlem Renaissance.* Chicago: University of Chicago Press, 1987.

Baker, Houston A., and Patricia Redmond, eds. *Afro-American Literary Study in the 1990s.* Chicago: University of Chicago Press, 1989.

Balibar, Etienne, and Immanuel Wallerstein. *Race, Nation, Class: Ambiguous Identities.* London: Verso, 1991.

Bassett, John. *Harlem in Review: Critical Reactions to Black American Writers, 1917–1939.* London: Associated University Presses, 1992.

Bobo, Jacqueline. "Images of Black People in Cinema." In *Women in Film: An International Guide,* ed. Annette Kuhn, 43–46, 110–111, 332–333. New York: Ballantine Books, 1991.

———. "Black Women in Fiction and Nonfiction: Images of Power and Powerlessness." *Wide Angle* 13, nos. 3 and 4 (July–October 1991), 72–81.

———. "The Female Spectator." *Camera Obscura* 20–21 (May–September 1989), 9, 100–103, 338.

———. "Sifting Through the Controversy: Reading *The Color Purple.*" *Callaloo* 12, no. 2 (Spring 1989), 332–342.

———. " 'The Subject Is Money': Reconsidering the Black Film Audience as a Theoretical Paradigm." *Black American Literature Forum* 25, no. 2 (Summer 1991), 421–432.

Bobo, Jacqueline, and Ellen Seiter. "Black Feminism and Media Criticism." *Screen* 32, no. 3 (Fall 1991), 286–302.

Bogle, Donald. *Blacks in Film and Television: An Encyclopedia.* New York: Garland Publications, 1988.

———. *Brown Sugar: Eighty Years of America's Black Female Superstars.* New York: Harmony Books, 1980.

Brantlinger, Patrick. *Bread and Circuses: Theories of Mass Culture as Social Decay.* Ithaca, N.Y.: Cornell University Press, 1983.

———. *Crusoe's Footprints: Cultural Studies in Britain and America.* New York: Routledge, 1990.

Braudy, Leo. *Native Informant: Essays on Film, Fiction, and Popular Culture.* New York: Oxford University Press, 1991.

Campbell, Mary Schmidt. *Harlem Renaissance: Art of Black America.* New York: Studio Museum of Harlem; Harry N. Abrams, 1987.

Carby, Hazel. *Reconstructing Womanhood: The Emergence of the Afro-American Woman Novelist.* New York: Oxford University Press, 1987.

Carey, James W. *Communication as Culture: Essays on Media and Society.* Boston: Unwin, 1988.

Cham, Mbye B., and Claire Andrade-Watkins, eds. *Blackframes: Critical Perspectives on Black Independent Cinema.* Cambridge: MIT Press, 1988.

Cone, James H. *A Black Theology of Liberation.* 1970; Maryknoll, N.Y.: Orbis Books, 1990.

_____. *For My People: Black Theology and the Black Church.* Maryknoll, N.Y.: Orbis Books, 1984.

_____. *Speaking the Truth: Ecumenism, Liberation, and Black Theology.* Grand Rapids, Mich.: W. B. Eerdmans Publishing Co., 1986.

Cross, William E. *Shades of Black: Diversity in African-American Identity.* Philadelphia, Pa.: Temple University Press, 1991.

Crouch, Stanley. *Notes of a Hanging Judge: Essays and Reviews, 1979–1989.* New York: Oxford University Press, 1990.

Dates, Jannette L., and William Barlow, eds. *Split Image: African Americans and the Mass Media.* Washington, D.C.: Howard University Press, 1990.

Davis, F. James. *Who Is Black?: One Nation's Definition.* University Park: Pennsylvania State University Press, 1991.

Diawara, Manthia, ed. *Black American Cinema: History, Theory, and Criticism.* New York: Routledge, 1993, forthcoming.

Dundes, Alan, ed. *Mother Wit from the Laughing Barrel: Readings in the Interpretation of Afro-American Folklore.* 1973; Jackson: University Press of Mississippi, 1990.

Early, Gerald Lyn. *Tuxedo Junction: Essays on American Culture.* New York: Ecco Press, 1989.

Ferguson, Russell, et al., eds. *Discourses: Conversations in Postmodern Art and Culture.* Cambridge: MIT Press in association with the New Museum of Contemporary Art, New York, 1990.

_____, eds. *Out There: Marginalization and Contemporary Cultures.* Cambridge: MIT Press in association with the New Museum of Contemporary Art, New York, 1990.

Fusco, Coco. "Fantasies of Oppositionality." *Afterimage* 16, no. 5 (December 1988), 6–9.

_____"Sublime Abjection: An Interview with Andres Serrano." *Third Text* 16/17 (Autumn/Winter 1991), 173–187.

Gates, Henry Louis. *Figures in Black: Words, Signs, and the "Racial" Self.* New York: Oxford University Press, 1987.

_____. *Loose Canons: Notes on the Culture Wars.* New York: Oxford University Press, 1992.

_____. *The Signifying Monkey: A Theory of Afro-American Literary Criticism.* New York: Oxford University Press, 1988.

_____, ed. *Reading Black, Reading Feminist: A Critical Anthology.* New York: Meridian Books, 1990.

Gay, Geneva, and Willie L. Baber. *Expressively Black: The Cultural Basis of Ethnic Identity.* New York: Praeger, 1987.

Girgus, Sam B., ed. *The American Self: Myth, Ideology, and Popular Culture.* Albuquerque: University of New Mexico Press, 1981.

Gray, John. *Blacks in Film and Television: A Pan-African Bibliography of Films, Filmmakers, and Performers.* New York: Greenwood Press, 1990.

Grossberg, Lawrence, Cary Nelson, and Paula Treichler, eds. *Cultural Studies.* New York: Routledge, 1992.

Hall, Stuart. *Minimal Selves.* ICA Document 6. London: Institute of Contemporary Arts, 1988.

_____. "New Ethnicities." *Black Film / British Cinema,* ICA Document 7, ed. Kobena Mercer. London: Institute of Contemporary Arts, 1988. Reprinted in *'Race,' Culture, and Difference,* ed. J. Donald and A. Ratansi, 252–260. London: Sage, 1992.

_____. "The Whites of Their Eyes: Racist Ideologies and the Media." In *The Media Reader,* ed. Manuel Alvarado and John O. Thompson, 7–23. London: BFI Publishing, 1990.

Hall, Stuart, et al., eds. *Culture, Media, Language: Working Papers in Cultural Studies.* London: Hutchinson, 1980.

Hebdige, Dick. *Subculture: The Meaning of Style.* London: Methuen, 1979.

Hill, George H. *African American Television Experience: A Researcher's Bibliography of Scholarly Writings.* Los Angeles: Daystar Publishing Co., 1987.

_____. *Black Women in Television: An Illustrated History and Bibliography.* New York: Garland Publications, 1990.

Hill, George H., and Sylvia Saversoon Hill. *Blacks on Television: A Selectively Annotated Bibliography.* Metuchen, N.J.: Scarecrow Press, 1985.

Hogan, Lawrence D. *A Black National News Service: the Associated Negro Press and Claude Barnett, 1919–1945.* Rutherford: Farleigh Dickinson University Press; London: Associated University Presses, 1984.

Holloway, Joseph, ed. *Africanisms in American Culture.* Bloomington: Indiana University Press, 1990.

hooks, bell. *Black Looks: Race and Representation.* Boston: South End Press, 1992.

_____. *Yearning: Race, Gender, and Cultural Politics.* Boston: South End Press, 1990.

hooks, bell, and Cornel West. *Breaking Bread: Insurgent Black Intellectual Life.* Boston: South End Press, 1991.

Hopkins, Dwight N. *Black Theology USA and South Africa: Politics, Culture, and Liberation.* Vol. 4. Maryknoll, N.Y.: Orbis Books, in association with The Bishop Henry McNeal Turner Studies in North American Black Religion, 1989.

Ikonne, Chidi, et al., eds. *Black Culture and Black Consciousness in Literature.* Ibadan, Nigeria: Heinemann Educational Books, 1987.

Joyce, Donald Franklin. *Gatekeepers of Black Culture: Black-Owned Book Publishing in the United States, 1817–1981.* Westport, Conn.: Greenwood Press, 1983.

LaCapra, Dominick, ed. *The Bounds of Race: Perspectives on Hegemony and Resistance.* Ithaca, N.Y.: Cornell University Press, 1991.

Lee, Spike, and Terry McMillan. *Five for Five: The Films of Spike Lee.* New York: Stewart, Tabori & Chang, 1991. Distributed in the United States by Workman Publishers.

Levine, Lawrence W. *Black Culture and Black Consciousness: Afro-American Folk Thought from Slavery to Freedom.* New York: Oxford University Press, 1978.

_____. *Highbrow / Lowbrow: The Emergence of Cultural Hierarchy in America.* Cambridge: Harvard University Press, 1988.

Lipsitz, George. *Time Passages: Collective Memory and American Popular Culture.* Minneapolis: University of Minnesota Press, 1990.

Lorde, Audre. *Sister Outsider: Essays and Speeches.* Trumansburg, N.Y.: The Crossing Press, 1984.

Lubiano, Wahneema. "But Compared to What?: Reading Realism, Representation, and Essentialism in *School Daze, Do the Right Thing,* and the Spike Lee Discourse." *Black American Literature Forum* 25 (Summer 1991), 253–82.

MacDonald, Fred J. *Blacks and White TV: Afro-Americans in Television Since 1948.* Chicago: Nelson-Hall, 1983.

Naremore, James, and Patrick Brantlinger, eds. *Modernity and Mass Culture.* Bloomington: Indiana University Press, 1991.

Nesteby, James R. *Black Images in American Films, 1896–1954: The Interplay Between Civil Rights and Film Culture.* Washington, D.C.: University Press of America, 1982.

O'Brien, Mark, and Craig Little. *Reimaging America: The Arts of Social Change.* Philadelphia, Pa.: New Society Publishers, 1990.

_____. *Voices of Dissent.* Bloomington: Indiana University Press, 1990.

Omi, Michael. *Racial Formation in the United States: From the 1960s to the 1980s.* New York: Routledge & Kegan Paul, 1986.

Orisawayi, Dele, and Ernest Emenyonu. *Literature and Black Aesthetics.* Ibadan, Nigeria: Heinemann Educational Books, 1990.

Owusu, Kwesi. *The Struggle for Black Arts in Britain: What We Can Consider.* London: Comedia Publishing Group, 1986.

_____, ed. *Storms of the Heart: An Anthology of Black Arts and Culture* (exhibition catalogue). London: Camden Press, 1988.

Perry, Margaret. *The Harlem Renaissance: An Annotated Bibliography and Commentary.* Vol. 2. *Critical Studies on Black Life and Culture.* New York: Garland Publications, 1982.

Profile of Black Museums. Nashville, Tenn.: American Association for State and Local History in association with African-American Museums Association, 1988.

Pryse, Marjorie, and Hortense J. Spillers. *Conjuring: Black Women, Fiction, and Literary Tradition.* Bloomington: Indiana University Press, 1985.

Rampersad, Arnold. *The Life of Langston Hughes.* New York: Oxford University Press, 1986–1988.

Ross, Andrew. *No Respect: Intellectuals and Popular Culture.* London: Routledge, 1989.

Ross, Andrew, and Constance Penley, eds. *Technoculture.* Minneapolis: University of Minnesota Press, 1991.

Rutherford, Jonathan, ed. *Identity: Community, Culture, Difference.* London: Lawrence & Wishart, 1990.

Sanders, Clinton R. *Marginal Conventions: Popular Culture, Mass Media, and Social Deviance.* Bowling Green, Ohio: Bowling Green University Popular Press, 1990.

Schneider, Cynthia, and Brian Wallis. *Global Television*. New York: Wedge Press, 1988.

Seiter, Ellen, et al., eds. *Remote Control: Television Audiences and Cultural Power*. New York: Routledge, 1989.

Shaw, Harry B. *Perspectives on Black Popular Culture*. Bowling Green, Ohio: Bowling Green University Popular Press, 1990.

Silk, Catherine. *Racism and Anti-Racism in American Popular Culture: Portrayals of African-Americans in Fiction and Film*. New York: Manchester University Press, 1990.

Singh, Amritjit, William S. Shiver, and Stanley Brodwin, eds. *The Harlem Renaissance: Revaluations*. Vol. 17. Critical Studies on Black Life and Culture. New York: Garland Publications, 1989.

Smith, Valerie. *Self-Discovery and Authority in Afro-American Narrative*. Cambridge: Harvard University Press, 1987.

Southern, Eileen. *African-American Traditions in Song, Sermon, Tale, and Dance, 1600s 1920. An Annotated Bibliography of Literature, Collections, and Artwork*. New York: Greenwood Press, 1990.

Spillers, Hortense J. *Comparative American Identities: Race, Sex, and Nationality in the Modern Text*. New York: Routledge, 1992.

Spivak, Gayatri Chakravorty. *The Post-Colonial Critic: Interviews, Strategies, Dialogues*. ed. Sarah Harasym. New York: Routledge, 1990.

Stallybrass, Peter, and Allon White. *The Politics and Poetics of Transgression*. Ithaca, N.Y.: Cornell University Press, 1986.

Swift, Jeannine, ed. *Dream and Reality: The Modern Black Struggle for Freedom and Equality*. New York: Greenwood Press, 1991.

Szwed, John, et al. *Afro-American Folk Culture: An Annotated Bibliography of Materials from North, Central, and South America, and the West Indies*. Philadelphia, Pa.: Institute for the Study of Human Issues, 1978.

Tate, Greg. *Flyboy in the Buttermilk: Essays on Contemporary America*. New York: Simon & Schuster, 1992.

Taylor, Patrick. *The Narrative of Liberation: Perspectives on Afro-Caribbean Literature, Popular Culture, and Politics*. Ithaca, N.Y.: Cornell University Press, 1989.

Thompson, Robert Farris. *Flash of the Spirit: African and Afro-American Art and Philosophy*. New York: Random House, 1983.

Trinh T. Minh-ha, *When the Moon Waxes Red: Representation, Gender, and Cultural Politics*. New York: Routledge, 1992.

Van Deburg, William L. *Slavery and Race in American Popular Culture*. Madison: University of Wisconsin Press, 1984.

Wall, Cheryl, ed. *Changing Our Own Words: Essays on Writing by Black Women*. New Brunswick, N.J.: Rutgers University Press, 1989.

Wallace, Michele. *Black Macho and the Myth of the Superwoman*. 1979; London: Verso, 1990.

_____. *Invisibility Blues: From Pop to Theory*. London: Verso, 1990.

West, Cornel. *The Ethical Dimensions of Marxist Thought*. New York: Monthly Review Press, 1991.

_____. *Prophesy Deliverance!: An Afro-American Revolutionary Christianity*. Philadelphia, Pa.: Westminister Press, 1982.

_____. *Prophetic Fragments*. Trenton, N.J.: Africa World Press, 1988.

Wilentz, Gay Alden. *Binding Cultures: Black Women Writers in Africa and the Diaspora.* Bloomington: Indiana University Press, 1992.

Williams, Raymond. *Television: Technology and Cultural Form.* New York: Schocken, 1975.

Wilmore, Gayraud S. *Black Religion and Black Radicalism: An Interpretation of the Religious History of Afro-American People.* Maryknoll, N.Y.: Orbis Books, 1983.

Wilson, Clint C. *Black Journalists in Paradox: Historical Perspectives and Current Dilemmas.* New York: Greenwood Press, 1991.

Wintz, Cary D. *Black Culture and the Harlem Renaissance.* Houston: Rice University Press, 1988.

Wolseley, Roland Edgar. *The Black Press, U.S.A.* Ames: Iowa State University Press, 1990.

Gender, Sexuality, and Black Images in Popular Culture

Art History / Aesthetics
Black Images and Representation
Gender and Culture
Sexuality

Als, Hilton. "Negro Faggotry." *Black Film Review* 5, no. 5 (Summer 1989), 18–19.

Bailey, Frankie Y. *Out of the Woodpile: Black Characters in Crime and Detective Fiction.* New York: Greenwood Press, 1991.

Bibby, Deidre L. *Augusta Savage and the Art Schools of Harlem.* New York: Schomburg Center for Research in Black Culture, 1988.

Blount, Marcellus, and George Cunningham. *Theorizing Black Male Subjectivity.* New York: Routledge, forthcoming.

Boffin, Tessa, and Sunil Gupta. *Ecstatic Antibodies: Resisting the AIDS Mythology.* London: Rivers Oram Press, 1990.

Bogle, Donald. *Toms, Coons, Mulattoes, Mammies, and Bucks: An Interpretive History of Blacks in American Films.* 1973; New York: Continuum, 1992.

Boime, Albert. *The Art of Exclusion: Representing Blacks in the Nineteenth Century.* Washington, D.C.: Smithsonian Institution Press, 1990.

Boskin, Joseph. *Sambo: The Rise and Demise of an American Jester.* New York: Oxford University Press, 1986.

Brown, Mary Ellen. *Television and Women's Culture: The Politics of the Popular.* London: Sage, 1990.

Carter, Erica, and Simon Watney. *Taking Liberties: AIDS and Cultural Politics.* London: Serpent's Tail, 1989.

Collins, Patricia Hill. *Black Feminist Thought: Knowledge, Consciousness, and the Politics of Empowerment.* London: Harper Collins Academic, 1990.

Conwill, Kinshasha, Mary Schmidt Campbell, and Sharon F. Patton, eds. *Memory and Metaphor: The Art of Romare Bearden 1940–1987.* New York: Oxford University Press, 1991.

Crimp, Douglas, ed. *AIDS: Cultural Analysis/Cultural Activism.* Cambridge: MIT Press, 1988.

Dabydeen, David. *Hogarth's Blacks: Images of Blacks in Eighteenth-Century English Art.* Athens: University of Georgia Press, 1987.

The Decade Show: Frameworks of Identity in the 1980s (exhibition catalogue). New York: Museum of Contemporary Hispanic Art/New

Museum of Contemporary Art/The Studio Museum in Harlem, 1990.

Ely, Melvin Patrick. *The Adventures of Amos 'n' Andy: A Social History of an American Phenomenon.* New York: Maxwell Macmillan International, 1991.

Ferris, William R. *Afro-American Folk Art and Crafts.* Boston: G. K. Hall, 1983.

Frechette, David. "What's Wrong with This Picture." *Black Film Review* 5, no. 3 (Summer 1989), 22–23.

Fry, Gladys-Marie. *Stitched from the Soul: Slave Quilts from the Antebellum South.* New York: Dutton Studio Books, in association with the Museum of American Folk Art, 1990.

Fusco, Coco. "Uncanny Dissonance: The Work of Lorna Simpson." In *Lorna Simpson* (exhibition catalogue). ed. Lynn Schwarzer. Hamilton, N.Y.: Dana Arts Center, Colgate University, 1991.

_____. "Vernacular Memories." *Art in America* 79, no. 12 (December 1991), 99–103, 133.

Goldsby, Jackie. "What it Means to Be Colored Me." *Out/Look* no. 9 (Summer 1990), 8–17.

Grey Art Gallery. *Interrogating Identity* (exhibition catalogue). New York: Grey Art Gallery and Study Center, 1991.

Gupta, Sunil. "Desire and Black Men." *Ten.8* no. 22 (1986), 17–22.

Guy-Sheftall, Beverly. *Daughters of Sorrow: Attitudes Toward Black Women, 1880–1920.* Brooklyn, N.Y.: Carlson, 1990.

Hartigan, Linda Roscoe. *Sharing Traditions: Five Black Artists in Nineteenth-Century America.* Washington, D.C.: Smithsonian Institution Press, 1985.

Hatt, Michael. "'Making a Man of Him': Masculinity and the Black Body in Mid-Nineteenth Century American Sculpture." *The Oxford Art Journal* 15, no. 1 (1992), 21–35.

Hemphill, Essex, and Joseph Beam. *Brother to Brother: New Writings by Black Gay Men.* Boston: Alyson Publications, 1991.

hooks, bell. *Ain't I A Woman: Black Women and Feminism.* Boston: South End Press, 1981.

_____. *Feminist Theory from Margin to Center.* Boston: South End Press, 1984.

_____. *Talking Back: Thinking Feminist, Thinking Black.* Boston: South End Press, 1989.

Julien, Isaac, and Kobena Mercer. "True Confessions: A Discourse on Images of Black Male Sexuality." In *Male Order: Unwrapping Masculinity,* ed. Rowena Chapman and Jonathan Rutherford, 97–164. London: Lawrence & Wishart, 1988.

Ladislas, Bugner, ed. *The Image of the Black in Western Art,* 4 vols. New York: William Morrow & Co., 1976.

Lippard, Lucy R. *Mixed Blessings: New Art in Multicultural America.* New York: Pantheon, 1990.

Livingston, Jane. *Black Folk Art in America, 1930–1980.* Jackson: University Press of Mississippi, 1982.

McElroy, Guy C., ed. *Facing History: The Black Image in American Art, 1710–1940.* San Francisco: Bedford Arts Publishers in association with the Corcoran Gallery of Art, Washington, D.C., 1990.

Mercer, Kobena. "Dark and Lovely: Notes on Black Gay Image-Making." *Ten.8* (1991).

_____. "Imaging the Black Man's Sex." In *Photography/Politics: Two,* ed. Pat Holland, Jo

Spence, and Simon Watney, 61–69. London: Comedia/Methuen, 1987, 61–69.

———. "Looking for Trouble." *Transition* 51, 184–197.

———. "Skin Head Sex Thing: Racial Difference and the Homoerotic Imaginary." In *How Do I Look?: Queer Film and Video,* ed. Bad Object-Choices, 169–210. Seattle: Bay Press, 1991.

Mercer, Kobena, Jacqueline Rose, Gayatri Chakravorty Spivak, and Angela McRobbie. "Sexual Identities: Questions of Difference." *Undercut,* no. 17 (Spring 1988), 19–30.

Navarro, Ray. "Shocking Pink Praxis: Race and Gender on the ACT UP Frontlines." In *Inside/Out: Lesbian Theories, Gay Theories,* ed. Diana Fuss. New York: Routledge, 1991.

Navarro, Ray, and Catherine Saalfield. "Not Just Black and White: AIDS, Media and People of Color." *The Independent* 12, no. 6 (1989), 18–23.

Nederveen Pieterse, Jan. *White on Black: Images of Africa and Blacks in Western Popular Culture.* New Haven: Yale University Press, 1992.

Powell, Richard J. *The Blues Aesthetic: Black Culture and Modernism* (exhibition catalogue). Washington, D.C.: Washington Project for the Arts, 1989.

———. *Homecoming: William H. Johnson and Afro-America, 1938–1946.* New York: Rizzoli, 1991.

Roberts, John W. *From Trickster to Badman: The Black Folk Hero in Slavery and Freedom.* Philadelphia: University of Pennsylvania Press, 1989.

Robinson, Jontyle Theresa. *Three Masters: Eldzier Cortor, Hughie Lee-Smith, and Archibald John Motley, Jr.* (exhibition catalogue). New York: Kenkeleba Gallery.

Schwartzman, Myron. *Romare Bearden: His Life and Art.* New York: Harry N. Abrams, 1990.

Sieber, Roy. *African Textiles and Decorative Arts.* New York: Museum of Modern Art, 1972.

Simmons, Ron. "Other Options." *Black Film Review* 5, no. 3 (Summer 1989), 20–22.

Sims, Lowery Stokes. "Aspects of Performance in the Work of Black American Women Artists." In *Feminist Art Criticism: An Anthology,* ed. Arlene Raven, Cassandra Langer, and Joanna Ellen Freuh, 207–225. Ann Arbor, Mich.: UMI Research Press, 1988.

———. "Bob Colescott Ain't Just Misbehavin'." *Artforum* 22, no. 7 (March 1984), 56–59.

———. "The Mirror the Other: The Politics of Esthetics." *Artforum* 28, no. 7 (March 1990), 111–115.

———. "The New Exclusionism." *Art Papers* 12, no. 4 (July/August 1988), 37–38.

Smith, Jessie Carney, ed. *Images of Blacks in American Culture: A Reference Guide to Information Sources.* New York: Greenwood Press, 1988.

Thompson, Robert Farris. *African Art in Motion.* Berkeley: University of California Press, 1974.

Washington, M. Bunch. *The Art of Romare Bearden: The Prevalence of Ritual.* New York: Harry N. Abrams, 1972.

Watney, Simon. *Policing Desire: Pornography, AIDS, and the Media.* Minneapolis: University of Minnesota Press, 1989.

Wilson, Judith. "Down to the Crossroads: The Art of Alison Saar." *Third Text* 10 (Spring 1990), 25–44.

_____. "Lifting 'the Veil': Henry O. Tanner's *The Banjo Lesson* and *The Thankful Poor.*" *Contributions in Black Studies* 9/10 (Fall 1992), 101–125.

_____. "In Memory of the News and of Our Selves: The Art of Adrian Piper." *Third Text* 16/17 (Autumn/Winter 1991), 39–64.

_____. *Novae: William H. Johnson and Bob Thompson* (exhibition catalogue). Los Angeles: California Afro-American Museum, 1990, 23–31.

_____. "Optical Illusions: Images of Miscegenation in Nineteenth and Twentieth-Century American Art." *American Art* 5, no. 3 (Summer 1991), 89–107.

Young, Lola. "Where Do We Go From Here? Musings on 'The Other Story.' " *The Oxford Art Journal* 13, no. 2 (1990), 51–54.

The Urban Context

Economics
Education
History
Sociology

Albelda, Randy, et al. *Mink Coats Don't Trickle Down: The Economic Attack on Women and People of Color.* Boston: South End Press, 1988.

Allen, Walter Recharde. *College in Black and White: African American Students in Predominantly White and in Historically Black Public Universities.* Albany: State University of New York Press, 1991.

Amott, Teresa, and Julie Matthaei. *Race, Gender, and Work: A Multicultural Economic History of Women in the United States.* Boston: South End Press, 1991.

Barnes, Annie S. *Single Parents in Black America: A Study in Culture and Legitimacy.* Bristol, Ind.: Wyndham Hall Press, 1987.

Bennett, Lerone. *Before the Mayflower: A History of Black America.* 6th ed. Chicago: Johnson, 1987.

Berry, Mary Frances, and John W. Blassingame. *Long Memory: The Black Experience in America.* New York: Oxford University Press, 1982.

Borchert, James. *Alley Life in Washington: Family, Community, Religion, and Folklife in the City 1850–1970.* Urbana: University of Illinois Press, 1980.

Browne, Ray Broadus. *Popular Culture and Curricula.* Bowling Green, Ohio: Bowling Green University Popular Press, 1972.

Chambers, Iain. *Popular Culture: The Metropolitan Experience.* New York: Methuen, 1986.

Clark, Kenneth Bancroft. *Dark Ghetto: Dilemmas of Social Power.* Middletown, Conn.: Wesleyan University Press, 1989.

Cross, Theodore L. *The Black Power Imperative: Racial Inequality.* New York: Faulkner, 1984.

Cruse, Harold. *The Crisis of the Negro Intellectual.* New York: William Morrow & Co., 1984.

_____. *Plural but Equal: A Critical Study of Blacks and Minorities in America's Plural Society.* New York: William Morrow & Co., 1987.

Dorr, Aimee. *Children and Television.* New York: Sage, 1987.

Foner, Philip Sheldon. *Organized Labor and the Black Worker, 1619–1981.* 2nd ed. New York: International Publishers, 1982.

Foner, Philip S., and Herbert Shapiro, eds. *American Communism and Black Americans: A Documentary, 1919–1929*. Philadelphia, Pa.: Temple University Press, 1987.

Foner, Philip S., and Herbert Shapiro, eds. *American Communism and Black Americans: A Documentary History, 1930–1934*. Philadelphia, Pa.: Temple University Press, 1991.

Frazier, Edward Franklin. *The Negro Family in the United States*. Chicago: University of Chicago Press, 1966.

Frazier, Edward Franklin. *Black Bourgeoisie*. New York: Free Press, 1965.

Frey, Sylvia R. *Water from the Rock: Black Resistance in a Revolutionary Age*. Princeton, N.J.: Princeton University Press, 1991.

Gatewood, Willard B. *Aristocrats of Color: The Black Elite, 1880–1920*. Bloomington: Indiana University Press, 1990.

Genovese, Eugene. *In Red and Black: Marxian Explorations in American History*. Knoxville: University of Tennessee Press, 1984.

———. *Roll, Jordan, Roll: The World the Slaves Made*. New York: Vintage, 1974.

Georgakas, Dan, and Marvin Surkin. *Detroit: I Do Mind Dying: A Study in Urban Revolution*. New York: St. Martin's Press, 1975.

Gibbs, Jewelle Taylor. *Young, Black, and Male in America: An Endangered Species*. Dover, Mass.: Auburn House Publishing Co., 1988.

Giddings, Paula. *When and Where I Enter: The Impact of Black Women on Race and Sex in America*. New York: Bantam Books, 1984.

Goldsmith, William, and Edward Blakely. *Separate Societies: Poverty and Inequality in U.S. Cities*. Philadelphia, Pa.: Temple University Press, 1992.

Gottlieb, Peter. *Making Their Own Way: Southern Blacks' Migration to Pittsburgh, 1916–1930*. Urbana: University of Illinois Press, 1987.

Greenberg, Cheryl L. *"Or Does it Explode?": Black Harlem in the Great Depression*. New York: Oxford University Press, 1991.

Grossberg, Lawrence. "Teaching the Popular." In *Theory in the Classroom*, ed. Cary Nelson. Urbana: University of Illinois Press, 1986.

Hagedorn, John, and Perry Macon. *People and Folks: Gangs, Crime, and the Underclass in a Rustbelt City*. Chicago: Lake View Press, 1988.

Hampton, Robert L. *Black Family Violence: Current Research and Theory*. Lexington, Mass.: Lexington Books, 1991.

Harris, William Hamilton. *Keeping the Faith: A. Philip Randolph, Milton P. Webster, and the Brotherhood of Sleeping Car Porters, 1925–1937*. Urbana: University of Illinois Press, 1977.

Harrison, Alferdteen, ed. *Black Exodus: The Great Migration from the American South*. Jackson: University Press of Mississippi, 1991.

Hine, Darlene Clark. *Black Women's History: Theory and Practice*. Brooklyn, N.Y.: Carlson, 1990.

Hirsch, Arnold R. *Making the Second Ghetto: Race and Housing in Chicago*. Cambridge: Cambridge University Press, 1983.

Hogan, Lloyd L. *Principles of Black Political Economy*. Boston: Routledge & Kegan Paul, 1984.

Jennings, James. *Black Activism in Urban America*. Detroit, Mich.: Wayne State University Press, 1992.

Jones, Jacqueline. *Labor of Love, Labor of Sorrow: Black Women, Work, and the Family from Slavery to the Present.* New York: Random House, 1985.

Jordan, Winthrop D. *White Over Black: American Attitudes Toward the Negro, 1550–1812.* 1969; New York: W. W. Norton, 1977.

Kasinitz, Philip. *Caribbean New York: Black Immigrants and the Politics of Race.* Ithaca, N.Y.: Cornell University Press, 1992.

Katzman, David M. *Before the Ghetto: Black Detroit in the Nineteenth Century.* Urbana: University of Illinois Press, 1975.

King, Mel. *Chain of Change: Struggles for Black Community Development.* Boston: South End Press, 1981.

Lemann, Nicholas. *The Promised Land: The Great Black Migration and How It Changed America.* New York: A. A. Knopf, 1991.

Lewis, David L. *When Harlem Was in Vogue.* New York: Knopf, 1981.

Lincoln, C. Eric, and Lawrence H. Mamiya. *The Black Church in the African American Experience.* Durham, N.C.: Duke University Press, 1990.

Lipsitz, George. *Class and Culture in Cold War America: A "Rainbow at Midnight."* New York: Praeger, 1981.

———. *A Life in the Struggle: Ivory Perry and the Culture of Opposition.* Philadelphia, Pa.: Temple University Press, 1988.

Lusane, Clarence, and Dennis Desmond. *Pipe Dream Blues: Racism and the War on Drugs.* Boston: South End Press, 1991.

Madhubuti, Haki R. *Black Men, Obsolete, Single, Dangerous?: Afrikan American Families in Transition: Essays in Discovery, Solution, and Hope.* Chicago: Third World Press, 1990.

Malson, Micheline, et al., eds. *Black Women in America: Social Science Perspectives.* Chicago: University of Chicago Press, 1988.

McLaughlin, Eugene. *Out of Order?: Policing Black People.* London: Routledge, 1991.

Meier, August, and Elliott M. Rudwick. *From Plantation to Ghetto.* New York: Hill and Wang, 1976.

Naison, Mark. *Communists in Harlem During the Depression.* Urbana: University of Illinois Press, 1983.

National Urban League. *Black Americans and Public Policy: Perspectives of the National Urban League.* New York: The League, 1988.

Olaquiaga, Celeste. *Megalopolis: Contemporary Cultural Sensibilities.* Minneapolis: University of Minnesota Press, 1992.

Osofsky, Gilbert. *Harlem: The Making of a Ghetto, 1890–1930.* New York: Harper & Row, 1966.

Patterson, James T. *America's Struggle Against Poverty, 1900–1985.* Cambridge: Harvard University Press, 1986.

Pinkney, Alphonso. *The Myth of Black Progress.* Cambridge: Cambridge University Press, 1984.

Raboteau, Albert J. *Slave Religion: "The Invisible Institution" in the Antebellum South.* New York: Oxford University Press, 1978.

Ramdin, Ron. *The Making of the Black Working Class in Britain.* Aldershots, Hants, England; Brookfield, Vt.: Gower Publishing Co., 1987.

Rabinowitz, Howard N. *Race Relations in the Urban South, 1865–1890.* New York: Oxford University Press, 1978.

Rose, Harold M. *Race, Place, and Risk: Black Homicide in Urban America.* Albany, N.Y.: State University of New York Press, 1990.

Salem, Dorothy C. *To Better Our World: Black Women in Organized Reform, 1890–1920*. Brooklyn, N.Y.: Carlson, 1990.

Saxton, Alexander. *The Rise and Fall of the White Republic: Class Politics and Mass Culture in Nineteenth-Century America*. London: Verso, 1990.

Scott, Kesho Yvonne. *The Habit of Surviving: Black Women's Strategies for Life*. New Brunswick, N.J.: Rutgers University Press, 1991.

Simms, Margaret C., and Julianne Malveaux, eds. *Slipping Through the Cracks: The Status of Black Women*. New Brunswick, N.J.: Transaction Books, 1986.

Smith, John David. *Black Slavery in the Americas: An Interdisciplinary Bibliography, 1865–1980*. Westport, Conn.: Greenwood Press, 1982.

Solomos, John. *Black Youth, Racism, and the State*. Cambridge: Cambridge University Press, 1988.

Spear, Allan H. *Black Chicago: The Making of a Negro Ghetto 1890–1920*. Chicago: University of Chicago Press, 1967.

Tidwell, William A. *The State of Black America*. New York: National Urban League, 1992.

Tolbert, Emory J. *The UNIA and Black Los Angeles: Ideology and Community in the American Garvey Movement*. Los Angeles: Center for Afro-American Studies, University of California, 1980.

Trotter, Joe William. *Black Milwaukee: The Making of an Industrial Proletariat, 1915–1945*. Urbana: University of Illinois Press, 1985.

Walker, Clarence. *Deromanticizing Black History: Critical Essays and Reappraisals*. Knoxville: University of Tennessee Press, 1991.

Wallace, Phyliss Ann, Linda Datcher, and Julianne Malveaux. *Black Women in the Labor Force*. Cambridge: MIT Press, 1980.

Wilson, Joseph, and Thomas Weissinger. *Black Labor in America, 1865–1983: A Selected Annotated Bibliography*. Westport, Conn.: Greenwood Press, 1986.

Wilson, William Julius. *The Truly Disadvantaged*. Chicago: University of Chicago Press, 1987.

_____, ed. *The Ghetto Underclass: Social Science Perspectives*. Newbury Park, Calif.: Sage, 1989.

Yee, Shirley J. *Black Women Abolitionists: A Study in Activism, 1828–1860*. Knoxville: University of Tennessee Press, 1992.

The Production of Black Popular Culture

Dance
Film and Video
Music
Photography
Theater

Adamczyk, Alice J. *Black Dance: An Annotated Bibliography*. New York: Garland Publications, 1989.

Arroyo, José. "Look Back and Talk Black: The Films of Isaac Julien in Postmodern Britain." *Jump Cut,* no. 36 (1991).

Bailey, David A. "Photographic Animateur: The Photographs of Rotimi Fani-Kayode in Relation to Black Photographic Practice." *Third Text* 13 (Winter 1990/1991): 57–62.

Baldwin, James. *The Devil Finds Work: An Essay* [on film]. 1976; New York: Dell, 1990.

Baraka, Imamu Amiri. *The Music: Reflections on*

Jazz and the Blues. New York: William Morrow & Co., 1987.

_____. *Blues People: Negro Music in White America.* New York: William Morrow & Co., 1963.

Bordwell, David, Janet Staiger, and Kristin Thompson. *Classical Hollywood Cinema: Film, Style, and Mode of Production to 1960.* New York: Columbia University Press, 1985.

Brooks, Tilford. *America's Black Musical Heritage.* Englewood Cliffs, N.J.: Prentice-Hall, 1984.

Brown, Rae Linda. *Music, Printed and Manuscript, in the James Weldon Johnson Memorial Collection of Negro Arts and Letters: An Annotated Catalog.* Vol. 23. Critical Studies on Black Life and Culture, New York: Garland Publications, 1982.

Cantor, Louis. *Wheelin' on Beale: How WDIA-Memphis Became the Nation's First All-Black Radio Station and Created the Sound that Changed America.* New York: Pharos Books, 1992.

Chambers, Iain. *Urban Rhythms: Pop Music and Popular Culture.* New York: St. Martin's Press, 1985.

Chernoff, John Miller. *African Rhythm and African Sensibility: Aesthetics and Social Action in African-American Musical Idioms.* Chicago: University of Chicago Press, 1979.

Chevigny, Paul. *Gigs: Jazz and the Cabaret Laws in New York City.* London: Routledge, 1991.

Costello, Mark, and David Foster Wallace, eds. *Signifying Rappers: Rap and Race in the Urban Present.* New York: Ecco Press, 1990.

De Lerma, Dominique. *Black Music and Musicians in the New Grove Dictionary of American Music and the New Harvard Dictionary of Music.* Chicago: Center for Black Music Research, 1989.

Dennison, Sam. *Scandalize My Name: Black Imagery in American Popular Music.* Vol. 13. Critical Studies on Black Life and Culture, New York: Garland Publications, 1982.

Diawara, Manthia. "The Absent One: The Avant-Garde and the Black Imaginary in *Looking for Langston.*" *Wide Angle* 13, nos. 3 and 4 (July–October 1991).

Ellison, Mary. *Lyrical Protest: Black Music's Struggle Against Discrimination.* New York: Praeger, 1989.

Emery, Lynne Fauley. *Black Dance in the United States from 1619 to Today.* Salem, N.H.: Ayer, 1988.

Finn, Julio. *The Bluesman: The Musical Heritage of Black Men and Women in the Americas.* New York: Quartet Books, 1986.

Floyd, Samuel A. *Black Music in the United States: An Annotated Bibliography of Selected Reference and Research Materials.* Millwood, N.Y.: Kraus International Publications, 1983.

_____, ed. *Black Music in the Harlem Renaissance: A Collection of Essays.* New York: Greenwood Press, 1990.

Garofalo, Reebee. *Rockin' the Boat: Mass Music and Mass Movements.* Boston: South End Press, 1992.

George, Nelson. *The Death of Rhythm and Blues.* New York: Pantheon Books, 1988.

_____. *Where Did Our Love Go?: The Rise and Fall of the Motown Sound.* New York: St. Martin's Press, 1985.

Gilroy, Paul. "Sounds Authentic: Black Music, Ethnicity, and the Challenge of a Changing Same." *Black Music Research Journal* 11, no. 2 (1991), 111–137.

Gill, Glenda Eloise. *White Grease Paint on Black Performers: A Study of the Federal Theatre of 1935–1939.* New York: P. Long, 1988.

Gray, John. *Black Theatre and Performance: A Pan-African Bibliography.* New York: Greenwood Press, 1990.

Griffin, Ada Gay. "What's Mine Is Not Mine/What's Mine Is Ours/What's Mine Is Yours/What's Yours Is Yours (Power Sharing in America)." *Felix* 1, no. 2 (Spring 1992).

Hall, Stuart, and David Bailey, eds. "The Critical Decade: Black Photography in the 1980s." *Ten.8* (1992).

Harrison, Daphne Duval. *Black Pearls: Blues Queens of the 1920s.* New Brunswick, N.J.: Rutgers University Press, 1988.

Haskins, James. *Black Dance in America: A History Through its People.* New York: T. Y. Crowell, 1990.

———. *Black Music in America.* New York: T. Y. Crowell, 1987.

Hazzard-Gordon, Katrina. *Jookin': The Rise of Social Dance Formations in African-American Culture.* Philadelphia, Pa.: Temple University Press, 1990.

Hebdige, Dick. *Cut 'n' Mix: Culture, Identity, and Caribbean Music.* London: Methuen, 1987.

Hill, George H. *Black Media in America: A Resource Guide.* Boston: G. K. Hall, 1984.

Hyatt, Marshall. *The Afro-American Cinematic Experience: An Annotated Bibliography and Filmography.* Wilmington, Del.: Scholarly Resources, Inc., 1983.

Kebede, Ashenafi. *Roots of Black Music: The Vocal, Instrumental, and Dance Heritage of Africa and Black America.* Englewood Cliffs, N.J.: Prentice-Hall, 1982.

Kochman, Thomas, ed. *Rappin' and Stylin' Out: Communication in Urban Black America.* Urbana: University of Illinois Press, 1972.

Kofsky, Frank. *Black Nationalism and the Revolution in Music.* New York: Pathfinder Press, 1970.

Long, Richard A. *Black Dance: The Black Tradition in American Dance.* New York: Rizzoli, 1989.

McKee, Margaret. *Beale, Black and Blue: Life and Music on Black America's Main Street.* Baton Rouge: Louisiana State University Press, 1981.

McRobbie, Angela. *Zootsuits and Second-Hand Dresses: An Anthology of Fashion and Music.* Boston: Unwin-Hyman, 1988.

Meadows, Eddie S. *Jazz Reference and Research Materials: A Bibliography.* New York: Garland Publications, 1981.

Mercer, Kobena. "Black Art and the Burden of Representation." *Third Text* 10 (Spring 1990), 61–78.

———. "Diaspora Culture and the Dialogic Imagination: The Aesthetic of Black Independent Film in Britain." In *The Media Reader,* ed. Manuel Alvarado and John O. Thompson, 24–35. London: BFI Publishing, 1990.

———, ed. *Black Film/British Cinema.* ICA Document 7. London: Institute of Contemporary Arts, 1988.

Merriam, Alan P. *African Music in Perspective.* Vol. 6. Critical Studies on Black Life and Culture. New York: Garland Publications, 1982.

Molette, Carlton W., and Barbara J. Molette. *Black Theatre: Premise and Presentation.* Bristol, Ind.: Wyndham Hall Press, 1986.

Morrow, Bradford, ed. *Conjunctions: 16.* Annandale-on-Hudson, N.Y.: Bard College, 1991.

Moutoussamy-Ashe, Jeanne. *Viewfinders: Black Women Photographers.* New York: Dodd, Mead, 1986.

Murray, Albert. *Stomping the Blues.* 1976; New York: Da Capo Press, 1989.

———. *Train Whistle Guitar.* 1974; Boston: Northeastern University Press, 1989.

Oliver, Paul, ed. *Black Music in Britain: Essays on the Afro-Asiatic Contribution to Popular Music.* Milton Keynes, England; Philadelphia, Pa.: Open University Press, 1990.

Palmer, Robert. *Deep Blues: A Musical and Cultural History of the Mississippi Delta.* Middlesex, U.K.: Penguin, 1981.

Parish, James Robert, and George H. Hill. *Black Action Films: Plots, Critiques, Casts, and Credits for 235 Theatrical and Made-for-Television Releases.* Jefferson, N.C.: McFarland, 1989.

Perkins, Eric, ed. *Droppin' Science: Critical Essays on Rap Music and Hip-Hop Culture.* Philadelphia, Pa.: Temple University Press, forthcoming.

Riis, Thomas Lawrence. *Just Before Jazz: Black Musical Theater in New York, 1890–1915.* Washington, D.C.: Smithsonian Institution Press, 1989.

Roach, Hildred. *Black American Music: Past and Present.* 1976; Malabar, Fla.: R. E. Krieger Publishing Co., 1985.

Rochon, Valerie J. *The African American Dance Directory.* New York: V. J. Rochon (5009 Broadway #106, New York, N.Y. 10034), 1984.

Rose, Tricia. "Never Trust a Big Butt and a Smile." *Camera Obscura,* no. 24 (1990), 105–120.

———. "Orality and Technology: Rap Music and Afro-American Cultural Resistance." *Journal of Popular Music and Society* 13, no. 4 (1989), 35–44.

Rosenthal, David. *Hard Bop: Jazz and Black Music, 1955–1965.* New York: Oxford University Press, 1992.

Shaw, Arnold. *Black Popular Music in America: From the Spirituals, Minstrels, and Ragtime to Soul, Disco, and Hip Hop.* New York: Schirmer Books, 1986.

———. *The Jazz Age: Popular Music in the 1920s.* New York: Oxford University Press, 1987.

Skowronski, JoAnn. *Black Music in America: A Bibliography.* Metuchen, N.J.: Scarecrow Press, 1981.

Small, Christopher. *Music of the Common Tongue: Survival and Celebration in Afro-American Music.* New York: Riverrun Press, 1987.

———. *Music, Society, and Education: An Examination of the Function of Music in Western, Eastern, and African Cultures with Its Impact on Society and Its Use in Education.* New York: Schirmer Books, 1977.

Southern, Eileen. *The Music of Black Americans: A History.* New York: W. W. Norton, 1983.

Stewart, Gary. *Breakout: Profiles in African Rhythm.* Chicago: University of Chicago Press, 1992.

Theide, Nancy, and Alain Ambrosei, eds. *Video: The Changing World.* Montreal: Black Rose Books, 1991.

Thorpe, Edward. *Black Dance.* London: Chatto & Windus, 1989.

Toop, David. *Rap Attack 2: African Rap to Global Hip Hop.* Revised edition. New York: Serpent's Tail, 1991.

Walker–Hill, Helen. *Piano Music by Black Women Composers: A Catalog of Solo and Ensemble Works.* New York: Greenwood Press, 1992.

Williams, Mance. *Black Theatre in the 1960s and 1970s.* Westport, Conn.: Greenwood Press, 1985.

Willis-Thomas, Deborah. *Black Photographers, 1840–1940: An Illustrated Bio-Bibliography.* New York: Garland Publications, 1985.

Willis-Thomas, Deborah, and Howard Dodson. *Black Photographers Bear Witness: 100 Years of Social Protest* (exhibition catalogue). Williamstown, Mass.: Williams College Museum of Art, 1989.

Wilson, Judith. "What Are We Doing Here? Cultural Difference in Photographic Theory and Practice." *S.F. Camerawork Quarterly* 17, no. 3 (Fall 1990).

Woll, Allen. *Black Musical Theatre: From Coontown to Dreamgirls.* Baton Rouge: Louisiana State University Press, 1989.

Film and Video Sources

Black Filmmaker Foundation, 375 Greenwich Street, New York, N.Y. 10013. (212) 941-3944.

California Newsreel, 149 Ninth Street/420, San Francisco, Ca. 94103. (415) 621-6196.

The Cinema Guild, 1697 Broadway, Suite 802, New York, N.Y. 10019. (212) 246-5522.

Direct Cinema, P.O. 69799, Los Angeles, Calif. 90069. (213) 652-8000.

Electronic Arts Intermix, 536 Broadway, 9th floor, New York, N.Y. 10012. (212) 966-4605.

Filmmakers Library, 124 East 40th Street, New York, N.Y. 10016. (212) 808-4980.

First Run/Icarus Films, 153 Waverly Place, New York, N.Y. 10014. (212) 727-1711.

Frameline, P.O. Box 14792, San Francisco, Ca. 94114. (415) 861-5245.

Media Network, 39 West 14th Street, New York, N.Y. 10011. (212) 929-2663.

PBS Video, Public Broadcasting Service, 1320 Braddock Place, Alexandria, Va. 22314-1698. (800) 344-3337.

Schomburg Center for Research in Black Culture, The New York Public Library, 515 Malcolm X Boulevard, New York, N.Y. 10037-1801. (212) 491-2200.

Third World Newsreel, 335 West 38th Street, 5th floor, New York, N.Y. 10018. (212) 947-9277.

Video Data Bank at The School of the Art Institute of Chicago, 37 South Wabash Avenue, Chicago, Ill. 60603. (312) 899-5172.

William Greaves Productions, Inc., 230 West 55th Street, New York, N.Y. 10019. (212) 246-7221.

Women Make Movies, 225 Lafayette Street, New York, N.Y. 10012. (212) 925-0606.

Do the Right Thing: Postnationalism and Essentialism

Diaspora Studies
Law and Civil Rights
Nationalism
Politics

Abraham, Kinfe. *The Politics of Black Nationalism: From Harlem to Soweto.* Trenton, N.J.: Africa World Press, 1991.

Asante, Molefi Kete. *Afrocentricity.* Trenton, N.J.: Africa World Press, 1988.

Bell, Derrick A. *And We Are Not Saved: The Elusive Quest for Racial Justice.* New York: Basic Books, 1987.

_____. *Faces at the Bottom of the Well.* New York: Basic Books, 1992.

Benson, Peter. *Black Orpheus: Transition, and Modern Cultural Awakening in Africa.* Berkeley: University of California Press, 1986.

Bhat, Ashok, et al., eds. *Britain's Black Population: A New Perspective.* Aldershots, Hants, England; Brookfield, Vt.: Gower Publishing Co., 1988.

The Black Americas 1492–1992. Vol. 25. *Report on the Americas,* ed. North American Congress on Latin America. 1992.

Bonnett, Aubrey W., and G. Llewellyn Watson, eds. *Emerging Perspectives on the Black Diaspora.* Lanham: University Press of America, 1990.

Bositis, David A. *Black Political Participation: Patterns and Trends in Voting Representation.* Washington, D.C.: University Press of America, 1992.

Brown, Colin. *Black and White Britain: The Third PSI Survey.* London: Heinemann, 1984.

Brown, Wilmette. *Black Women and the Peace Movement.* Bristol, Ind.: Falling Wall Press, 1984.

Carson, Claybourne. *The Eyes on the Prize Civil Rights Reader.* New York: Viking, 1991.

Chambers, Iain. *Border Dialogues: Journeys in Postmodernity.* New York: Routledge, 1990.

Chirimuuta, Richard C. *AIDS, Africa, and Racism.* London: Free Association Books, 1989.

Cone, James. *Martin and Malcolm and America: A Dream or a Nightmare.* Maryknoll, N.Y.: Orbis Books, 1991.

Crawford, Vicki L., Jacqueline Anne Rouse, and Barbara Woods, eds. *Women in the Civil Rights Movement: Trailblazers and Torchbearers, 1941–1965.* Brooklyn, N.Y.: Carlson, 1990.

Cross, Malcolm, and Hans Entzinger, eds. *Lost Illusions: Caribbean Minorities in Britain and the Netherlands.* London: Routledge, 1988.

Daniels, Therese, and Jane Gerson. *The Colour Black: Black Images in British Television.* London: BFI Publishing, 1989.

Davis, Angela Yvonne. *Violence Against Women and the Ongoing Challenge to Racism.* Latham, N.Y.: Kitchen Table Women of Color Press, 1985.

_____. *Women, Culture, and Politics.* New York: Random House, 1989.

_____. *Women, Race, and Class.* New York: Random House, 1981.

Diawara, Manthia. *African Cinema: Politics and Culture.* Bloomington: Indiana University Press, 1992.

Downing, John D. A. *Film and Politics in the Third World.* New York: Automedia, 1987.

Drake, St. Clair. *Black Folk Here and There: An Essay in History and Anthropology.* 1987; Los Angeles: Center for Afro-American Studies, University of California, 1990.

Elkins, W. F. *Black Power in the Caribbean: The Beginnings of the Modern National Movement.* New York: Revisionist Press, 1977.

Fontaine, Pierre-Michel, ed. *Race, Class, and Power in Brazil.* Los Angeles: Center for Afro-American Studies, 1985.

Fraginals, Manuel Morena, ed. *Africa in Latin America: Essays on History, Culture, and Socialization.* New York: Holmes & Meier, 1984.

Franklin, Vincent. *Black Self-Determination: A Cultural History.* Westport, Conn.: L. Hill, 1984.

Fryer, Peter. *Black People in the British Empire: An Introduction.* London: Pluto, 1988.

———. *Staying Power: The History of Black People in Britain.* London: Pluto Press, 1984.

Fusco, Coco, ed. *Young, British, and Black.* Buffalo, N.Y.: Hallwalls/Contemporary Arts Center, 1988.

Gershoni, Yekutiel. *Black Colonialism: The Americo-Liberian Scramble for the Hinterland.* Boulder, Colo.: Westview Press, 1985.

Gilroy, Paul. *"There Ain't No Black in the Union Jack": The Cultural Politics of Race and Nation.* London: Hutchinson, 1987.

———. "Wearing Your Art on Your Sleeve: Notes Toward a Diaspora Theory of Black Ephemera." *Ten.8* 2, no. 3 (1992), 128–137.

Goulbourne, Harry, ed. *Black Politics in Britain. Papers from the Conference on Black People and British Politics.* Warwick University, 1987, Aldershot; Brookfield: Avebury, 1990.

Graham, Richard, ed. *The Idea of Race in Latin America, 1870–1940.* Austin: University of Texas Press, 1990.

Haines, Herbert H. *Black Radicals and the Civil Rights Mainstream, 1954–1970.* Knoxville: University of Tennessee Press, 1988.

Hall, Stuart, and Martin Jacques. *The Hard Road to Renewal: Thatcherism and the Crisis of the Left.* New York: Verso, 1988.

Hall, Stuart, and Tony Jefferson. *Resistance Through Ritual: Youth Subcultures in Post-War Britain.* Boston: Unwin, 1976.

Hall, Stuart, et al., eds. *Policing the Crisis: Mugging, the State, and Law and Order.* New York: Holmes & Meier, 1978.

Henry, Charles P. *Culture and African American Politics.* Bloomington: Indiana University Press, 1990.

Hiro, Dilip. *Black British, White British.* London: Grafton, 1991.

Jacobs, Brian D. *Black Politics and Urban Crisis in Britain.* Cambridge: Cambridge University Press, 1986.

Jenkins, Craig J. *Channeling Black Insurgency: Elite Patronage and Professional SMOs in the Development of the Civil Rights Movement.* New Haven: Institute for Social and Policy Studies, 1986.

Jones, Simon. *Black Culture, White Youth: The Reggae Tradition from JA to UK.* Houndmills, Basingstoke, Hampshire: Macmillan Education, 1988.

La Guerre, John Gaffar. *Enemies of Empire.* St. Augustine, Trinidad: University of the West Indies, 1984.

Lampschreur, Willem, and Joost Divendal, eds. *Culture in Another South Africa.* New York: Olive Branch, 1989.

Marable, Manning. *African and Caribbean Politics: From Kwame Nkrumah to Maurice Bishop.* London: Verso, 1987.

———. *Black American Politics: From the Washington Marches to Jesse Jackson.* London: Verso, 1985.

———. *Blackwater: Historical Studies in Race, Class Consciousness, and Revolution.* Dayton, Ohio: Black Praxis Press, 1981.

_____. *The Crisis of Color and Democracy: Essays on Race, Class, and Power.* Monroe, Maine: Common Courage Press, 1992.

_____. *How Capitalism Underdeveloped Black America: Problems in Race, Political Economy, and Society.* Boston: South End Press, 1983.

_____. *Race, Reform, and Rebellion: The Second Reconstruction in Black America, 1945–1990.* Jackson: University Press of Mississippi, 1991.

_____. *W.E.B. Du Bois: Black Radical Democrat.* Boston: Twayne Publishers, 1986.

McCartney, John. *Black Power Ideologies: An Essay in African-American Political Thought.* Philadelphia, Pa.: Temple University Press, 1992.

Meier, August, and John H. Bracey. *Black Protest in the Sixties.* New York: M. Weiner, 1991.

Michael, Colette. *Negritude: An Annotated Bibliography.* West Cornwall, Conn.: Locust Hill Press, 1988.

Morris, Aldon D. *The Origins of the Civil Rights Movement: Black Communities Organizing for Change.* New York: Free Press, 1984.

Morrison, Toni, ed. *Race-ing Justice, En-gendering Power: Essays on Anita Hill, Clarence Thomas and the Construction of Social Reality.* New York: Pantheon, 1992.

Moses, Wilson Jeremiah. *Alexander Crummell: A Study of Civilization and Discontent.* New York; Oxford: Oxford University Press, 1989.

_____. *Black Messiahs and Uncle Toms.* University Park: Pennsylvania State University Press, 1982.

_____. *The Golden Age of Black Nationalism, 1850–1925.* 1978; New York: Oxford University Press, 1988.

Nascimento, Abdias do. *Brazil, Mixture or Massacre?: Essays in the Genocide of a Black People.* 2nd ed. Dover, Mass.: Majority Press, 1989.

Nodal, Roberto. *Black Culture in Latin America: An Updated Bibliography.* Milwaukee: Department of Afro-American Studies, University of Wisconsin, 1977.

Okpaku, Joseph Ohiomogben, et al., eds. *The Arts and Civilization of Black and African Peoples.* 1986 ed., World Black and African Festival of the Arts and Culture. Lagos, Nigeria: Centre for Black and African Arts and Civilization, 1977.

Pohlmann, Marcus D. *Black Politics in Conservative America.* New York: Longman, 1990.

Proceedings of the Conference on Latin American Popular Culture. Vol. 10. *Studies in Latin American Popular Culture,* 1991.

Quaynor, Thomas. *A Documented History of Black Consciousness.* New York: Vantage Press, 1986.

Reed, Adolph. *The Jesse Jackson Phenomenon: The Crisis of Purpose in American Politics.* New Haven: Yale University Press, 1986.

Retamar, Roberto Fernandez. *Caliban and Other Essays.* Minneapolis: University of Minnesota Press, 1989.

Robinson, Armstead L., and Patricia Sullivan, eds. *New Directions in Civil Rights Studies.* Carter G. Woodson Institute Series in Black Studies. Charlottesville: University Press of Virginia, 1991.

Robinson, Cedric J. *Black Marxism: The Making of the Black Radical Tradition*. London: Zed Books, 1983.

Sewell, Tony. *Garvey's Children: The Legacy of Marcus Garvey*. Trenton, N.J.: Africa World Press, 1990.

Sivanandan, Ambalavaner. *Communities of Resistance: Writings on Black Struggles for Socialism*. London: Verso, 1990.

Solomon, Irvin D. *Feminism and Black Activism in Contemporary America: An Ideological Assessment*. New York: Greenwood Press, 1989.

Stuckey, Sterling. *Slave Culture: Nationalist Theory and the Foundations of Black America*. New York: Oxford University Press, 1987.

Terborg-Penn, Rosalyn, and Sharon Harley. *Women in Africa and the African Diaspora*. Washington, D. C.: Howard University Press, 1987.

University of Michigan Center for Afro-American and African Studies. *Black Immigration and Ethnicity in the United States: An Annotated Bibliography*. Westport, Conn.: Greenwood Press, 1985.

Wallerstein, Immanuel. *Frantz Fanon: Reason and Violence*. New York: Institute of African Studies, Columbia University, 1970.

_____. *Africa and the Modern World*. Trenton, N.J.: Africa World Press, 1986.

Waters, Ronald W. *Black Presidential Politics in America: A Strategic Approach*. Albany: State University of New York Press, 1988.

Williams, Patricia J. *The Alchemy of Race and Rights: Diary of a Law Professor*. Cambridge: Harvard University Press, 1991.

Woldemikael, Tekle Mariam. *Becoming Black American: Haitians and American Institutions in Evanston, Illinois*. New York: AMS Press, 1989.

Wright, Bruce. *Black Robes, White Justice*. Secaucus, N.J.: Lyle Stuart, 1987.

Notes on Contributors

Houston A. Baker, Jr. is Director of the Center for the Study of Black Literature and Culture at the University of Pennsylvania. He is the author of a number of books devoted to black literature and culture, including the forth-coming *Black Studies, Rap, and the Academy,* which will be published by University of Chicago Press in 1993.

Jacqueline Bobo is Assistant Professor of Radio, Television, and Motion Pictures at the University of North Carolina, Chapel Hill. She is currently completing a manuscript on Black women and film titled *Credible Witness: Black Women, Film Theory, Spectatorship*, forthcoming from Columbia University Press. She is also the guest editor of an issue of the *Quarterly Review of Film & Video* devoted to the topic "Black Feminism and Media Studies," which will be available in Spring 1993.

Hazel V. Carby is Professor of English and Afro-American Studies at Yale University and is the author of *Reconstructing Womanhood: The Emergence of the Afro-American Woman Novelist* (1987).

Angela Y. Davis has been teaching, writing, and lecturing about African-American and women's social theories and practices for the last twenty years, during which she has also been active in a number of organizations concerned with issues of social justice. She presently teaches in the History of Consciousness program at the University of California, Santa Cruz.

Gina Dent is a Ph.D. candidate in the Department of English and Comparative Literature at Columbia University.

Manthia Diawara is Professor of Film and Comparative Literature and Director of Africana Studies at New York University. His most recent book is *African Cinema, Politics and Culture* published by Indiana University Press, and he is editor of the forthcoming book *Black American Cinema*, which will be published by Routledge in 1993.

Coco Fusco is a New York–based writer, curator, and media artist. Her articles have appeared in many publications, including *The Village Voice*, *The Nation*, and *Third Text*. She has lectured widely and curated numerous international media exhibitions, including *Internal Exiles: New Films and Videos from Chile* (1990) and *The Hybrid State Film Series* (1991). Co-producer of the video documentary, *Havana Postmodern* (1989), she has collaborated with Guillermo Gómez-Pena on two interdisciplinary arts projects: *Norte:Sur* (1990) and *1992: The Year of the White Bear* (1992).

Henry Louis Gates, Jr. is the W.E.B. Du Bois Professor of the Humanities and Director of the W.E.B. Du Bois Institute for Afro-American Research at Harvard University. He is Chairman of the Department of Afro-American Studies at Harvard and is a professor in the English Department. His most recent book is *Loose Canons* (1992). He is general editor of the *Schomburg Library of Nineteenth-Century Black Women Writers* and, with K. Anthony Appiah, of *Transition* magazine, and Director of the Black Periodical Literature Project.

Paul Gilroy teaches at Goldsmiths' College of the University of London. He has also worked as a musician and journalist. He is the author of *"There Ain't No Black in the Union Jack": The Cultural Politics of Race and Nation* (1987) and *Promised Lands*, a study of black Atlantic cultural history, which will be published by Random Century in 1993.

Ada Gay Griffin is an independent producer and Executive Director of Third World Newsreel. She is a black feminist from western Pennsylvania and is collaborating with Michelle Parkerson on a film documentary on the life and work of black/lesbian/mother/poet/warrior Audre Lorde.

Stuart Hall is professor of sociology at Open University, Milton Keynes, England. His books include *Minimal Selves* (1988), *The Hard Road to Renewal: Thatcherism and the Crisis of the Left*, with Martin Jacques (1988), and *Resistance Through Ritual: Youth Subcultures in Post-War Britain*, with Tony Jefferson (1976).

He is co-editor of *Culture, Media, Language: Working Papers in Cultural Studies* (1980) and of a special issue of *Ten.8* entitled "The Critical Decade: Black Photography in the 1980s" (1992).

Thomas Allen Harris is a producer, writer, and curator who has worked as a staff producer in public television. His films and videos include *Splash*, *Black Body*, and *All in the Family*. He is currently working in collaboration with Phillip Mallory Jones and Carlos de Jesus on *First World Order*, a series of videotapes that explore African diasporic expression.

bell hooks is a writer and teacher who speaks widely on issues of race, class, and gender. She is Associate Professor of English and Women's Studies at Oberlin College. Her most recent books are *Black Looks: Race, Gender, and Cultural Politics* (1992), *Yearning: Race, Gender, and Culture* (1990), and *Talking Back* (1989).

Arthur Jafa is a filmmaker who was born in Tupelo, Mississippi, raised in Clarksdale, Mississippi, and attended Howard University.

John Jeffries is Chair for the Committee on Urban Studies and Assistant Professor of Urban Policy in the Analysis and Management Program at the Graduate School of Management and Urban Policy, New School for Social Research.

Jacquie Jones is Editor of *Black Film Review* and Assistant Director of the Black Film Institute at the University of the District of Columbia. She has programmed Black film for various festivals and organizations including The Festival of New Latin American Cinema (Havana, Cuba), Filmfest D. C., and The Smithsonian Institution. Her articles on film have appeared in a number of publications including *Cineaste*, where she is editorial associate, *American Visions*, *Wide Angle*, and *In These Times*.

Isaac Julien lives in London where he works as a film director. Currently completing a short film, *The Attendant* for Channel 4 Television, his 1992 two-part documentary series *Black and White in Colour* for BBC2-TV was shown in the

1992 New York Film Festival. His feature *Young Soul Rebels* (1991) gained the International Critics Week Prize in Cannes. *Looking for Langston* (1989), his prize-winning short film on Langston Hughes, was recently broadcast on PBS.

Lisa Kennedy is Arts Editor for *The Village Voice* and has written for *The Village Voice* and *Mother Jones*.

Julianne Malveaux is an economist, writer, and columnist whose weekly column appears nationally through the King Features Syndicate. She is a regular contributor to *Ms.* and *USA Today*, a weekly contributor to the *San Francisco Sun Reporter*, contributor of the "Left Coast" column to *Emerge Magazine*, and a monthly column to *Black Issues in Higher Education*. She also provides regular radio and television commentary on sociopolitical issues, especially on CNN's "Crier & Co." and on the PBS show "To the Contrary."

Manning Marable is Professor of Political Science and History, University of Colorado, Boulder. He is the author of eight books, including *Black American Politics* (1985), *W.E.B. Du Bois: Black Radical Democrat* (1986), and *The Crisis of Color and Democracy* (1992). He is currently completing a biography of Malcolm X and a comprehensive study of Black intellectuals in the twentieth century. Professor Marable's political commentary series "Along the Color Line" appears in over two hundred fifty newspapers and is broadcast by more than fifty radio stations internationally.

Kofi Natambu is a writer and cultural critic. His work has appeared in many national literary magazines and newspapers. He is the author of two books: *The Melody Never Stops* (1991) and *Intervals* (1983). He is also the founding editor of the literary magazine *Solid Ground: A New World Journal*. Currently, he is Visiting Professor in Fine Arts & the Social Sciences, University of California, Irvine.

Marlon T. Riggs is a prize-winning producer, director, and writer. His videos include the feature-length documentary *Color Adjustment* (1991), *Tongues Untied* (1989), and *Ethnic Notions* (1985). Currently he is working on *Black is...Black Ain't*. He teaches at the University of California, Berkeley.

Tricia Rose is a native New Yorker who was trained at Yale College and Brown University and is currently Assistant Professor of American Studies at Rutgers University. She writes on black cultural theory and popular culture and is the author of a forthcoming book on rap music and the politics of black cultural practice.

Valerie Smith is author of *Self-Discovery and Authority in Afro-American Narrative* (1987) and editor of *African American Writers* (1991). She is a black feminist critic who teaches and writes about ideologies of race and gender as they are represented in film and literature. An associate professor of English at University of California, Los Angeles, she is currently working on a book on black feminism and contemporary culture.

Greg Tate is a staff writer for *The Village Voice* and a founding member of the Black Rock Coalition. He also contributes to *Spin* and *Downbeat*. Author of *Flyboy in the Buttermilk: Essays on Contemporary America* (1992), he lives and thrives in Harlem.

Michele Wallace is Associate Professor of English and Women's Studies at City College of New York and City University of New York Graduate Center. She is author of *Black Macho and the Myth of the Superwoman* (1979) and *Invisibility Blues: From Pop to Theory (1990).*

Cornel West is Professor of Theology and Director of the Afro-American Studies Program at Princeton University. He is the author of *Prophesy, Deliverance! An Afro-American Revolutionary Christianity* (1982), *Prophetic Fragments* (1988), *The American Evasion of Philosophy* (1989), *The Ethical Dimensions of Marxist Thought* (1991), and co-editor of *Out There: Marginalization and Contemporary Cultures.*

Sherley Anne Williams is a writer whose books include *Dessa Rose* (1986) and *Working Cotton*, forthcoming. She also has published many works of short fiction, poetry, drama, and nonfiction prose.

Judith Wilson is an art critic and historian. A former *Ms.* editor, she has also been a book review columnist and contributing editor for *Essence* and an art reviewer for *The Village Voice*. Since 1979, she has written extensively about African-American visual artists and is the author of numerous exhibition catalogue essays. She is currently Acting Assistant Professor in the McIntire Department of Art, University of Virginia, and a Ph.D. candidate at Yale University.

Facing page 1, courtesy Greta Schiller and Jezebel Productions; pages 31, 34, 140,152, 166, 219, 256, 326, courtesy of the artists; page 36, © 1966 Robert Sengstacke; pages 46, 76, 136, 298, 299, 321, 336, 337, UPI/Bettmann Newsphotos; pages 50, 188, 274, 276, © 1992 by New African Visions, Incorporated, the photographers, from the book *Songs of My People*; pages 52, 146, courtesy Women Make Movies; page 62, courtesy Frameline; pages 71, 94, 111, 128, 286, courtesy Photofest; page 84, courtesy of the artist and Pat Hearn Gallery, New York; pages 92, 225, 304, courtesy Prestige, a division of Miramax Films; page 100, courtesy of Jonathan Lee and Fear of Disclosure; page 108, 202, courtesy of the artist and Josh Baer Gallery, New York; page 115, left, courtesy The Corcoran Gallery of Art; page 115, right, photograph by Mario Carrieri, courtesy The Menil Foundation and Ministero per i Beni Culturali e Ambientali; page 117, courtesy National Museum of American Art, Smithsonian Institution, Gift of The Harmon Foundation; page 150, photograph by Peter Muscato, Collection of Elaine and Werner Dannheisser, courtesy of the artist and Andrea Rosen Gallery, New York; page 181, courtesy Kofi Natambu; page 210, photograph by Lee Stalsworth, courtesy Hirshhorn Museum and Sculpture Garden, Smithsonian Institution, from "Works: Houston Conwill," August 2–October 29, 1989; page 212, courtesy Demolished by Neglect; page 220, © Jack Mitchell; page 230, courtesy Third World Newsreel; page 235, courtesy California Newsreel and New Decade Productions; page 244, photograph by Todd Schroeder; page 252, courtesy Arthur Jafa; page 262, photograph by David Lee; page 278, courtesy Rachel Weiss and Polarities, Inc.; page 280, courtesy Magnum Photos, Inc. and Susan Meiselas; page 318, photograph by Ivan Dalla Tana, courtesy Tony Shafrazi Gallery and The Estate of Keith Haring.